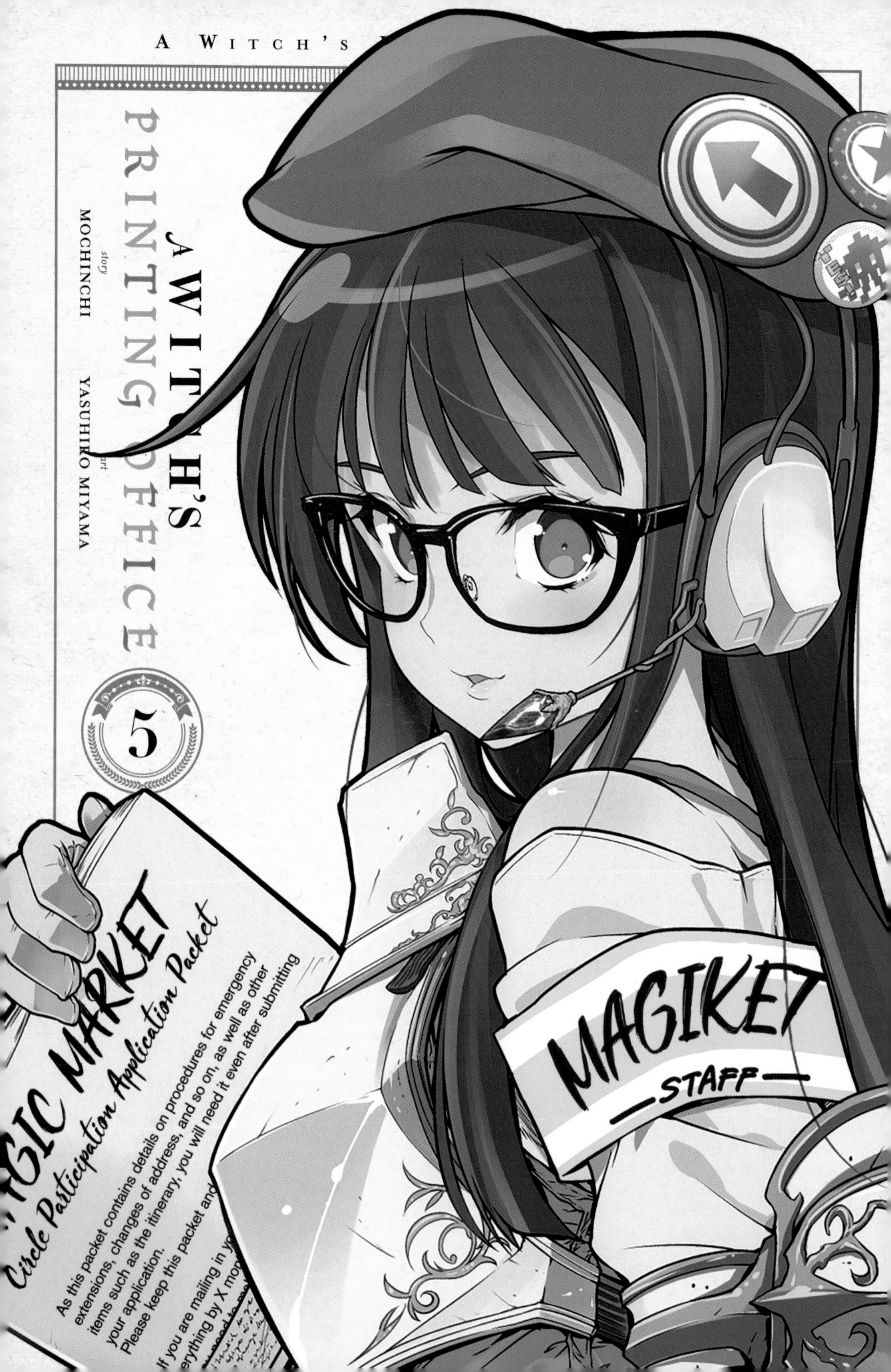
A WITCH'S
A WIT H'S
PRINTING OFFICE
story
MOCHINCHI
art
YASUHIRO MIYAMA
5
GIC MARKET
Circle Participation Application Packet
As this packet contains details on procedures for emergency
extensions, changes of address, and so on, as well as other
items such as the itinerary, you will need it even after submitting
your application.
Please keep this packet and
If you are mailing in yo
erything by X mo
MAGIKET
—STAFF—

A Witch's Printing Office

CONTENTS

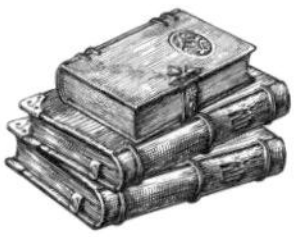

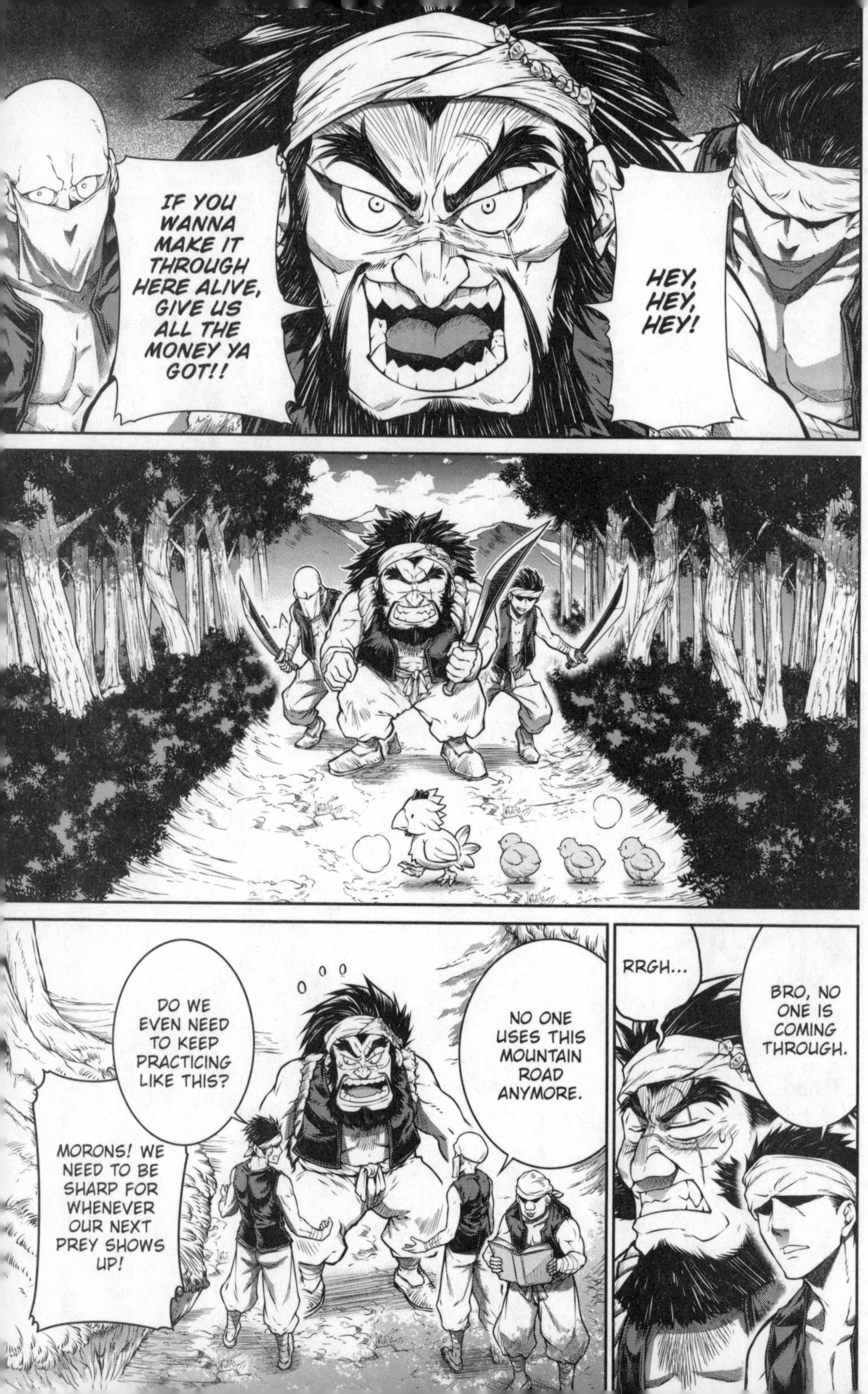
HEY, HEY, HEY!
IF YOU WANNA MAKE IT THROUGH HERE ALIVE, GIVE US ALL THE MONEY YA GOT!!
BRO, NO ONE IS COMING THROUGH.
RRGH...
NO ONE USES THIS MOUNTAIN ROAD ANYMORE.
DO WE EVEN NEED TO KEEP PRACTICING LIKE THIS?
MORONS! WE NEED TO BE SHARP FOR WHENEVER OUR NEXT PREY SHOWS UP!

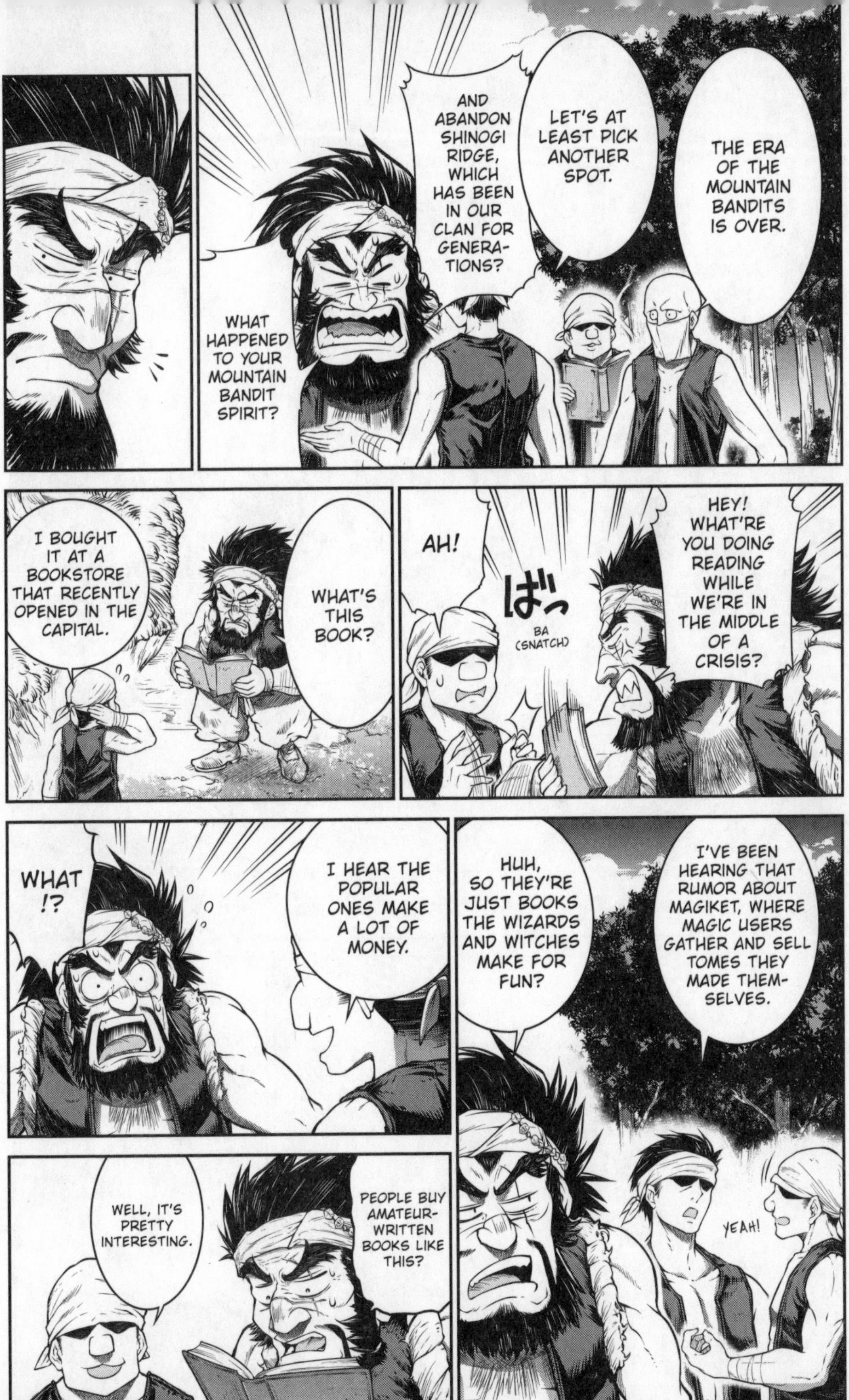
THE ERA OF THE MOUNTAIN BANDITS IS OVER.
LET'S AT LEAST PICK ANOTHER SPOT.
AND ABANDON SHINOGI RIDGE, WHICH HAS BEEN IN OUR CLAN FOR GENERATIONS?
WHAT HAPPENED TO YOUR MOUNTAIN BANDIT SPIRIT?
HEY! WHAT'RE YOU DOING READING WHILE WE'RE IN THE MIDDLE OF A CRISIS?
ばっ
BA (SNATCH)
AH!
WHAT'S THIS BOOK?
I BOUGHT IT AT A BOOKSTORE THAT RECENTLY OPENED IN THE CAPITAL.
I'VE BEEN HEARING THAT RUMOR ABOUT MAGIKET, WHERE MAGIC USERS GATHER AND SELL TOMES THEY MADE THEM-SELVES.
HUH, SO THEY'RE JUST BOOKS THE WIZARDS AND WITCHES MAKE FOR FUN?
YEAH!
I HEAR THE POPULAR ONES MAKE A LOT OF MONEY.
WHAT !?
PEOPLE BUY AMATEUR-WRITTEN BOOKS LIKE THIS?
WELL, IT'S PRETTY INTERESTING.

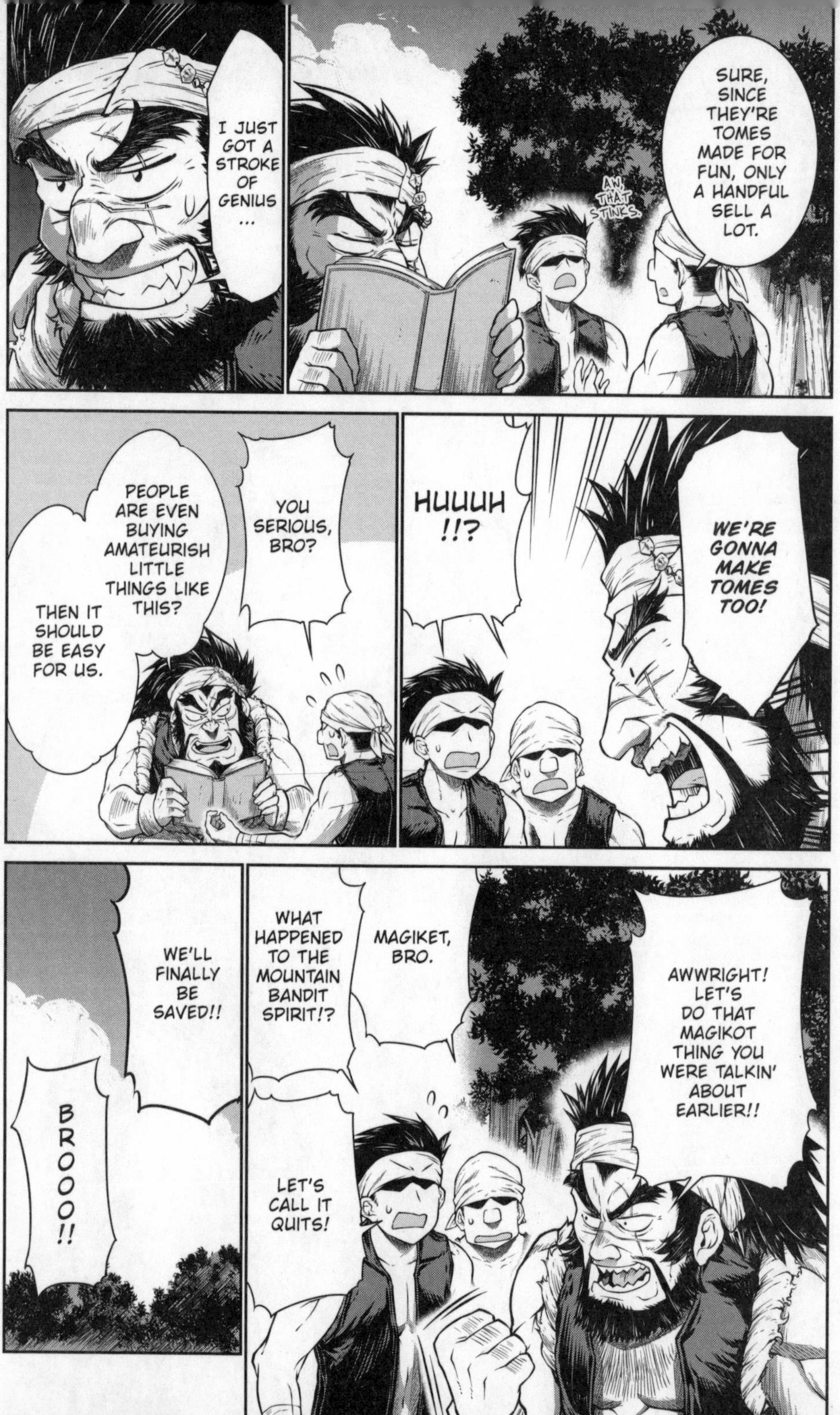

SURE, SINCE THEY'RE TOMES MADE FOR FUN, ONLY A HANDFUL SELL A LOT.
AW, THAT STINKS.
I JUST GOT A STROKE OF GENIUS...
WE'RE GONNA MAKE TOMES TOO!
HUUUH!!?
YOU SERIOUS, BRO?
PEOPLE ARE EVEN BUYING AMATEURISH LITTLE THINGS LIKE THIS?
THEN IT SHOULD BE EASY FOR US.
AWWRIGHT! LET'S DO THAT MAGIKOT THING YOU WERE TALKIN' ABOUT EARLIER!!
MAGIKET, BRO.
WHAT HAPPENED TO THE MOUNTAIN BANDIT SPIRIT!?
LET'S CALL IT QUITS!
WE'LL FINALLY BE SAVED!!
BROOOO!!

Chapter 26

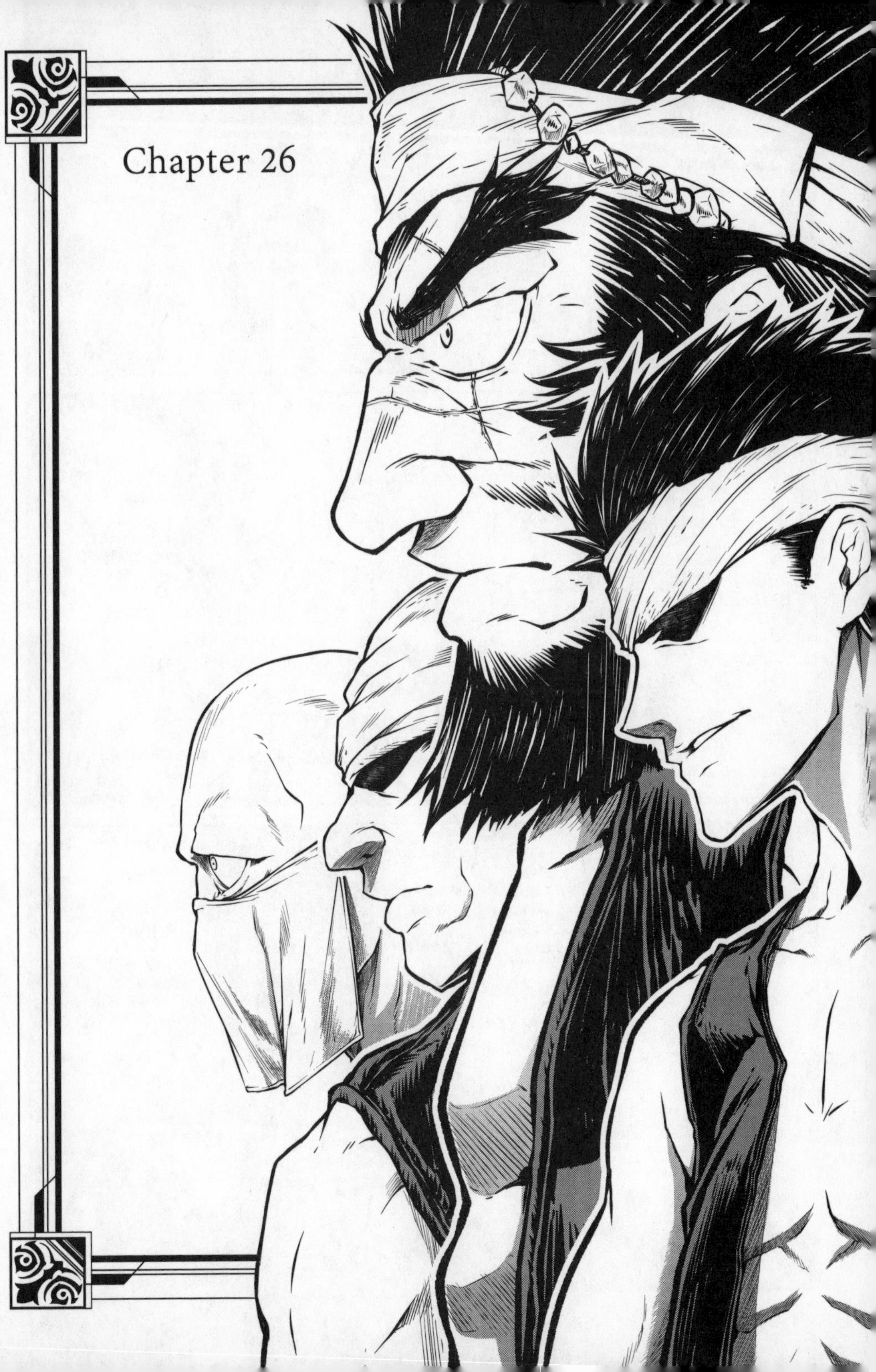

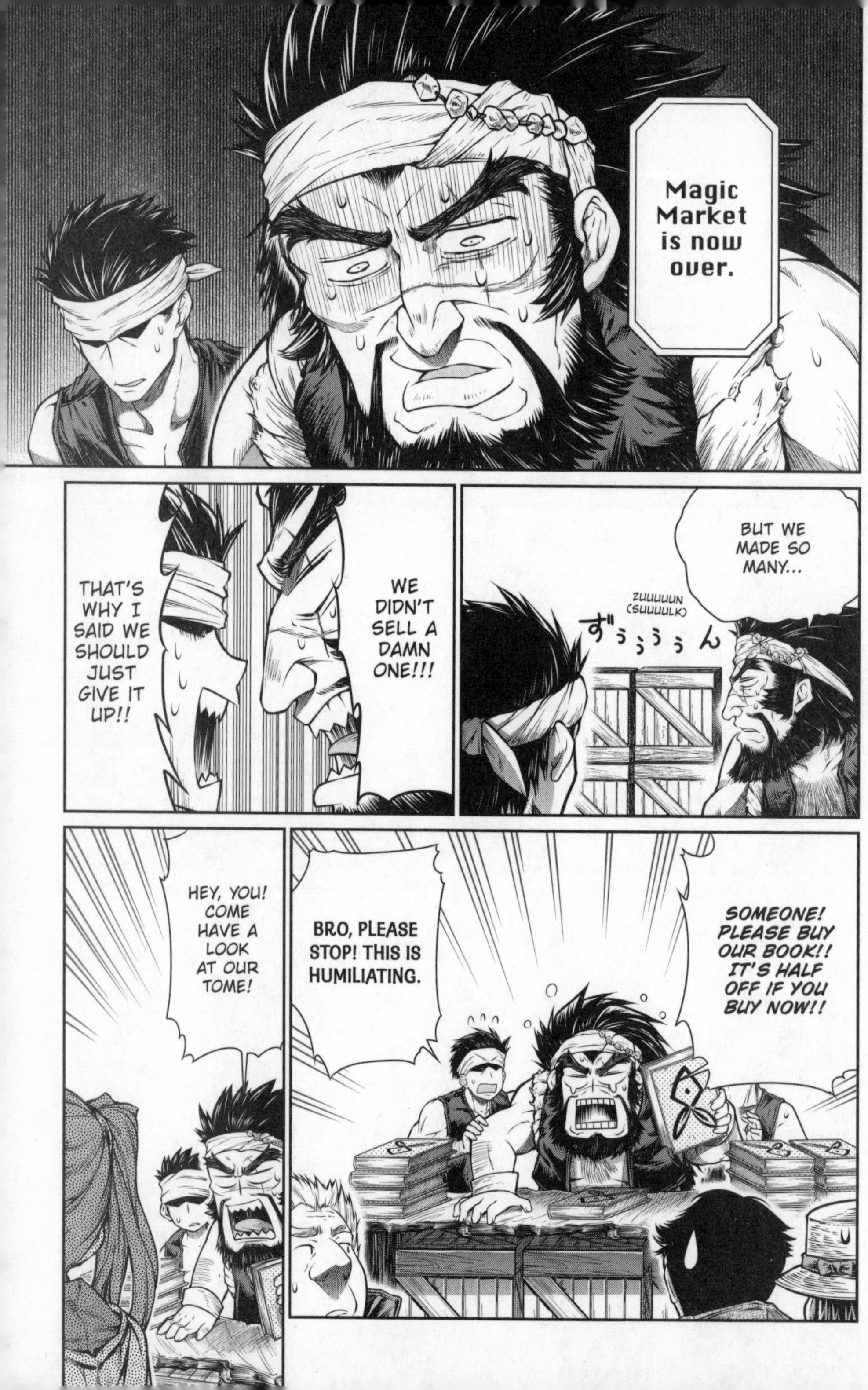
Magic Market is now over.
BUT WE MADE SO MANY...
ZUUUUUN (SUUUULK)
ずぅぅうぅん
WE DIDN'T SELL A DAMN ONE!!!
THAT'S WHY I SAID WE SHOULD JUST GIVE IT UP!!
SOMEONE! PLEASE BUY OUR BOOK!! IT'S HALF OFF IF YOU BUY NOW!!
BRO, PLEASE STOP! THIS IS HUMILIATING.
HEY, YOU! COME HAVE A LOOK AT OUR TOME!

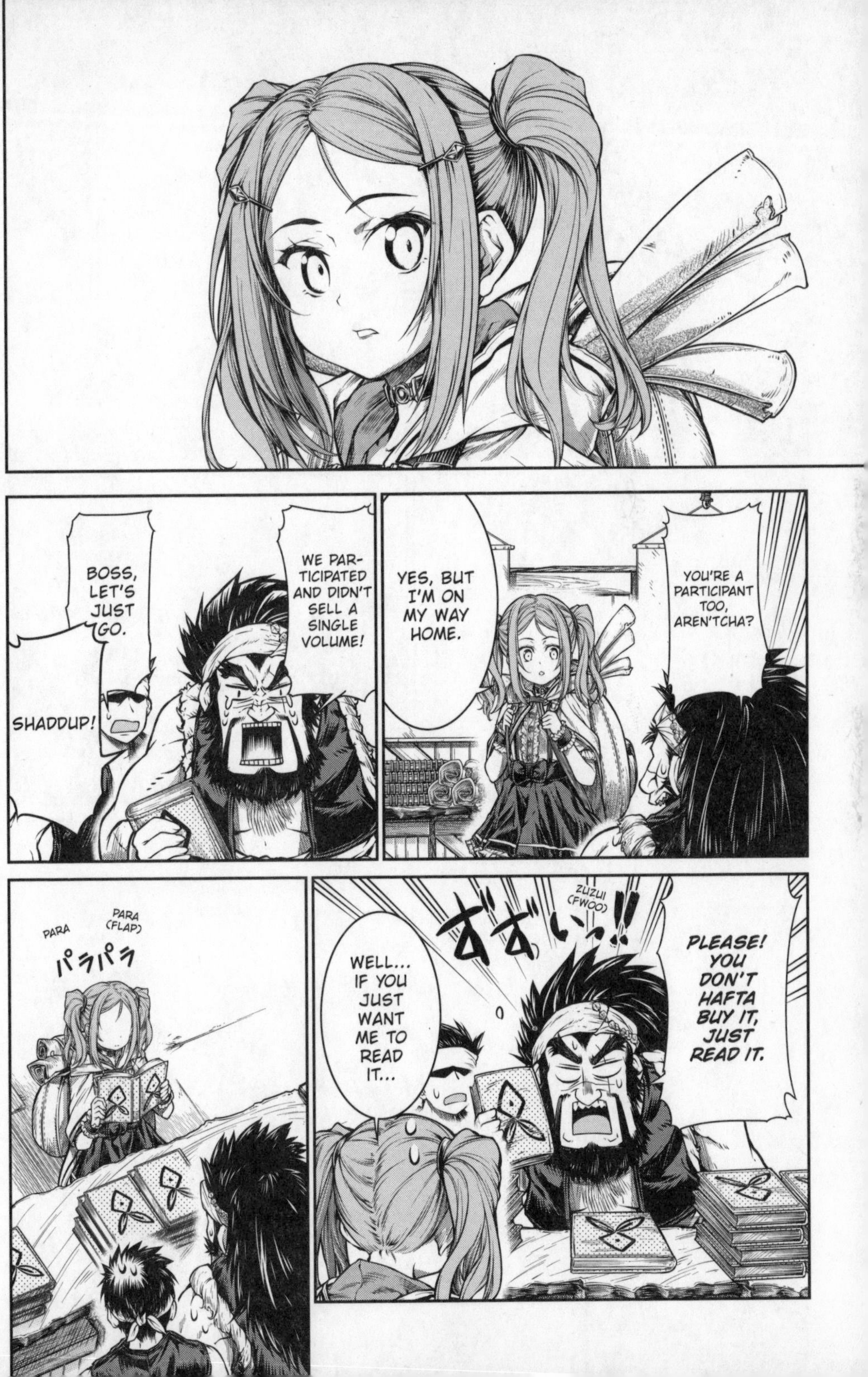
YOU'RE A PARTICIPANT TOO, AREN'TCHA?
YES, BUT I'M ON MY WAY HOME.
WE PARTICIPATED AND DIDN'T SELL A SINGLE VOLUME!
BOSS, LET'S JUST GO.
SHADDUP!
PLEASE! YOU DON'T HAFTA BUY IT, JUST READ IT.
ずずいっ!!
ZUZUI (FWOO)
WELL... IF YOU JUST WANT ME TO READ IT...
パラパラ
PARA PARA (FLAP)

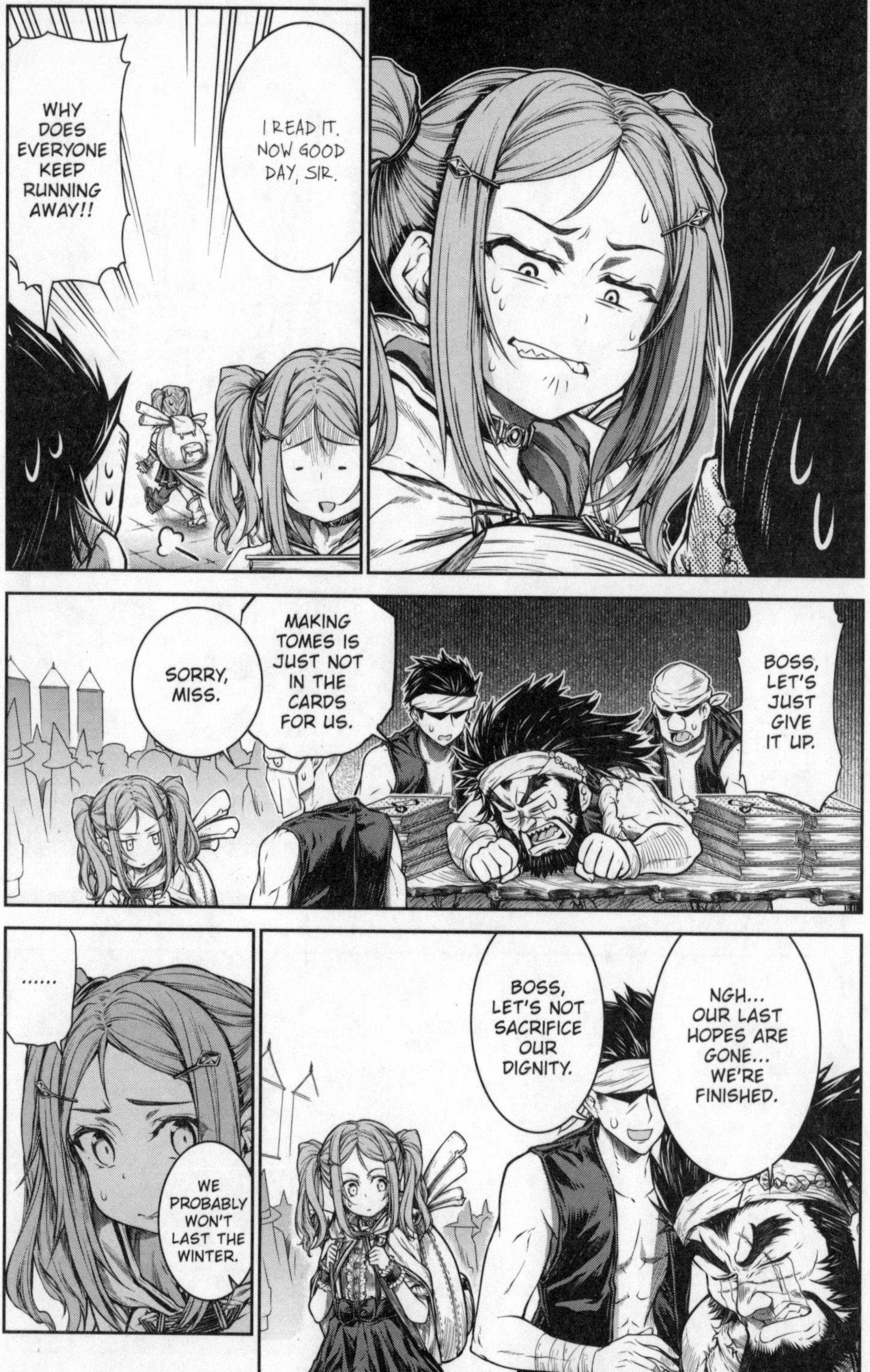
I READ IT. NOW GOOD DAY, SIR.
WHY DOES EVERYONE KEEP RUNNING AWAY!!
BOSS, LET'S JUST GIVE IT UP.
MAKING TOMES IS JUST NOT IN THE CARDS FOR US.
SORRY, MISS.
NGH... OUR LAST HOPES ARE GONE... WE'RE FINISHED.
BOSS, LET'S NOT SACRIFICE OUR DIGNITY.
......
WE PROBABLY WON'T LAST THE WINTER.

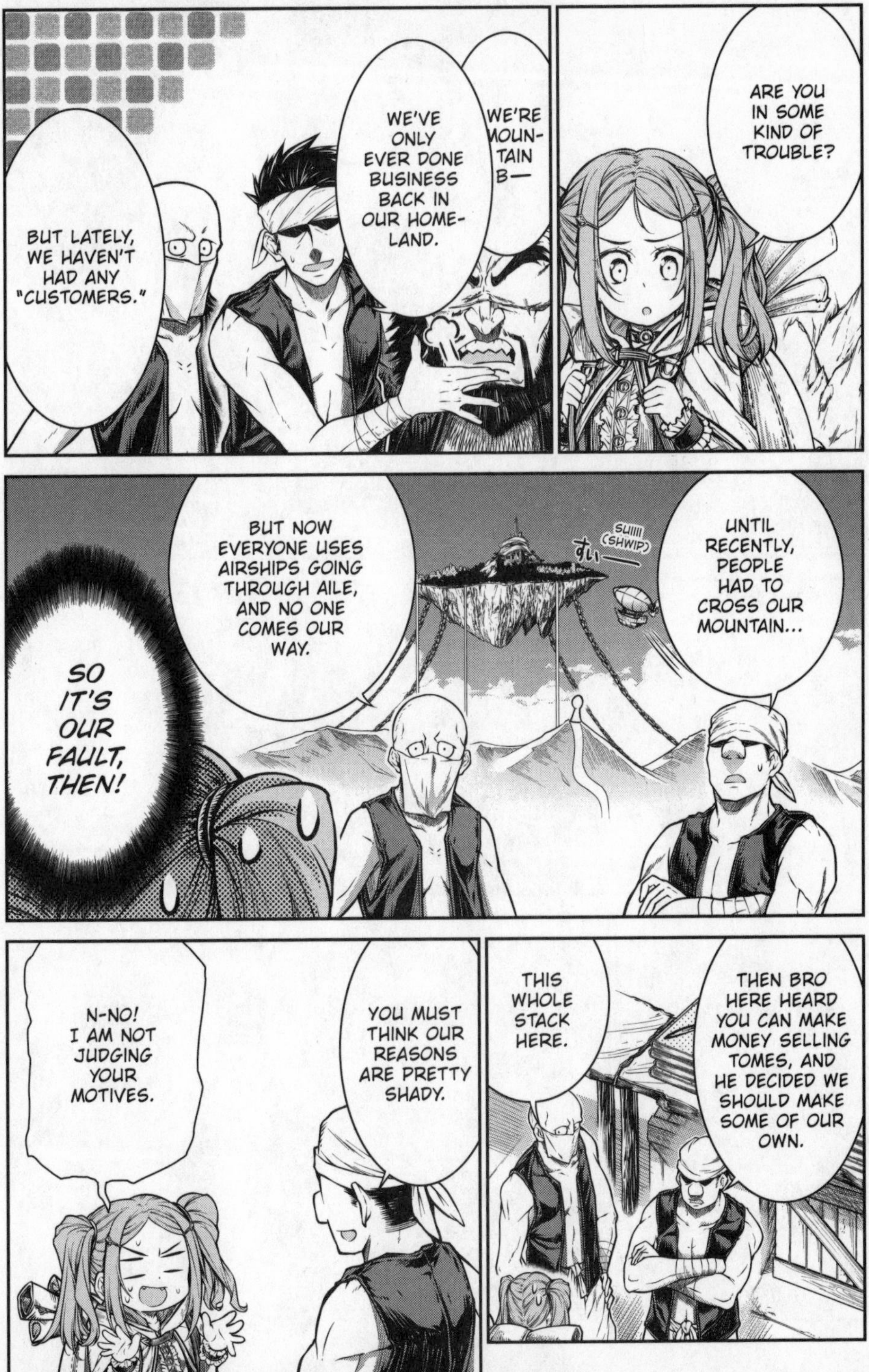
ARE YOU IN SOME KIND OF TROUBLE?
WE'RE MOUN-TAIN B—
WE'VE ONLY EVER DONE BUSINESS BACK IN OUR HOME-LAND.
BUT LATELY, WE HAVEN'T HAD ANY "CUSTOMERS."
UNTIL RECENTLY, PEOPLE HAD TO CROSS OUR MOUNTAIN...
すい—
SUIIII (SHWIP)
BUT NOW EVERYONE USES AIRSHIPS GOING THROUGH AILE, AND NO ONE COMES OUR WAY.
SO IT'S OUR FAULT, THEN!
THEN BRO HERE HEARD YOU CAN MAKE MONEY SELLING TOMES, AND HE DECIDED WE SHOULD MAKE SOME OF OUR OWN.
THIS WHOLE STACK HERE.
YOU MUST THINK OUR REASONS ARE PRETTY SHADY.
N-NO! I AM NOT JUDGING YOUR MOTIVES.

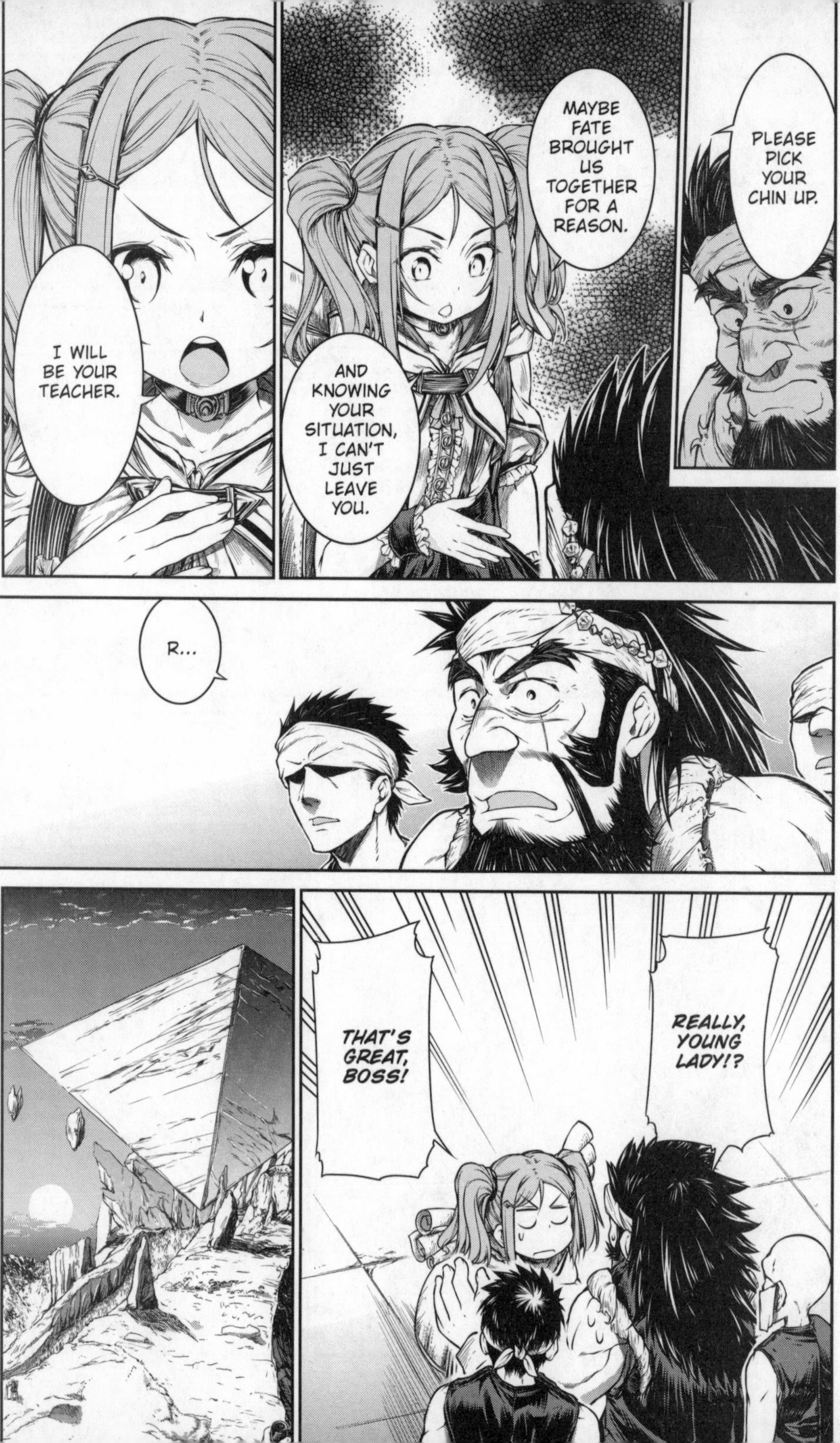
PLEASE PICK YOUR CHIN UP.
MAYBE FATE BROUGHT US TOGETHER FOR A REASON.
AND KNOWING YOUR SITUATION, I CAN'T JUST LEAVE YOU.
I WILL BE YOUR TEACHER.
R...
REALLY, YOUNG LADY!?
THAT'S GREAT, BOSS!

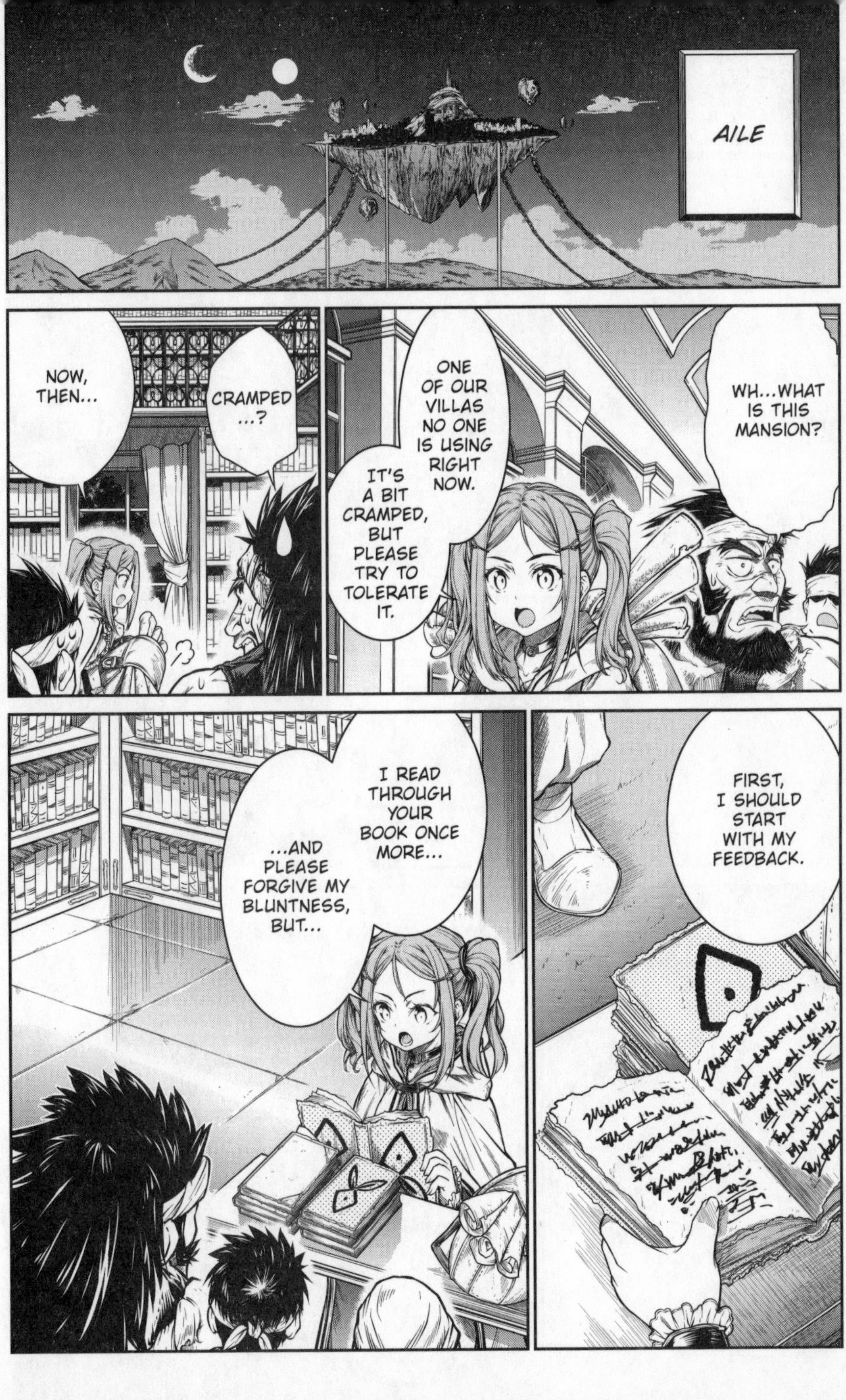
AILE
WH...WHAT IS THIS MANSION?
ONE OF OUR VILLAS NO ONE IS USING RIGHT NOW.
IT'S A BIT CRAMPED, BUT PLEASE TRY TO TOLERATE IT.
CRAMPED ...?
NOW, THEN...
FIRST, I SHOULD START WITH MY FEEDBACK.
I READ THROUGH YOUR BOOK ONCE MORE...
...AND PLEASE FORGIVE MY BLUNTNESS, BUT...

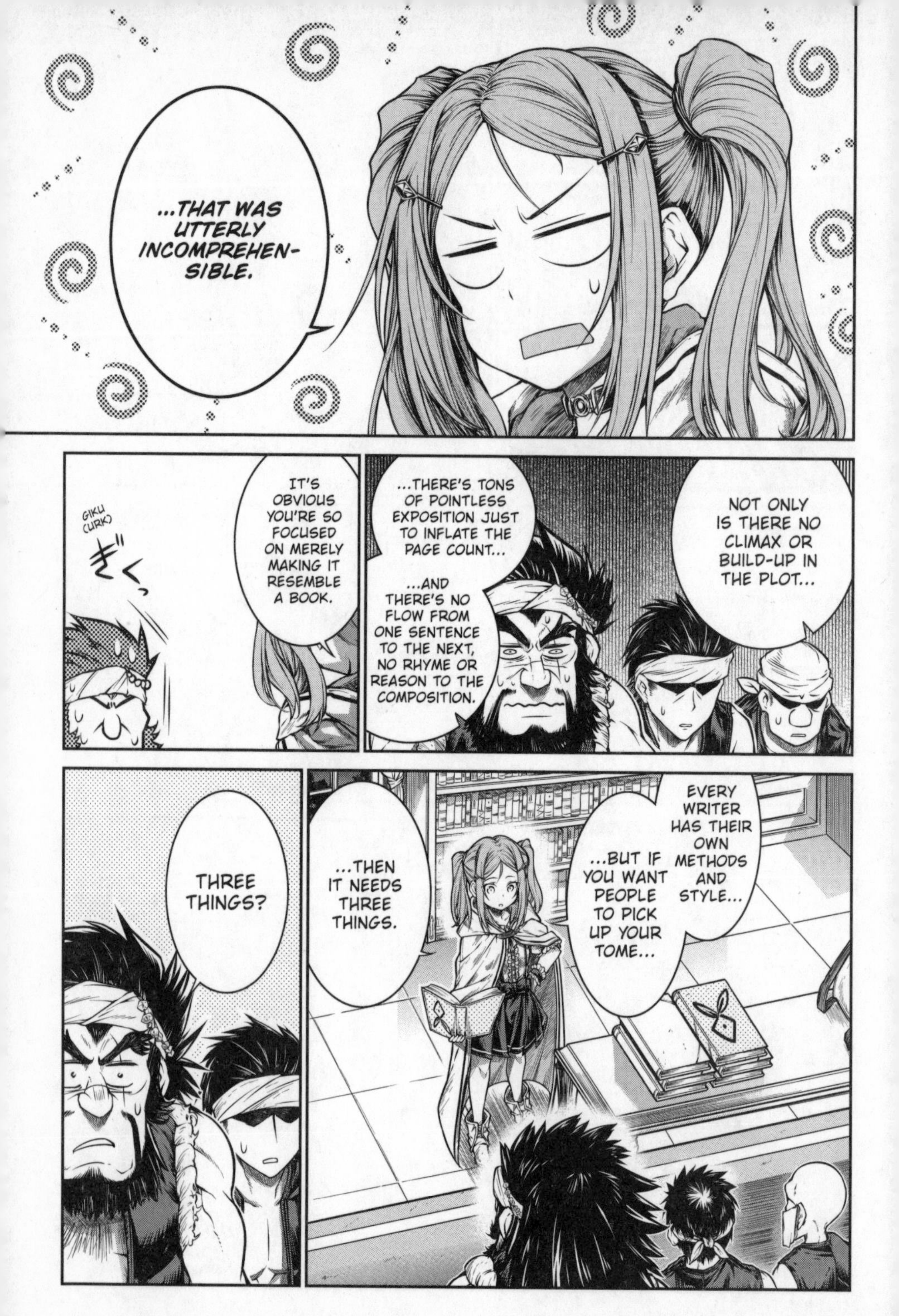
...THAT WAS UTTERLY INCOMPREHEN-SIBLE.
NOT ONLY IS THERE NO CLIMAX OR BUILD-UP IN THE PLOT...
...THERE'S TONS OF POINTLESS EXPOSITION JUST TO INFLATE THE PAGE COUNT...
...AND THERE'S NO FLOW FROM ONE SENTENCE TO THE NEXT, NO RHYME OR REASON TO THE COMPOSITION.
IT'S OBVIOUS YOU'RE SO FOCUSED ON MERELY MAKING IT RESEMBLE A BOOK.
ぎくっ
GIKU (URK)
EVERY WRITER HAS THEIR OWN METHODS AND STYLE...
...BUT IF YOU WANT PEOPLE TO PICK UP YOUR TOME...
...THEN IT NEEDS THREE THINGS.
THREE THINGS?

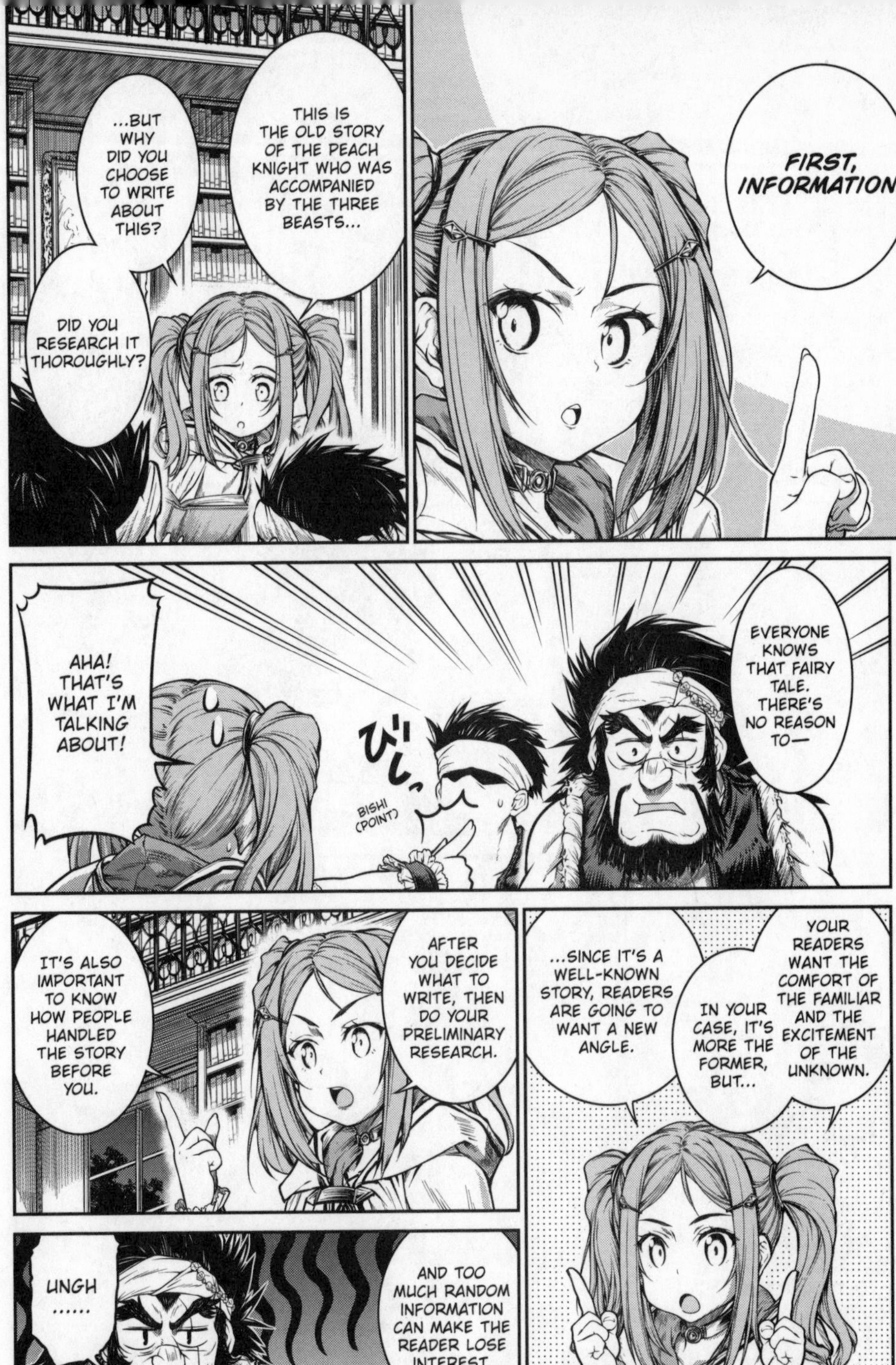
FIRST, INFORMATION.
THIS IS THE OLD STORY OF THE PEACH KNIGHT WHO WAS ACCOMPANIED BY THE THREE BEASTS...
...BUT WHY DID YOU CHOOSE TO WRITE ABOUT THIS?
DID YOU RESEARCH IT THOROUGHLY?
EVERYONE KNOWS THAT FAIRY TALE. THERE'S NO REASON TO—
びしっ
BISHI (POINT)
AHA! THAT'S WHAT I'M TALKING ABOUT!
YOUR READERS WANT THE COMFORT OF THE FAMILIAR AND THE EXCITEMENT OF THE UNKNOWN.
IN YOUR CASE, IT'S MORE THE FORMER, BUT...
...SINCE IT'S A WELL-KNOWN STORY, READERS ARE GOING TO WANT A NEW ANGLE.
AFTER YOU DECIDE WHAT TO WRITE, THEN DO YOUR PRELIMINARY RESEARCH.
IT'S ALSO IMPORTANT TO KNOW HOW PEOPLE HANDLED THE STORY BEFORE YOU.
AND TOO MUCH RANDOM INFORMATION CAN MAKE THE READER LOSE INTEREST.
UNGH ......

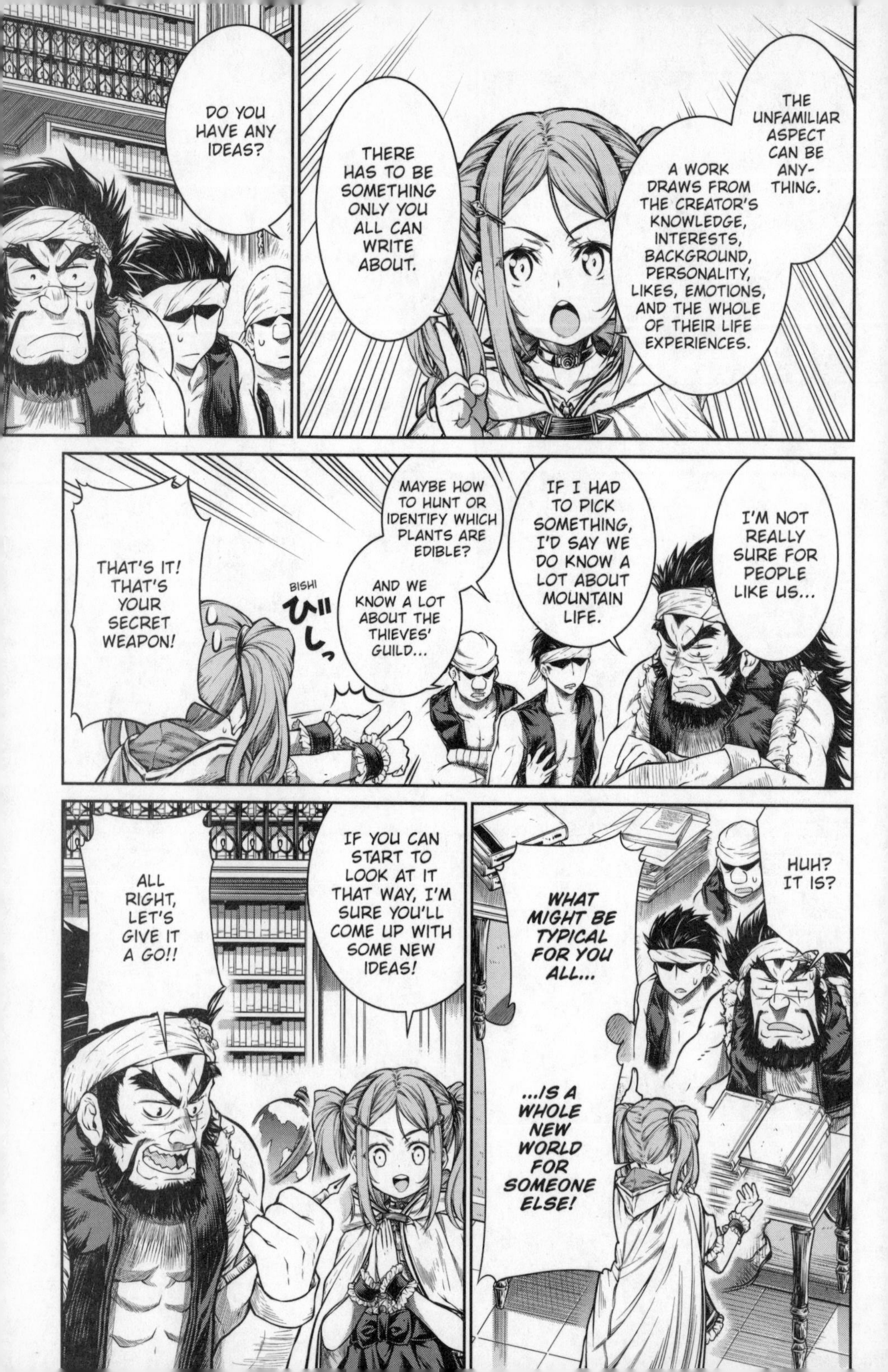
THE UNFAMILIAR ASPECT CAN BE ANY-THING.
A WORK DRAWS FROM THE CREATOR'S KNOWLEDGE, INTERESTS, BACKGROUND, PERSONALITY, LIKES, EMOTIONS, AND THE WHOLE OF THEIR LIFE EXPERIENCES.
THERE HAS TO BE SOMETHING ONLY YOU ALL CAN WRITE ABOUT.
DO YOU HAVE ANY IDEAS?
I'M NOT REALLY SURE FOR PEOPLE LIKE US...
IF I HAD TO PICK SOMETHING, I'D SAY WE DO KNOW A LOT ABOUT MOUNTAIN LIFE.
MAYBE HOW TO HUNT OR IDENTIFY WHICH PLANTS ARE EDIBLE?
AND WE KNOW A LOT ABOUT THE THIEVES' GUILD...
BISHI
びしっ
THAT'S IT! THAT'S YOUR SECRET WEAPON!
HUH? IT IS?
WHAT MIGHT BE TYPICAL FOR YOU ALL...
...IS A WHOLE NEW WORLD FOR SOMEONE ELSE!
IF YOU CAN START TO LOOK AT IT THAT WAY, I'M SURE YOU'LL COME UP WITH SOME NEW IDEAS!
ALL RIGHT, LET'S GIVE IT A GO!!

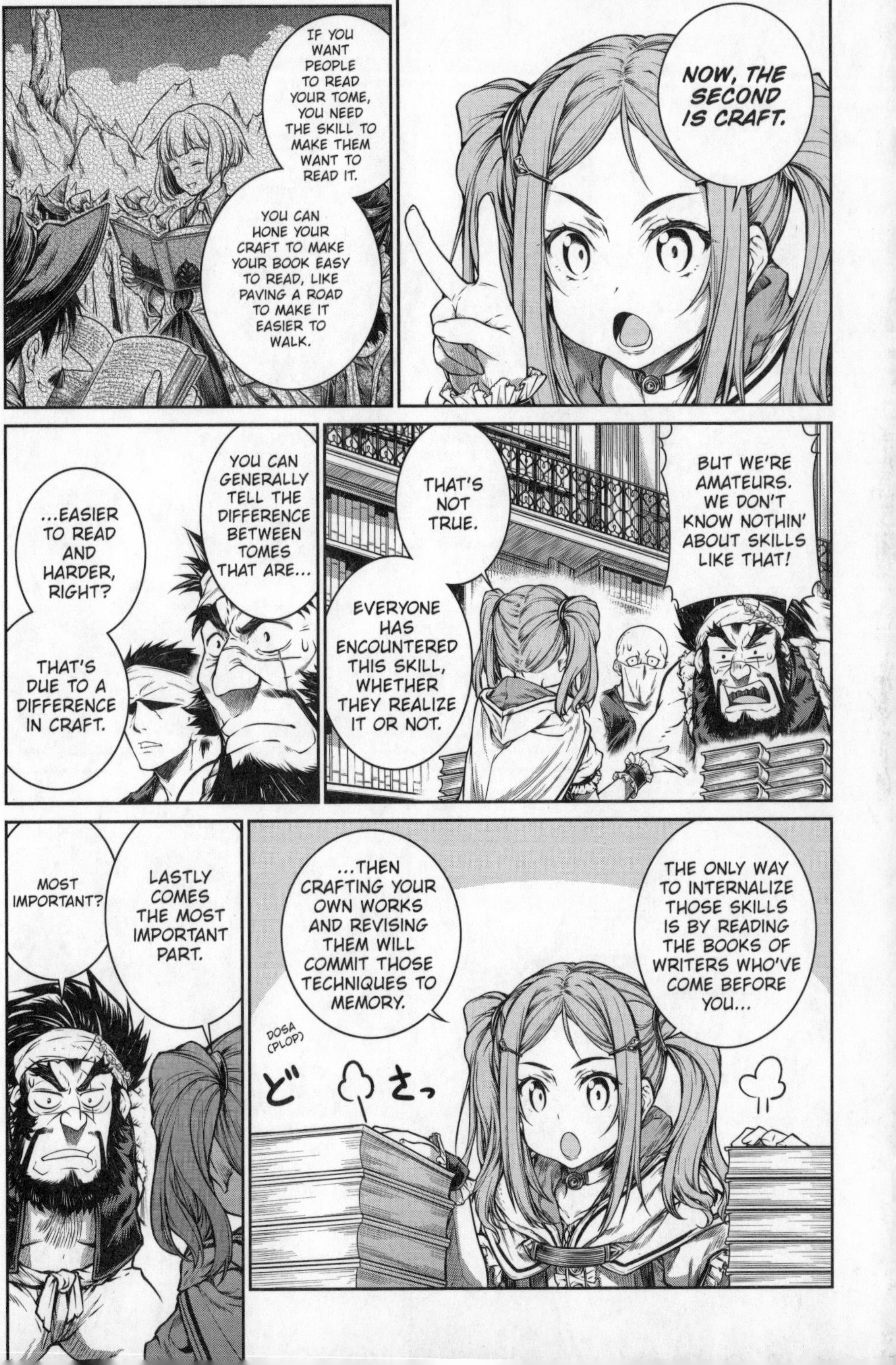
NOW, THE SECOND IS CRAFT.
IF YOU WANT PEOPLE TO READ YOUR TOME, YOU NEED THE SKILL TO MAKE THEM WANT TO READ IT.
YOU CAN HONE YOUR CRAFT TO MAKE YOUR BOOK EASY TO READ, LIKE PAVING A ROAD TO MAKE IT EASIER TO WALK.
BUT WE'RE AMATEURS. WE DON'T KNOW NOTHIN' ABOUT SKILLS LIKE THAT!
THAT'S NOT TRUE.
EVERYONE HAS ENCOUNTERED THIS SKILL, WHETHER THEY REALIZE IT OR NOT.
YOU CAN GENERALLY TELL THE DIFFERENCE BETWEEN TOMES THAT ARE...
...EASIER TO READ AND HARDER, RIGHT?
THAT'S DUE TO A DIFFERENCE IN CRAFT.
THE ONLY WAY TO INTERNALIZE THOSE SKILLS IS BY READING THE BOOKS OF WRITERS WHO'VE COME BEFORE YOU...
...THEN CRAFTING YOUR OWN WORKS AND REVISING THEM WILL COMMIT THOSE TECHNIQUES TO MEMORY.
DOSA (PLOP)
どさっ
LASTLY COMES THE MOST IMPORTANT PART.
MOST IMPORTANT?

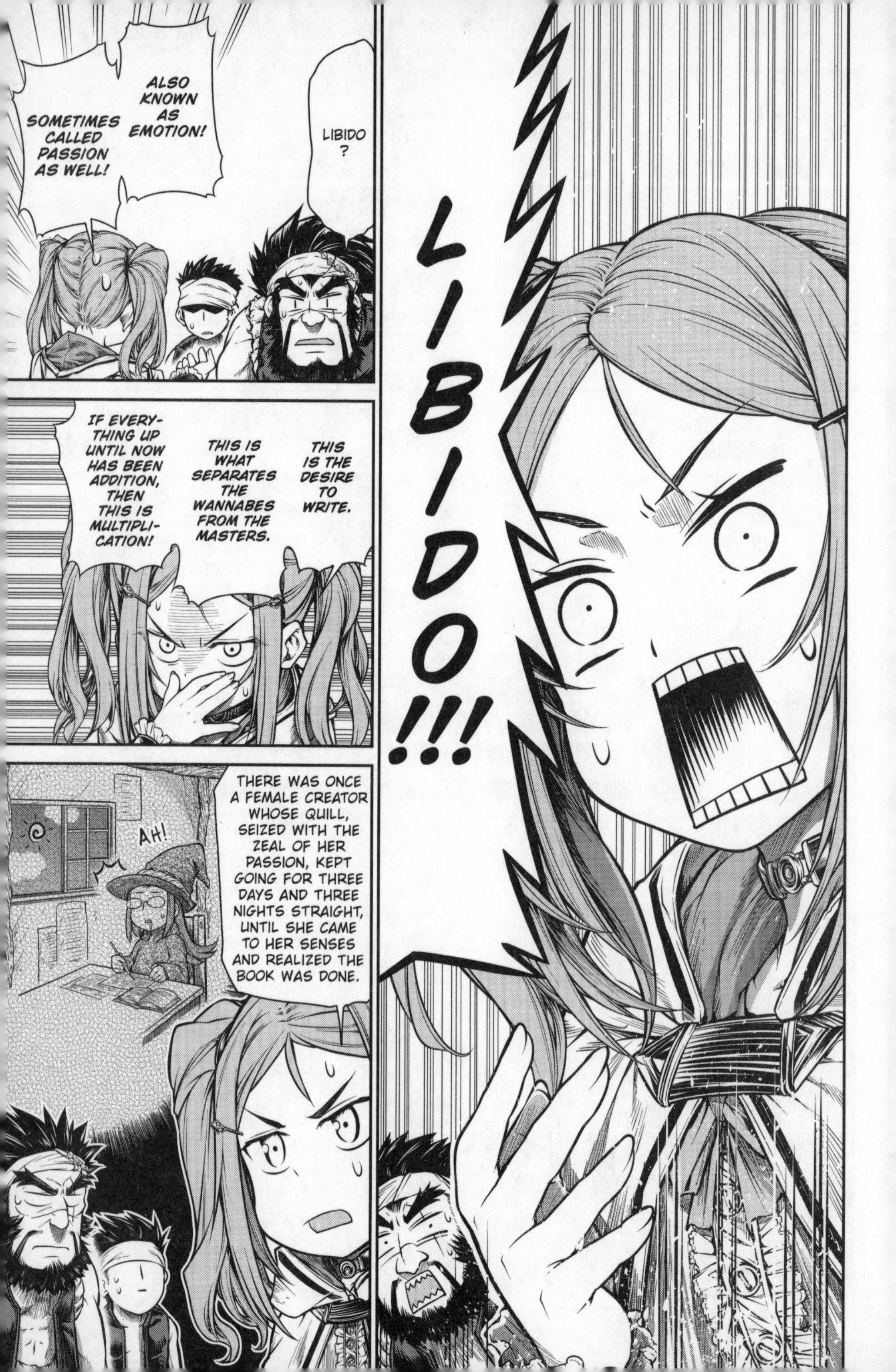
LIBIDO!!!
LIBIDO ?
ALSO KNOWN AS EMOTION!
SOMETIMES CALLED PASSION AS WELL!
THIS IS THE DESIRE TO WRITE.
THIS IS WHAT SEPARATES THE WANNABES FROM THE MASTERS.
IF EVERYTHING UP UNTIL NOW HAS BEEN ADDITION, THEN THIS IS MULTIPLICATION!
THERE WAS ONCE A FEMALE CREATOR WHOSE QUILL, SEIZED WITH THE ZEAL OF HER PASSION, KEPT GOING FOR THREE DAYS AND THREE NIGHTS STRAIGHT, UNTIL SHE CAME TO HER SENSES AND REALIZED THE BOOK WAS DONE.
AH!

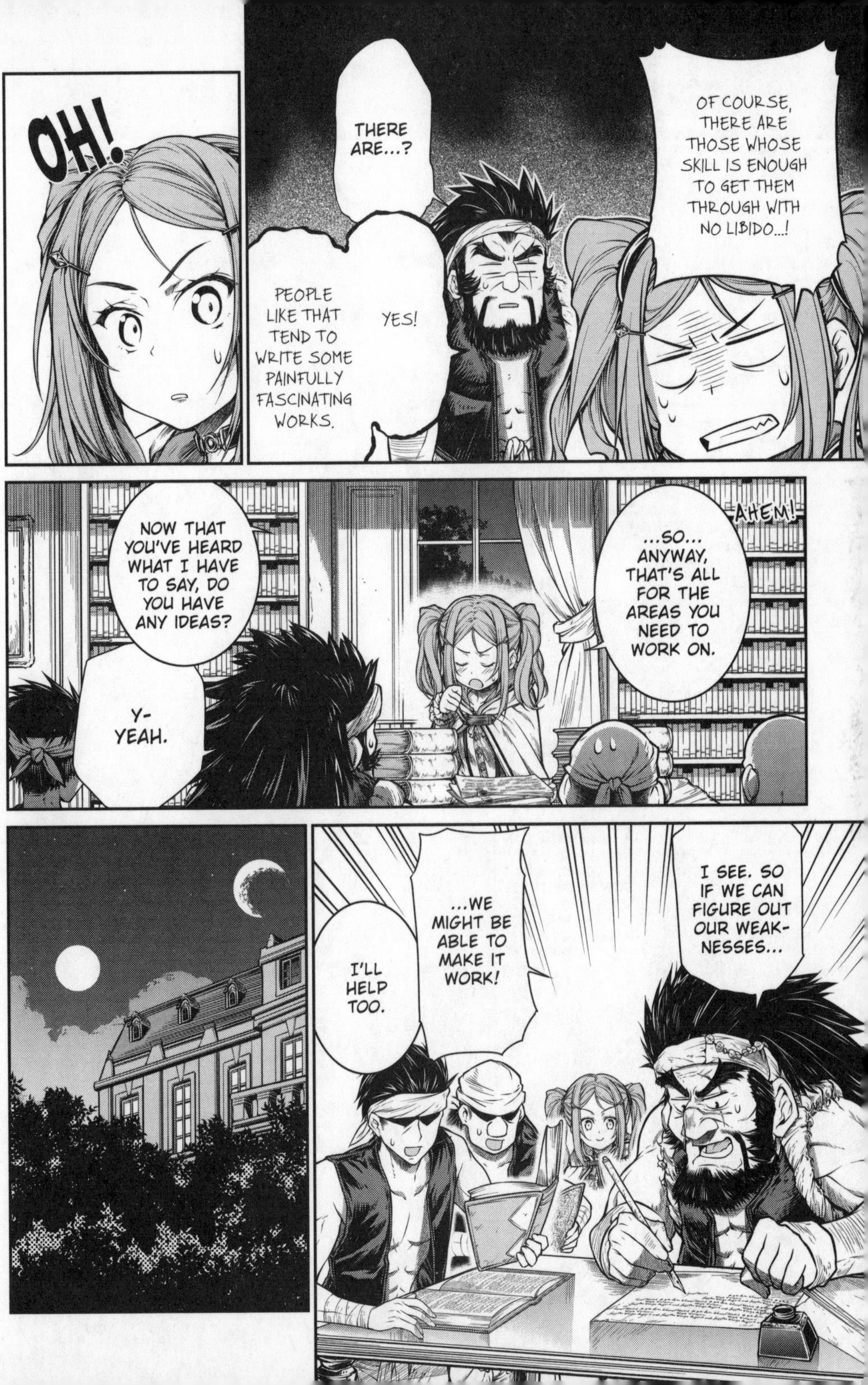
OF COURSE, THERE ARE THOSE WHOSE SKILL IS ENOUGH TO GET THEM THROUGH WITH NO LIBIDO...!
THERE ARE...?
YES!
PEOPLE LIKE THAT TEND TO WRITE SOME PAINFULLY FASCINATING WORKS.
OH!
AHEM!
...SO... ANYWAY, THAT'S ALL FOR THE AREAS YOU NEED TO WORK ON.
NOW THAT YOU'VE HEARD WHAT I HAVE TO SAY, DO YOU HAVE ANY IDEAS?
Y-YEAH.
I SEE. SO IF WE CAN FIGURE OUT OUR WEAK-NESSES...
...WE MIGHT BE ABLE TO MAKE IT WORK!
I'LL HELP TOO.

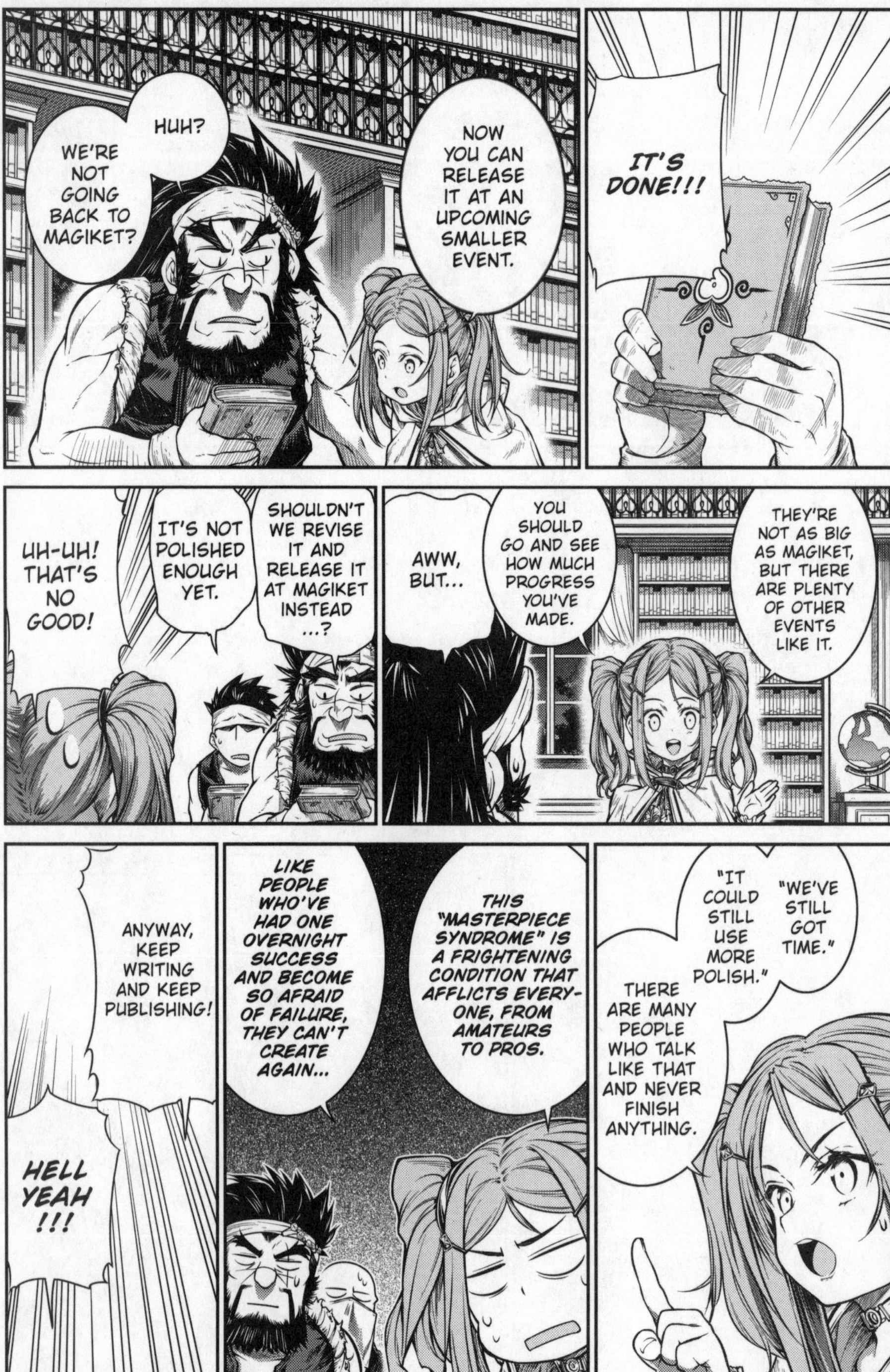
IT'S DONE!!!
NOW YOU CAN RELEASE IT AT AN UPCOMING SMALLER EVENT.
HUH? WE'RE NOT GOING BACK TO MAGIKET?
THEY'RE NOT AS BIG AS MAGIKET, BUT THERE ARE PLENTY OF OTHER EVENTS LIKE IT.
YOU SHOULD GO AND SEE HOW MUCH PROGRESS YOU'VE MADE.
AWW, BUT...
SHOULDN'T WE REVISE IT AND RELEASE IT AT MAGIKET INSTEAD ...?
IT'S NOT POLISHED ENOUGH YET.
UH-UH! THAT'S NO GOOD!
"WE'VE STILL GOT TIME."
"IT COULD STILL USE MORE POLISH."
THERE ARE MANY PEOPLE WHO TALK LIKE THAT AND NEVER FINISH ANYTHING.
THIS "MASTERPIECE SYNDROME" IS A FRIGHTENING CONDITION THAT AFFLICTS EVERY-ONE, FROM AMATEURS TO PROS.
LIKE PEOPLE WHO'VE HAD ONE OVERNIGHT SUCCESS AND BECOME SO AFRAID OF FAILURE, THEY CAN'T CREATE AGAIN...
ANYWAY, KEEP WRITING AND KEEP PUBLISHING!
HELL YEAH!!!

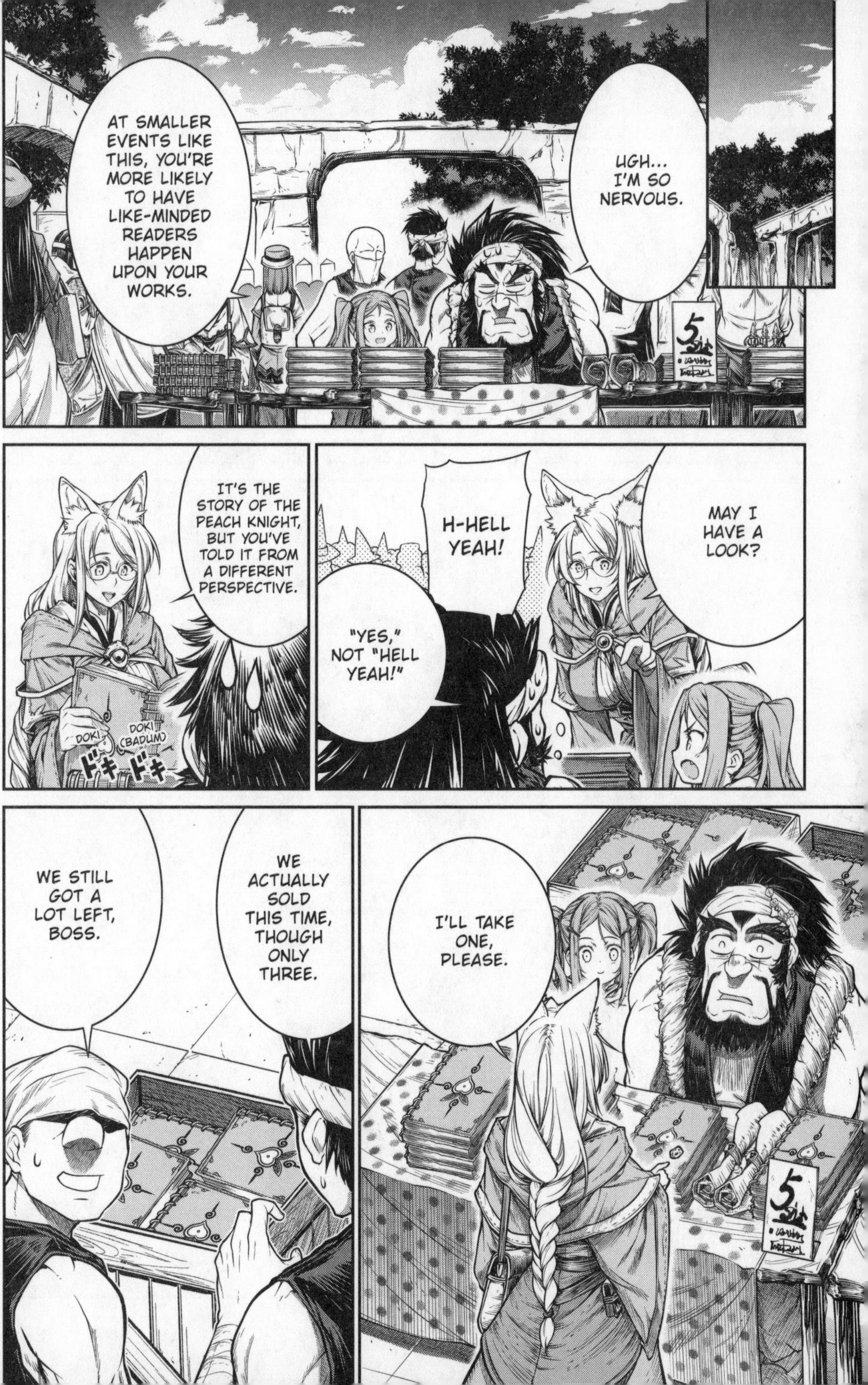
UGH... I'M SO NERVOUS.
AT SMALLER EVENTS LIKE THIS, YOU'RE MORE LIKELY TO HAVE LIKE-MINDED READERS HAPPEN UPON YOUR WORKS.
MAY I HAVE A LOOK?
H-HELL YEAH!
"YES," NOT "HELL YEAH!"
IT'S THE STORY OF THE PEACH KNIGHT, BUT YOU'VE TOLD IT FROM A DIFFERENT PERSPECTIVE.
DOKI DOKI (BADUM)
ドキドキ
I'LL TAKE ONE, PLEASE.
WE ACTUALLY SOLD THIS TIME, THOUGH ONLY THREE.
WE STILL GOT A LOT LEFT, BOSS.

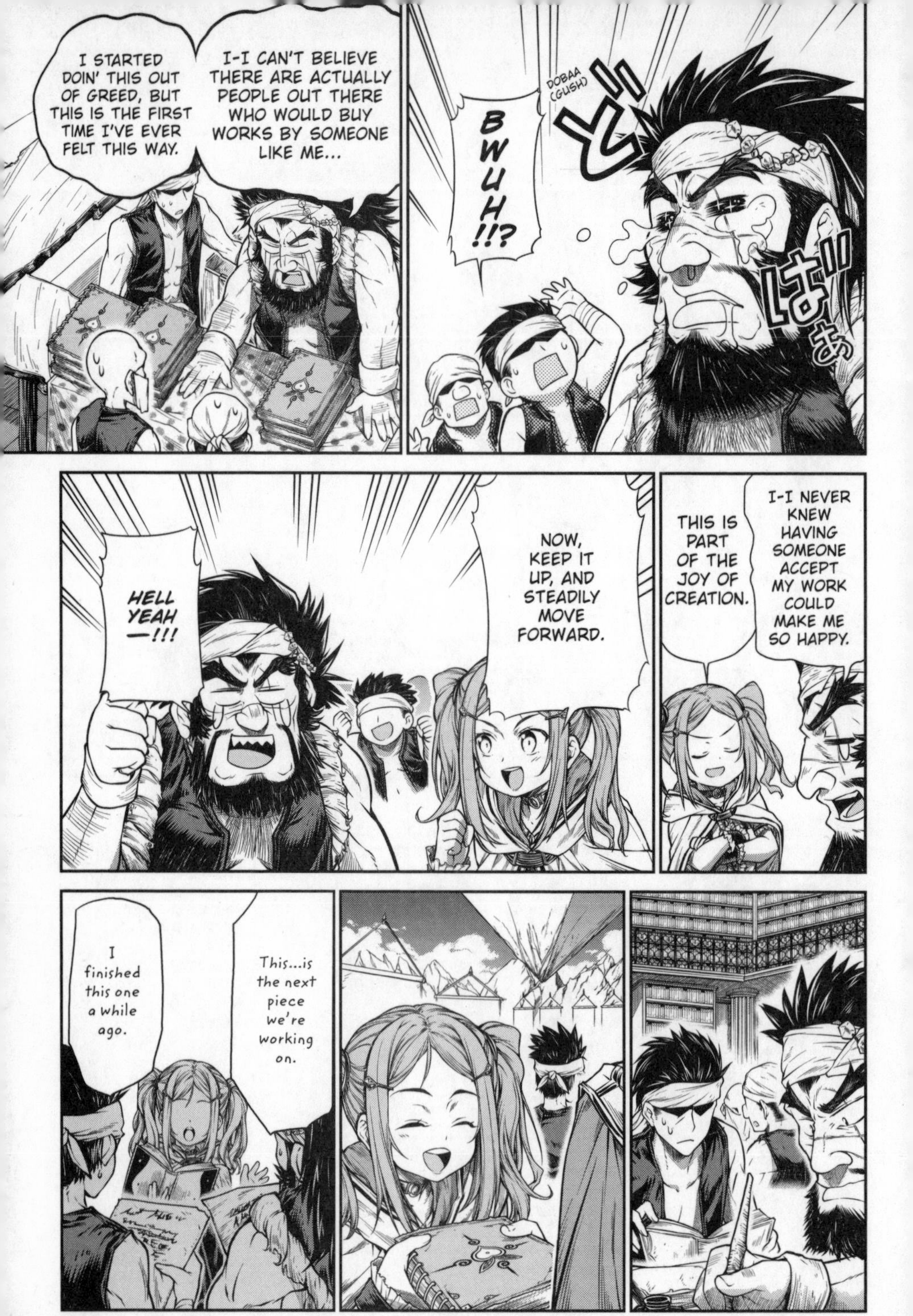
DOBAA (GUSH)
ど
BWUH!!?
ばぁ
I-I CAN'T BELIEVE THERE ARE ACTUALLY PEOPLE OUT THERE WHO WOULD BUY WORKS BY SOMEONE LIKE ME…
I STARTED DOIN' THIS OUT OF GREED, BUT THIS IS THE FIRST TIME I'VE EVER FELT THIS WAY.
I-I NEVER KNEW HAVING SOMEONE ACCEPT MY WORK COULD MAKE ME SO HAPPY.
THIS IS PART OF THE JOY OF CREATION.
NOW, KEEP IT UP, AND STEADILY MOVE FORWARD.
HELL YEAH—!!!
This…is the next piece we're working on.
I finished this one a while ago.

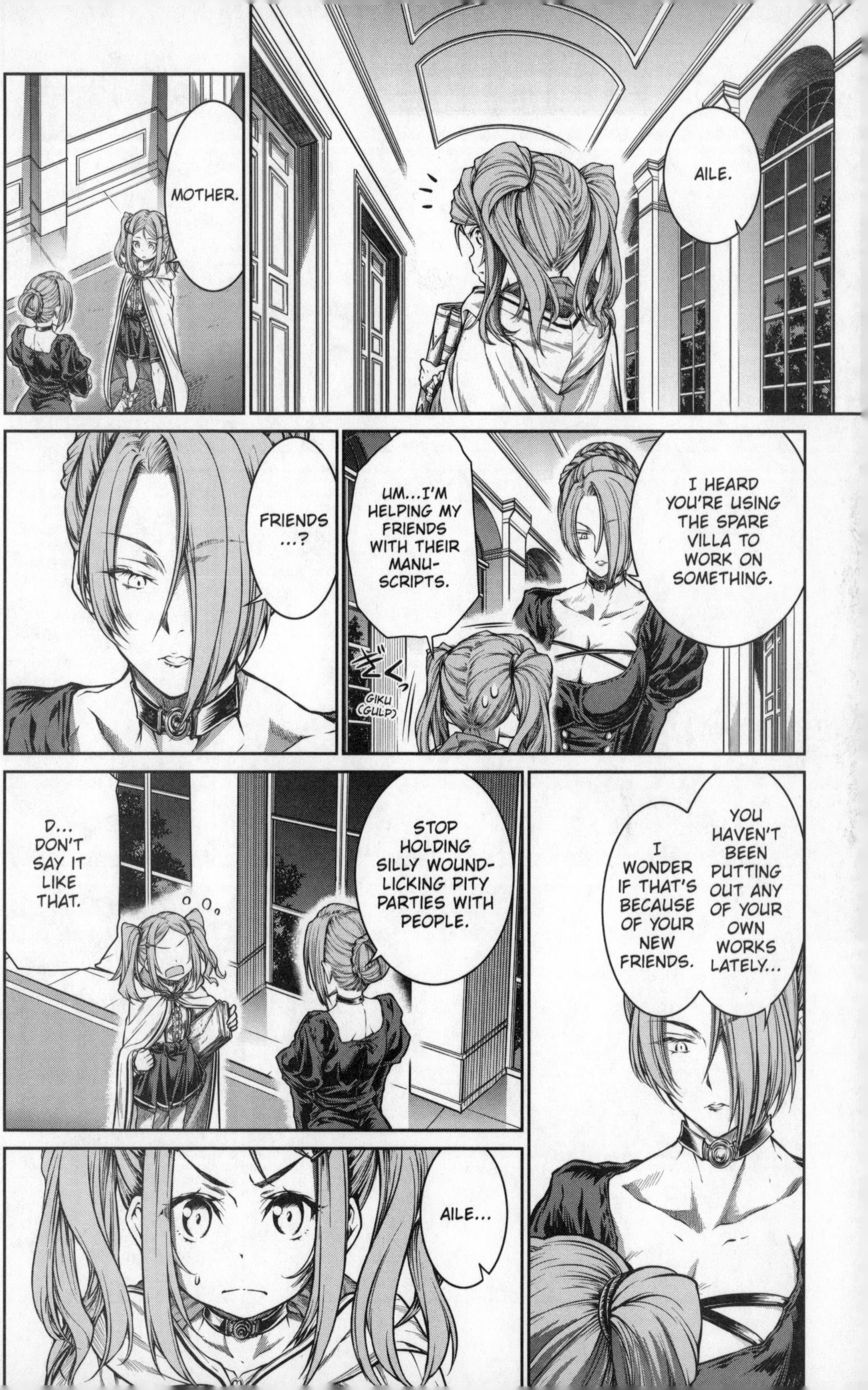
AILE.
MOTHER.
I HEARD YOU'RE USING THE SPARE VILLA TO WORK ON SOMETHING.
UM...I'M HELPING MY FRIENDS WITH THEIR MANU-SCRIPTS.
ぎくっ
GIKU (GULP)
FRIENDS ...?
YOU HAVEN'T BEEN PUTTING OUT ANY OF YOUR OWN WORKS LATELY...
I WONDER IF THAT'S BECAUSE OF YOUR NEW FRIENDS.
STOP HOLDING SILLY WOUND-LICKING PITY PARTIES WITH PEOPLE.
D... DON'T SAY IT LIKE THAT.
AILE...

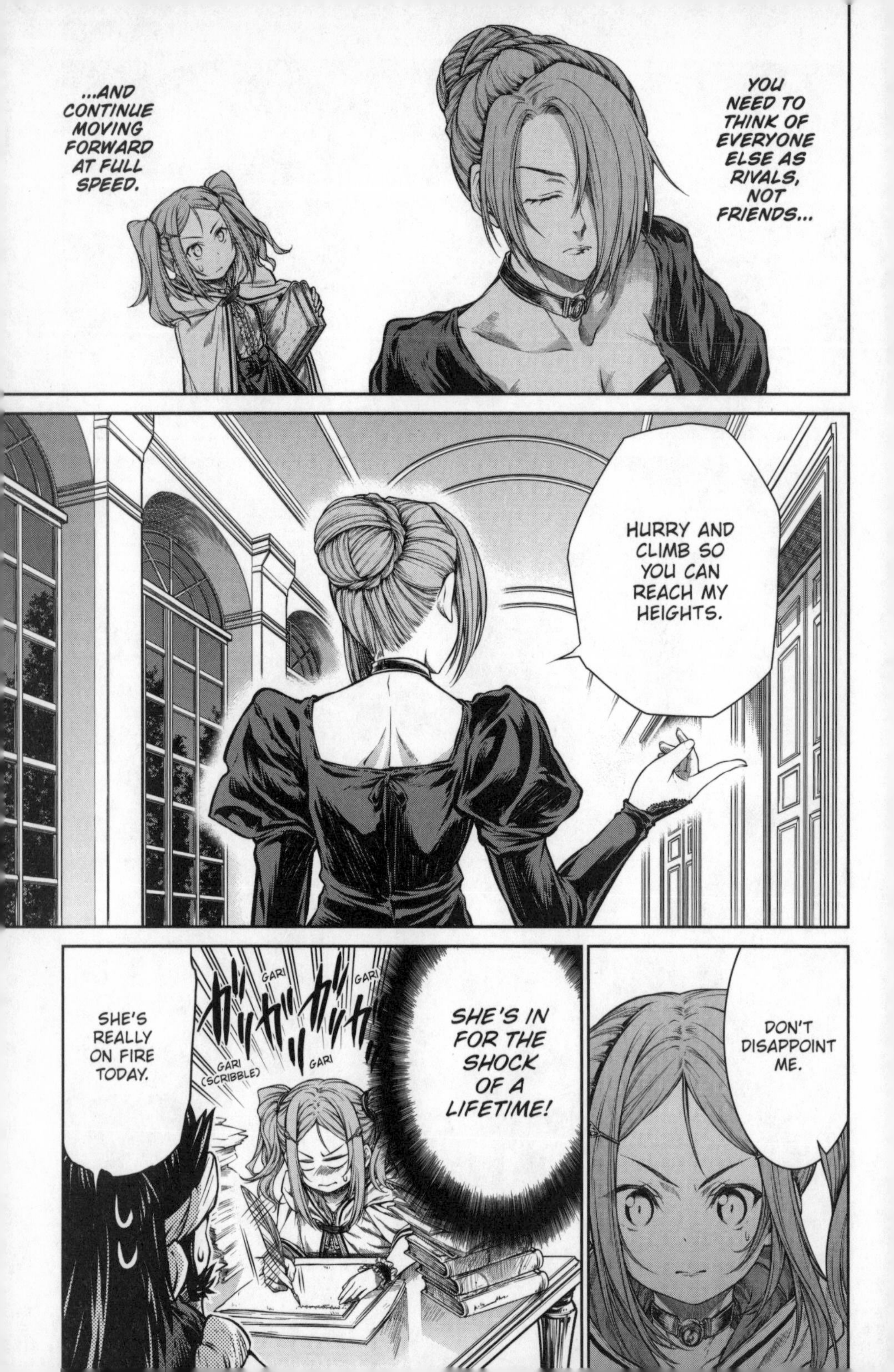
YOU NEED TO THINK OF EVERYONE ELSE AS RIVALS, NOT FRIENDS...
...AND CONTINUE MOVING FORWARD AT FULL SPEED.
HURRY AND CLIMB SO YOU CAN REACH MY HEIGHTS.
DON'T DISAPPOINT ME.
SHE'S IN FOR THE SHOCK OF A LIFETIME!
GARI
GARI
GARI
GARI (SCRIBBLE)
SHE'S REALLY ON FIRE TODAY.

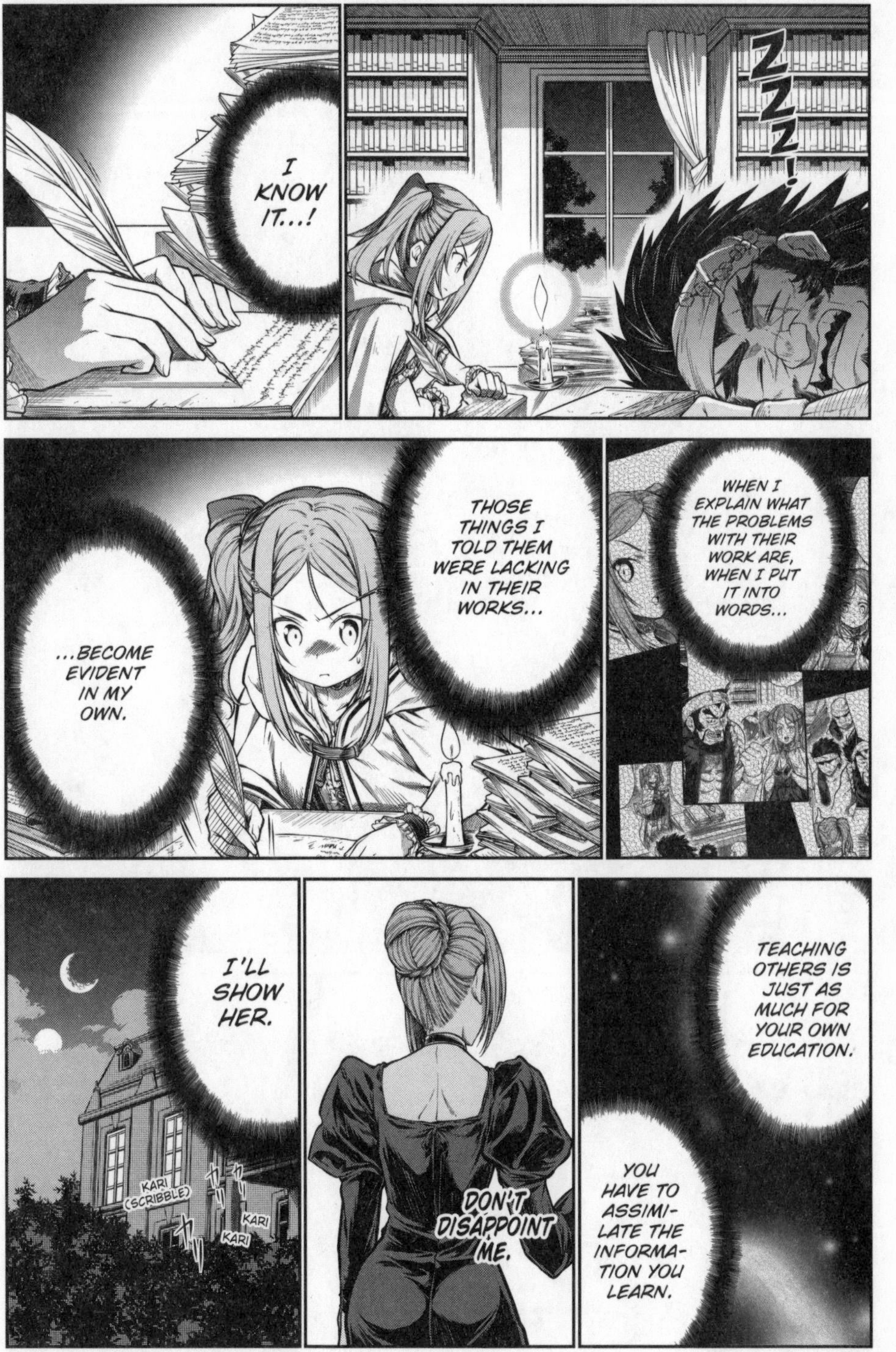
ZZZ!
I KNOW IT...!
WHEN I EXPLAIN WHAT THE PROBLEMS WITH THEIR WORK ARE, WHEN I PUT IT INTO WORDS...
THOSE THINGS I TOLD THEM WERE LACKING IN THEIR WORKS...
...BECOME EVIDENT IN MY OWN.
TEACHING OTHERS IS JUST AS MUCH FOR YOUR OWN EDUCATION.
YOU HAVE TO ASSIMI-LATE THE INFORMA-TION YOU LEARN.
DON'T DISAPPOINT ME.
I'LL SHOW HER.
KARI (SCRIBBLE)
KARI
KARI

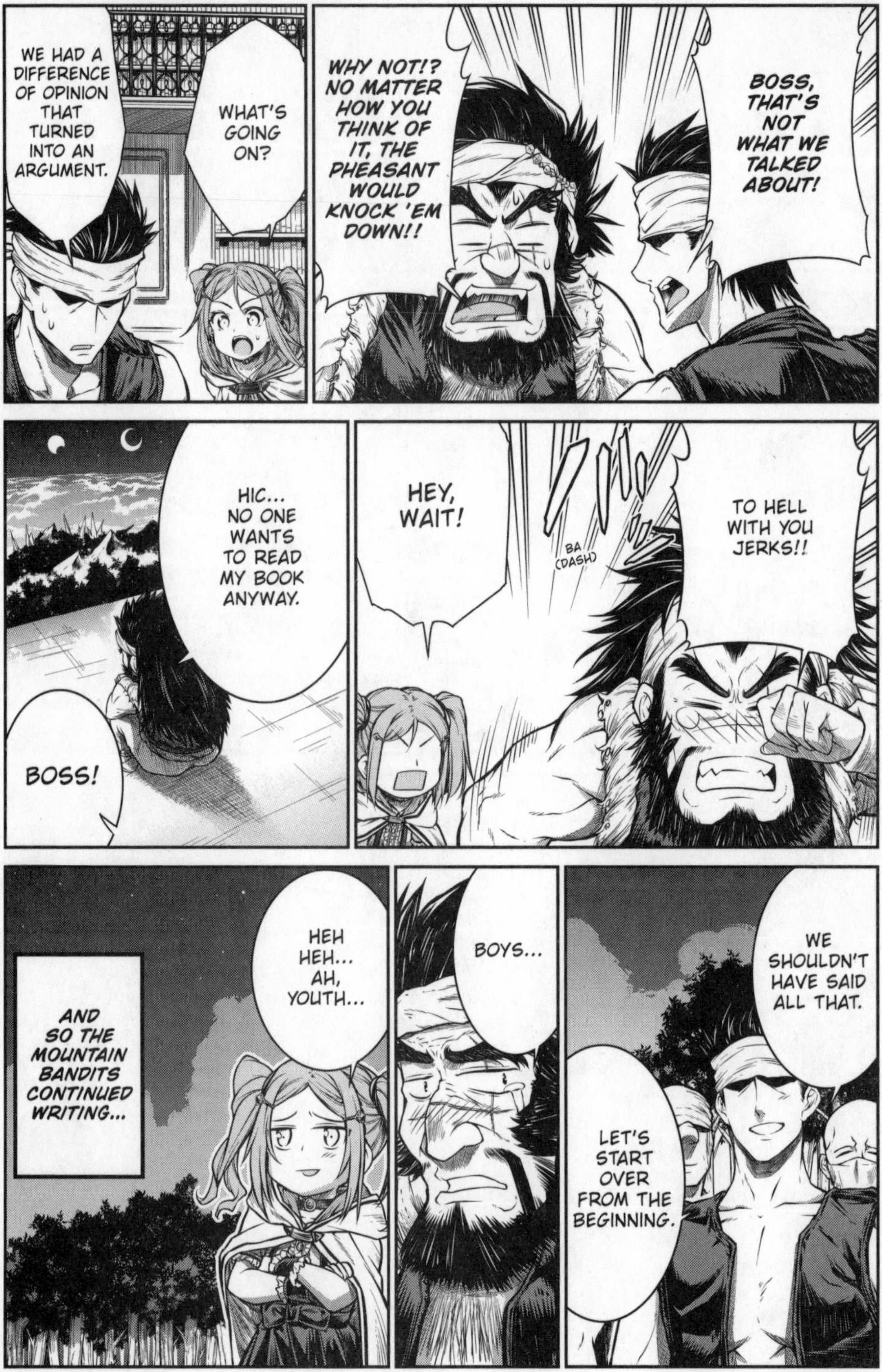
BOSS, THAT'S NOT WHAT WE TALKED ABOUT!
WHY NOT!? NO MATTER HOW YOU THINK OF IT, THE PHEASANT WOULD KNOCK 'EM DOWN!!
WHAT'S GOING ON?
WE HAD A DIFFERENCE OF OPINION THAT TURNED INTO AN ARGUMENT.
TO HELL WITH YOU JERKS!!
BA (DASH)
HEY, WAIT!
HIC... NO ONE WANTS TO READ MY BOOK ANYWAY.
BOSS!
WE SHOULDN'T HAVE SAID ALL THAT.
LET'S START OVER FROM THE BEGINNING.
BOYS...
HEH HEH... AH, YOUTH...
AND SO THE MOUNTAIN BANDITS CONTINUED WRITING...

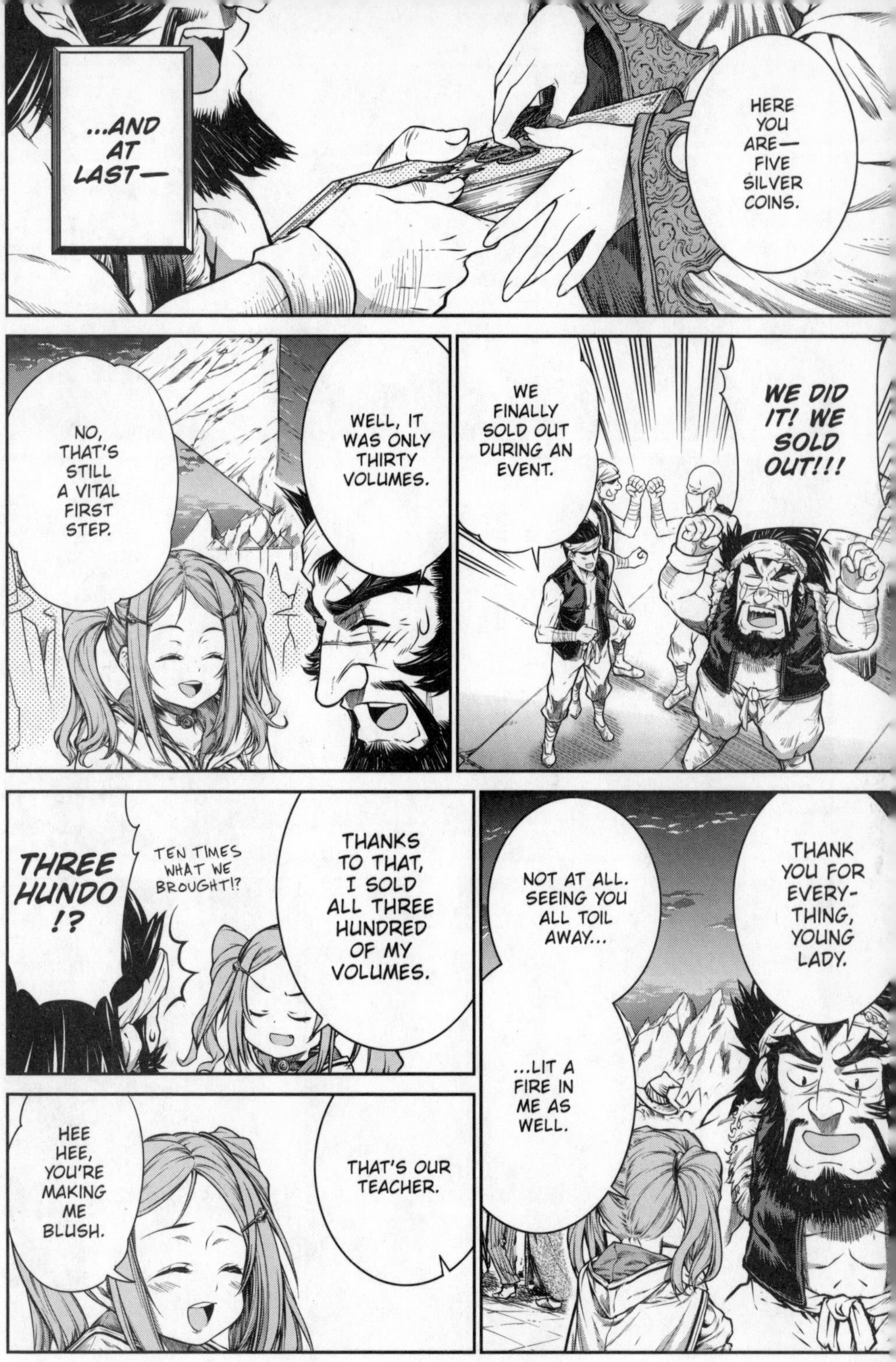
HERE YOU ARE— FIVE SILVER COINS.
...AND AT LAST—
WE DID IT! WE SOLD OUT!!!
WE FINALLY SOLD OUT DURING AN EVENT.
WELL, IT WAS ONLY THIRTY VOLUMES.
NO, THAT'S STILL A VITAL FIRST STEP.
THANK YOU FOR EVERY-THING, YOUNG LADY.
NOT AT ALL. SEEING YOU ALL TOIL AWAY...
...LIT A FIRE IN ME AS WELL.
THANKS TO THAT, I SOLD ALL THREE HUNDRED OF MY VOLUMES.
TEN TIMES WHAT WE BROUGHT!?
THREE HUNDO!?
THAT'S OUR TEACHER.
HEE HEE, YOU'RE MAKING ME BLUSH.

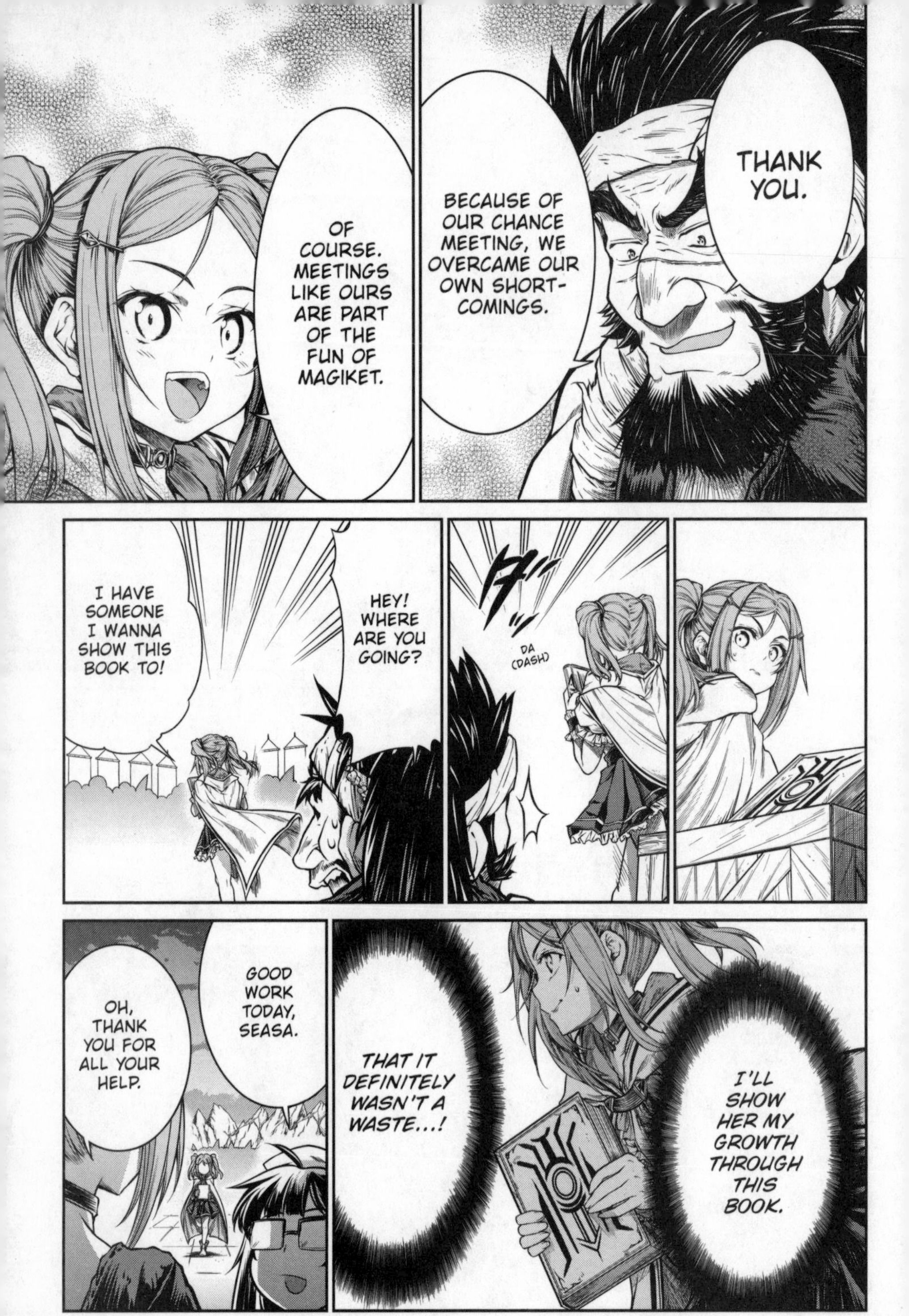
THANK YOU.
BECAUSE OF OUR CHANCE MEETING, WE OVERCAME OUR OWN SHORT-COMINGS.
OF COURSE. MEETINGS LIKE OURS ARE PART OF THE FUN OF MAGIKET.
DA (DASH)
HEY! WHERE ARE YOU GOING?
I HAVE SOMEONE I WANNA SHOW THIS BOOK TO!
I'LL SHOW HER MY GROWTH THROUGH THIS BOOK.
THAT IT DEFINITELY WASN'T A WASTE...!
GOOD WORK TODAY, SEASA.
OH, THANK YOU FOR ALL YOUR HELP.

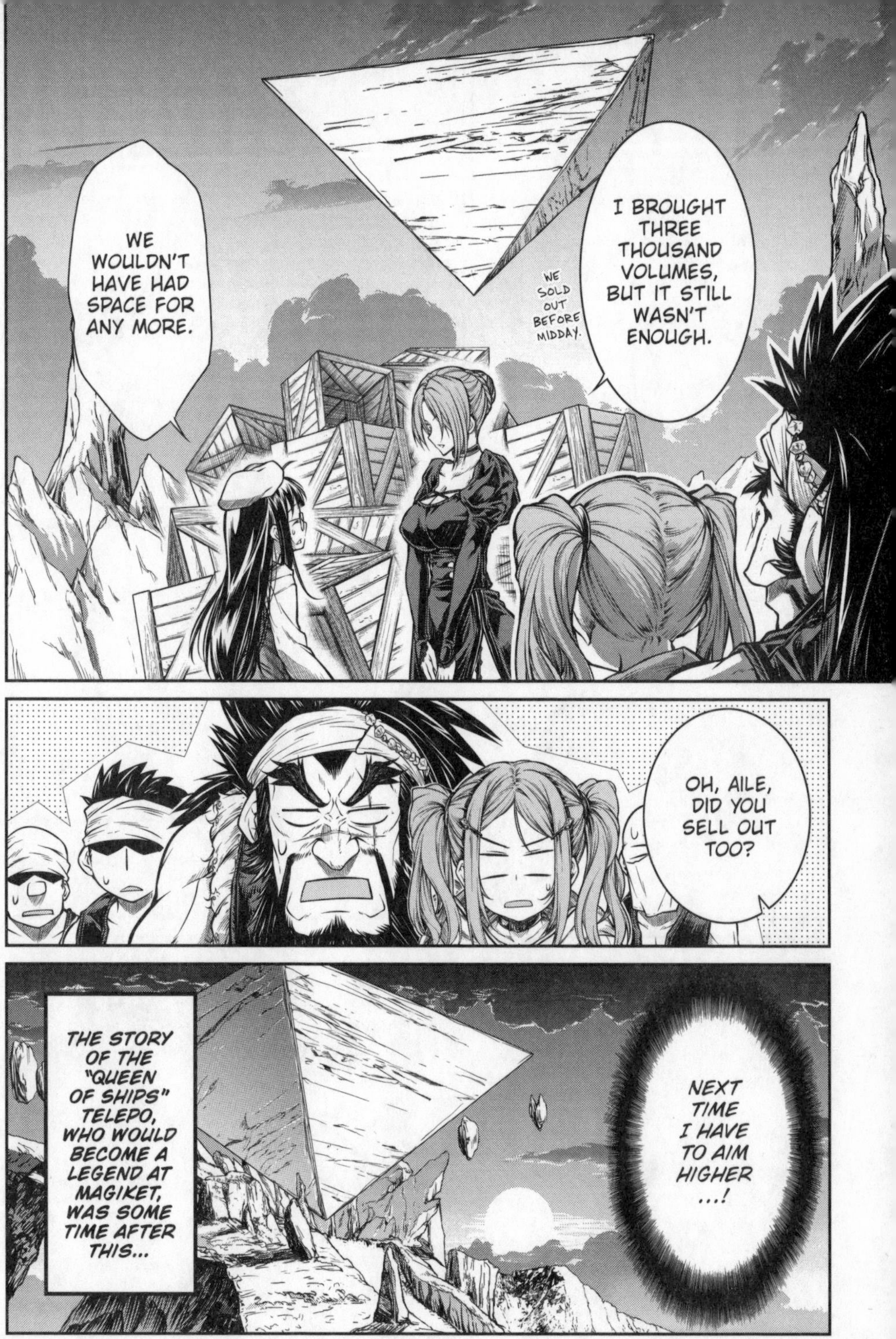
I BROUGHT THREE THOUSAND VOLUMES, BUT IT STILL WASN'T ENOUGH.
WE SOLD OUT BEFORE MIDDAY.
WE WOULDN'T HAVE HAD SPACE FOR ANY MORE.
OH, AILE, DID YOU SELL OUT TOO?
NEXT TIME I HAVE TO AIM HIGHER ...!
THE STORY OF THE "QUEEN OF SHIPS" TELEPO, WHO WOULD BECOME A LEGEND AT MAGIKET, WAS SOME TIME AFTER THIS...

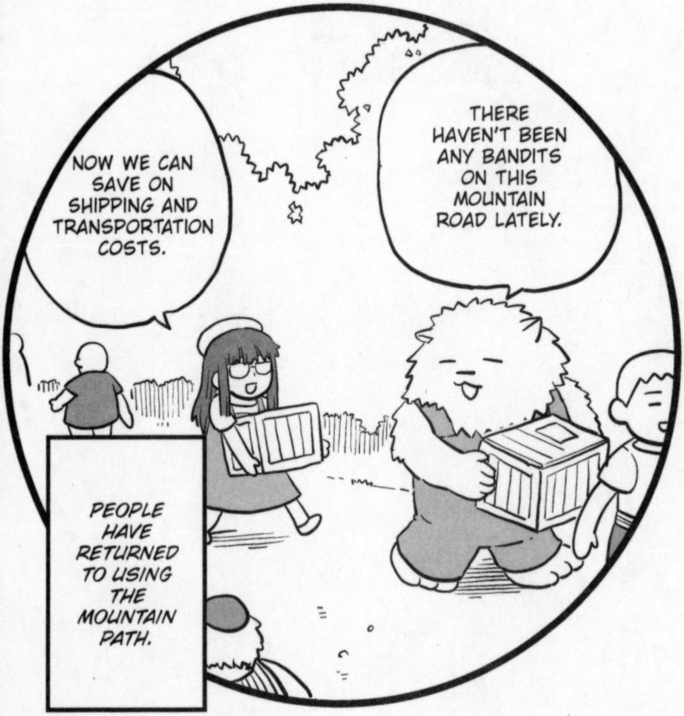
THERE HAVEN'T BEEN ANY BANDITS ON THIS MOUNTAIN ROAD LATELY.
NOW WE CAN SAVE ON SHIPPING AND TRANSPORTATION COSTS.
PEOPLE HAVE RETURNED TO USING THE MOUNTAIN PATH.

A WITCH'S PRINTING OFFICE

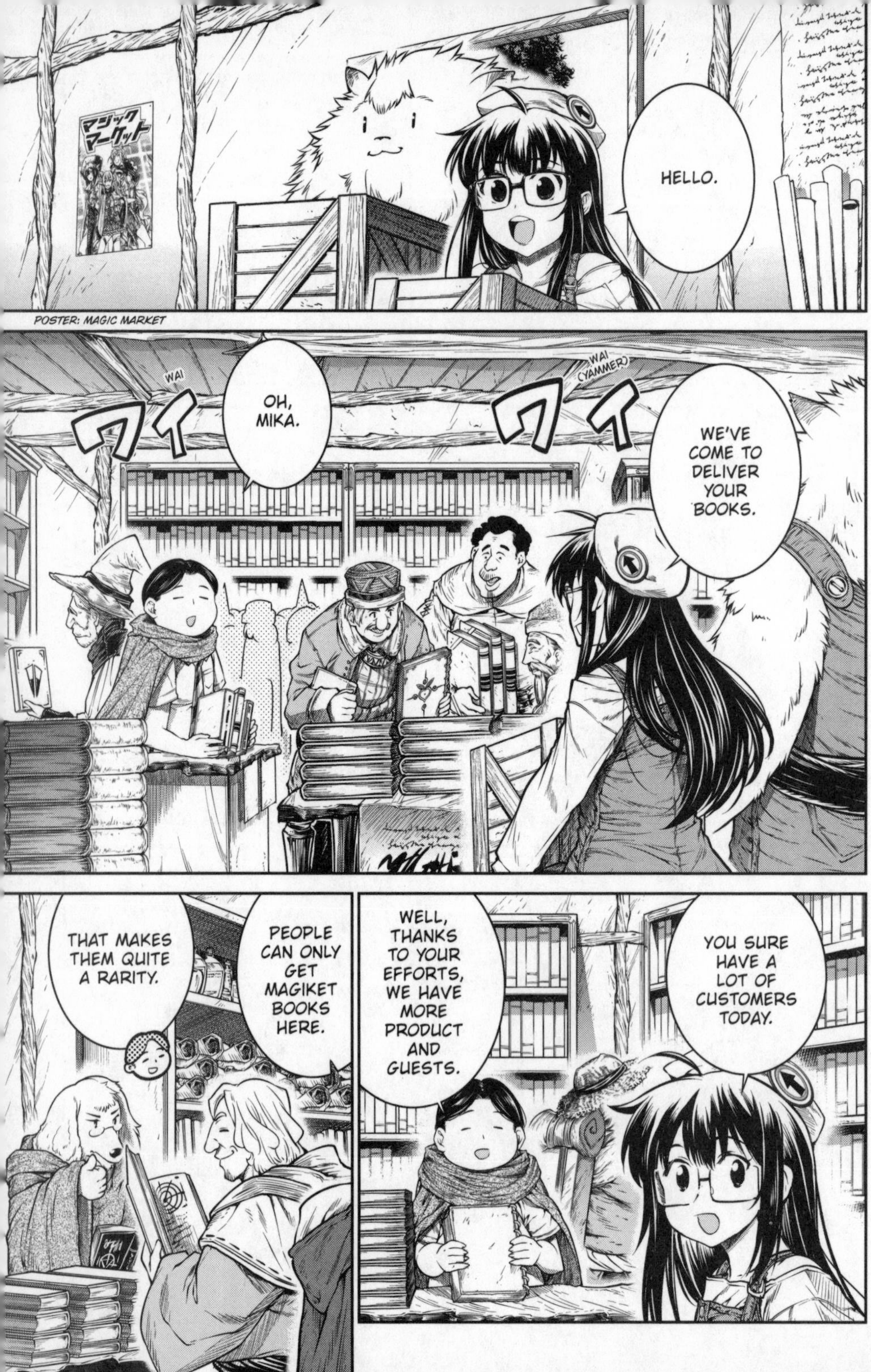
マジック
マーケット
HELLO.
POSTER: MAGIC MARKET
WE'VE COME TO DELIVER YOUR BOOKS.
WAI (YAMMER)
ワイ
OH, MIKA.
WAI
ワイ
YOU SURE HAVE A LOT OF CUSTOMERS TODAY.
WELL, THANKS TO YOUR EFFORTS, WE HAVE MORE PRODUCT AND GUESTS.
PEOPLE CAN ONLY GET MAGIKET BOOKS HERE.
THAT MAKES THEM QUITE A RARITY.

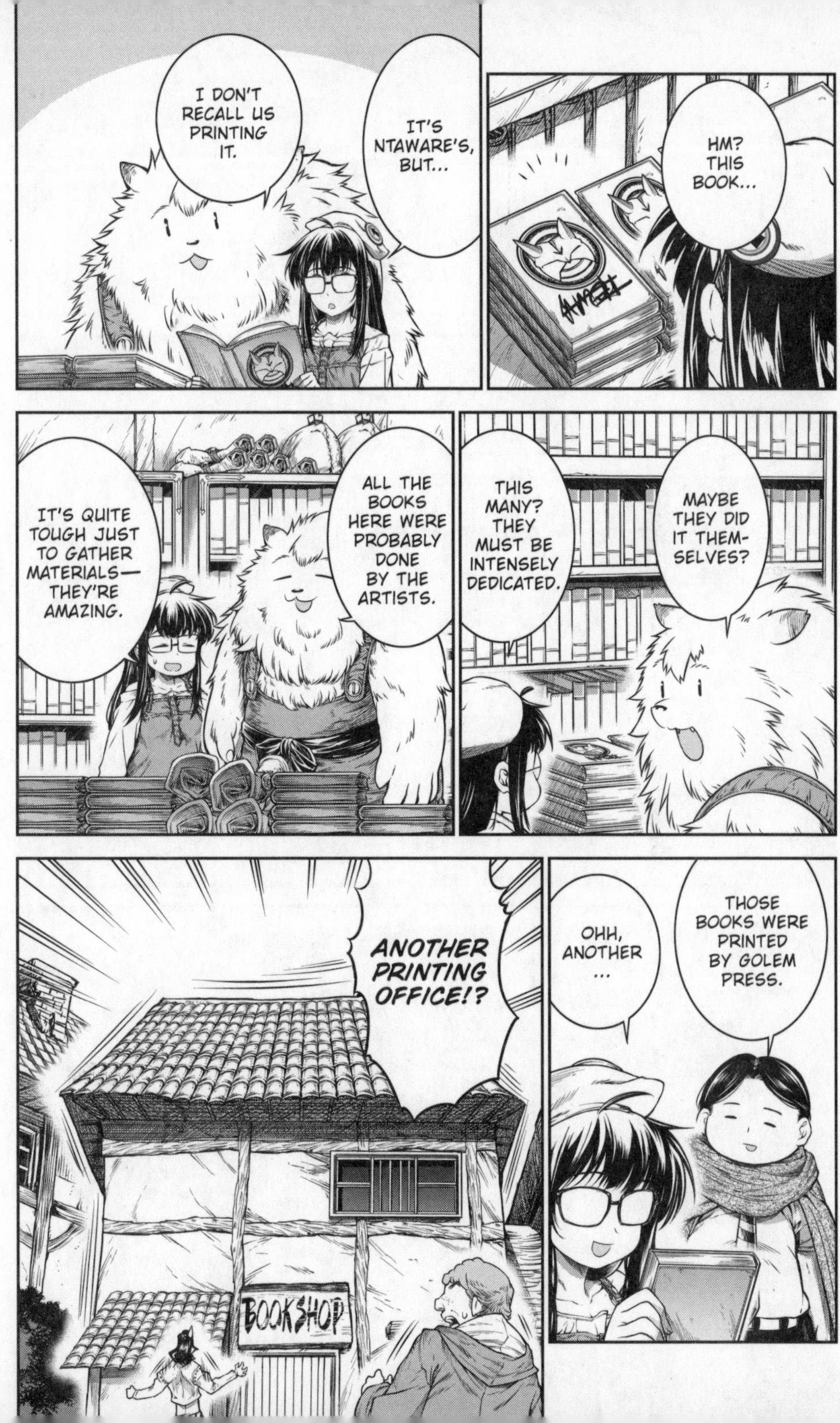
HM? THIS BOOK...
IT'S NTAWARE'S, BUT...
I DON'T RECALL US PRINTING IT.
MAYBE THEY DID IT THEMSELVES?
THIS MANY? THEY MUST BE INTENSELY DEDICATED.
ALL THE BOOKS HERE WERE PROBABLY DONE BY THE ARTISTS.
IT'S QUITE TOUGH JUST TO GATHER MATERIALS—THEY'RE AMAZING.
THOSE BOOKS WERE PRINTED BY GOLEM PRESS.
OHH, ANOTHER ...
ANOTHER PRINTING OFFICE!?
BOOKSHOP

Chapter 27

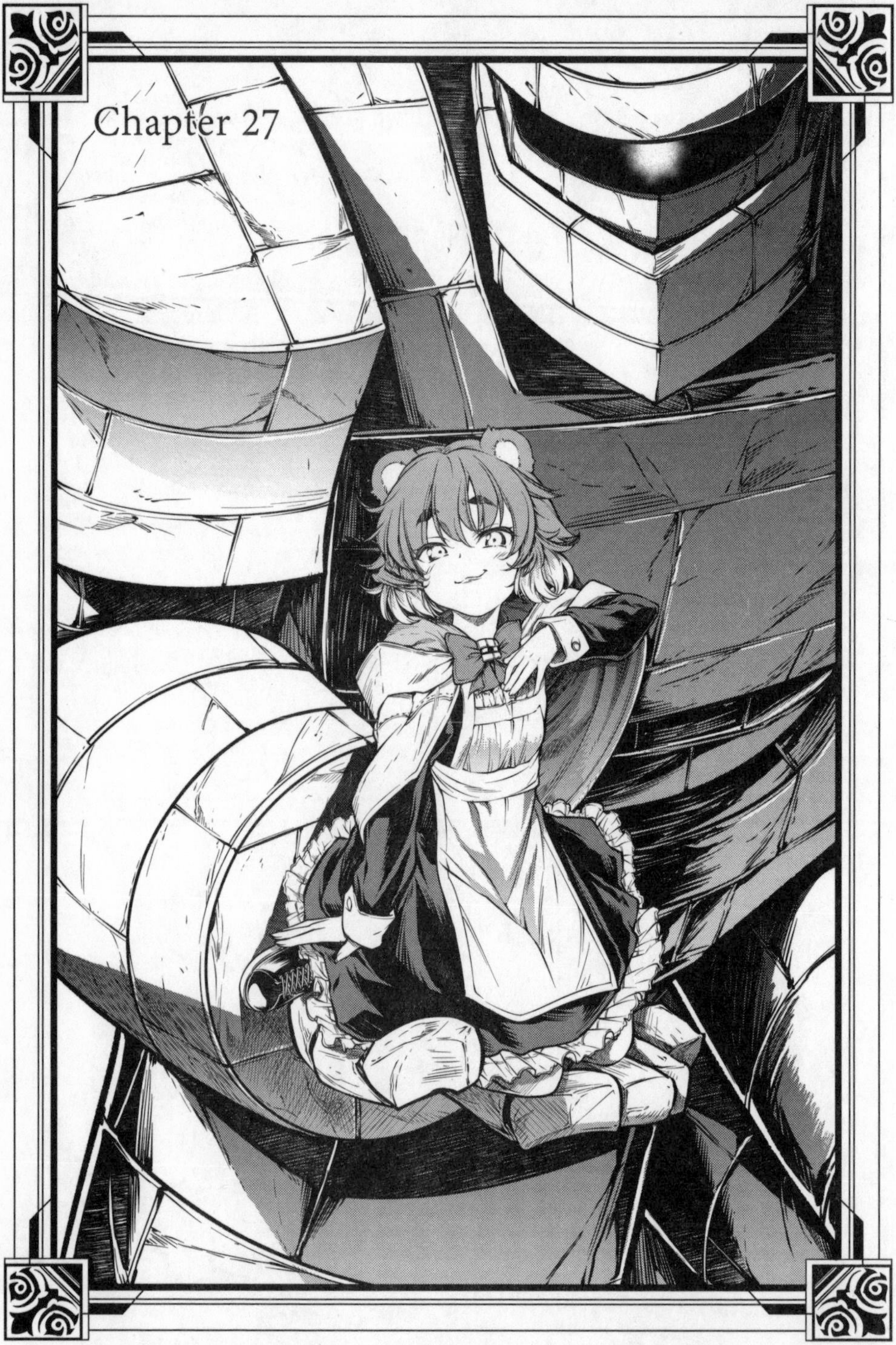

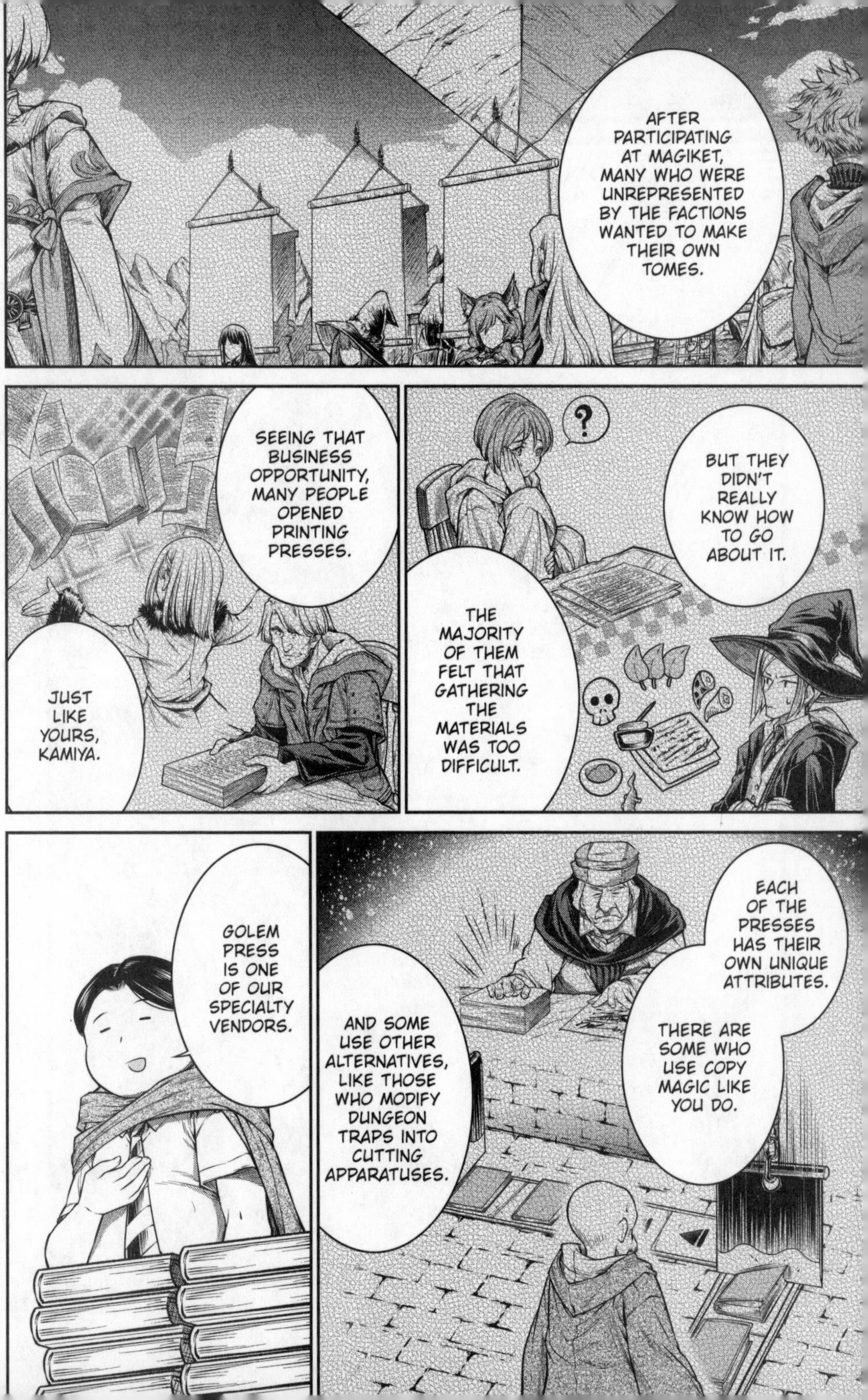
AFTER PARTICIPATING AT MAGIKET, MANY WHO WERE UNREPRESENTED BY THE FACTIONS WANTED TO MAKE THEIR OWN TOMES.
?
BUT THEY DIDN'T REALLY KNOW HOW TO GO ABOUT IT.
THE MAJORITY OF THEM FELT THAT GATHERING THE MATERIALS WAS TOO DIFFICULT.
SEEING THAT BUSINESS OPPORTUNITY, MANY PEOPLE OPENED PRINTING PRESSES.
JUST LIKE YOURS, KAMIYA.
EACH OF THE PRESSES HAS THEIR OWN UNIQUE ATTRIBUTES.
THERE ARE SOME WHO USE COPY MAGIC LIKE YOU DO.
AND SOME USE OTHER ALTERNATIVES, LIKE THOSE WHO MODIFY DUNGEON TRAPS INTO CUTTING APPARATUSES.
GOLEM PRESS IS ONE OF OUR SPECIALTY VENDORS.

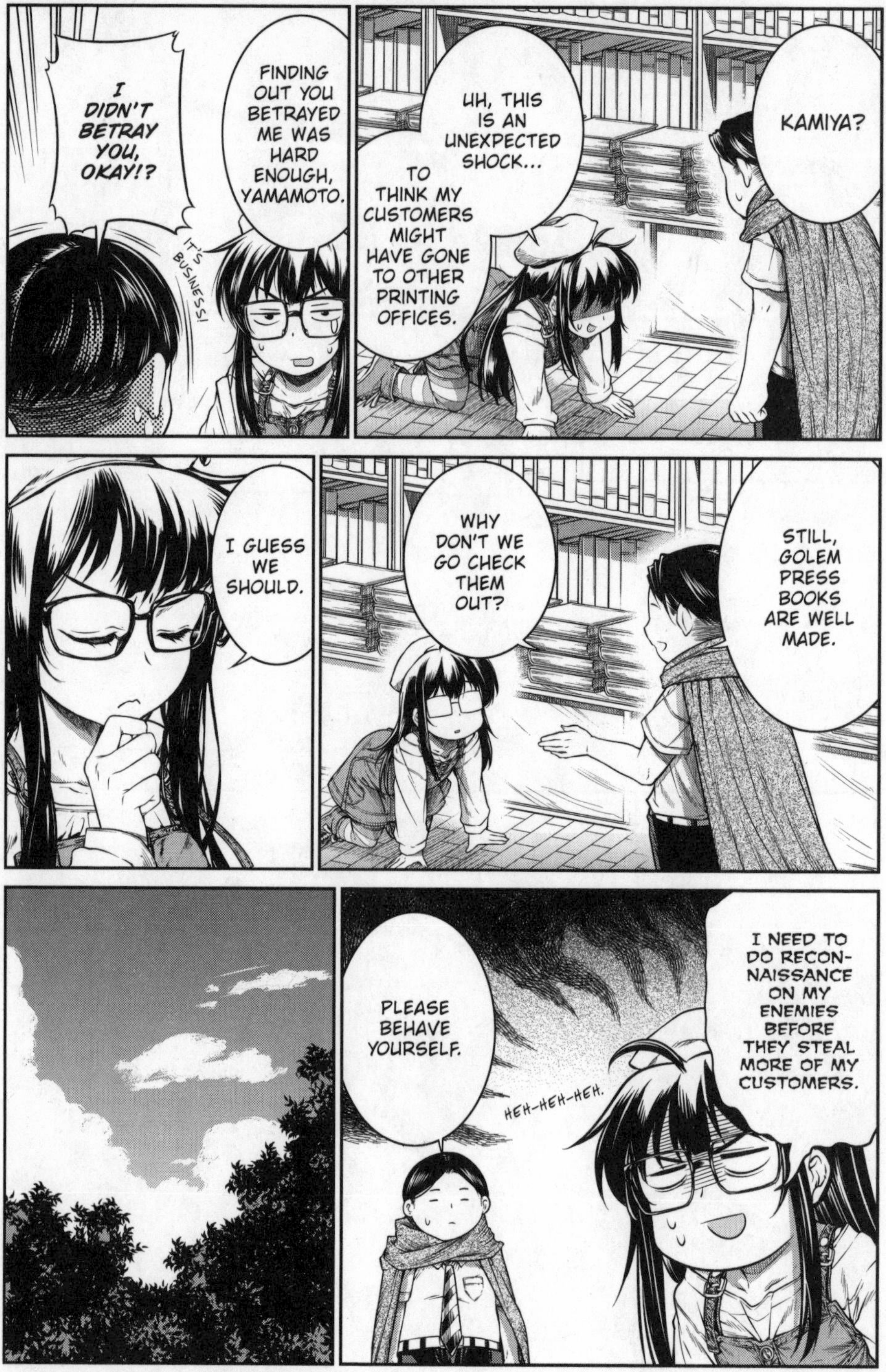
KAMIYA?
UH, THIS IS AN UNEXPECTED SHOCK...
TO THINK MY CUSTOMERS MIGHT HAVE GONE TO OTHER PRINTING OFFICES.
FINDING OUT YOU BETRAYED ME WAS HARD ENOUGH, YAMAMOTO.
I DIDN'T BETRAY YOU, OKAY!?
IT'S BUSINESS!
STILL, GOLEM PRESS BOOKS ARE WELL MADE.
WHY DON'T WE GO CHECK THEM OUT?
I GUESS WE SHOULD.
I NEED TO DO RECON-NAISSANCE ON MY ENEMIES BEFORE THEY STEAL MORE OF MY CUSTOMERS.
HEH-HEH-HEH.
PLEASE BEHAVE YOURSELF.

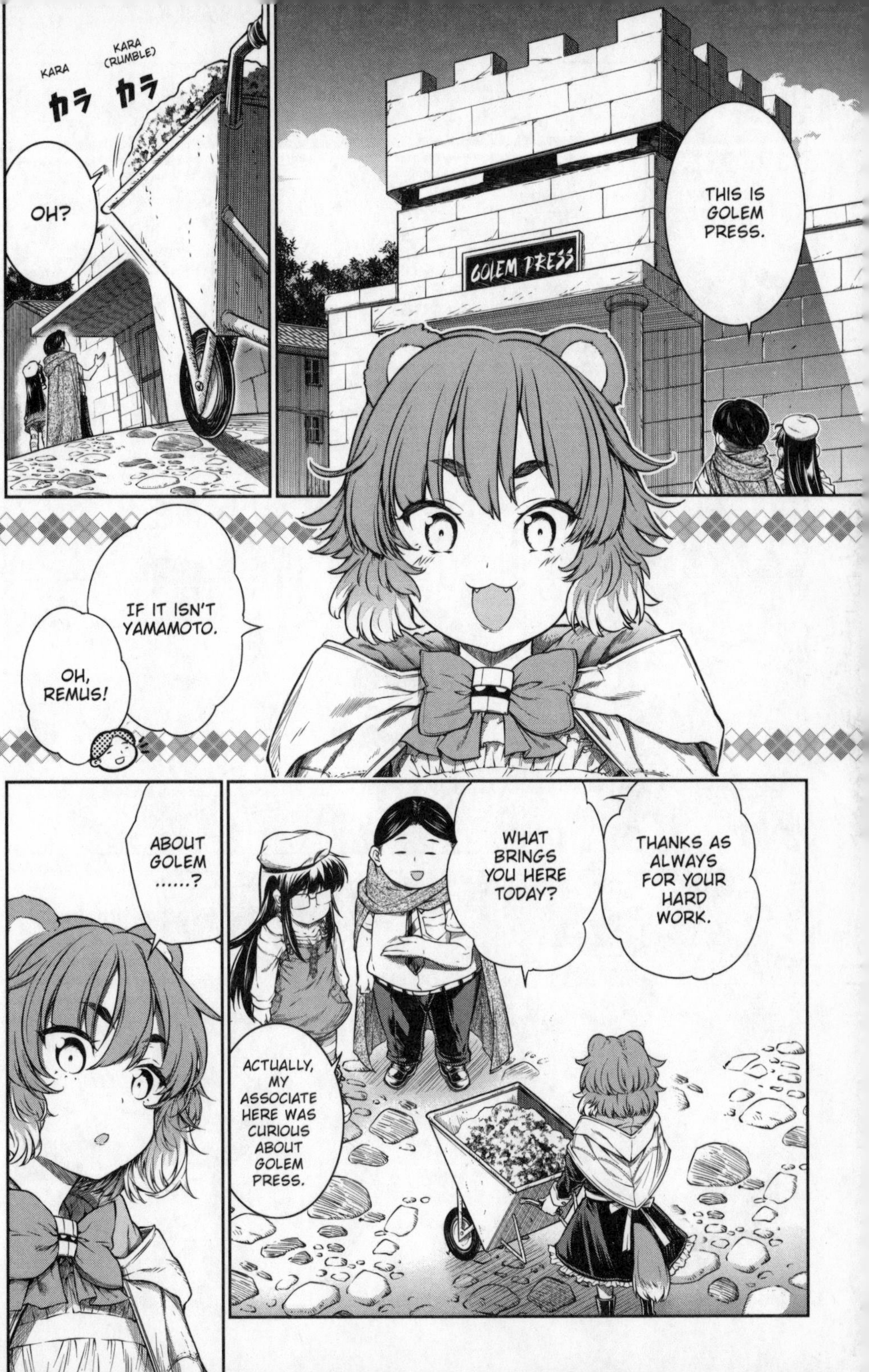

GOLEM PRESS
THIS IS GOLEM PRESS.
カラ
KARA (RUMBLE)
カラ
KARA
OH?
IF IT ISN'T YAMAMOTO.
OH, REMUS!
THANKS AS ALWAYS FOR YOUR HARD WORK.
WHAT BRINGS YOU HERE TODAY?
ACTUALLY, MY ASSOCIATE HERE WAS CURIOUS ABOUT GOLEM PRESS.
ABOUT GOLEM ......?

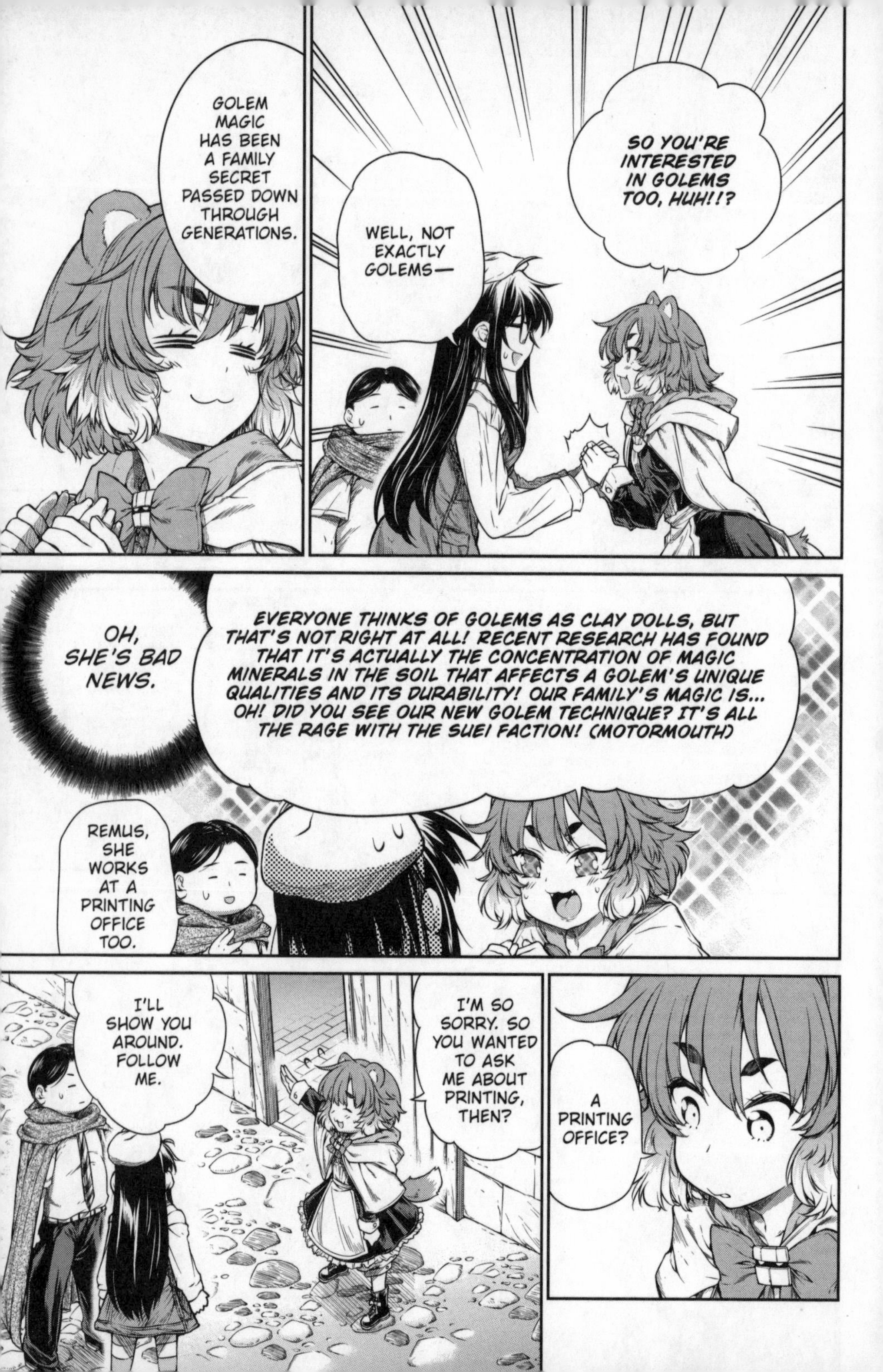
SO YOU'RE INTERESTED IN GOLEMS TOO, HUH!!?
WELL, NOT EXACTLY GOLEMS—
GOLEM MAGIC HAS BEEN A FAMILY SECRET PASSED DOWN THROUGH GENERATIONS.
EVERYONE THINKS OF GOLEMS AS CLAY DOLLS, BUT THAT'S NOT RIGHT AT ALL! RECENT RESEARCH HAS FOUND THAT IT'S ACTUALLY THE CONCENTRATION OF MAGIC MINERALS IN THE SOIL THAT AFFECTS A GOLEM'S UNIQUE QUALITIES AND ITS DURABILITY! OUR FAMILY'S MAGIC IS... OH! DID YOU SEE OUR NEW GOLEM TECHNIQUE? IT'S ALL THE RAGE WITH THE SUEI FACTION! (MOTORMOUTH)
OH, SHE'S BAD NEWS.
REMUS, SHE WORKS AT A PRINTING OFFICE TOO.
A PRINTING OFFICE?
I'M SO SORRY. SO YOU WANTED TO ASK ME ABOUT PRINTING, THEN?
I'LL SHOW YOU AROUND. FOLLOW ME.

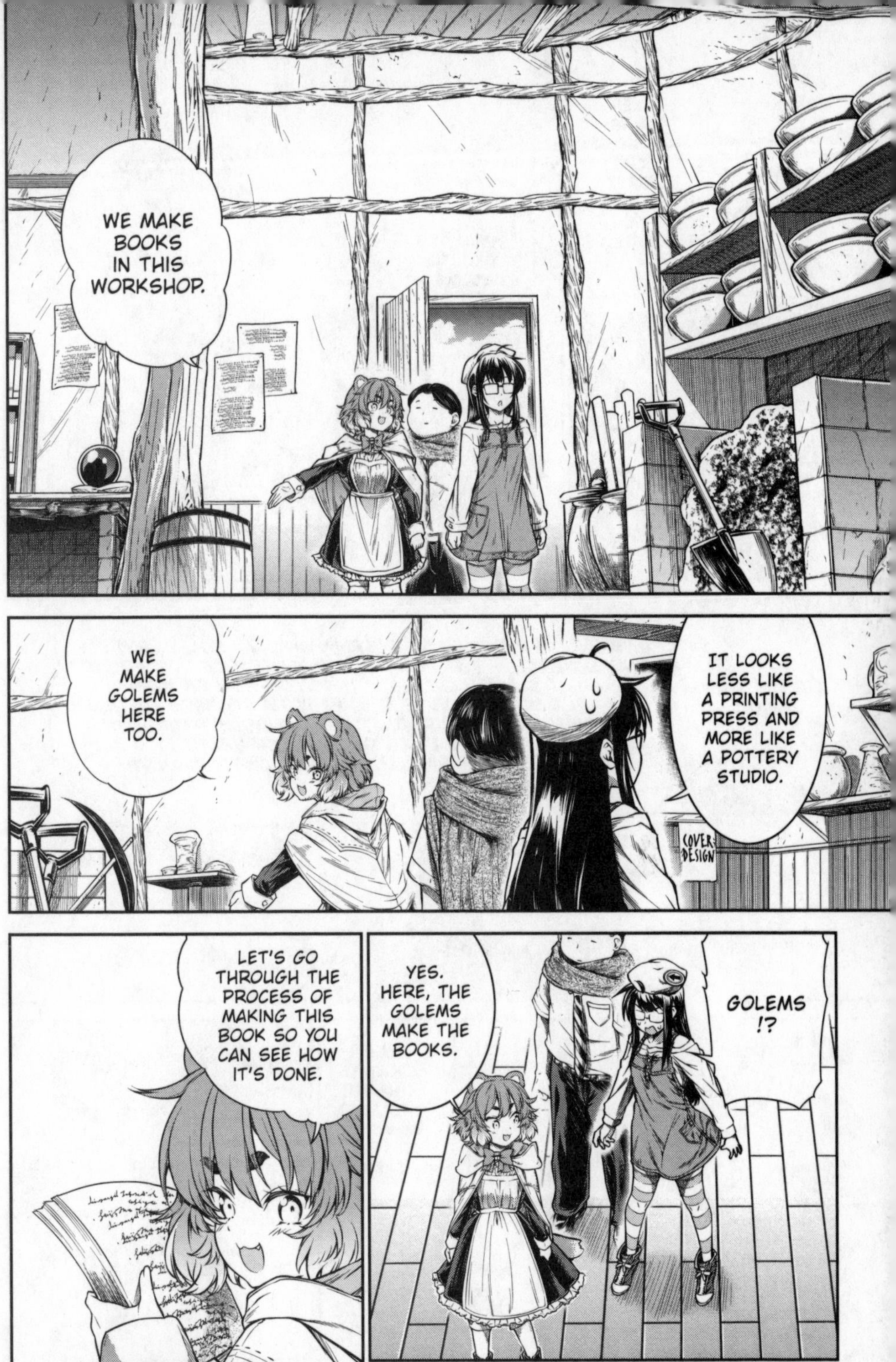
WE MAKE BOOKS IN THIS WORKSHOP.
IT LOOKS LESS LIKE A PRINTING PRESS AND MORE LIKE A POTTERY STUDIO.
WE MAKE GOLEMS HERE TOO.
COVER-DESIGN
GOLEMS !?
YES. HERE, THE GOLEMS MAKE THE BOOKS.
LET'S GO THROUGH THE PROCESS OF MAKING THIS BOOK SO YOU CAN SEE HOW IT'S DONE.

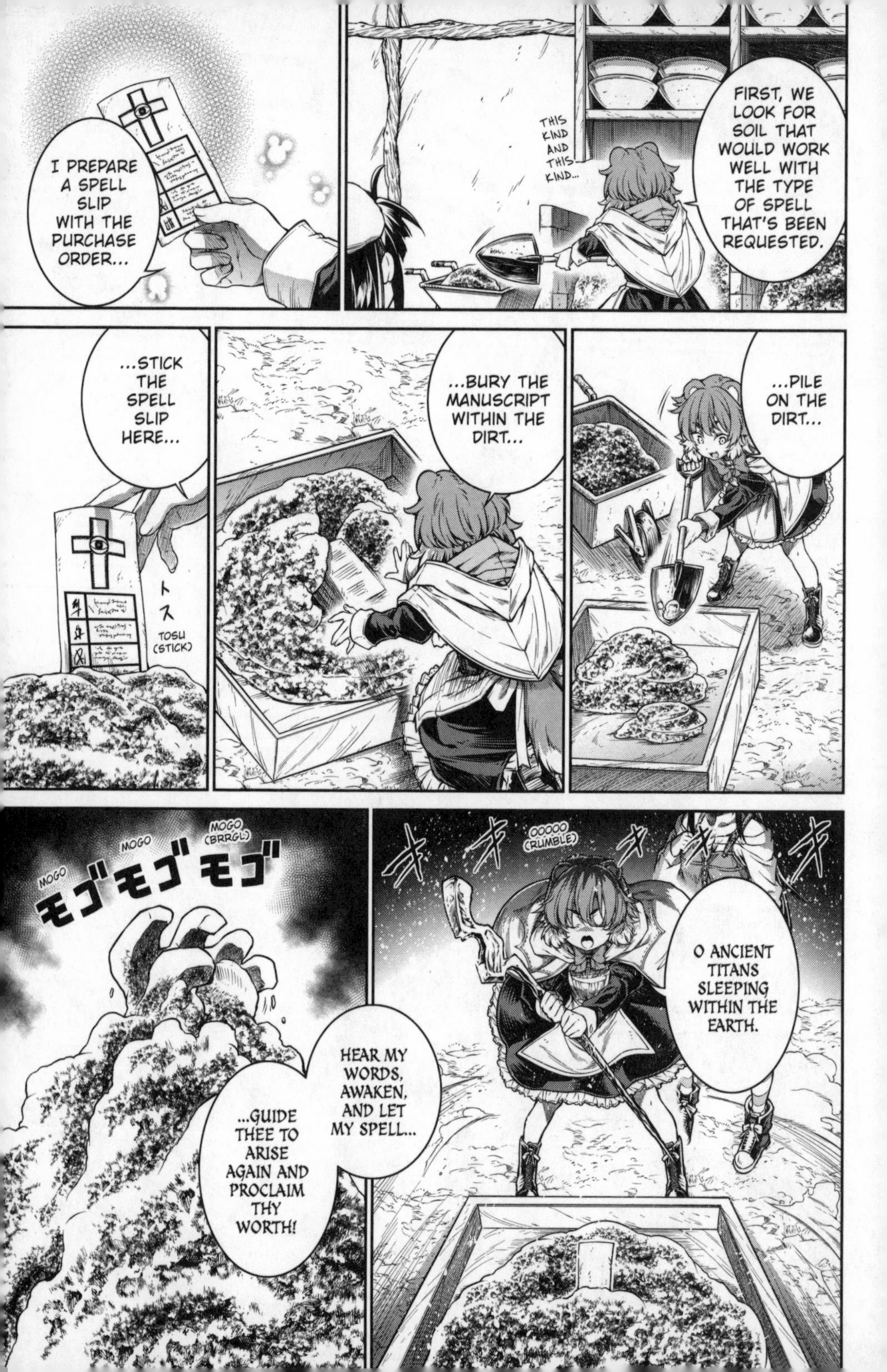
FIRST, WE LOOK FOR SOIL THAT WOULD WORK WELL WITH THE TYPE OF SPELL THAT'S BEEN REQUESTED.
THIS KIND AND THIS KIND...
I PREPARE A SPELL SLIP WITH THE PURCHASE ORDER...
...PILE ON THE DIRT...
...BURY THE MANUSCRIPT WITHIN THE DIRT...
...STICK THE SPELL SLIP HERE...
トス
TOSU (STICK)
オオオオ
OOOOO (RUMBLE)
O ANCIENT TITANS SLEEPING WITHIN THE EARTH.
モゴモゴモゴ
MOGO MOGO MOGO (BRRGL)
HEAR MY WORDS, AWAKEN, AND LET MY SPELL...
...GUIDE THEE TO ARISE AGAIN AND PROCLAIM THY WORTH!

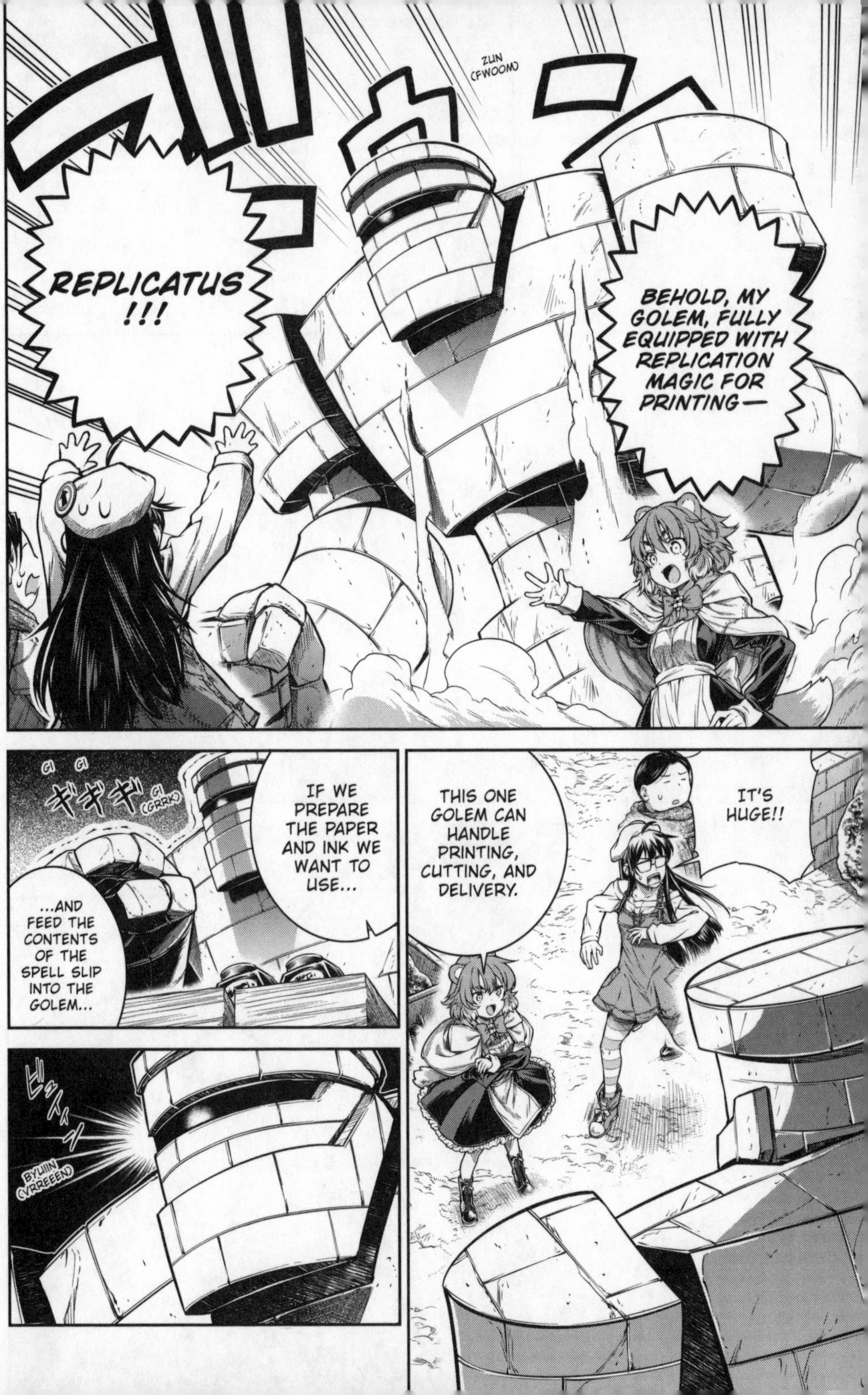

ZUN (FWOOM)
BEHOLD, MY GOLEM, FULLY EQUIPPED WITH REPLICATION MAGIC FOR PRINTING—
REPLICATUS !!!
IT'S HUGE!!
THIS ONE GOLEM CAN HANDLE PRINTING, CUTTING, AND DELIVERY.
GI GI GI (GRRK)
IF WE PREPARE THE PAPER AND INK WE WANT TO USE...
...AND FEED THE CONTENTS OF THE SPELL SLIP INTO THE GOLEM...
BYUIIN (VRREEEN)

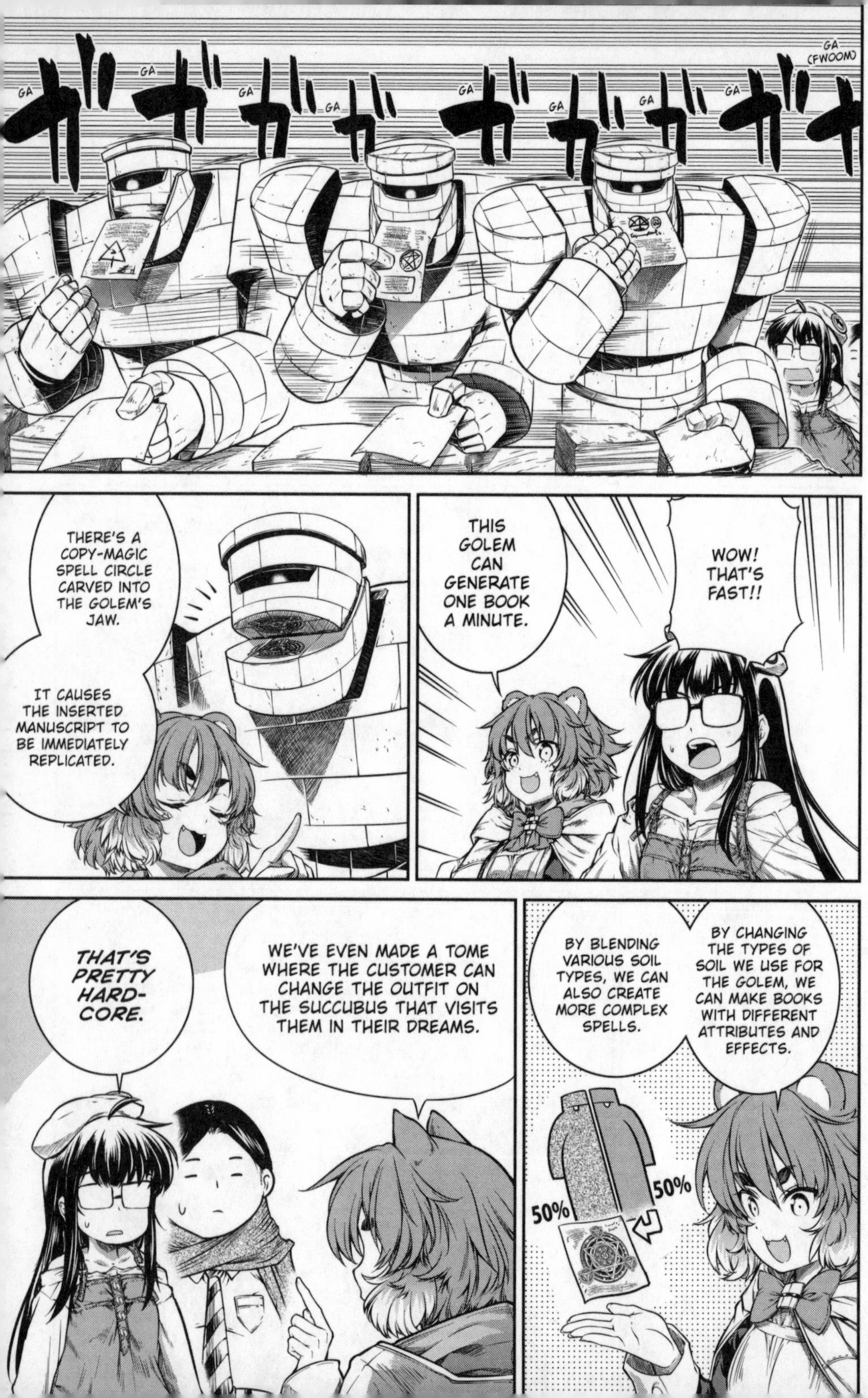
GA (FWOOM)
GA
GA
GA
GA
GA
GA
GA
GA
THIS GOLEM CAN GENERATE ONE BOOK A MINUTE.
WOW! THAT'S FAST!!
THERE'S A COPY-MAGIC SPELL CIRCLE CARVED INTO THE GOLEM'S JAW.
IT CAUSES THE INSERTED MANUSCRIPT TO BE IMMEDIATELY REPLICATED.
BY CHANGING THE TYPES OF SOIL WE USE FOR THE GOLEM, WE CAN MAKE BOOKS WITH DIFFERENT ATTRIBUTES AND EFFECTS.
BY BLENDING VARIOUS SOIL TYPES, WE CAN ALSO CREATE MORE COMPLEX SPELLS.
50%
50%
WE'VE EVEN MADE A TOME WHERE THE CUSTOMER CAN CHANGE THE OUTFIT ON THE SUCCUBUS THAT VISITS THEM IN THEIR DREAMS.
THAT'S PRETTY HARD-CORE.

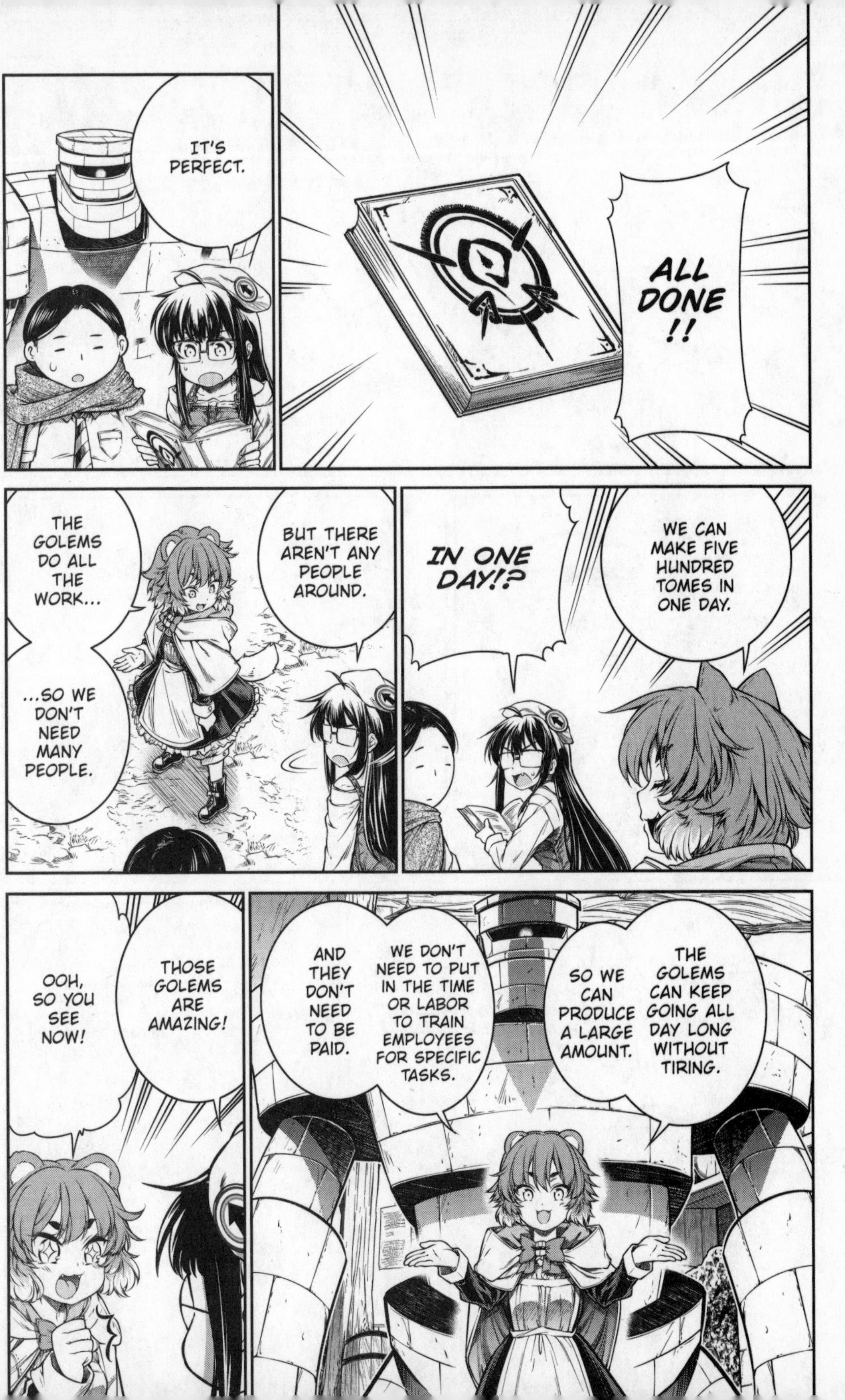
ALL DONE!!
IT'S PERFECT.
WE CAN MAKE FIVE HUNDRED TOMES IN ONE DAY.
IN ONE DAY!?
BUT THERE AREN'T ANY PEOPLE AROUND.
THE GOLEMS DO ALL THE WORK...
...SO WE DON'T NEED MANY PEOPLE.
THE GOLEMS CAN KEEP GOING ALL DAY LONG WITHOUT TIRING.
SO WE CAN PRODUCE A LARGE AMOUNT.
WE DON'T NEED TO PUT IN THE TIME OR LABOR TO TRAIN EMPLOYEES FOR SPECIFIC TASKS.
AND THEY DON'T NEED TO BE PAID.
THOSE GOLEMS ARE AMAZING!
OOH, SO YOU SEE NOW!

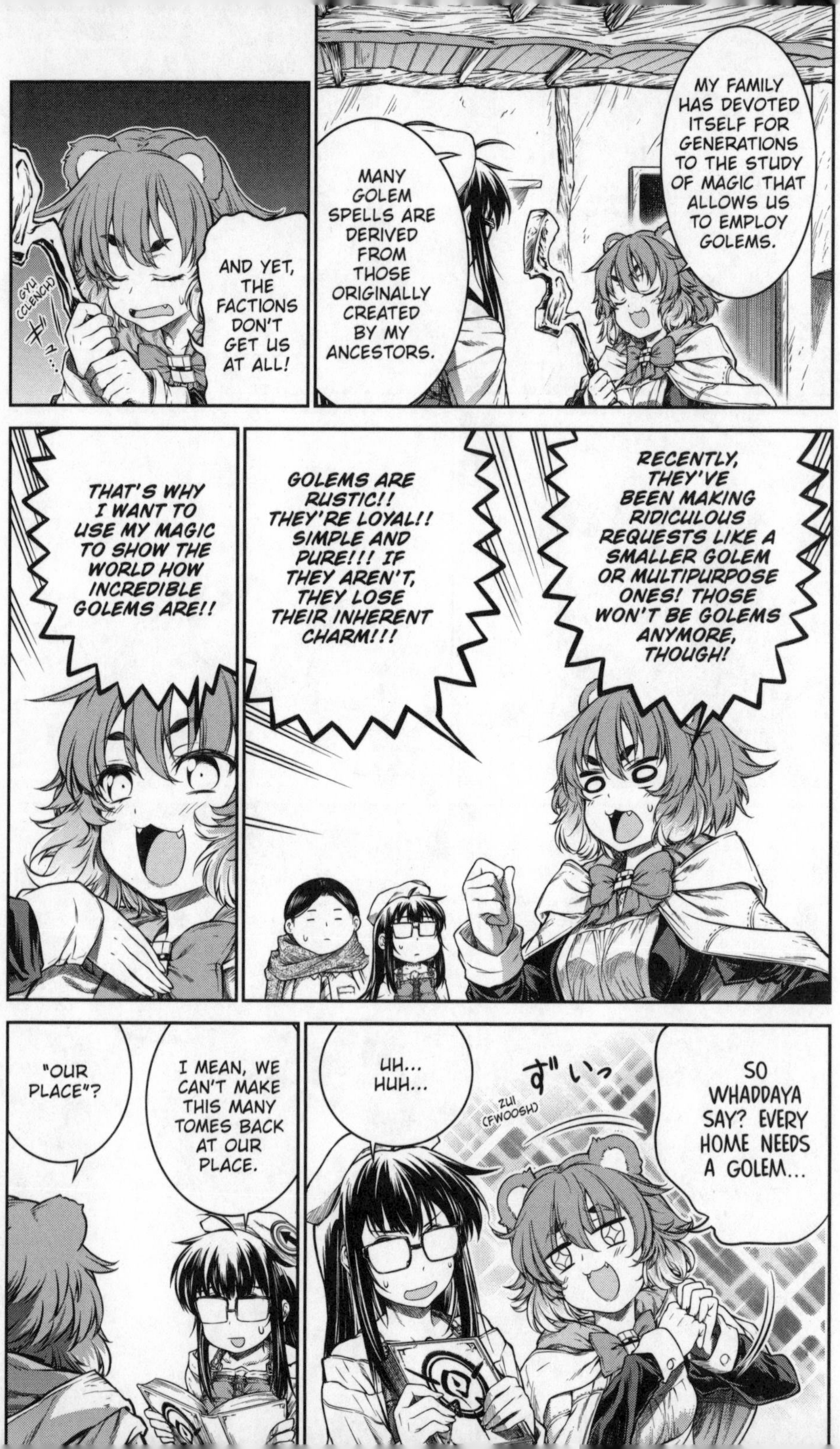
MY FAMILY HAS DEVOTED ITSELF FOR GENERATIONS TO THE STUDY OF MAGIC THAT ALLOWS US TO EMPLOY GOLEMS.
MANY GOLEM SPELLS ARE DERIVED FROM THOSE ORIGINALLY CREATED BY MY ANCESTORS.
GYU (CLENCH)
AND YET, THE FACTIONS DON'T GET US AT ALL!
RECENTLY, THEY'VE BEEN MAKING RIDICULOUS REQUESTS LIKE A SMALLER GOLEM OR MULTIPURPOSE ONES! THOSE WON'T BE GOLEMS ANYMORE, THOUGH!
GOLEMS ARE RUSTIC!! THEY'RE LOYAL!! SIMPLE AND PURE!!! IF THEY AREN'T, THEY LOSE THEIR INHERENT CHARM!!!
THAT'S WHY I WANT TO USE MY MAGIC TO SHOW THE WORLD HOW INCREDIBLE GOLEMS ARE!!
SO WHADDAYA SAY? EVERY HOME NEEDS A GOLEM...
ずいっ
ZUI (FWOOSH)
UH... HUH...
I MEAN, WE CAN'T MAKE THIS MANY TOMES BACK AT OUR PLACE.
"OUR PLACE"?

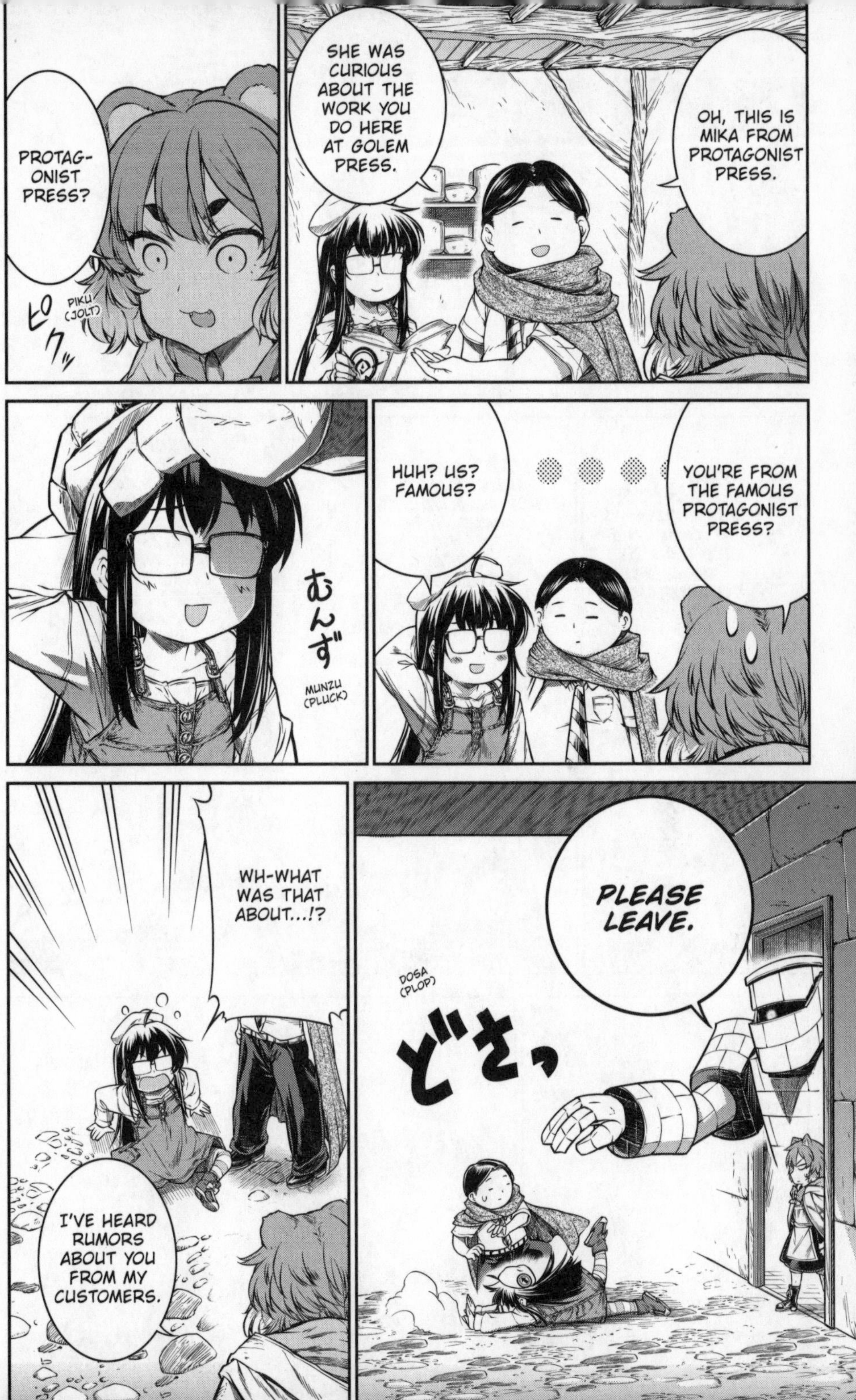
OH, THIS IS MIKA FROM PROTAGONIST PRESS.
SHE WAS CURIOUS ABOUT THE WORK YOU DO HERE AT GOLEM PRESS.
PROTAG-ONIST PRESS?
ピクッ
PIKU (JOLT)
YOU'RE FROM THE FAMOUS PROTAGONIST PRESS?
HUH? US? FAMOUS?
むんず
MUNZU (PLUCK)
PLEASE LEAVE.
どさっ
DOSA (PLOP)
WH-WHAT WAS THAT ABOUT...!?
I'VE HEARD RUMORS ABOUT YOU FROM MY CUSTOMERS.

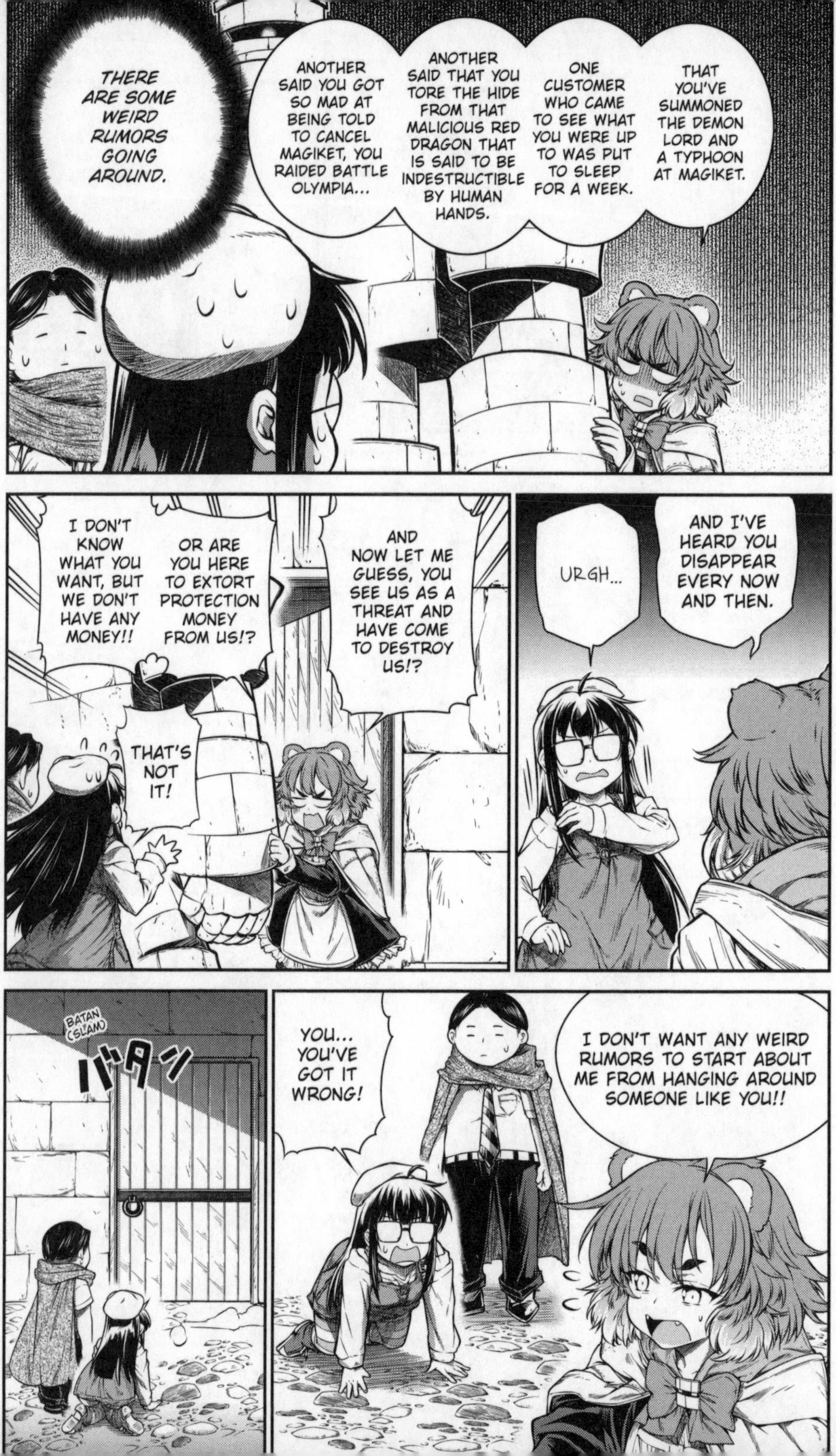
THAT YOU'VE SUMMONED THE DEMON LORD AND A TYPHOON AT MAGIKET.
ONE CUSTOMER WHO CAME TO SEE WHAT YOU WERE UP TO WAS PUT TO SLEEP FOR A WEEK.
ANOTHER SAID THAT YOU TORE THE HIDE FROM THAT MALICIOUS RED DRAGON THAT IS SAID TO BE INDESTRUCTIBLE BY HUMAN HANDS.
ANOTHER SAID YOU GOT SO MAD AT BEING TOLD TO CANCEL MAGIKET, YOU RAIDED BATTLE OLYMPIA...
THERE ARE SOME WEIRD RUMORS GOING AROUND.
AND I'VE HEARD YOU DISAPPEAR EVERY NOW AND THEN.
URGH...
AND NOW LET ME GUESS, YOU SEE US AS A THREAT AND HAVE COME TO DESTROY US!?
OR ARE YOU HERE TO EXTORT PROTECTION MONEY FROM US!?
I DON'T KNOW WHAT YOU WANT, BUT WE DON'T HAVE ANY MONEY!!
THAT'S NOT IT!
I DON'T WANT ANY WEIRD RUMORS TO START ABOUT ME FROM HANGING AROUND SOMEONE LIKE YOU!!
YOU... YOU'VE GOT IT WRONG!
BATAN (SLAM)
バタン

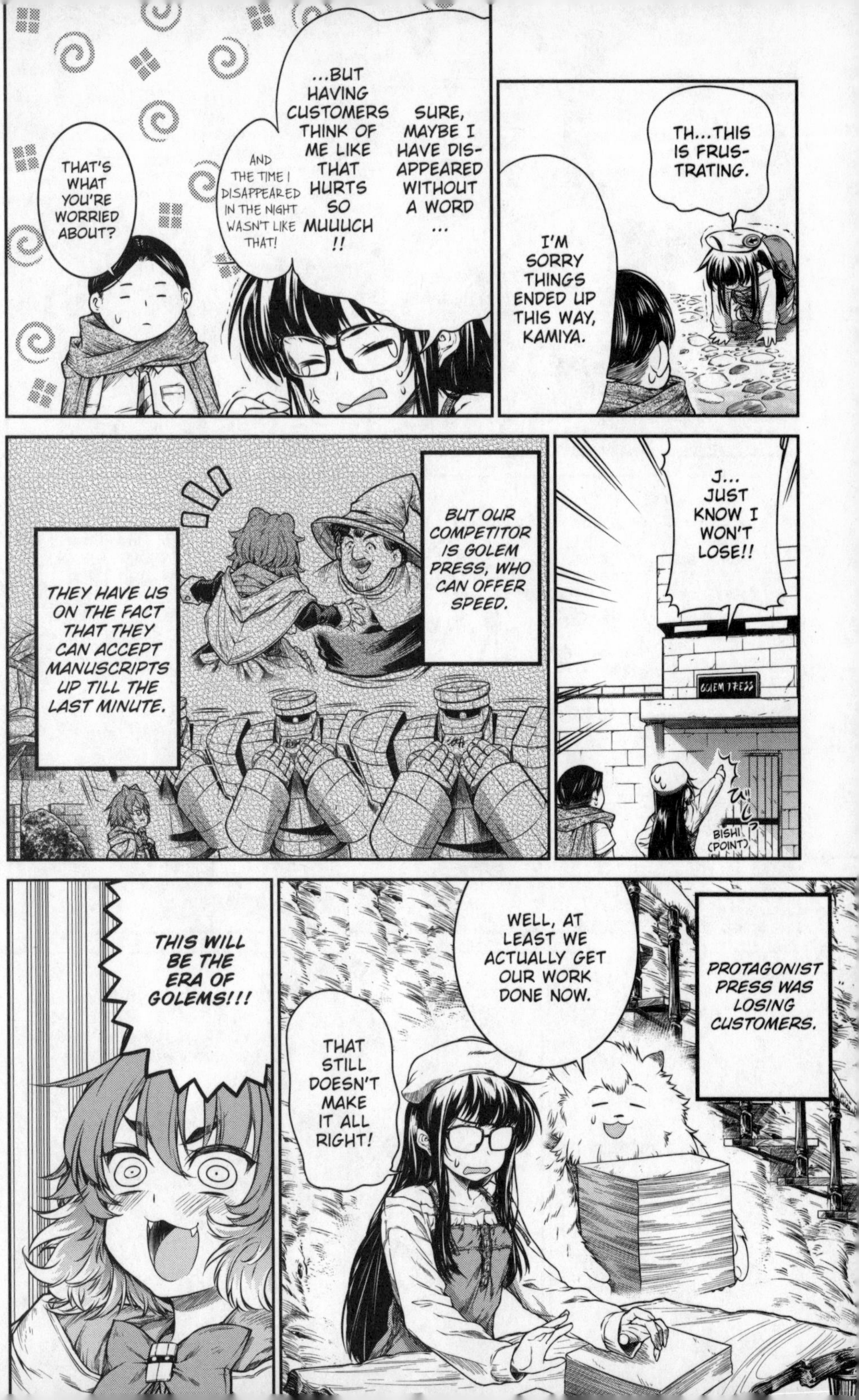
TH...THIS IS FRUS-TRATING.
I'M SORRY THINGS ENDED UP THIS WAY, KAMIYA.
SURE, MAYBE I HAVE DIS-APPEARED WITHOUT A WORD ...
...BUT HAVING CUSTOMERS THINK OF ME LIKE THAT HURTS SO MUUUCH !!
AND THE TIME I DISAPPEARED IN THE NIGHT WASN'T LIKE THAT!
THAT'S WHAT YOU'RE WORRIED ABOUT?
J... JUST KNOW I WON'T LOSE!!
GOLEM PRESS
BISHI (POINT)
BUT OUR COMPETITOR IS GOLEM PRESS, WHO CAN OFFER SPEED.
THEY HAVE US ON THE FACT THAT THEY CAN ACCEPT MANUSCRIPTS UP TILL THE LAST MINUTE.
PROTAGONIST PRESS WAS LOSING CUSTOMERS.
WELL, AT LEAST WE ACTUALLY GET OUR WORK DONE NOW.
THAT STILL DOESN'T MAKE IT ALL RIGHT!
THIS WILL BE THE ERA OF GOLEMS!!!

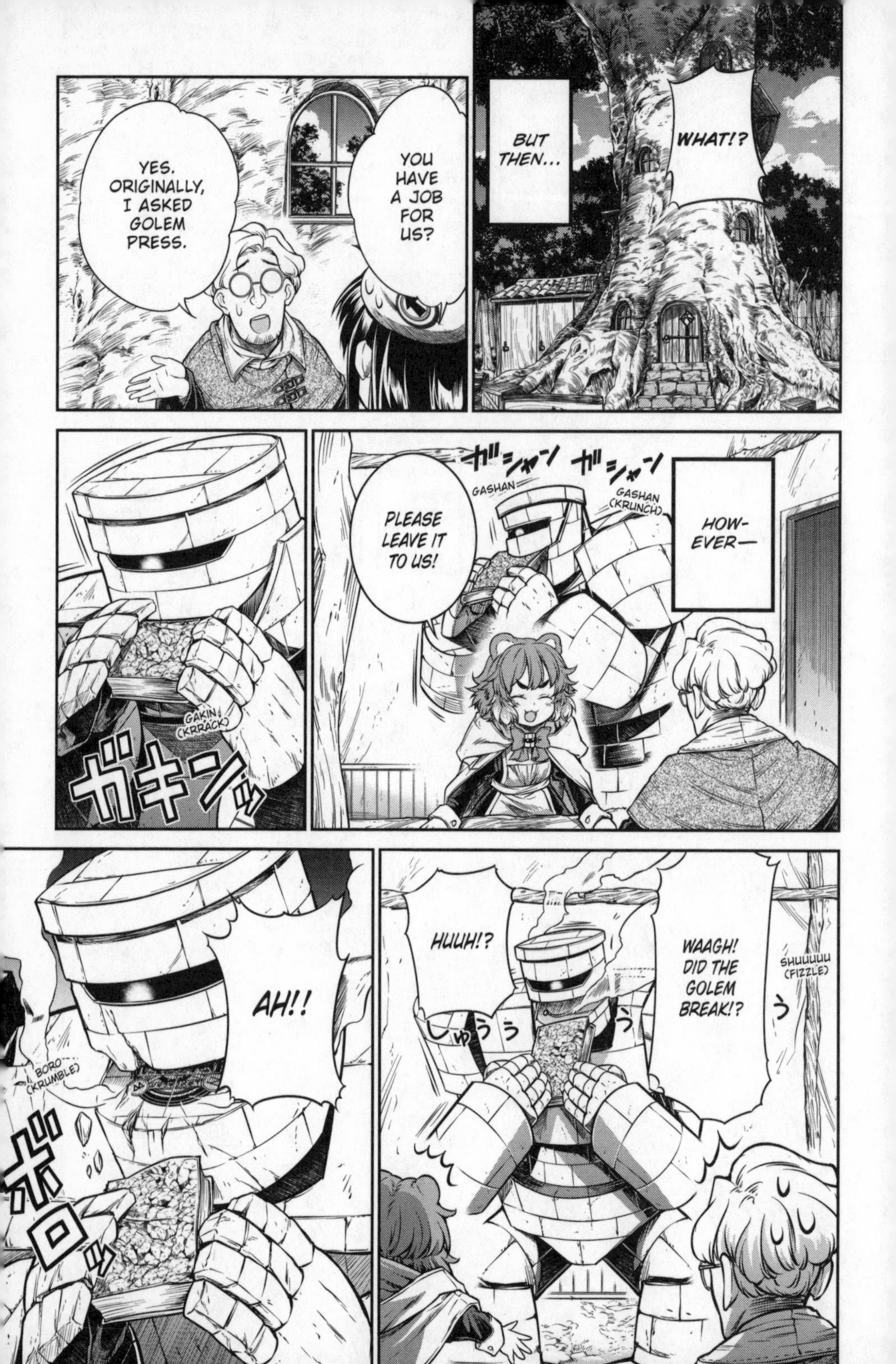
WHAT!?
BUT THEN...
YOU HAVE A JOB FOR US?
YES. ORIGINALLY, I ASKED GOLEM PRESS.
HOW-EVER—
ガシャン
GASHAN (KRUNCH)
ガシャン
GASHAN
PLEASE LEAVE IT TO US!
ガキーン
GAKIN (KRRACK)
SHUUUUU (FIZZLE)
WAAGH! DID THE GOLEM BREAK!?
HUUH!?
しゅううう
AH!!
BORO (KRUMBLE)
ボロッ

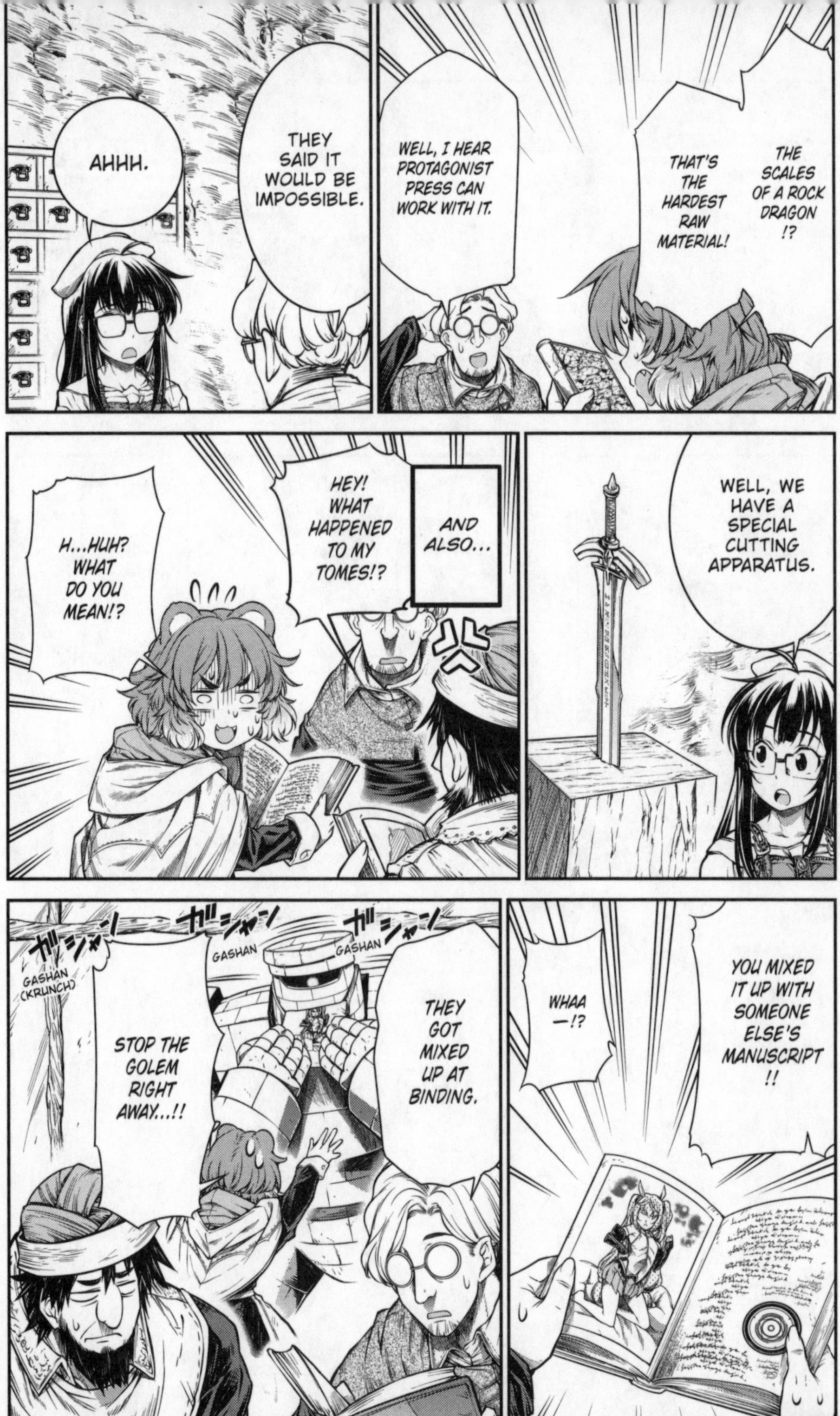
THE SCALES OF A ROCK DRAGON !?
THAT'S THE HARDEST RAW MATERIAL!
WELL, I HEAR PROTAGONIST PRESS CAN WORK WITH IT.
THEY SAID IT WOULD BE IMPOSSIBLE.
AHHH.
WELL, WE HAVE A SPECIAL CUTTING APPARATUS.
AND ALSO...
HEY! WHAT HAPPENED TO MY TOMES!?
H...HUH? WHAT DO YOU MEAN!?
YOU MIXED IT UP WITH SOMEONE ELSE'S MANUSCRIPT !!
WHAA —!?
ガシャン
GASHAN
THEY GOT MIXED UP AT BINDING.
ガシャン
GASHAN
STOP THE GOLEM RIGHT AWAY...!!
GASHAN (KRUNCH)

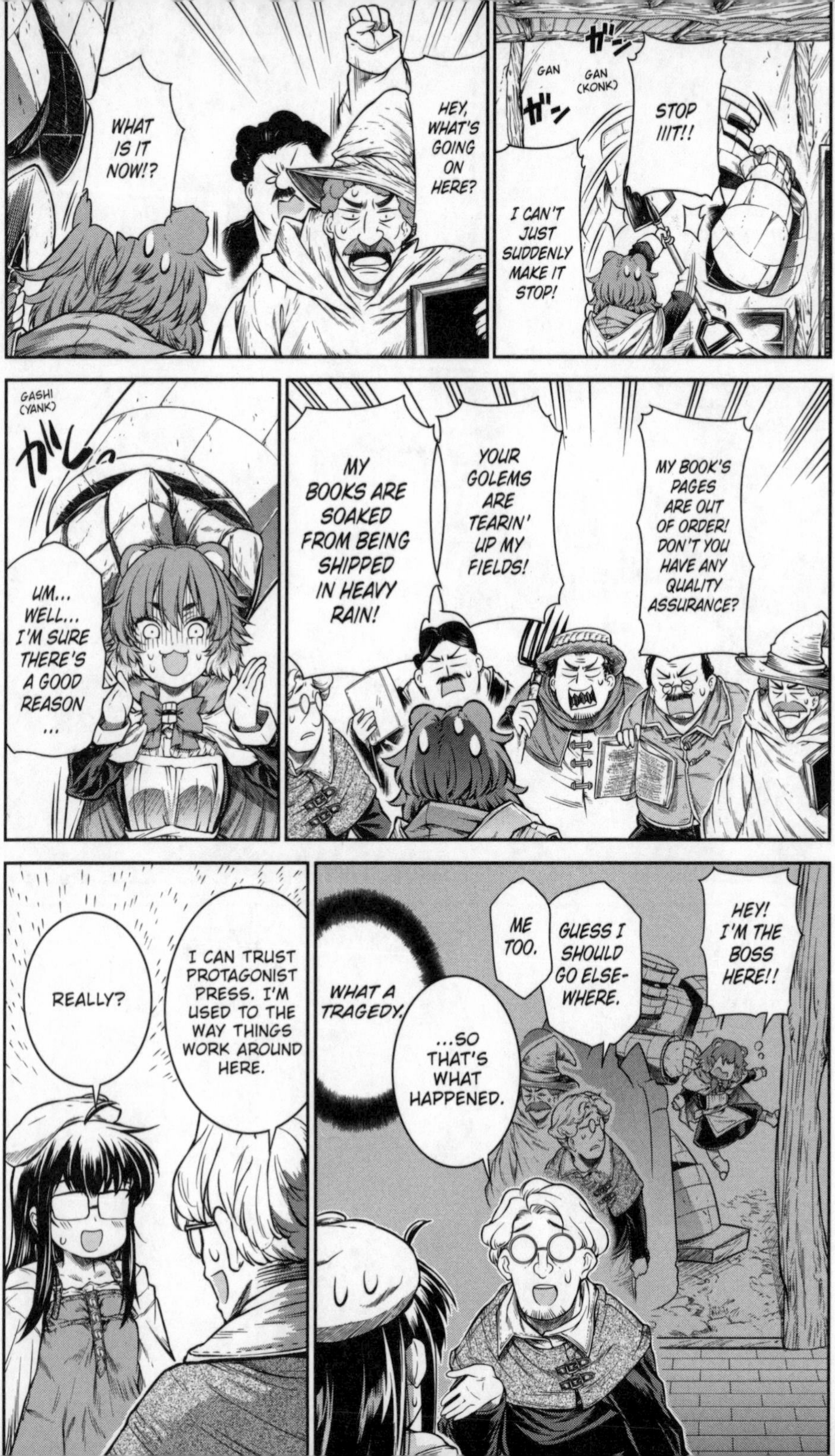
STOP IIIT!!
GAN (KONK)
GAN
I CAN'T JUST SUDDENLY MAKE IT STOP!
HEY, WHAT'S GOING ON HERE?
WHAT IS IT NOW!?
MY BOOK'S PAGES ARE OUT OF ORDER! DON'T YOU HAVE ANY QUALITY ASSURANCE?
YOUR GOLEMS ARE TEARIN' UP MY FIELDS!
MY BOOKS ARE SOAKED FROM BEING SHIPPED IN HEAVY RAIN!
GASHI (YANK)
UM... WELL... I'M SURE THERE'S A GOOD REASON ...
HEY! I'M THE BOSS HERE!!
GUESS I SHOULD GO ELSE-WHERE.
ME TOO.
WHAT A TRAGEDY.
...SO THAT'S WHAT HAPPENED.
I CAN TRUST PROTAGONIST PRESS. I'M USED TO THE WAY THINGS WORK AROUND HERE.
REALLY?

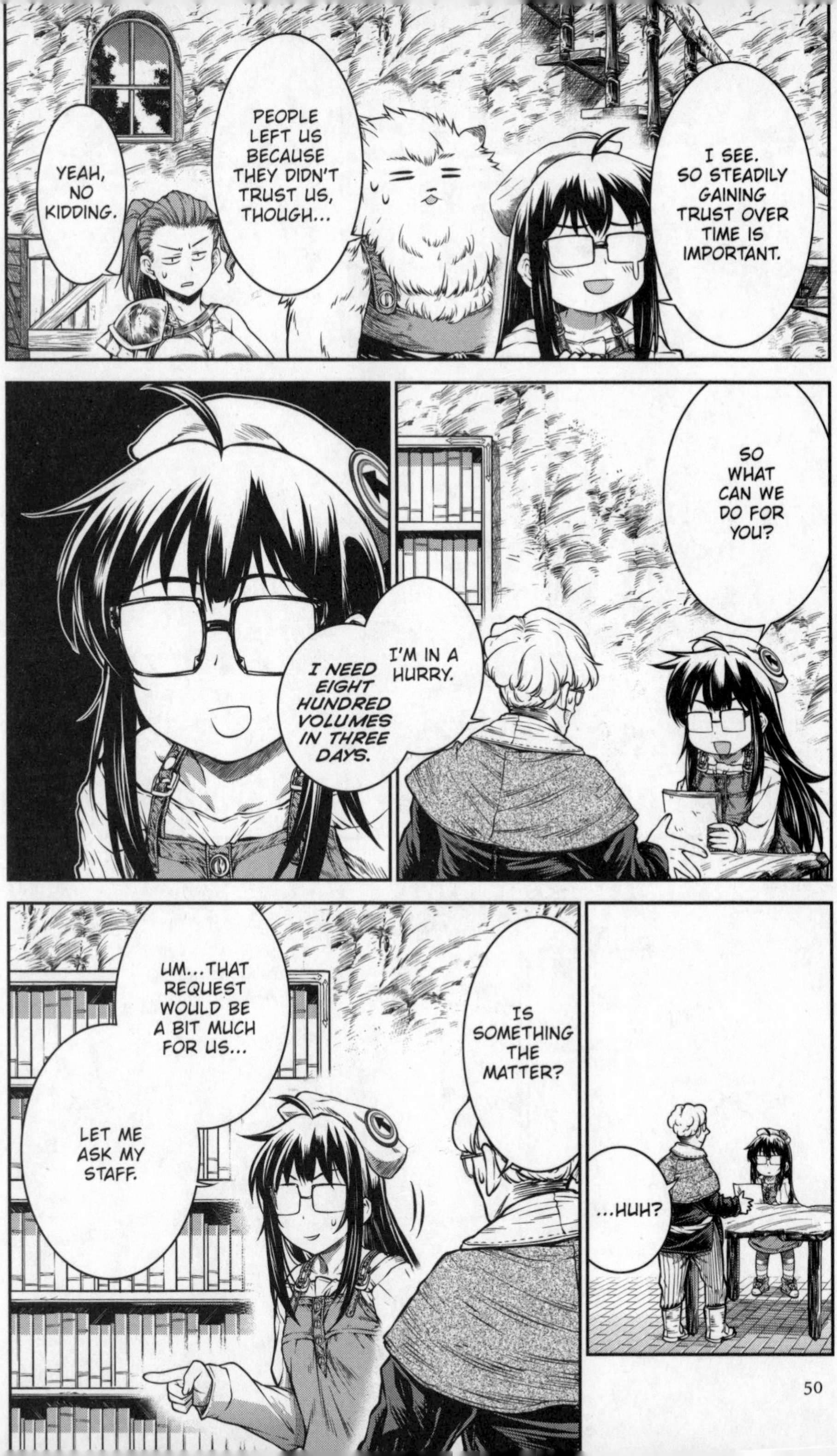
I SEE. SO STEADILY GAINING TRUST OVER TIME IS IMPORTANT.
PEOPLE LEFT US BECAUSE THEY DIDN'T TRUST US, THOUGH...
YEAH, NO KIDDING.
SO WHAT CAN WE DO FOR YOU?
I'M IN A HURRY.
I NEED EIGHT HUNDRED VOLUMES IN THREE DAYS.
...HUH?
IS SOMETHING THE MATTER?
UM...THAT REQUEST WOULD BE A BIT MUCH FOR US...
LET ME ASK MY STAFF.

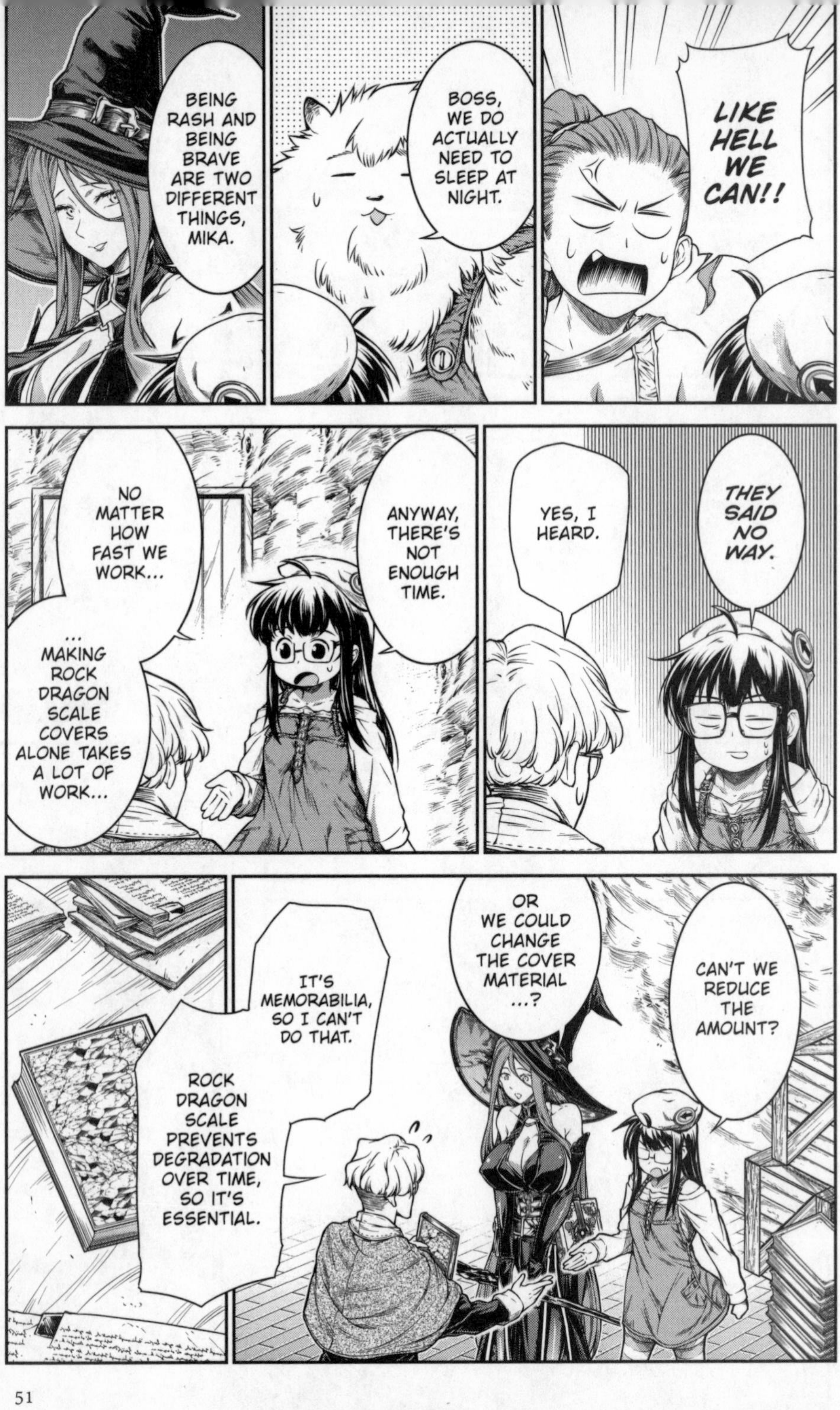
LIKE HELL WE CAN!!
BOSS, WE DO ACTUALLY NEED TO SLEEP AT NIGHT.
BEING RASH AND BEING BRAVE ARE TWO DIFFERENT THINGS, MIKA.
THEY SAID NO WAY.
YES, I HEARD.
ANYWAY, THERE'S NOT ENOUGH TIME.
NO MATTER HOW FAST WE WORK...
...MAKING ROCK DRAGON SCALE COVERS ALONE TAKES A LOT OF WORK...
CAN'T WE REDUCE THE AMOUNT?
OR WE COULD CHANGE THE COVER MATERIAL ...?
IT'S MEMORABILIA, SO I CAN'T DO THAT.
ROCK DRAGON SCALE PREVENTS DEGRADATION OVER TIME, SO IT'S ESSENTIAL.

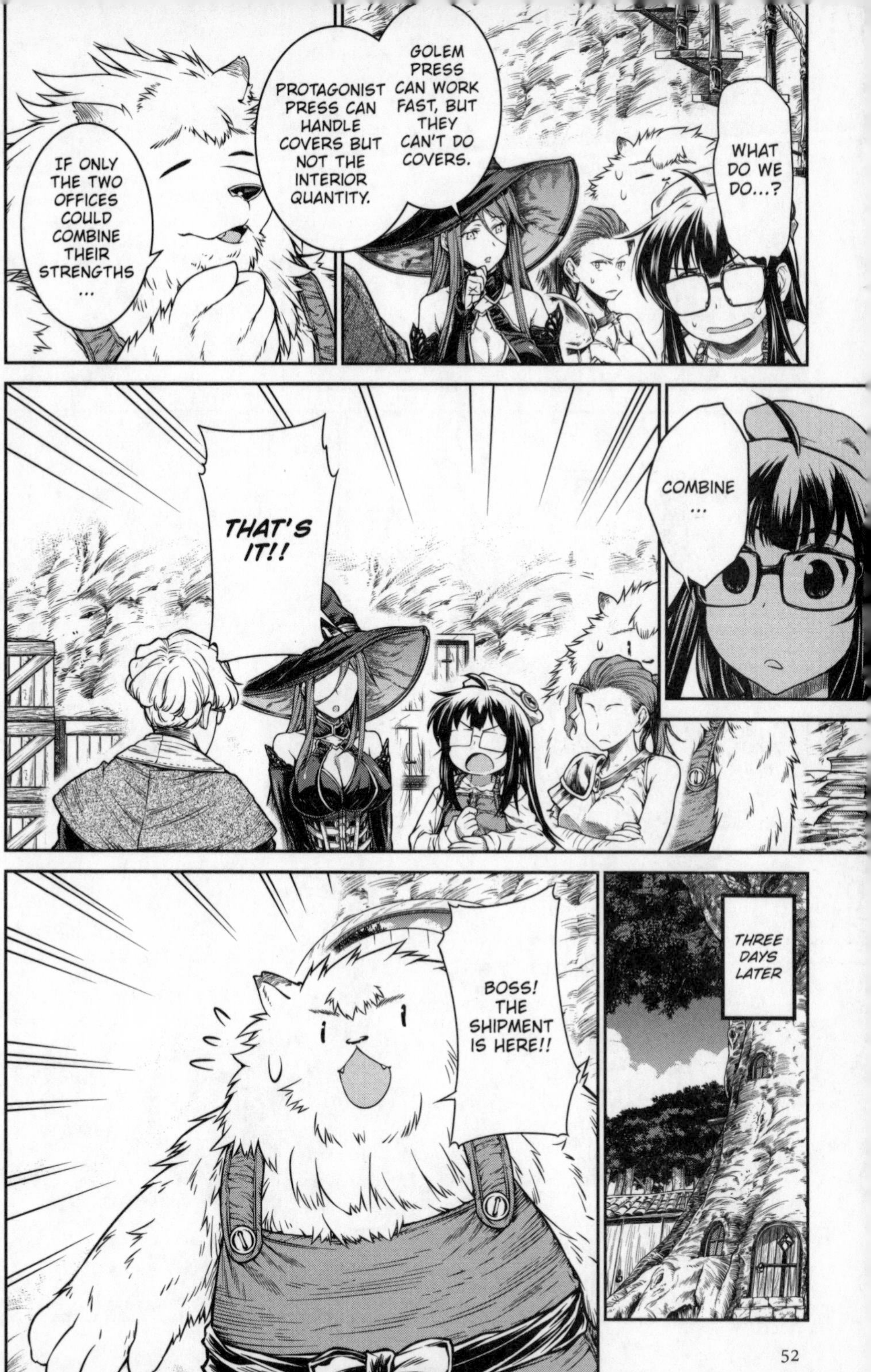
WHAT DO WE DO...?
GOLEM PRESS CAN WORK FAST, BUT THEY CAN'T DO COVERS.
PROTAGONIST PRESS CAN HANDLE COVERS BUT NOT THE INTERIOR QUANTITY.
IF ONLY THE TWO OFFICES COULD COMBINE THEIR STRENGTHS...
COMBINE...
THAT'S IT!!
THREE DAYS LATER
BOSS! THE SHIPMENT IS HERE!!

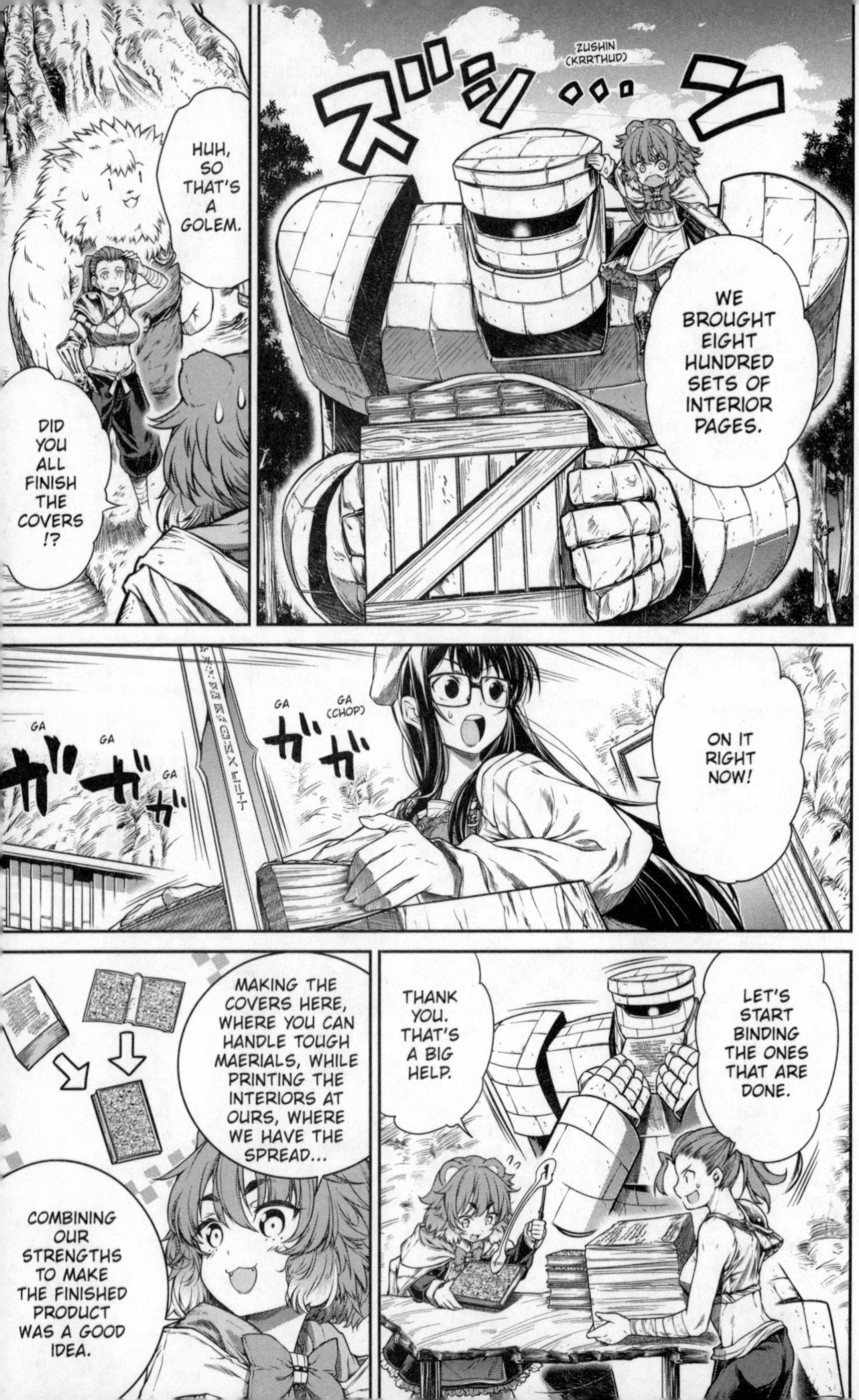
ZUSHIN (KRRTHUD)
WE BROUGHT EIGHT HUNDRED SETS OF INTERIOR PAGES.
HUH, SO THAT'S A GOLEM.
DID YOU ALL FINISH THE COVERS!?
ON IT RIGHT NOW!
GA
GA (CHOP)
GA
GA
GA
LET'S START BINDING THE ONES THAT ARE DONE.
THANK YOU. THAT'S A BIG HELP.
MAKING THE COVERS HERE, WHERE YOU CAN HANDLE TOUGH MAERIALS, WHILE PRINTING THE INTERIORS AT OURS, WHERE WE HAVE THE SPREAD...
COMBINING OUR STRENGTHS TO MAKE THE FINISHED PRODUCT WAS A GOOD IDEA.

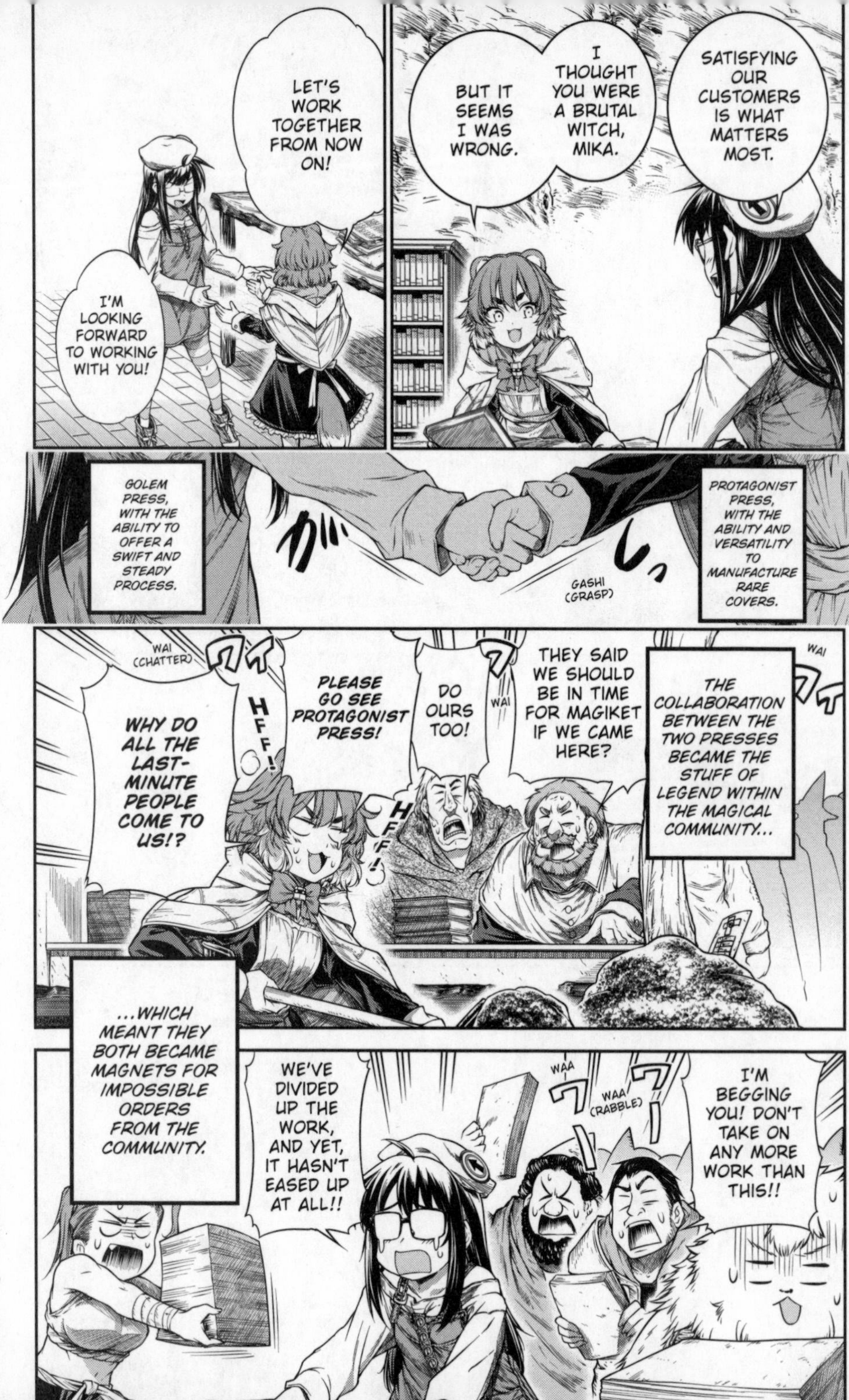
SATISFYING OUR CUSTOMERS IS WHAT MATTERS MOST.
I THOUGHT YOU WERE A BRUTAL WITCH, MIKA.
BUT IT SEEMS I WAS WRONG.
LET'S WORK TOGETHER FROM NOW ON!
I'M LOOKING FORWARD TO WORKING WITH YOU!
PROTAGONIST PRESS, WITH THE ABILITY AND VERSATILITY TO MANUFACTURE RARE COVERS.
GASHI (GRASP)
GOLEM PRESS, WITH THE ABILITY TO OFFER A SWIFT AND STEADY PROCESS.
THE COLLABORATION BETWEEN THE TWO PRESSES BECAME THE STUFF OF LEGEND WITHIN THE MAGICAL COMMUNITY...
WAI
THEY SAID WE SHOULD BE IN TIME FOR MAGIKET IF WE CAME HERE?
WAI
DO OURS TOO!
PLEASE GO SEE PROTAGONIST PRESS!
HFF!
HFF!
WAI (CHATTER)
WHY DO ALL THE LAST-MINUTE PEOPLE COME TO US!?
...WHICH MEANT THEY BOTH BECAME MAGNETS FOR IMPOSSIBLE ORDERS FROM THE COMMUNITY.
I'M BEGGING YOU! DON'T TAKE ON ANY MORE WORK THAN THIS!!
WAA (RABBLE)
WAA
WE'VE DIVIDED UP THE WORK, AND YET, IT HASN'T EASED UP AT ALL!!

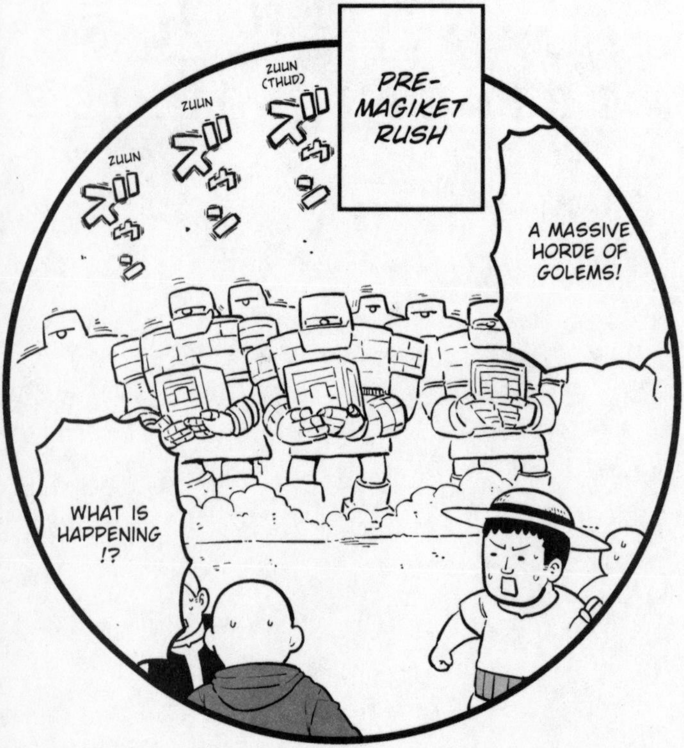
PRE-MAGIKET RUSH
ZUUN (THUD)
ZUUN
ZUUN
A MASSIVE HORDE OF GOLEMS!
WHAT IS HAPPENING !?

A WITCH'S PRINTING OFFICE

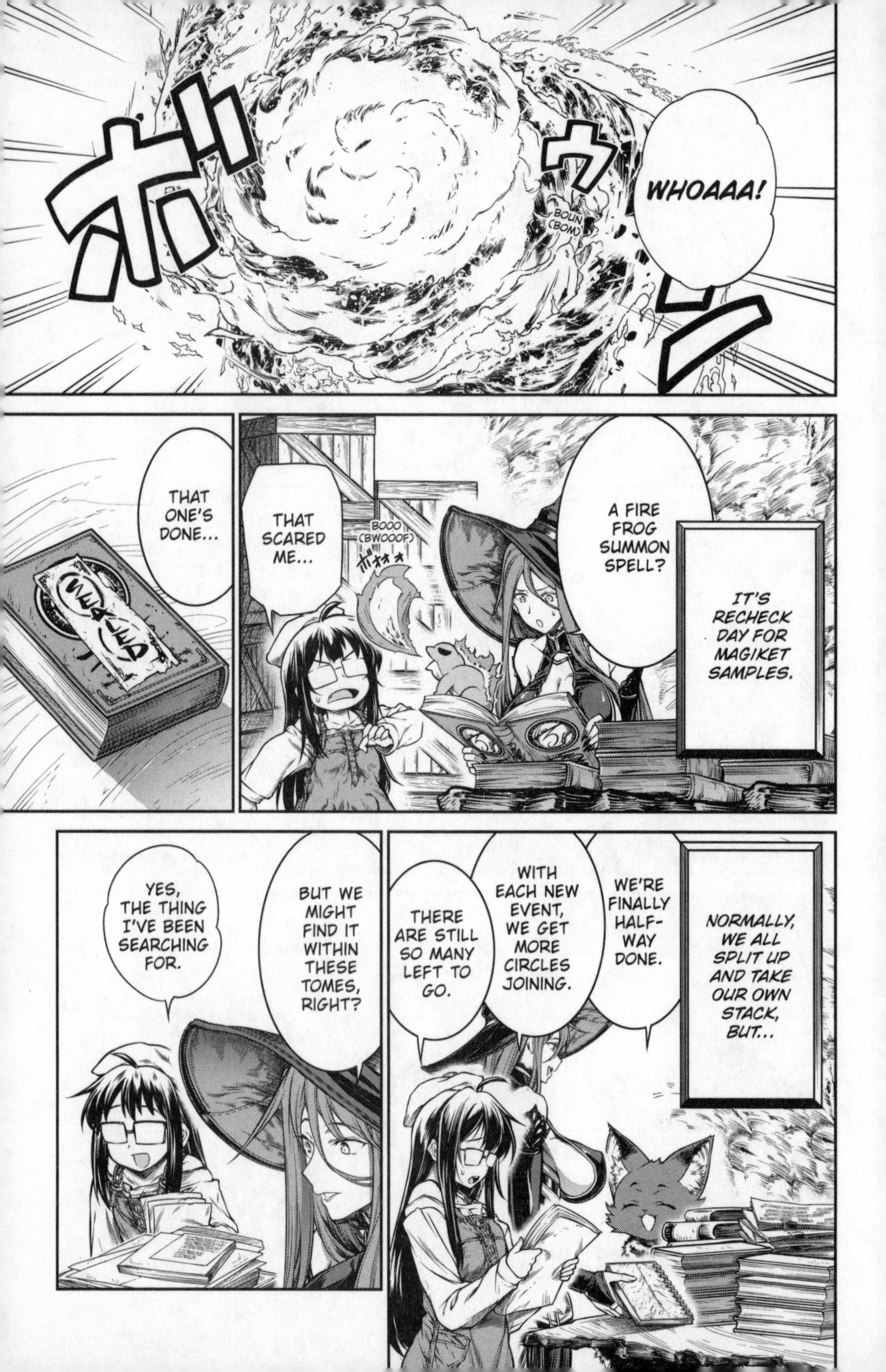
WHOAAA!
BOUN (BOM)
IT'S RECHECK DAY FOR MAGIKET SAMPLES.
A FIRE FROG SUMMON SPELL?
BOOO (BWOOOF)
THAT SCARED ME...
THAT ONE'S DONE...
SEALED
NORMALLY, WE ALL SPLIT UP AND TAKE OUR OWN STACK, BUT...
WE'RE FINALLY HALF-WAY DONE.
WITH EACH NEW EVENT, WE GET MORE CIRCLES JOINING.
THERE ARE STILL SO MANY LEFT TO GO.
BUT WE MIGHT FIND IT WITHIN THESE TOMES, RIGHT?
YES, THE THING I'VE BEEN SEARCHING FOR.

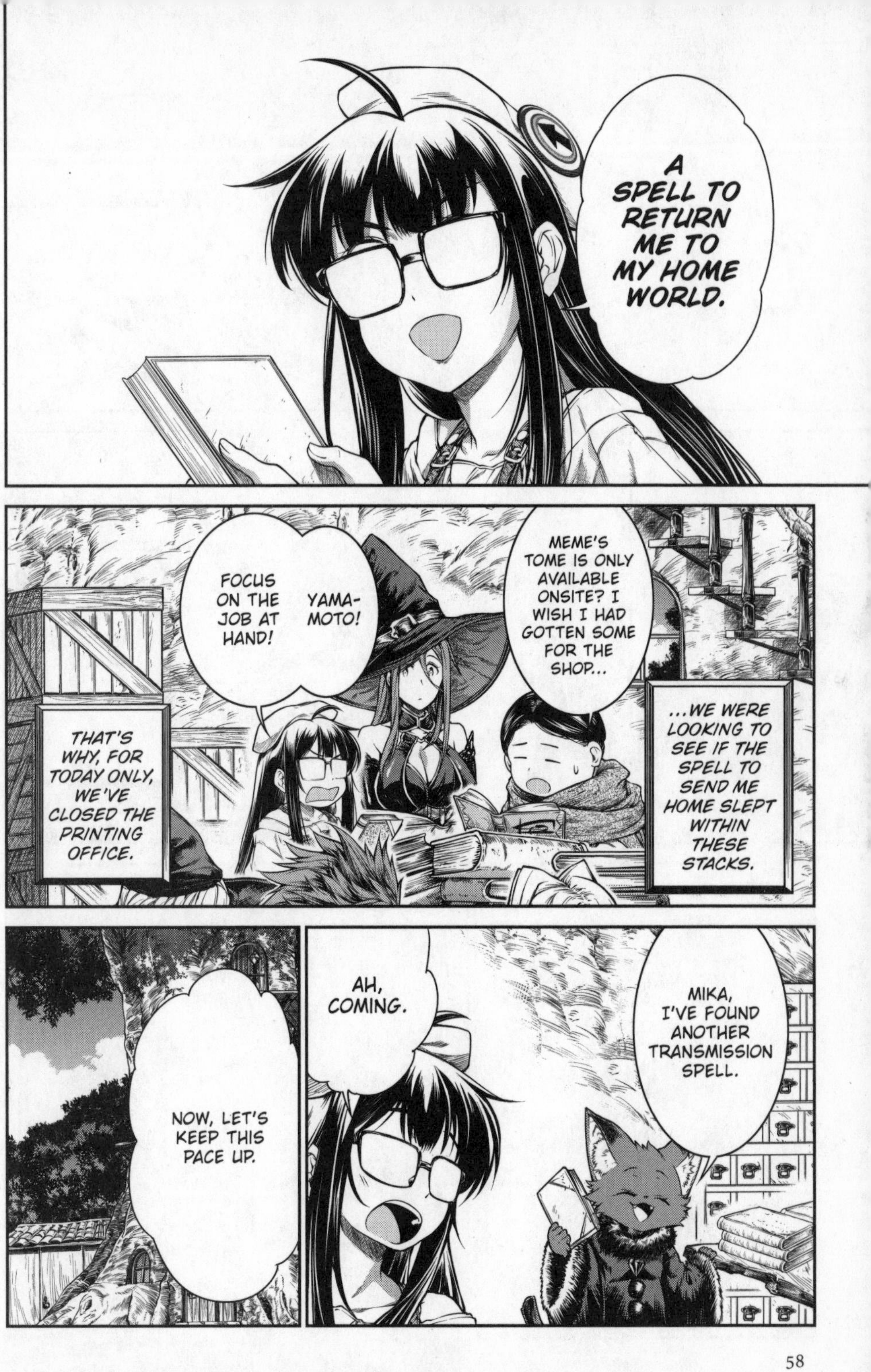
A SPELL TO RETURN ME TO MY HOME WORLD.
MEME'S TOME IS ONLY AVAILABLE ONSITE? I WISH I HAD GOTTEN SOME FOR THE SHOP...
...WE WERE LOOKING TO SEE IF THE SPELL TO SEND ME HOME SLEPT WITHIN THESE STACKS.
YAMA-MOTO! FOCUS ON THE JOB AT HAND!
THAT'S WHY, FOR TODAY ONLY, WE'VE CLOSED THE PRINTING OFFICE.
MIKA, I'VE FOUND ANOTHER TRANSMISSION SPELL.
AH, COMING.
NOW, LET'S KEEP THIS PACE UP.

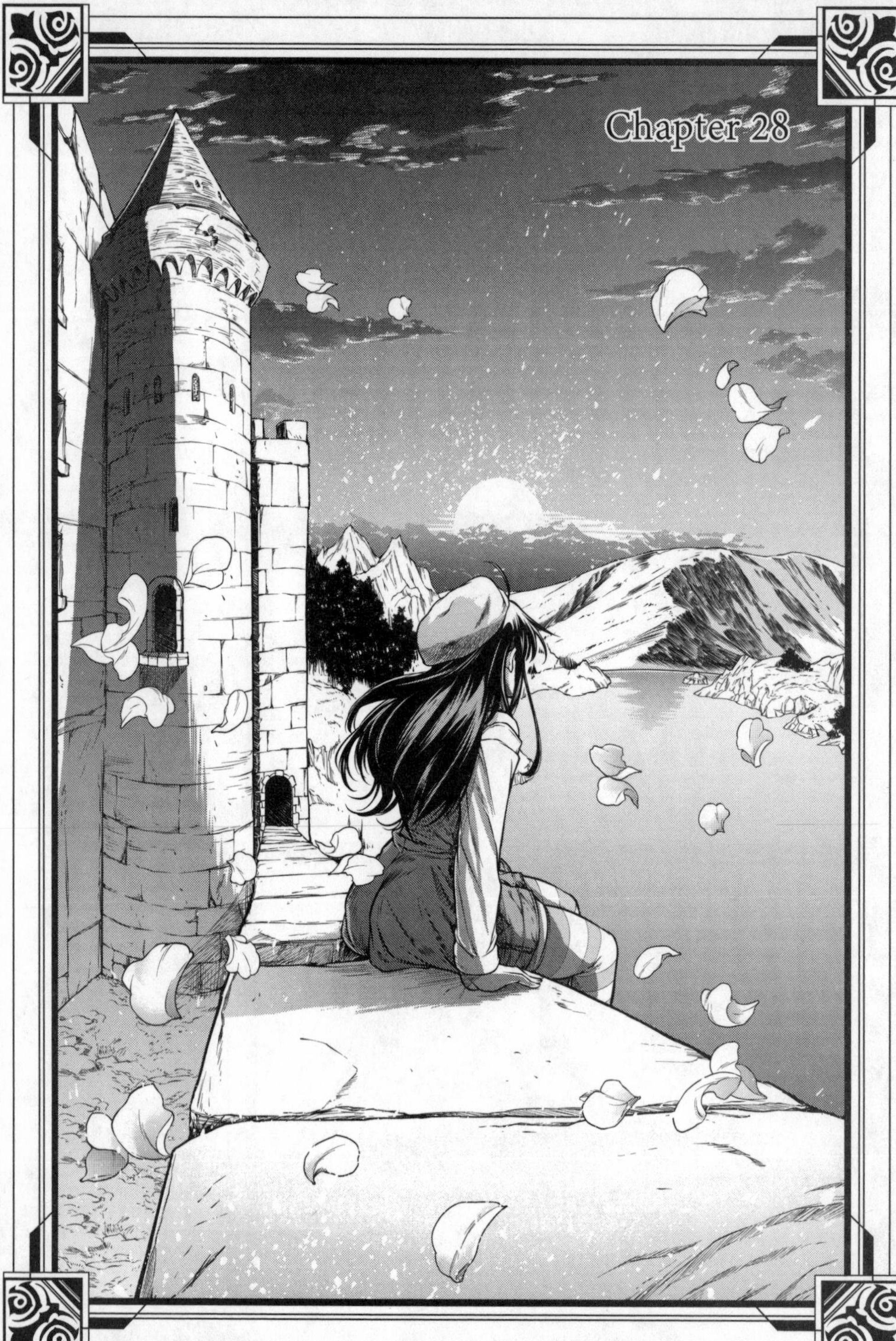
Chapter 28

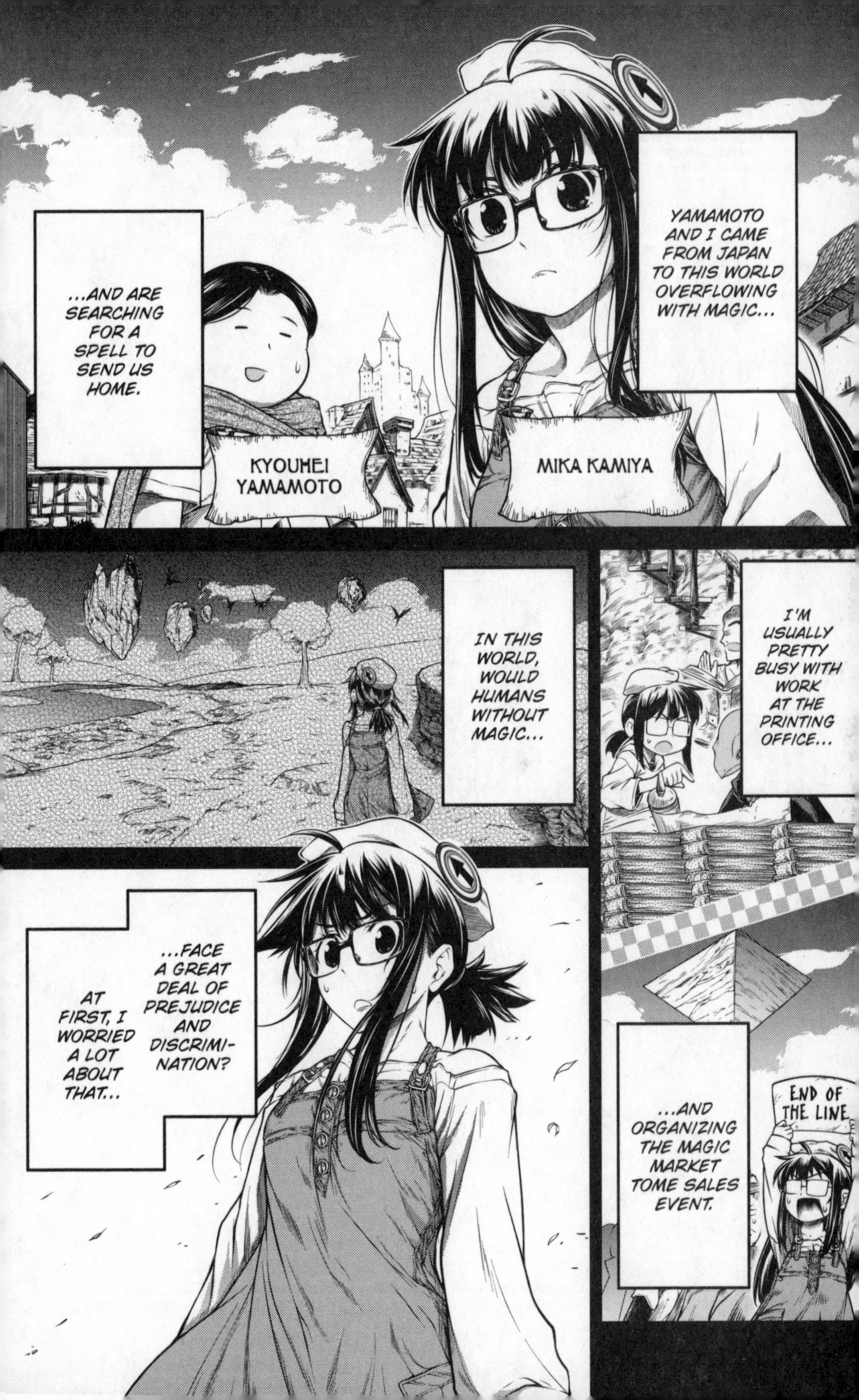
YAMAMOTO AND I CAME FROM JAPAN TO THIS WORLD OVERFLOWING WITH MAGIC...
...AND ARE SEARCHING FOR A SPELL TO SEND US HOME.
MIKA KAMIYA
KYOUHEI YAMAMOTO
I'M USUALLY PRETTY BUSY WITH WORK AT THE PRINTING OFFICE...
END OF THE LINE
...AND ORGANIZING THE MAGIC MARKET TOME SALES EVENT.
IN THIS WORLD, WOULD HUMANS WITHOUT MAGIC...
...FACE A GREAT DEAL OF PREJUDICE AND DISCRIMI-NATION?
AT FIRST, I WORRIED A LOT ABOUT THAT...

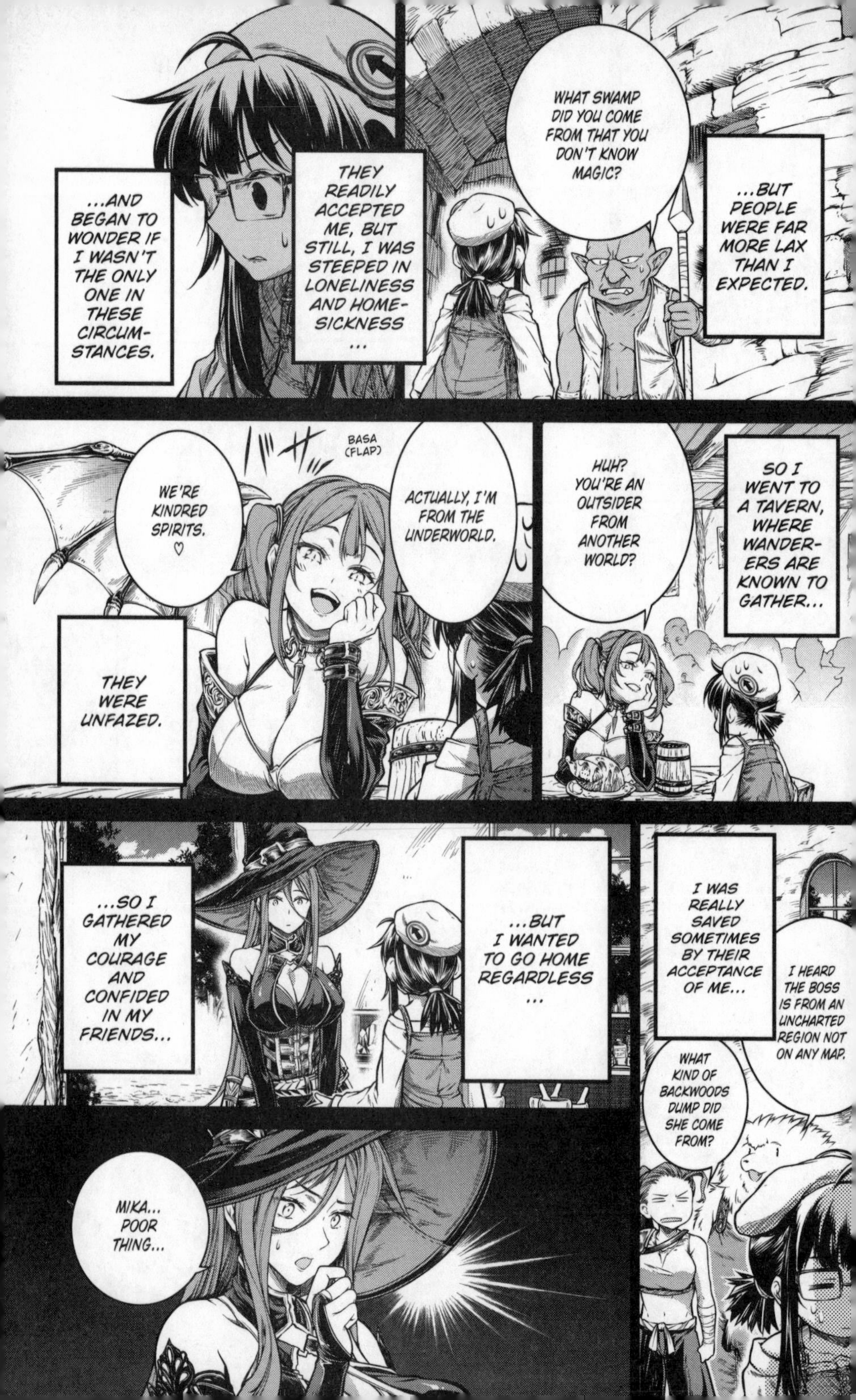
...BUT PEOPLE WERE FAR MORE LAX THAN I EXPECTED.
WHAT SWAMP DID YOU COME FROM THAT YOU DON'T KNOW MAGIC?
THEY READILY ACCEPTED ME, BUT STILL, I WAS STEEPED IN LONELINESS AND HOME-SICKNESS...
...AND BEGAN TO WONDER IF I WASN'T THE ONLY ONE IN THESE CIRCUM-STANCES.
SO I WENT TO A TAVERN, WHERE WANDER-ERS ARE KNOWN TO GATHER...
HUH? YOU'RE AN OUTSIDER FROM ANOTHER WORLD?
ACTUALLY, I'M FROM THE UNDERWORLD.
BASA (FLAP)
WE'RE KINDRED SPIRITS. ♡
THEY WERE UNFAZED.
I WAS REALLY SAVED SOMETIMES BY THEIR ACCEPTANCE OF ME...
I HEARD THE BOSS IS FROM AN UNCHARTED REGION NOT ON ANY MAP.
WHAT KIND OF BACKWOODS DUMP DID SHE COME FROM?
...BUT I WANTED TO GO HOME REGARDLESS...
...SO I GATHERED MY COURAGE AND CONFIDED IN MY FRIENDS...
...
MIKA... POOR THING...

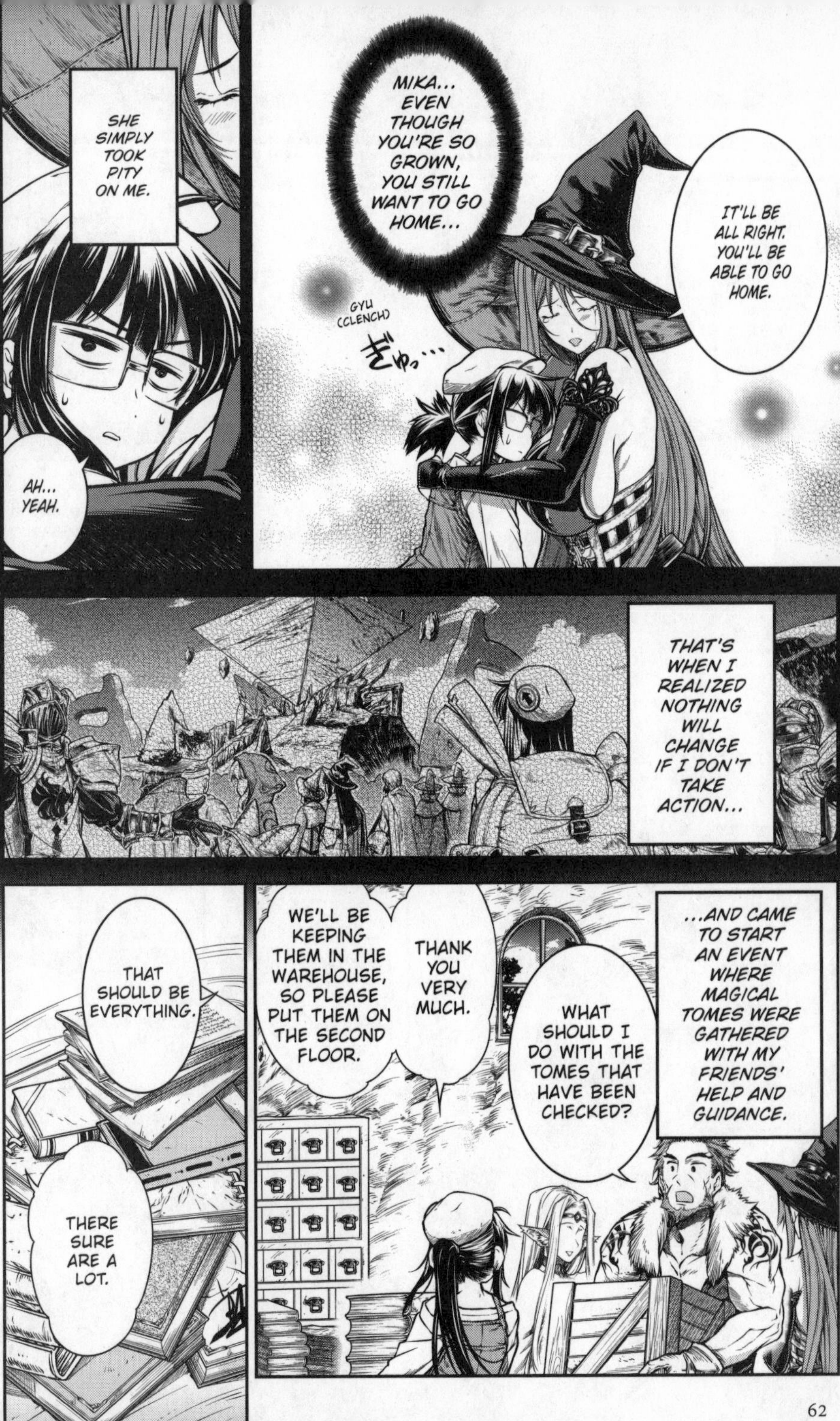
IT'LL BE ALL RIGHT. YOU'LL BE ABLE TO GO HOME.
MIKA... EVEN THOUGH YOU'RE SO GROWN, YOU STILL WANT TO GO HOME...
GYU (CLENCH)
ぎゅっ…
SHE SIMPLY TOOK PITY ON ME.
AH... YEAH.
THAT'S WHEN I REALIZED NOTHING WILL CHANGE IF I DON'T TAKE ACTION...
...AND CAME TO START AN EVENT WHERE MAGICAL TOMES WERE GATHERED WITH MY FRIENDS' HELP AND GUIDANCE.
WHAT SHOULD I DO WITH THE TOMES THAT HAVE BEEN CHECKED?
THANK YOU VERY MUCH.
WE'LL BE KEEPING THEM IN THE WAREHOUSE, SO PLEASE PUT THEM ON THE SECOND FLOOR.
THAT SHOULD BE EVERYTHING.
THERE SURE ARE A LOT.

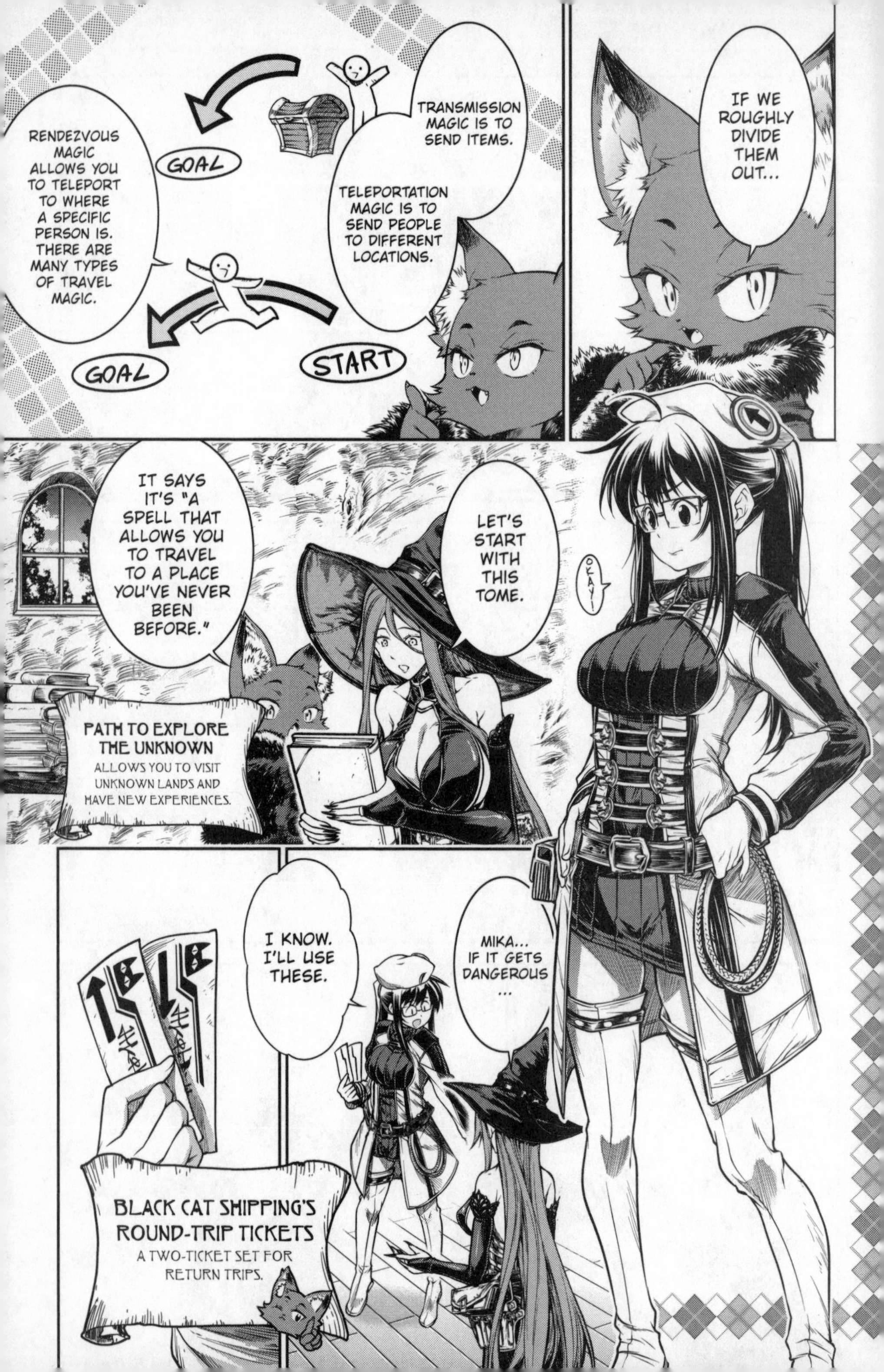

IF WE ROUGHLY DIVIDE THEM OUT...
TRANSMISSION MAGIC IS TO SEND ITEMS.
TELEPORTATION MAGIC IS TO SEND PEOPLE TO DIFFERENT LOCATIONS.
GOAL
START
GOAL
RENDEZVOUS MAGIC ALLOWS YOU TO TELEPORT TO WHERE A SPECIFIC PERSON IS. THERE ARE MANY TYPES OF TRAVEL MAGIC.
OKAY!
LET'S START WITH THIS TOME.
IT SAYS IT'S "A SPELL THAT ALLOWS YOU TO TRAVEL TO A PLACE YOU'VE NEVER BEEN BEFORE."
PATH TO EXPLORE THE UNKNOWN
ALLOWS YOU TO VISIT UNKNOWN LANDS AND HAVE NEW EXPERIENCES.
MIKA... IF IT GETS DANGEROUS ...
I KNOW. I'LL USE THESE.
BLACK CAT SHIPPING'S ROUND-TRIP TICKETS
A TWO-TICKET SET FOR RETURN TRIPS.

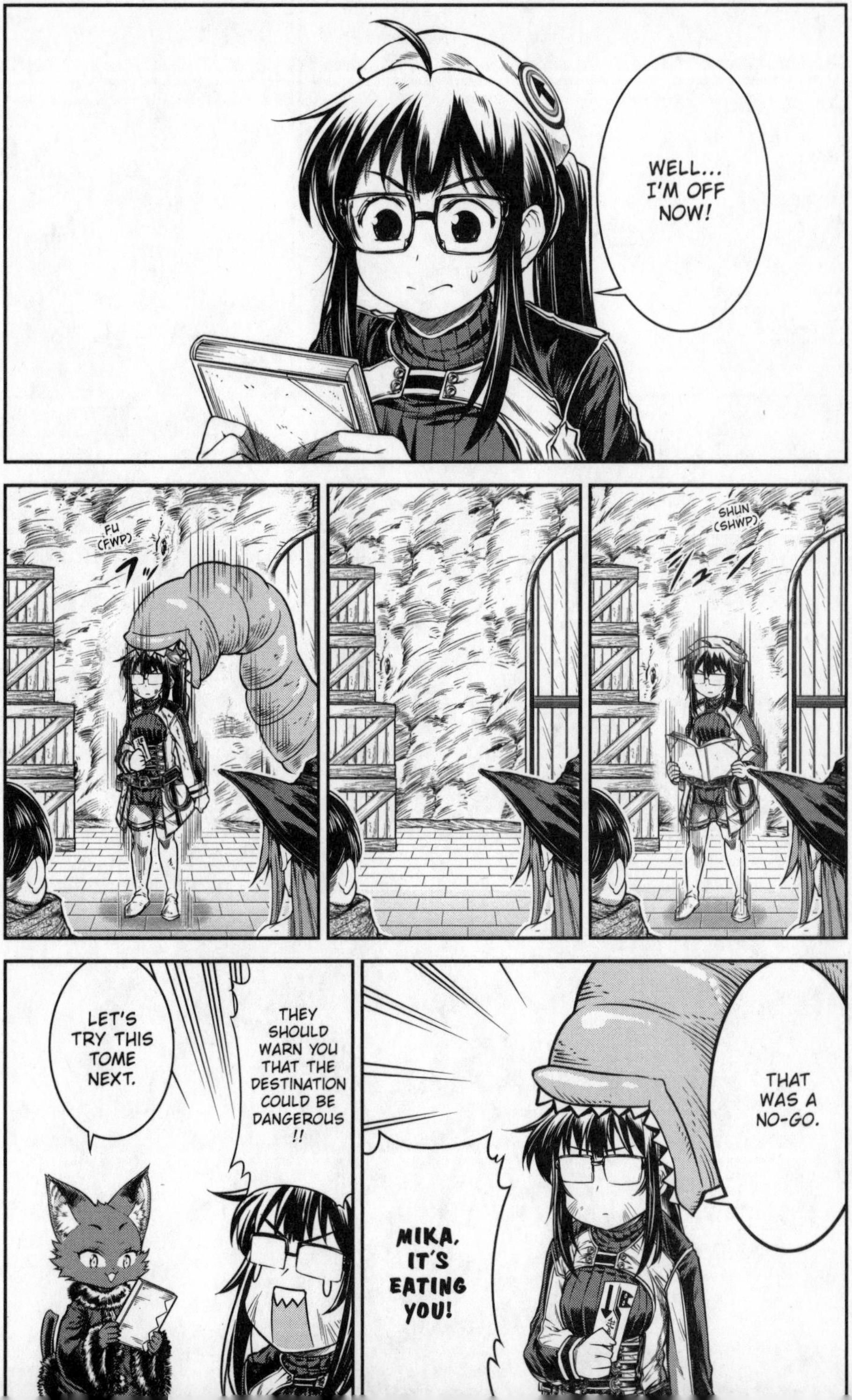
WELL... I'M OFF NOW!
SHUN (SHWP)
FU (FWP)
THAT WAS A NO-GO.
MIKA, IT'S EATING YOU!
THEY SHOULD WARN YOU THAT THE DESTINATION COULD BE DANGEROUS!!
LET'S TRY THIS TOME NEXT.

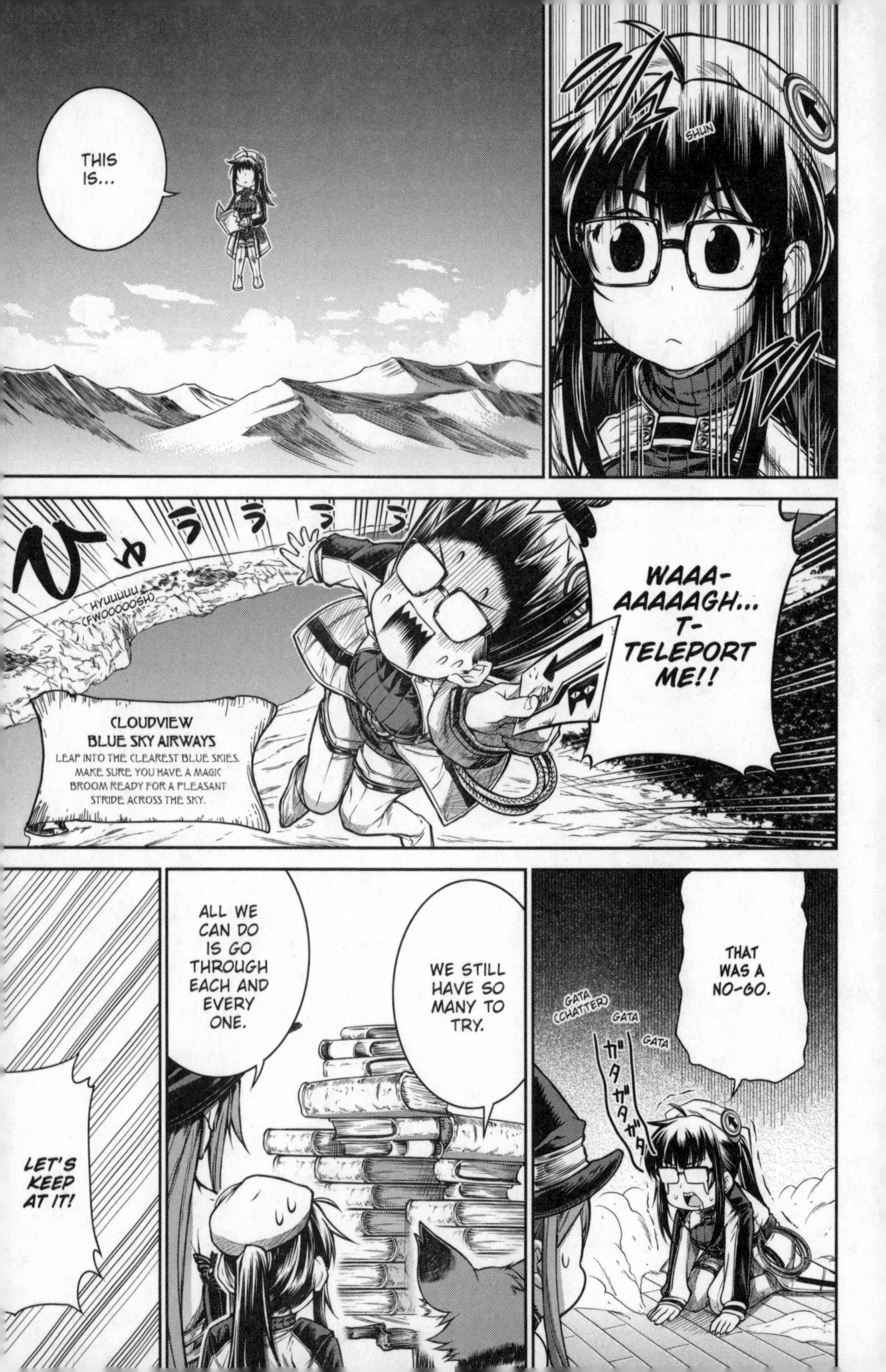

SHUN
THIS IS...
WAAA-AAAAAGH... T-TELEPORT ME!!
ひゅううう
HYUUUUU (FWOOOOOSH)
CLOUDVIEW BLUE SKY AIRWAYS
LEAP INTO THE CLEAREST BLUE SKIES. MAKE SURE YOU HAVE A MAGIC BROOM READY FOR A PLEASANT STRIDE ACROSS THE SKY.
THAT WAS A NO-GO.
ガタガタガタ
GATA (CHATTER) GATA GATA
WE STILL HAVE SO MANY TO TRY.
ALL WE CAN DO IS GO THROUGH EACH AND EVERY ONE.
LET'S KEEP AT IT!

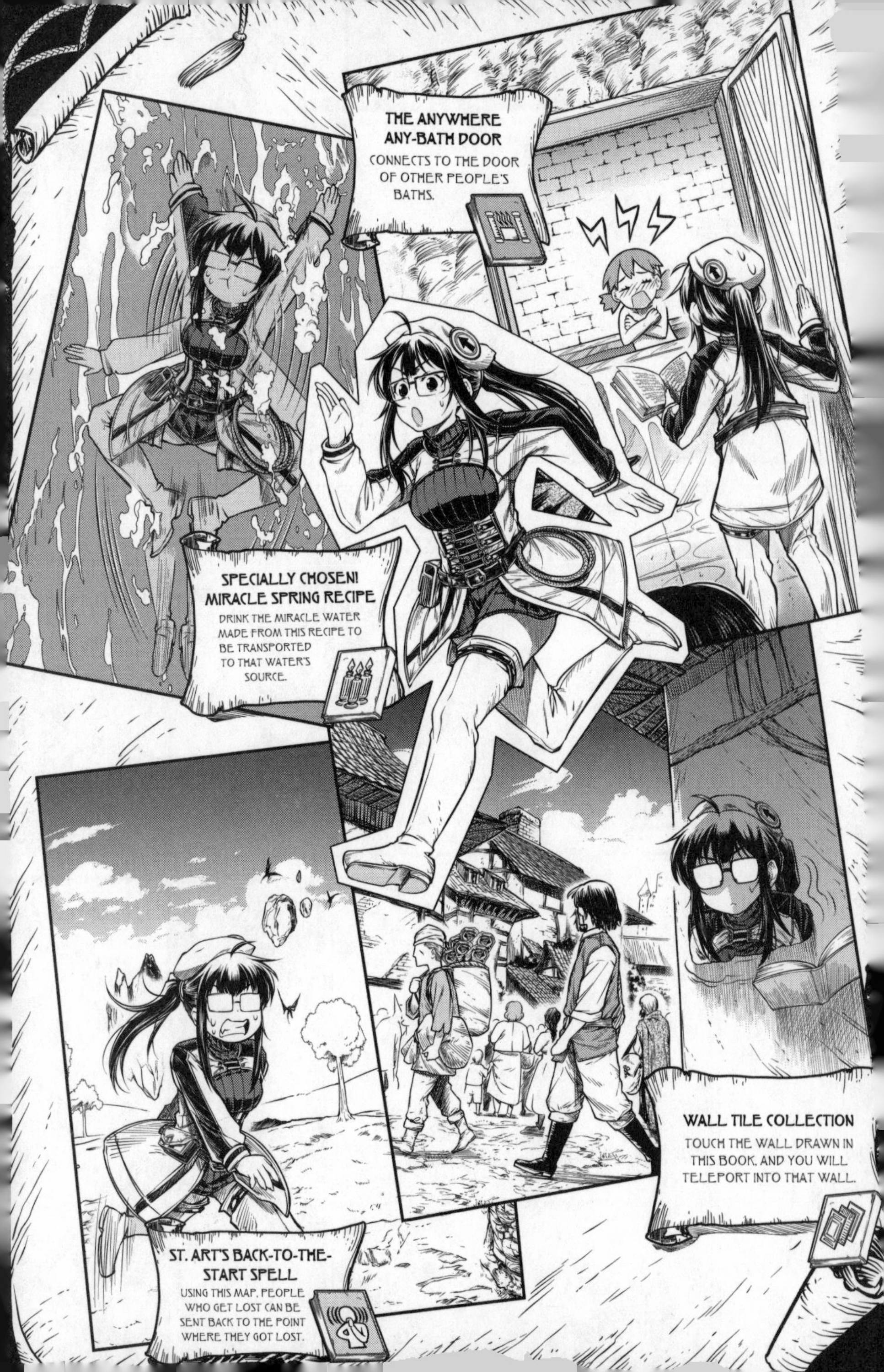

THE ANYWHERE ANY-BATH DOOR
CONNECTS TO THE DOOR OF OTHER PEOPLE'S BATHS.
SPECIALLY CHOSEN! MIRACLE SPRING RECIPE
DRINK THE MIRACLE WATER MADE FROM THIS RECIPE TO BE TRANSPORTED TO THAT WATER'S SOURCE.
WALL TILE COLLECTION
TOUCH THE WALL DRAWN IN THIS BOOK, AND YOU WILL TELEPORT INTO THAT WALL.
ST. ART'S BACK-TO-THE-START SPELL
USING THIS MAP, PEOPLE WHO GET LOST CAN BE SENT BACK TO THE POINT WHERE THEY GOT LOST.

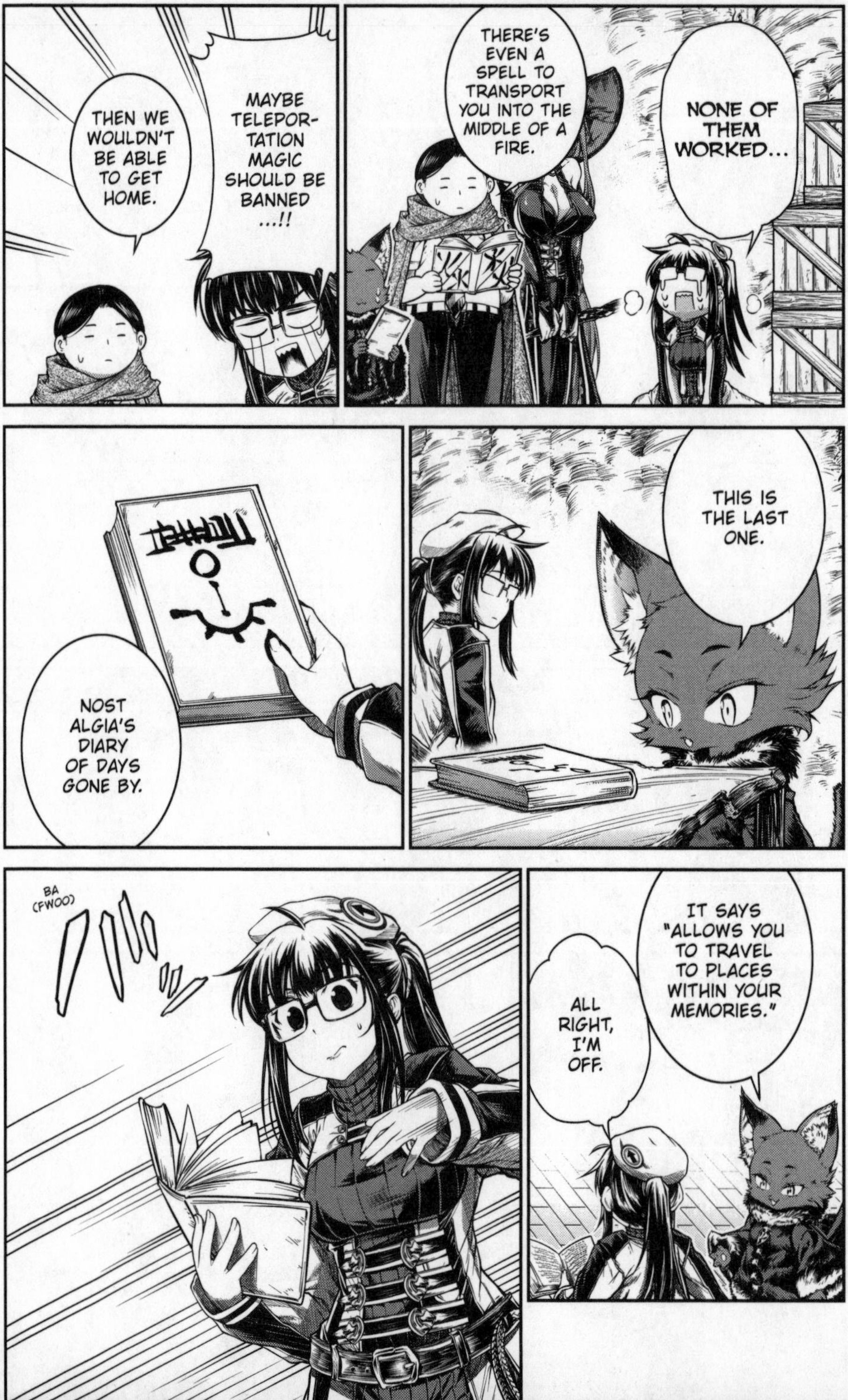
NONE OF THEM WORKED...
THERE'S EVEN A SPELL TO TRANSPORT YOU INTO THE MIDDLE OF A FIRE.
MAYBE TELEPORTATION MAGIC SHOULD BE BANNED...!!
THEN WE WOULDN'T BE ABLE TO GET HOME.
THIS IS THE LAST ONE.
NOST ALGIA'S DIARY OF DAYS GONE BY.
IT SAYS "ALLOWS YOU TO TRAVEL TO PLACES WITHIN YOUR MEMORIES."
ALL RIGHT, I'M OFF.
BA (FWOO)

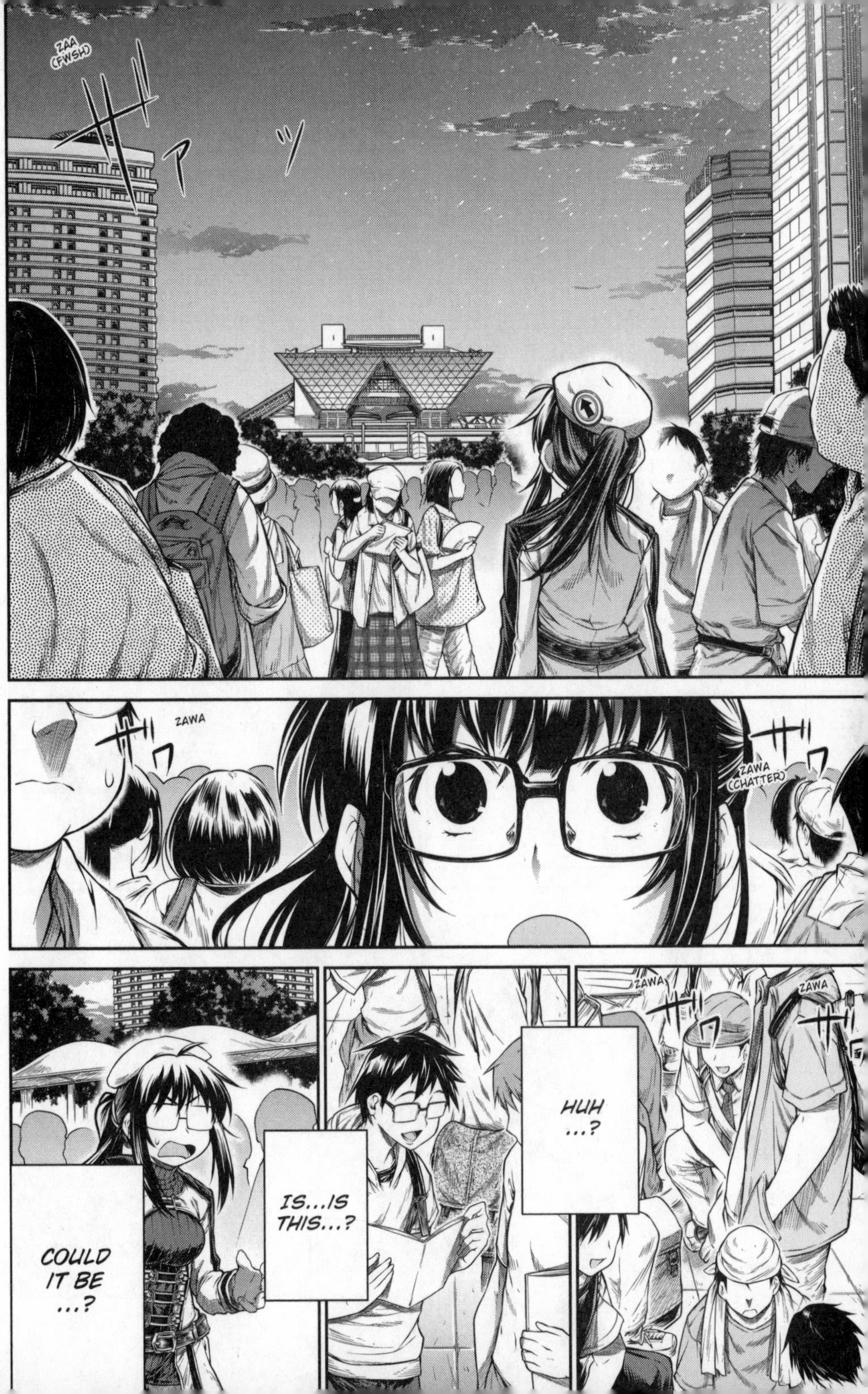
ZAA (FWSH)
ZAWA (CHATTER)
ZAWA
ZAWA
ZAWA
HUH ...?
IS...IS THIS...?
COULD IT BE ...?

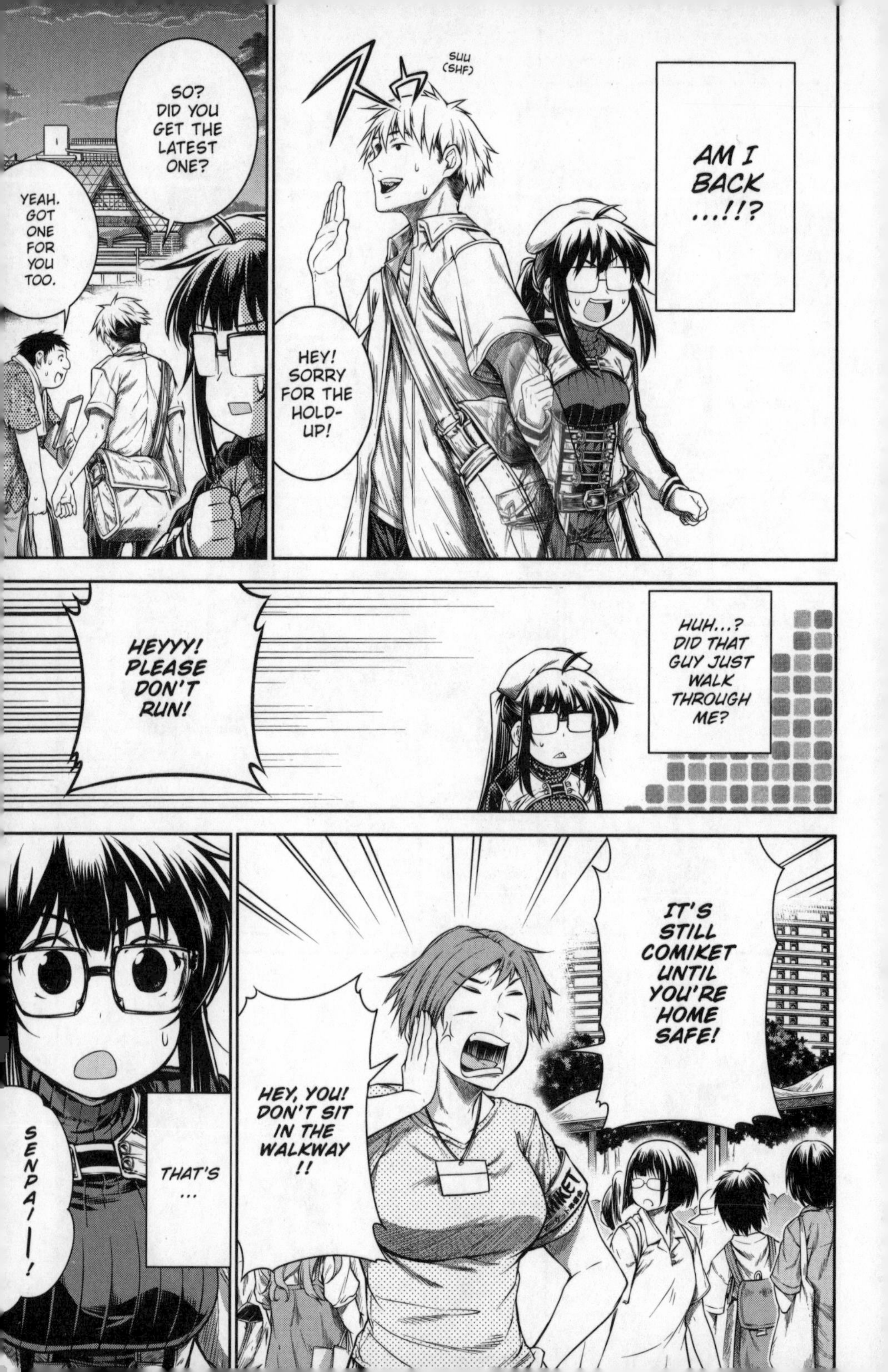
AM I BACK ...!!?
SUU (SHF)
HEY! SORRY FOR THE HOLD-UP!
SO? DID YOU GET THE LATEST ONE?
YEAH. GOT ONE FOR YOU TOO.
HUH...? DID THAT GUY JUST WALK THROUGH ME?
HEYYY! PLEASE DON'T RUN!
IT'S STILL COMIKET UNTIL YOU'RE HOME SAFE!
HEY, YOU! DON'T SIT IN THE WALKWAY!!
THAT'S ...
SENPAI!!

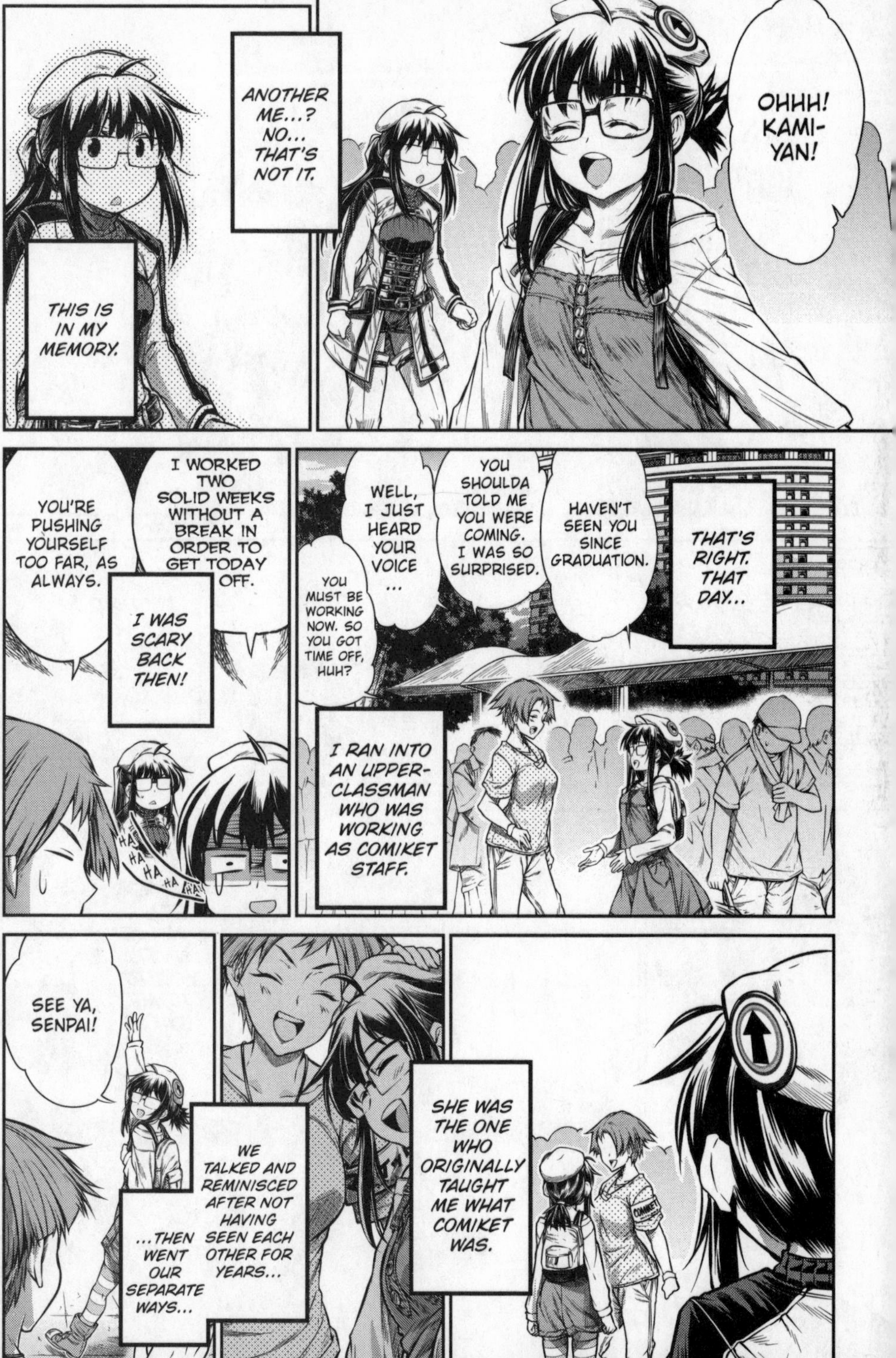
OHHH! KAMI-YAN!
ANOTHER ME...? NO... THAT'S NOT IT.
THIS IS IN MY MEMORY.
THAT'S RIGHT. THAT DAY...
HAVEN'T SEEN YOU SINCE GRADUATION.
YOU SHOULDA TOLD ME YOU WERE COMING. I WAS SO SURPRISED.
WELL, I JUST HEARD YOUR VOICE ...
YOU MUST BE WORKING NOW. SO YOU GOT TIME OFF, HUH?
I RAN INTO AN UPPER-CLASSMAN WHO WAS WORKING AS COMIKET STAFF.
I WORKED TWO SOLID WEEKS WITHOUT A BREAK IN ORDER TO GET TODAY OFF.
YOU'RE PUSHING YOURSELF TOO FAR, AS ALWAYS.
I WAS SCARY BACK THEN!
HA HA HA HA HA!
SHE WAS THE ONE WHO ORIGINALLY TAUGHT ME WHAT COMIKET WAS.
COMIKET
WE TALKED AND REMINISCED AFTER NOT HAVING SEEN EACH OTHER FOR YEARS...
SEE YA, SENPAI!
...THEN WENT OUR SEPARATE WAYS...

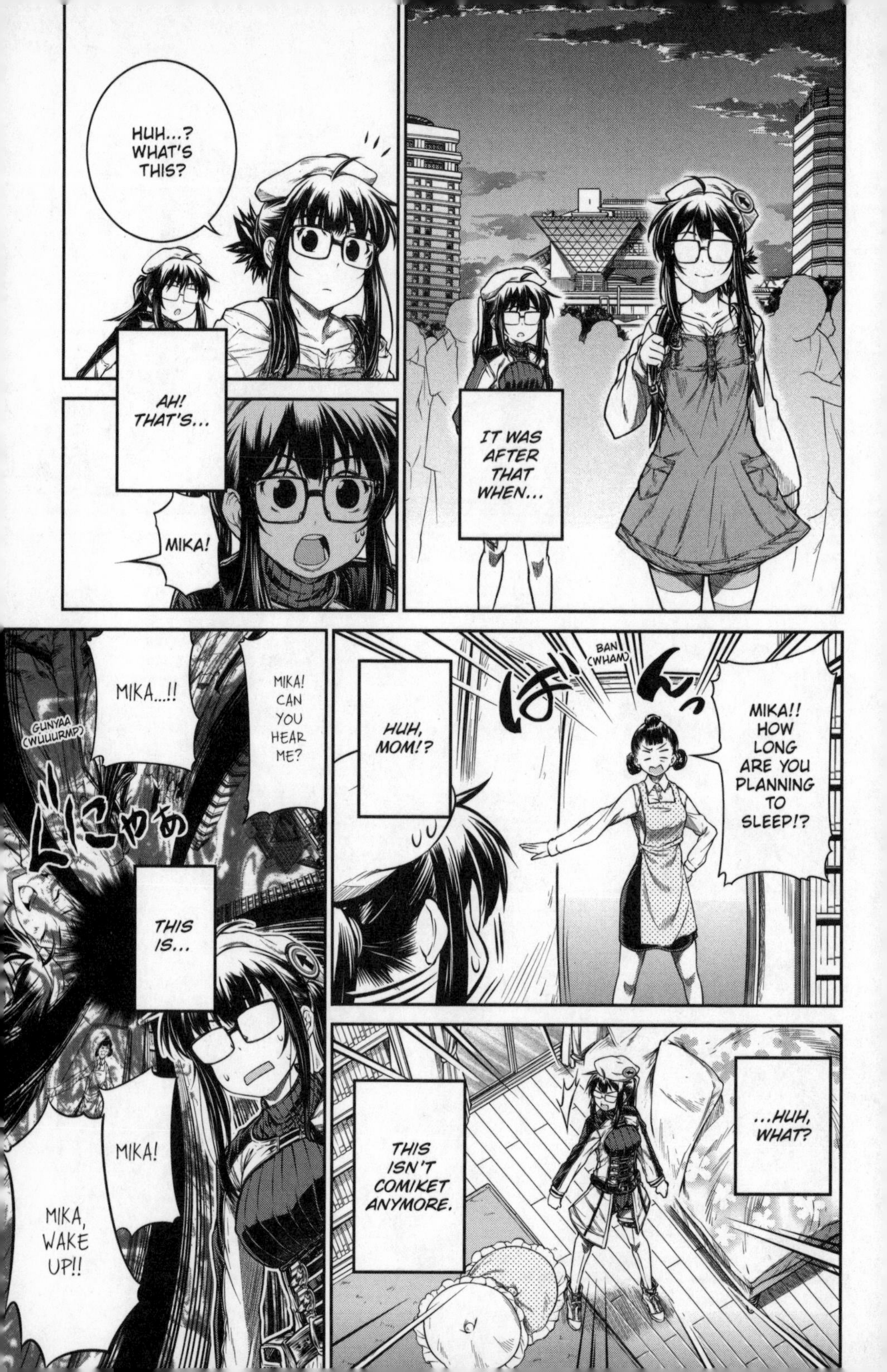
IT WAS AFTER THAT WHEN...
HUH...? WHAT'S THIS?
AH! THAT'S...
MIKA!
BAN (WHAM)
ばんっ
MIKA!! HOW LONG ARE YOU PLANNING TO SLEEP!?
HUH, MOM!?
...HUH, WHAT?
THIS ISN'T COMIKET ANYMORE.
MIKA! CAN YOU HEAR ME?
MIKA...!!
GUNYAA (WUUURMP)
THIS IS...
MIKA!
MIKA, WAKE UP!!

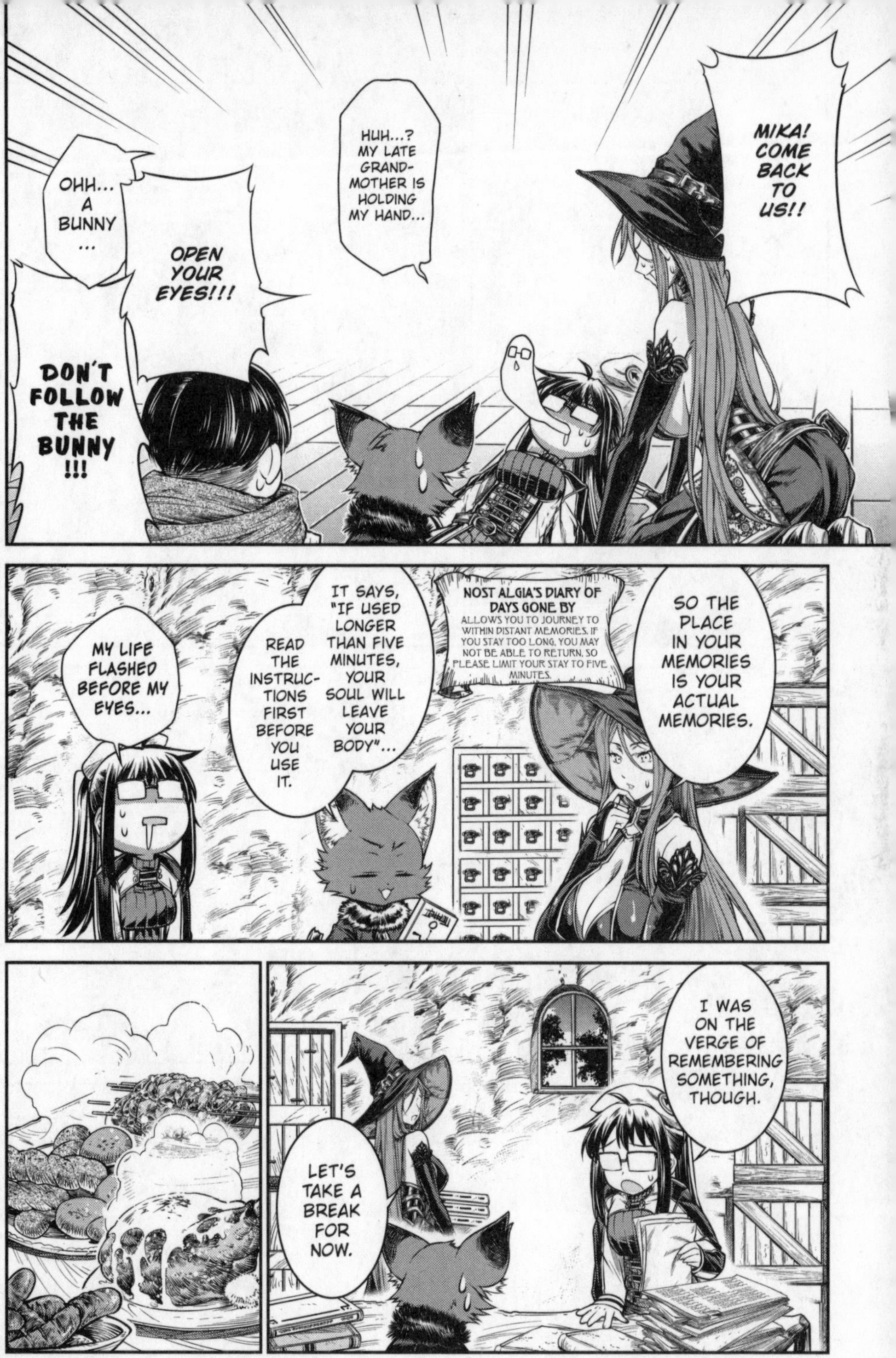
MIKA! COME BACK TO US!!
HUH...? MY LATE GRAND-MOTHER IS HOLDING MY HAND...
OPEN YOUR EYES!!!
OHH... A BUNNY...
DON'T FOLLOW THE BUNNY!!!
SO THE PLACE IN YOUR MEMORIES IS YOUR ACTUAL MEMORIES.
NOST ALGIA'S DIARY OF DAYS GONE BY
ALLOWS YOU TO JOURNEY TO WITHIN DISTANT MEMORIES. IF YOU STAY TOO LONG, YOU MAY NOT BE ABLE TO RETURN, SO PLEASE LIMIT YOUR STAY TO FIVE MINUTES.
IT SAYS, "IF USED LONGER THAN FIVE MINUTES, YOUR SOUL WILL LEAVE YOUR BODY"...
READ THE INSTRUC-TIONS FIRST BEFORE YOU USE IT.
MY LIFE FLASHED BEFORE MY EYES...
I WAS ON THE VERGE OF REMEMBERING SOMETHING, THOUGH.
LET'S TAKE A BREAK FOR NOW.

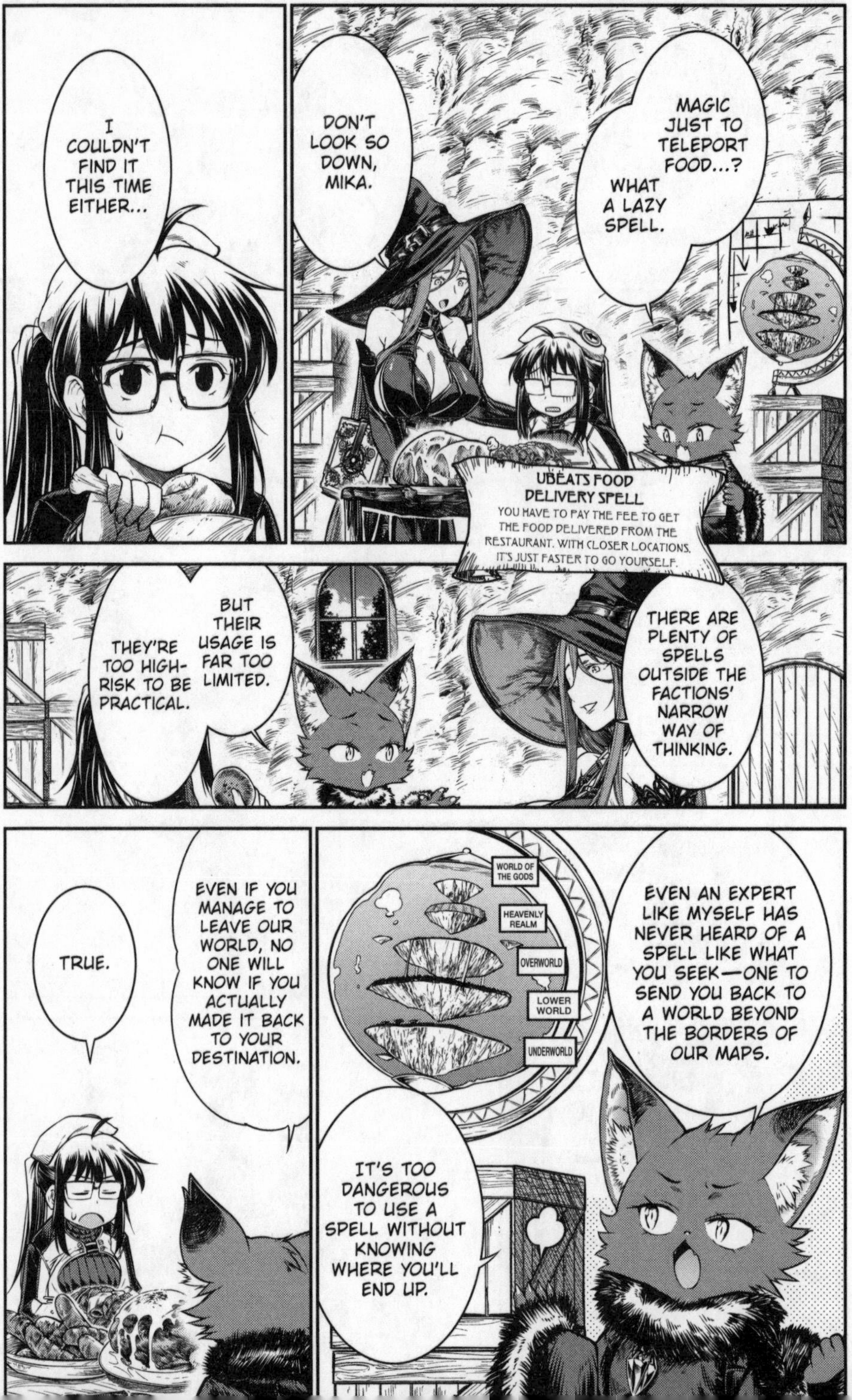
MAGIC JUST TO TELEPORT FOOD...?
WHAT A LAZY SPELL.
DON'T LOOK SO DOWN, MIKA.
UBEATS FOOD DELIVERY SPELL
YOU HAVE TO PAY THE FEE TO GET THE FOOD DELIVERED FROM THE RESTAURANT. WITH CLOSER LOCATIONS, IT'S JUST FASTER TO GO YOURSELF.
I COULDN'T FIND IT THIS TIME EITHER...
THERE ARE PLENTY OF SPELLS OUTSIDE THE FACTIONS' NARROW WAY OF THINKING.
BUT THEIR USAGE IS FAR TOO LIMITED.
THEY'RE TOO HIGH-RISK TO BE PRACTICAL.
EVEN AN EXPERT LIKE MYSELF HAS NEVER HEARD OF A SPELL LIKE WHAT YOU SEEK—ONE TO SEND YOU BACK TO A WORLD BEYOND THE BORDERS OF OUR MAPS.
WORLD OF THE GODS
HEAVENLY REALM
OVERWORLD
LOWER WORLD
UNDERWORLD
IT'S TOO DANGEROUS TO USE A SPELL WITHOUT KNOWING WHERE YOU'LL END UP.
EVEN IF YOU MANAGE TO LEAVE OUR WORLD, NO ONE WILL KNOW IF YOU ACTUALLY MADE IT BACK TO YOUR DESTINATION.
TRUE.

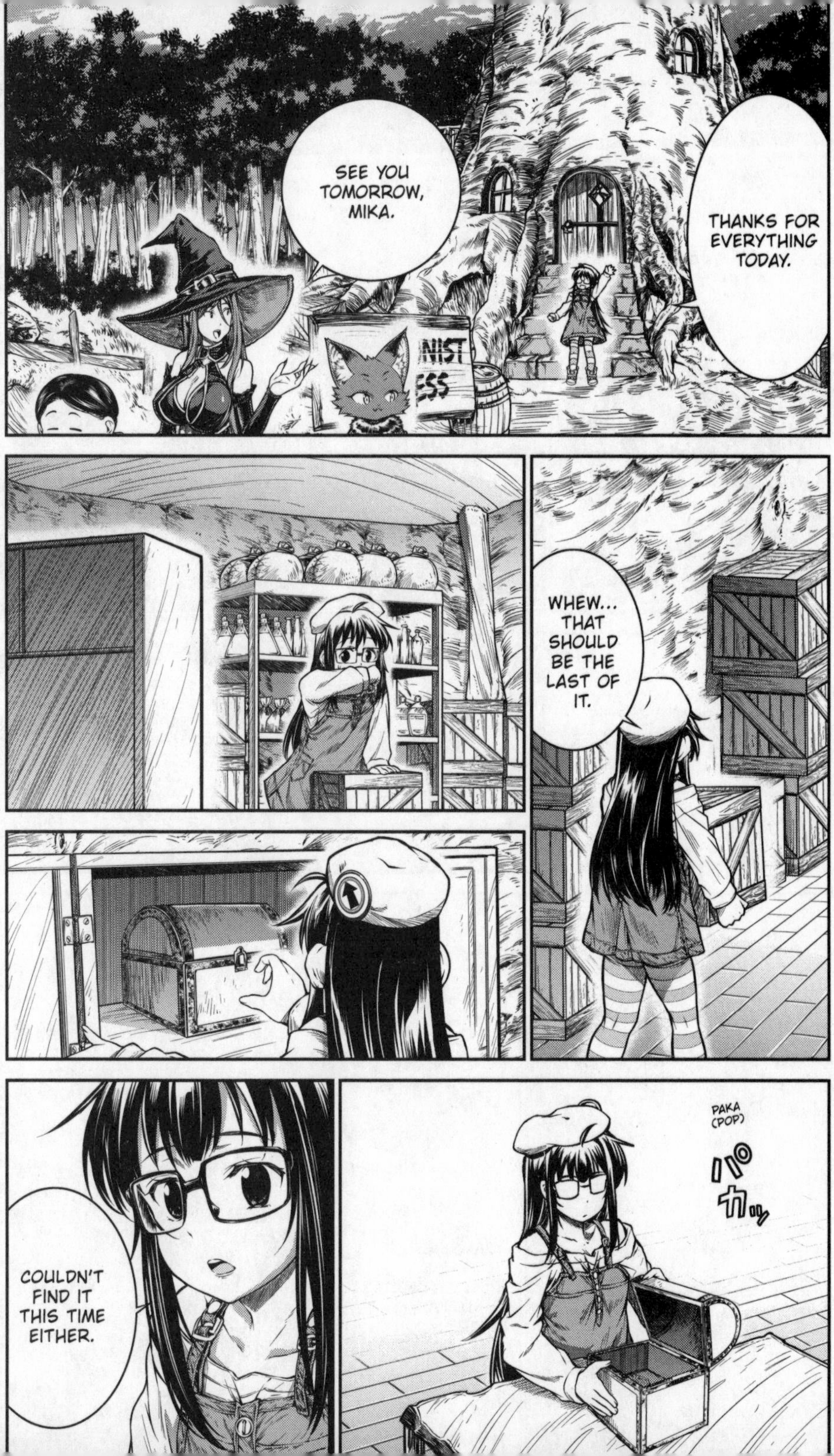
THANKS FOR EVERYTHING TODAY.
SEE YOU TOMORROW, MIKA.
WHEW... THAT SHOULD BE THE LAST OF IT.
PAKA (POP)
パカッ
COULDN'T FIND IT THIS TIME EITHER.

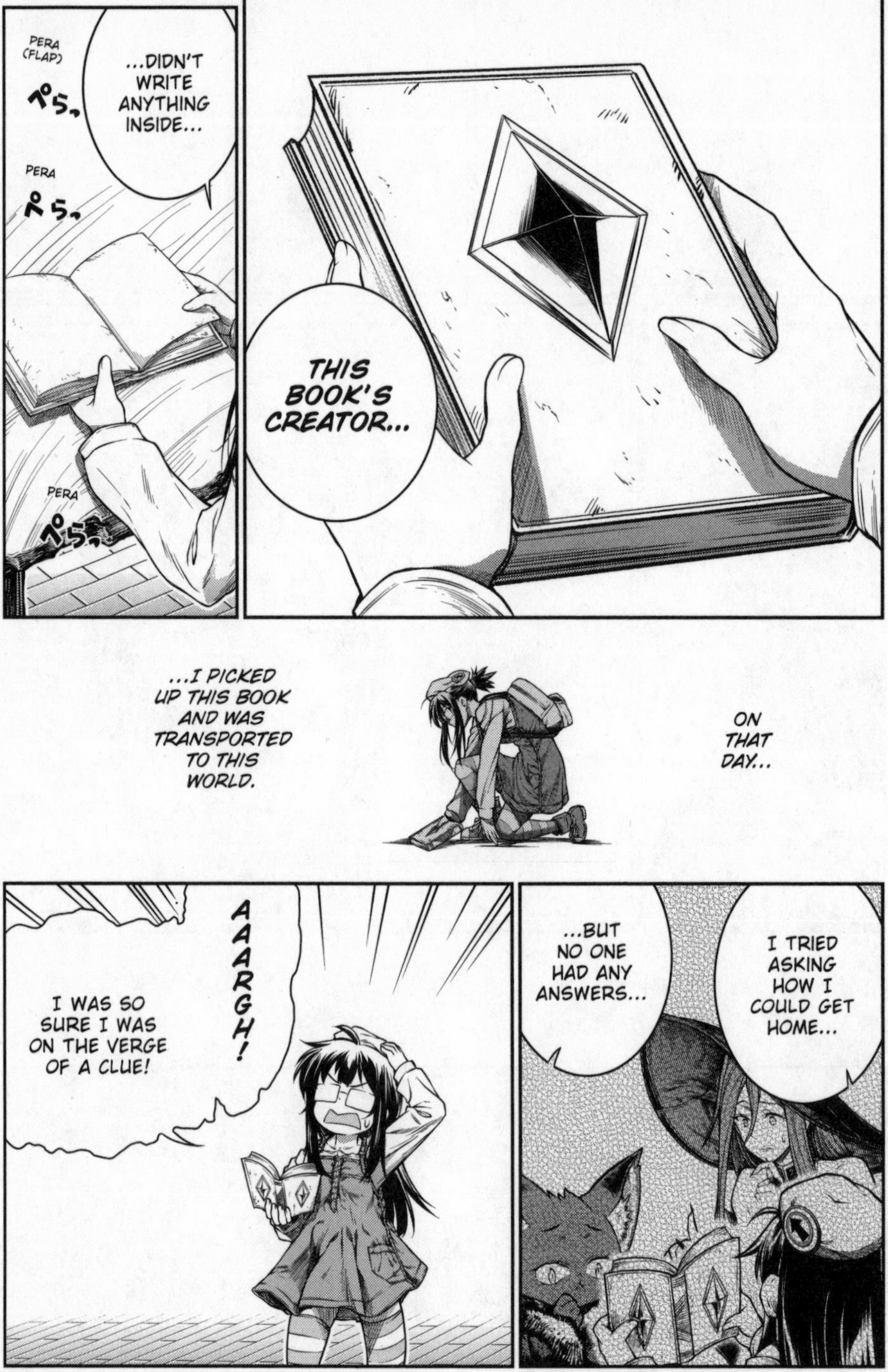
THIS BOOK'S CREATOR...
...DIDN'T WRITE ANYTHING INSIDE...
PERA (FLAP)
ぺらっ
PERA
ぺらっ
PERA
ぺらっ
ON THAT DAY...
...I PICKED UP THIS BOOK AND WAS TRANSPORTED TO THIS WORLD.
I TRIED ASKING HOW I COULD GET HOME...
...BUT NO ONE HAD ANY ANSWERS...
AAAARGH!
I WAS SO SURE I WAS ON THE VERGE OF A CLUE!

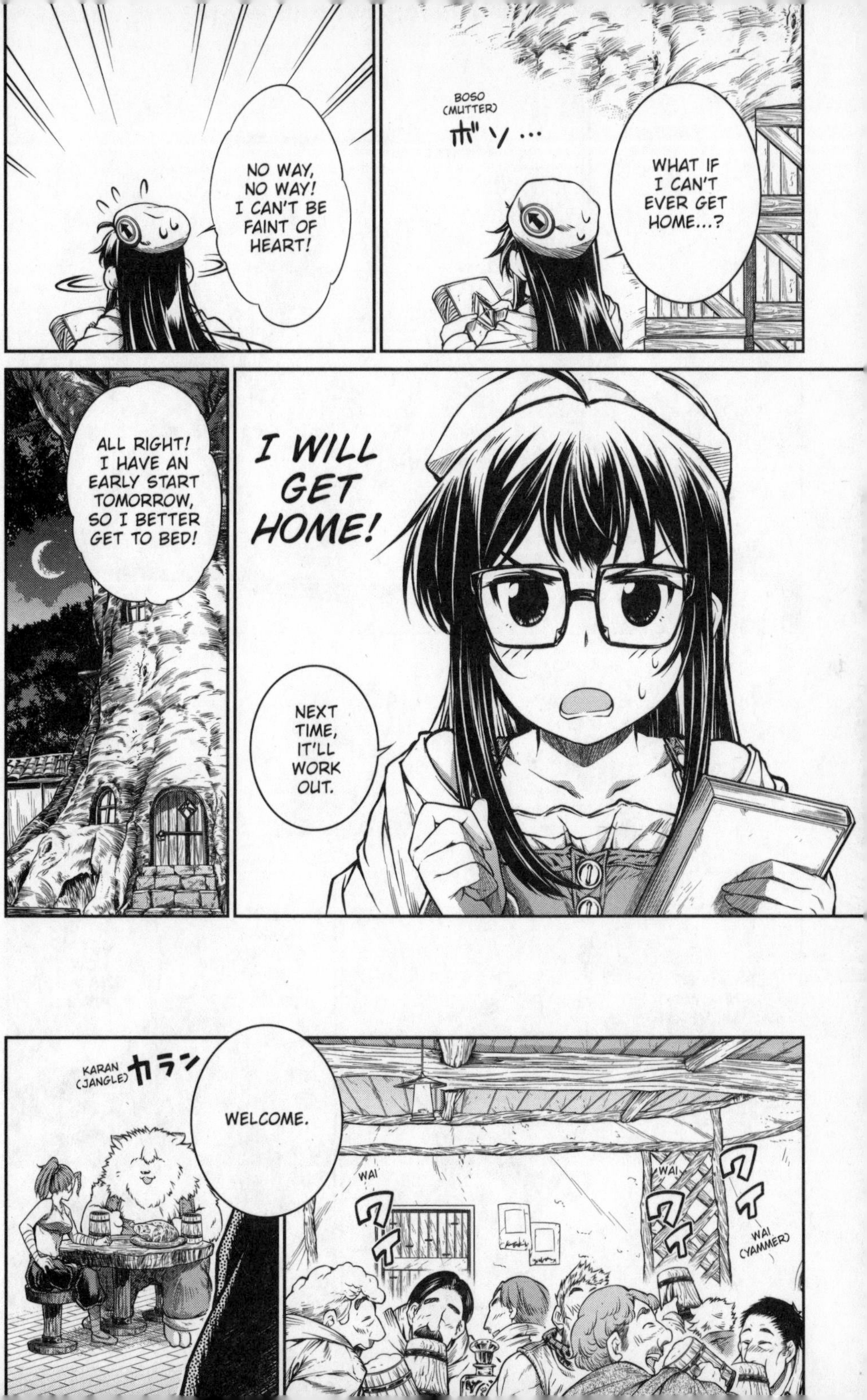
BOSO (MUTTER)
ボソ…
WHAT IF I CAN'T EVER GET HOME...?
NO WAY, NO WAY! I CAN'T BE FAINT OF HEART!
I WILL GET HOME!
NEXT TIME, IT'LL WORK OUT.
ALL RIGHT! I HAVE AN EARLY START TOMORROW, SO I BETTER GET TO BED!
WAI
ワイ
WAI (YAMMER)
ワイ
WAI
ワイ
WELCOME.
KARAN (JANGLE)
カラン

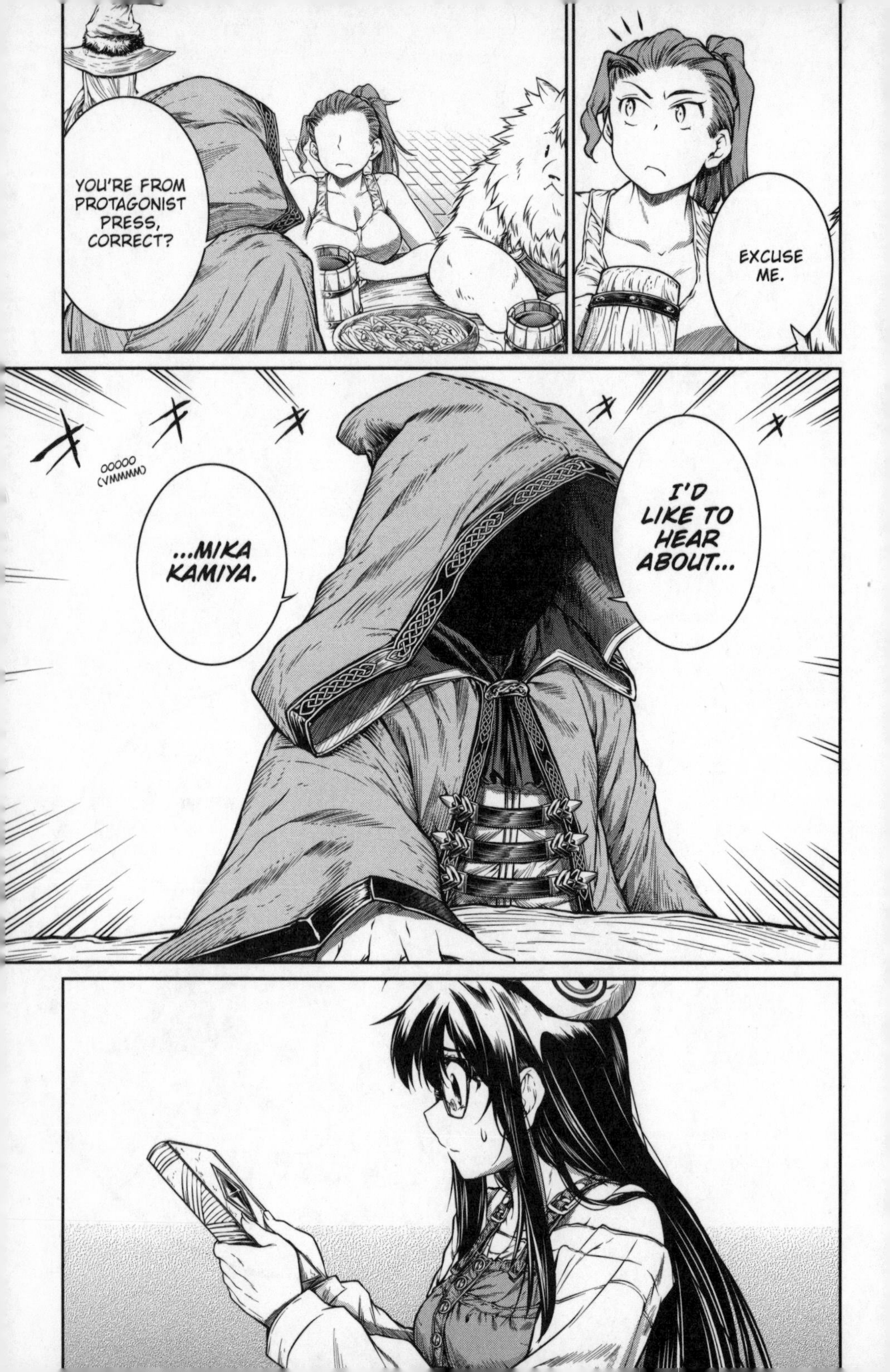
EXCUSE ME.
YOU'RE FROM PROTAGONIST PRESS, CORRECT?
I'D LIKE TO HEAR ABOUT...
OOOOO (VMMMM)
...MIKA KAMIYA.

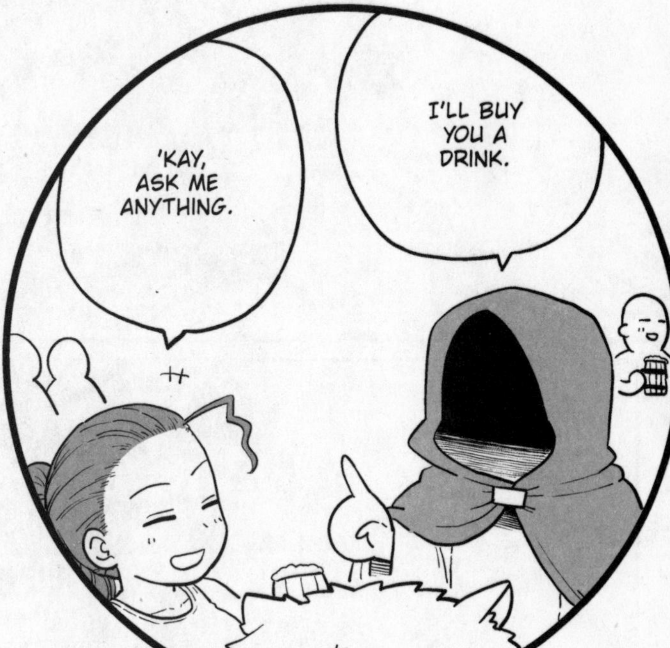
I'LL BUY YOU A DRINK.
'KAY, ASK ME ANYTHING.

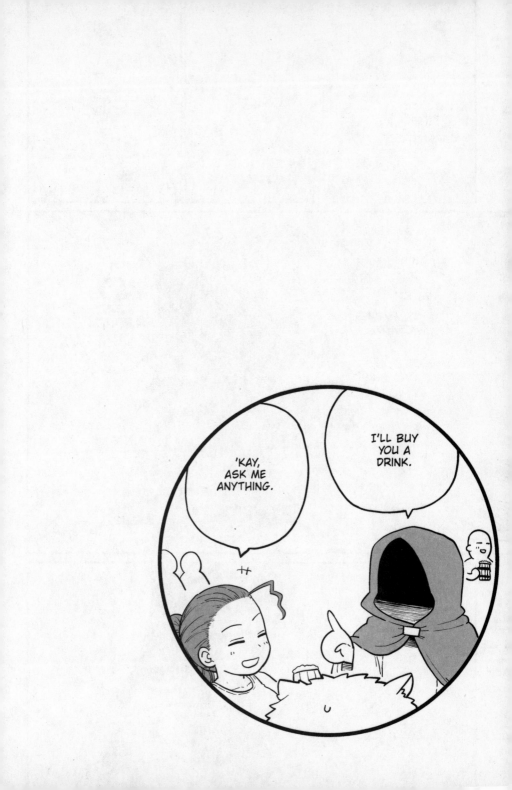

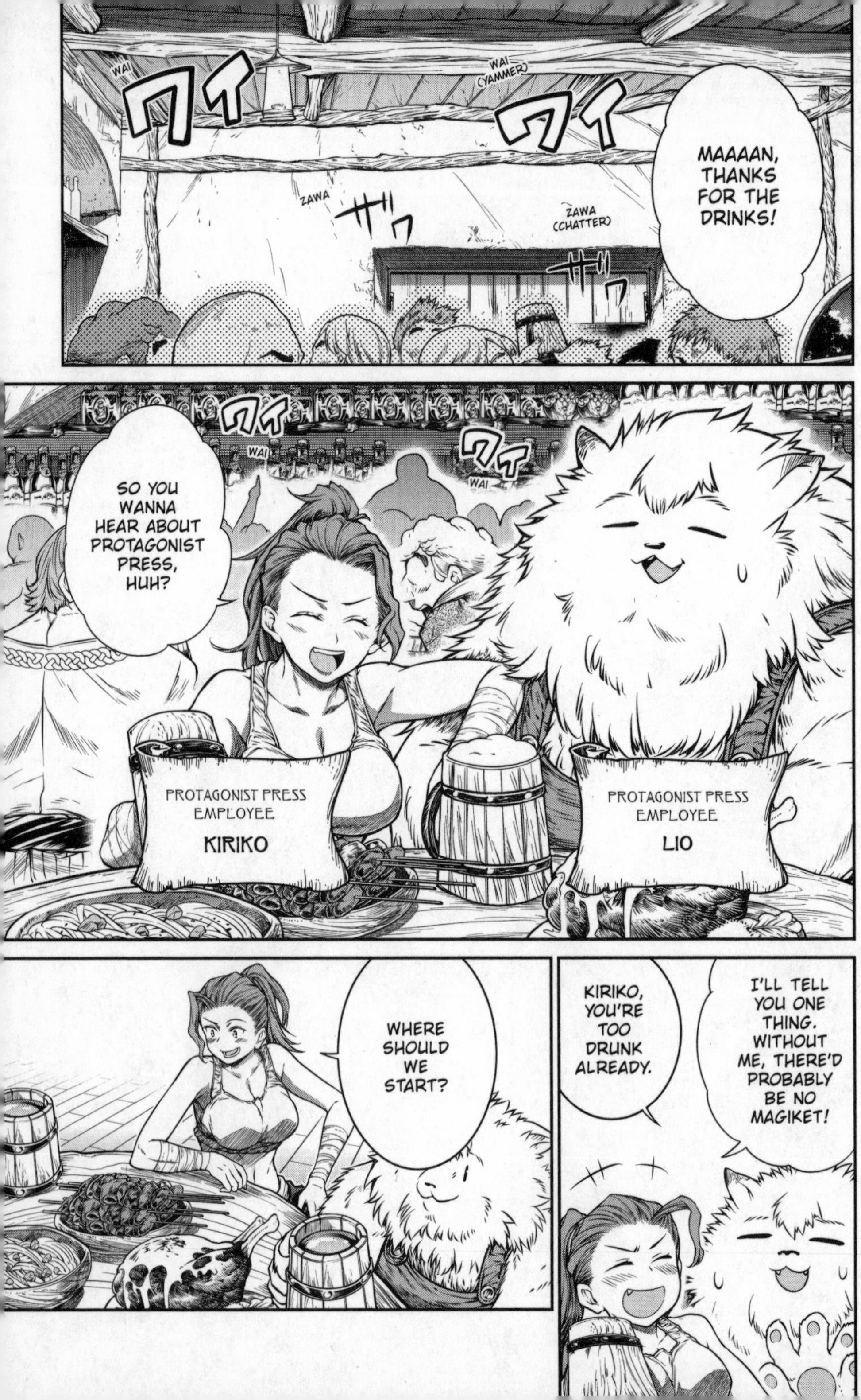

WAI (YAMMER)
MAAAAN, THANKS FOR THE DRINKS!
WAI
ZAWA (CHATTER)
ZAWA
WAI
WAI
SO YOU WANNA HEAR ABOUT PROTAGONIST PRESS, HUH?
PROTAGONIST PRESS EMPLOYEE LIO
PROTAGONIST PRESS EMPLOYEE KIRIKO
I'LL TELL YOU ONE THING. WITHOUT ME, THERE'D PROBABLY BE NO MAGIKET!
KIRIKO, YOU'RE TOO DRUNK ALREADY.
WHERE SHOULD WE START?

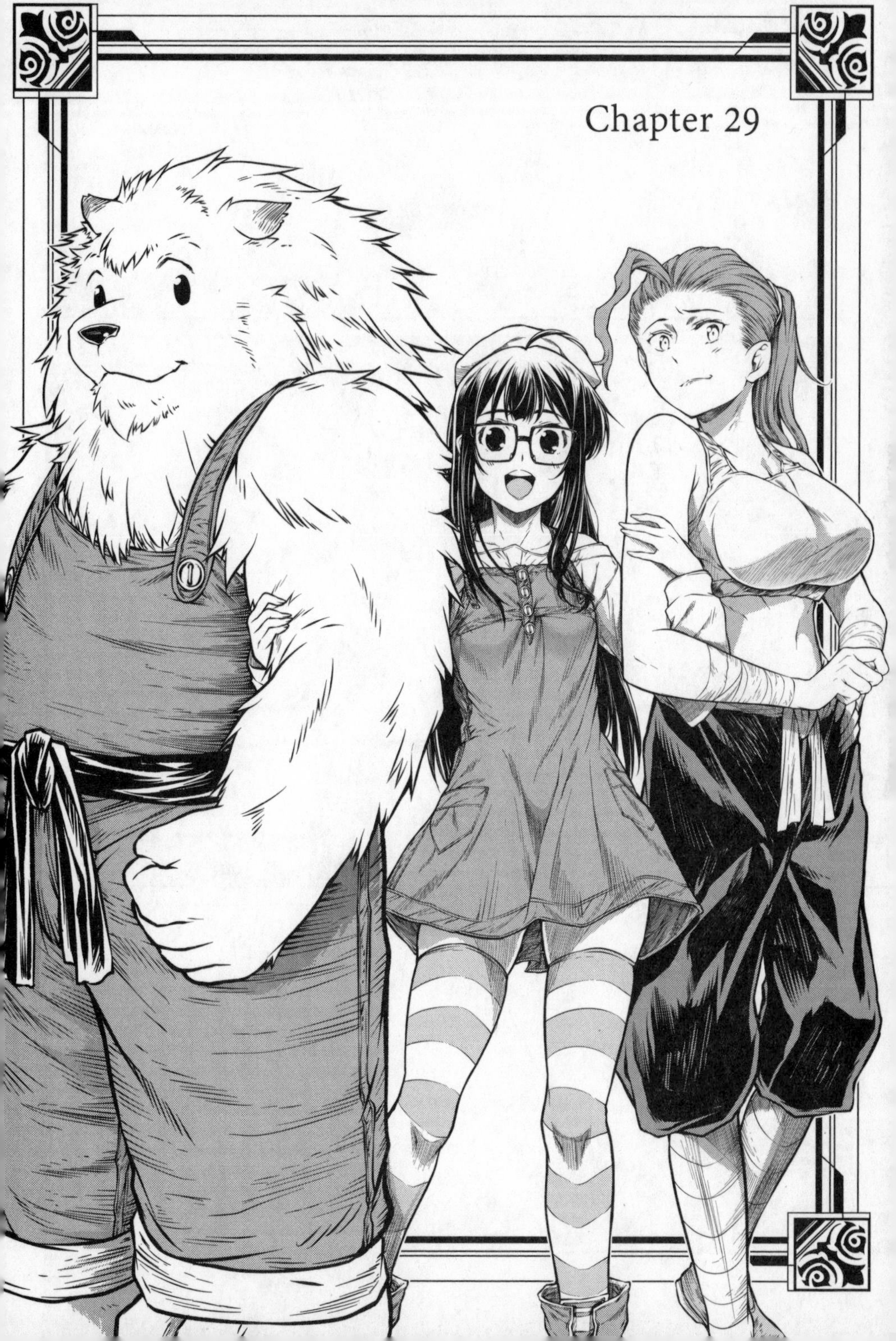
Chapter 29

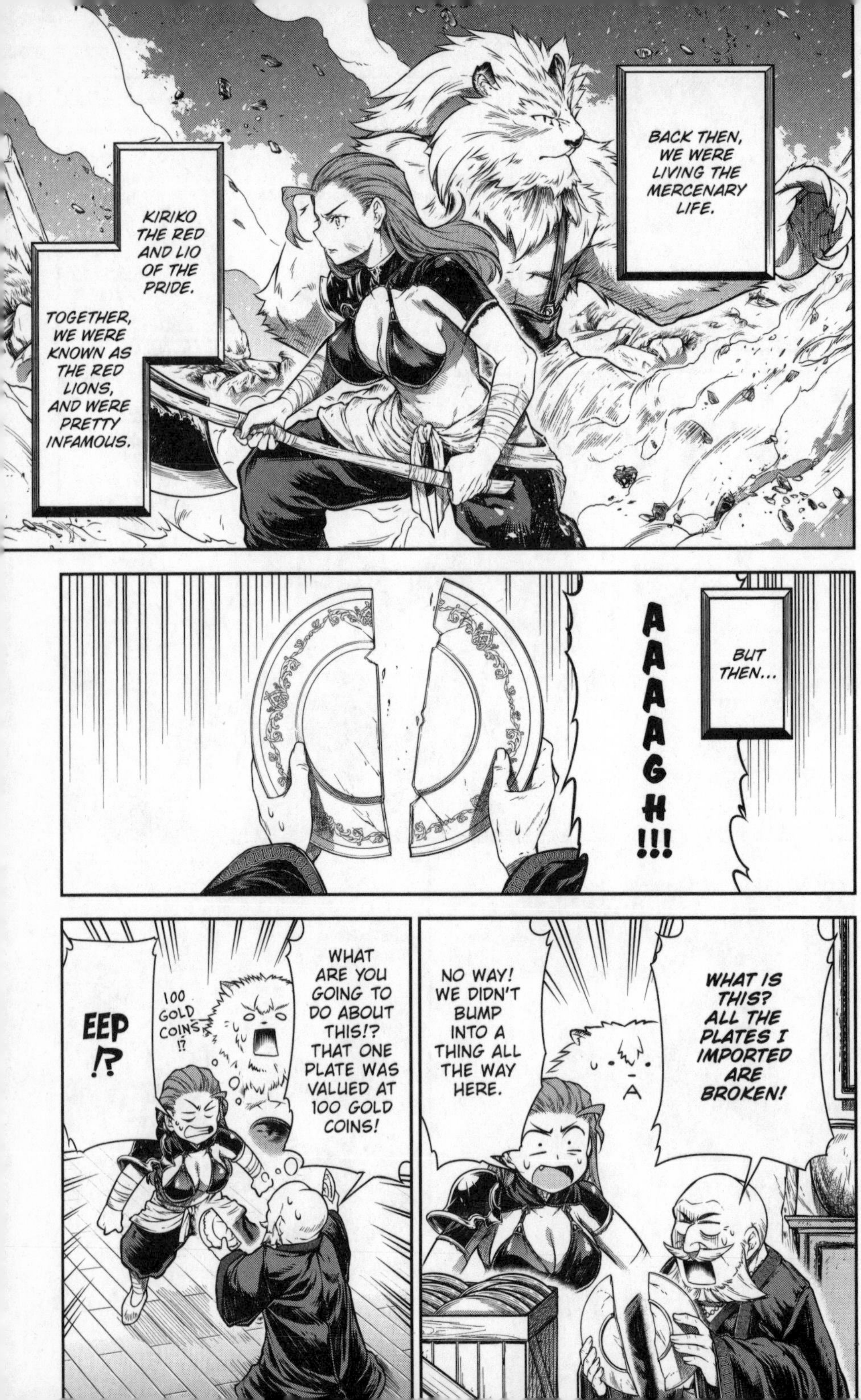
BACK THEN, WE WERE LIVING THE MERCENARY LIFE.
KIRIKO THE RED AND LIO OF THE PRIDE.
TOGETHER, WE WERE KNOWN AS THE RED LIONS, AND WERE PRETTY INFAMOUS.
BUT THEN...
AAAAGH!!!
WHAT IS THIS? ALL THE PLATES I IMPORTED ARE BROKEN!
NO WAY! WE DIDN'T BUMP INTO A THING ALL THE WAY HERE.
WHAT ARE YOU GOING TO DO ABOUT THIS!? THAT ONE PLATE WAS VALUED AT 100 GOLD COINS!
100 GOLD COINS!?
EEP!?

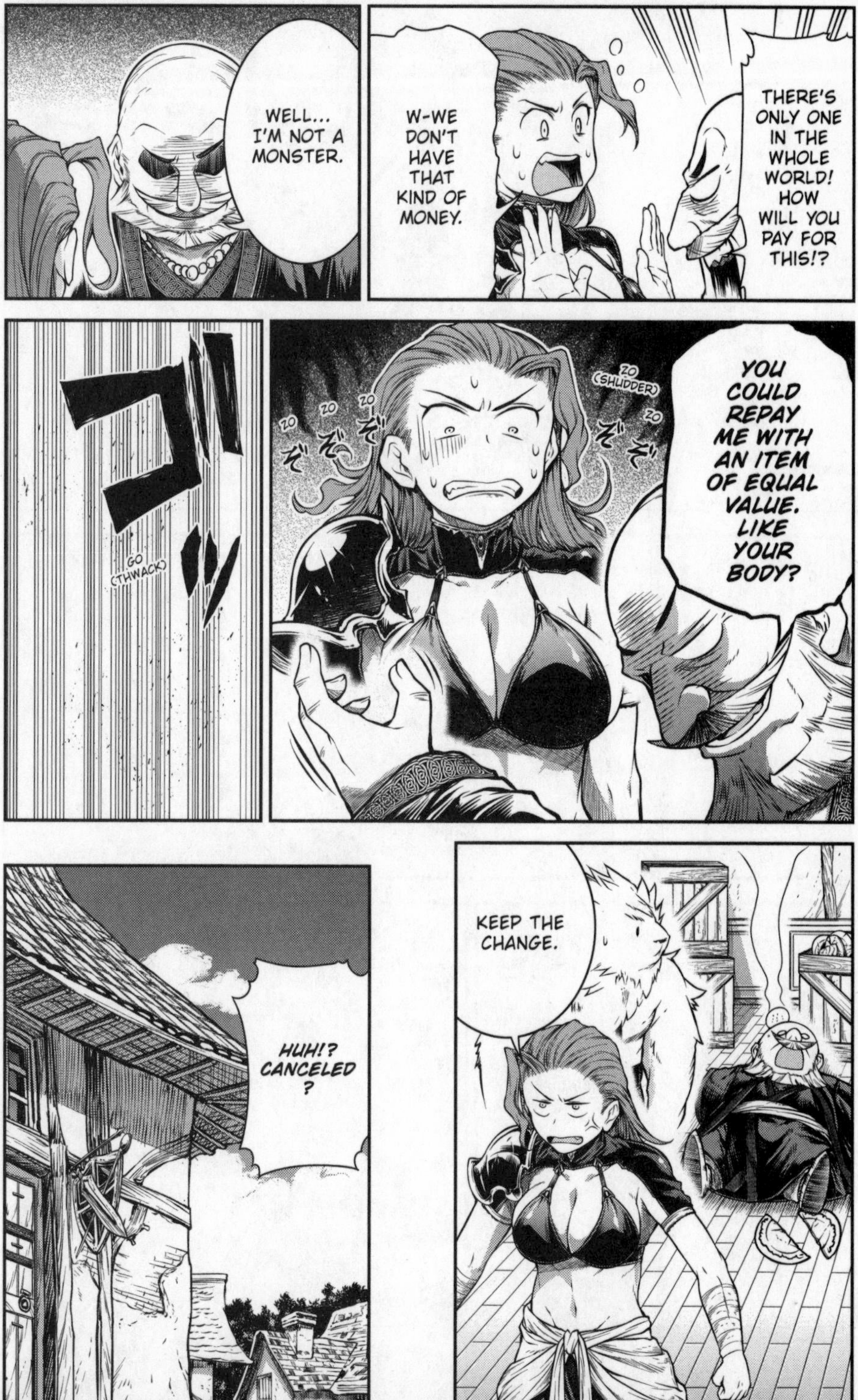
THERE'S ONLY ONE IN THE WHOLE WORLD! HOW WILL YOU PAY FOR THIS!?
W-WE DON'T HAVE THAT KIND OF MONEY.
WELL... I'M NOT A MONSTER.
YOU COULD REPAY ME WITH AN ITEM OF EQUAL VALUE. LIKE YOUR BODY?
ZO (SHUDDER)
ZO ZO ZO
ゴッ
GO (THWACK)
KEEP THE CHANGE.
HUH!? CANCELED?

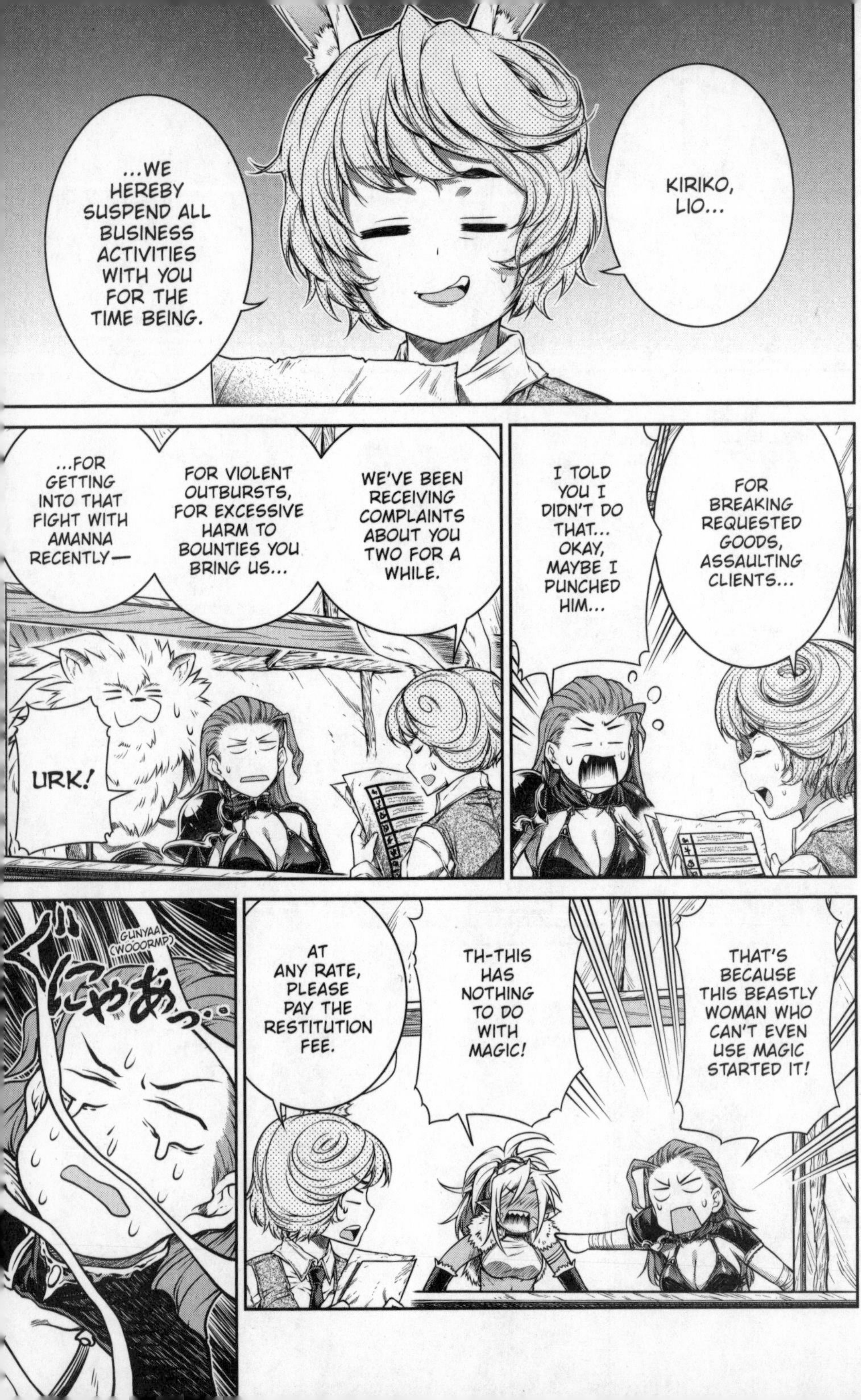
KIRIKO, LIO...
...WE HEREBY SUSPEND ALL BUSINESS ACTIVITIES WITH YOU FOR THE TIME BEING.
FOR BREAKING REQUESTED GOODS, ASSAULTING CLIENTS...
I TOLD YOU I DIDN'T DO THAT... OKAY, MAYBE I PUNCHED HIM...
WE'VE BEEN RECEIVING COMPLAINTS ABOUT YOU TWO FOR A WHILE.
FOR VIOLENT OUTBURSTS, FOR EXCESSIVE HARM TO BOUNTIES YOU BRING US...
...FOR GETTING INTO THAT FIGHT WITH AMANNA RECENTLY—
URK!
THAT'S BECAUSE THIS BEASTLY WOMAN WHO CAN'T EVEN USE MAGIC STARTED IT!
TH-THIS HAS NOTHING TO DO WITH MAGIC!
AT ANY RATE, PLEASE PAY THE RESTITUTION FEE.
ぐにゃあっ
GUNYAA (WOOORMP)

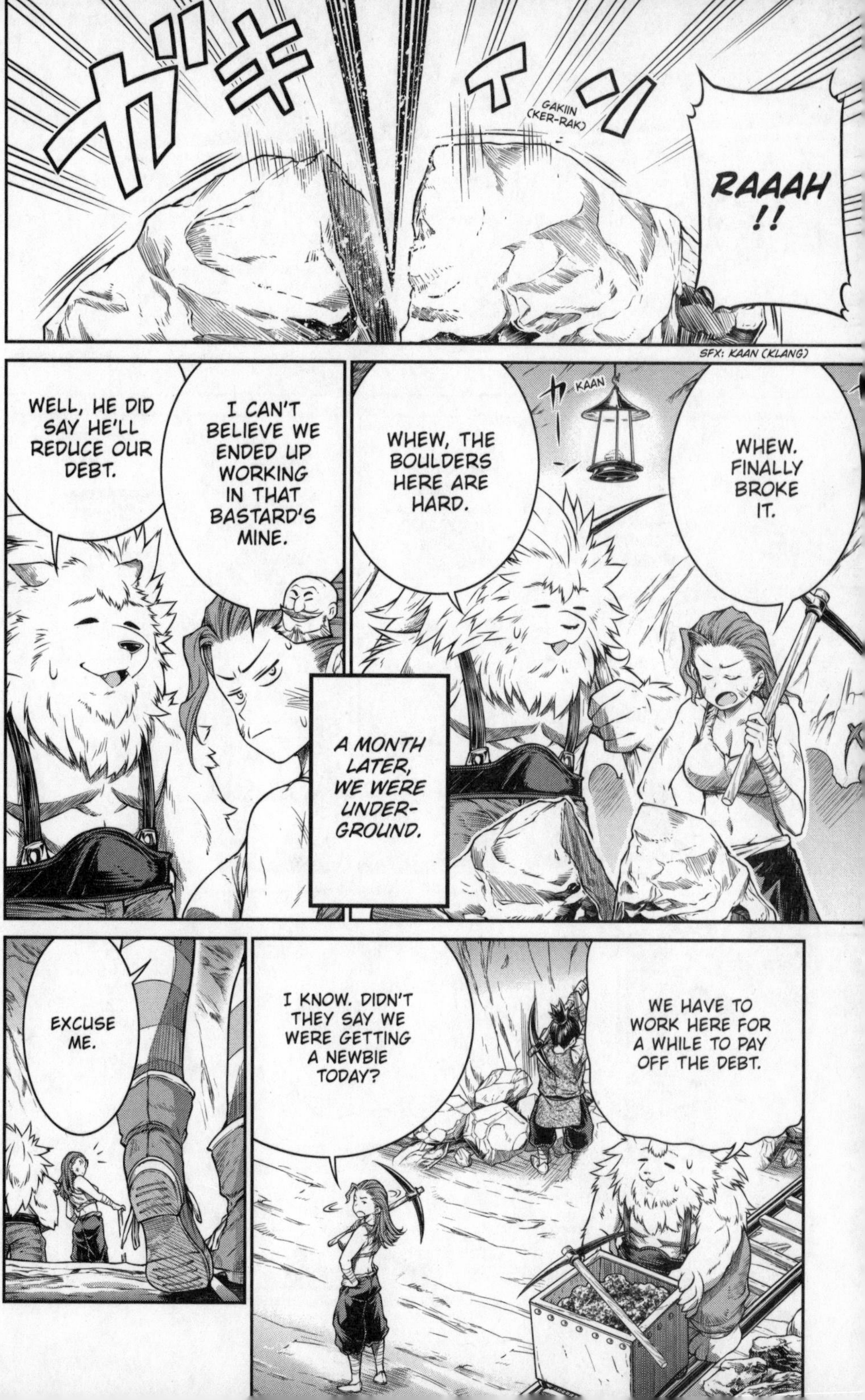
RAAAH!!
ガギィーン
GAKIIN (KER-RAK)
SFX: KAAN (KLANG)
WHEW. FINALLY BROKE IT.
KAAN
WHEW, THE BOULDERS HERE ARE HARD.
A MONTH LATER, WE WERE UNDERGROUND.
I CAN'T BELIEVE WE ENDED UP WORKING IN THAT BASTARD'S MINE.
WELL, HE DID SAY HE'LL REDUCE OUR DEBT.
WE HAVE TO WORK HERE FOR A WHILE TO PAY OFF THE DEBT.
I KNOW. DIDN'T THEY SAY WE WERE GETTING A NEWBIE TODAY?
EXCUSE ME.

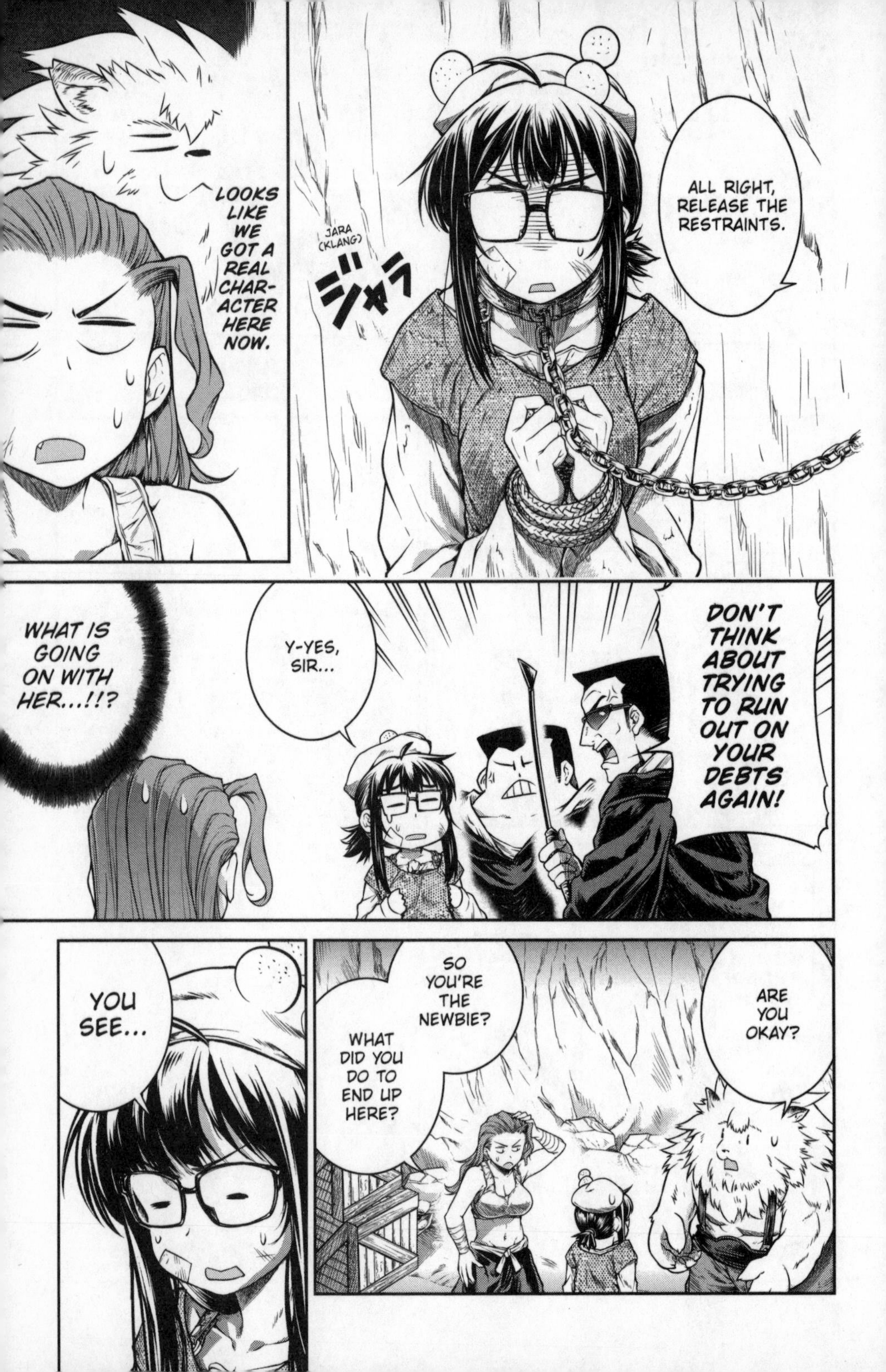
ALL RIGHT, RELEASE THE RESTRAINTS.
JARA (KLANG)
ジャラ
LOOKS LIKE WE GOT A REAL CHAR-ACTER HERE NOW.
DON'T THINK ABOUT TRYING TO RUN OUT ON YOUR DEBTS AGAIN!
Y-YES, SIR...
WHAT IS GOING ON WITH HER...!!?
ARE YOU OKAY?
SO YOU'RE THE NEWBIE?
WHAT DID YOU DO TO END UP HERE?
YOU SEE...

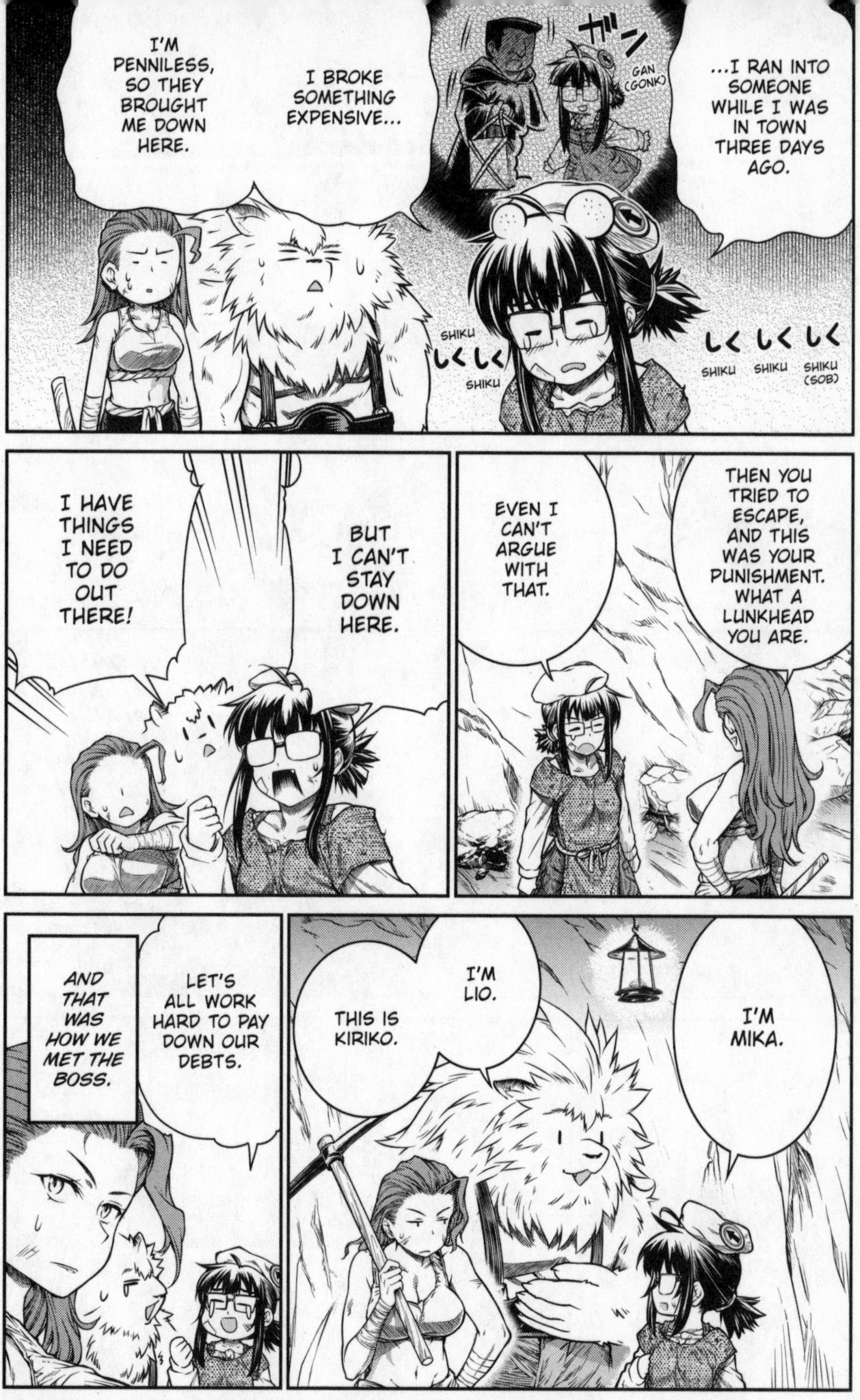
...I RAN INTO SOMEONE WHILE I WAS IN TOWN THREE DAYS AGO.
ガン
GAN (GONK)
I BROKE SOMETHING EXPENSIVE...
I'M PENNILESS, SO THEY BROUGHT ME DOWN HERE.
しくしくしく
SHIKU SHIKU SHIKU (SOB)
しくしく
SHIKU SHIKU
THEN YOU TRIED TO ESCAPE, AND THIS WAS YOUR PUNISHMENT. WHAT A LUNKHEAD YOU ARE.
EVEN I CAN'T ARGUE WITH THAT.
BUT I CAN'T STAY DOWN HERE.
I HAVE THINGS I NEED TO DO OUT THERE!
I'M MIKA.
I'M LIO.
THIS IS KIRIKO.
LET'S ALL WORK HARD TO PAY DOWN OUR DEBTS.
AND THAT WAS HOW WE MET THE BOSS.

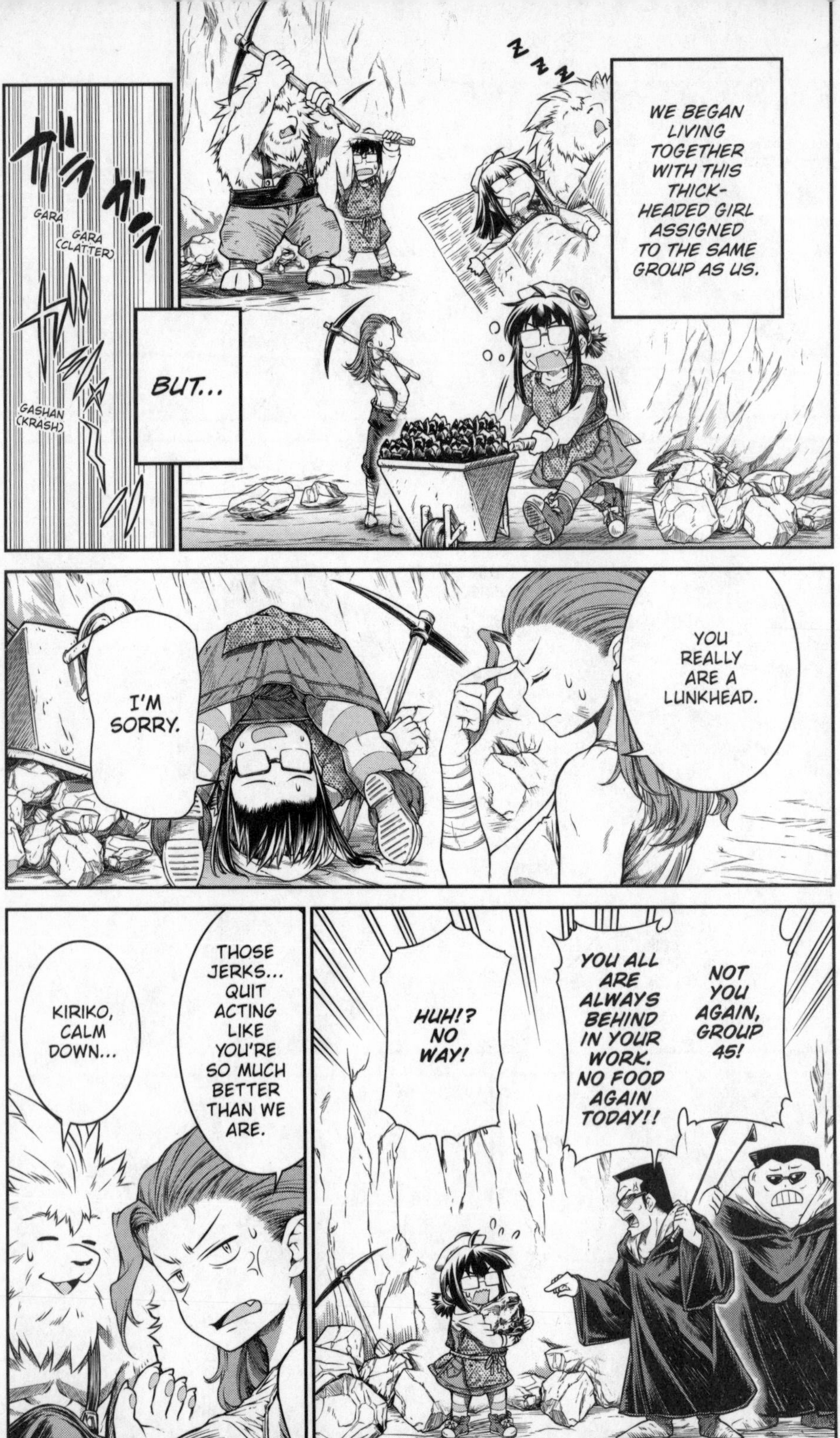
Z Z Z
WE BEGAN LIVING TOGETHER WITH THIS THICK-HEADED GIRL ASSIGNED TO THE SAME GROUP AS US.
BUT...
GARA GARA (CLATTER)
GASHAN (KRASH)
YOU REALLY ARE A LUNKHEAD.
I'M SORRY.
NOT YOU AGAIN, GROUP 45!
YOU ALL ARE ALWAYS BEHIND IN YOUR WORK. NO FOOD AGAIN TODAY!!
HUH!? NO WAY!
THOSE JERKS... QUIT ACTING LIKE YOU'RE SO MUCH BETTER THAN WE ARE.
KIRIKO, CALM DOWN...

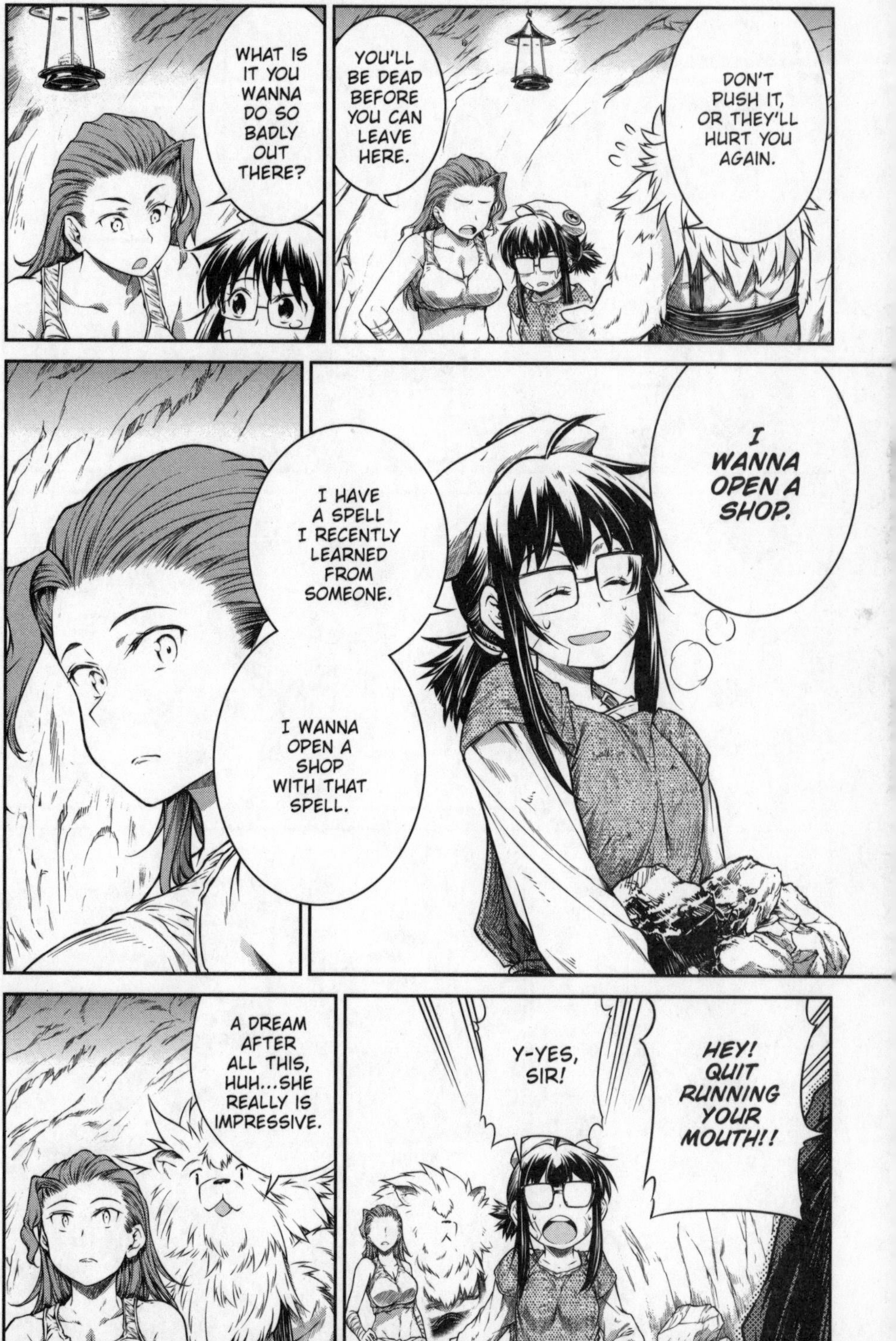
DON'T PUSH IT, OR THEY'LL HURT YOU AGAIN.
YOU'LL BE DEAD BEFORE YOU CAN LEAVE HERE.
WHAT IS IT YOU WANNA DO SO BADLY OUT THERE?
I WANNA OPEN A SHOP.
I HAVE A SPELL I RECENTLY LEARNED FROM SOMEONE.
I WANNA OPEN A SHOP WITH THAT SPELL.
HEY! QUIT RUNNING YOUR MOUTH!!
Y-YES, SIR!
A DREAM AFTER ALL THIS, HUH...SHE REALLY IS IMPRESSIVE.

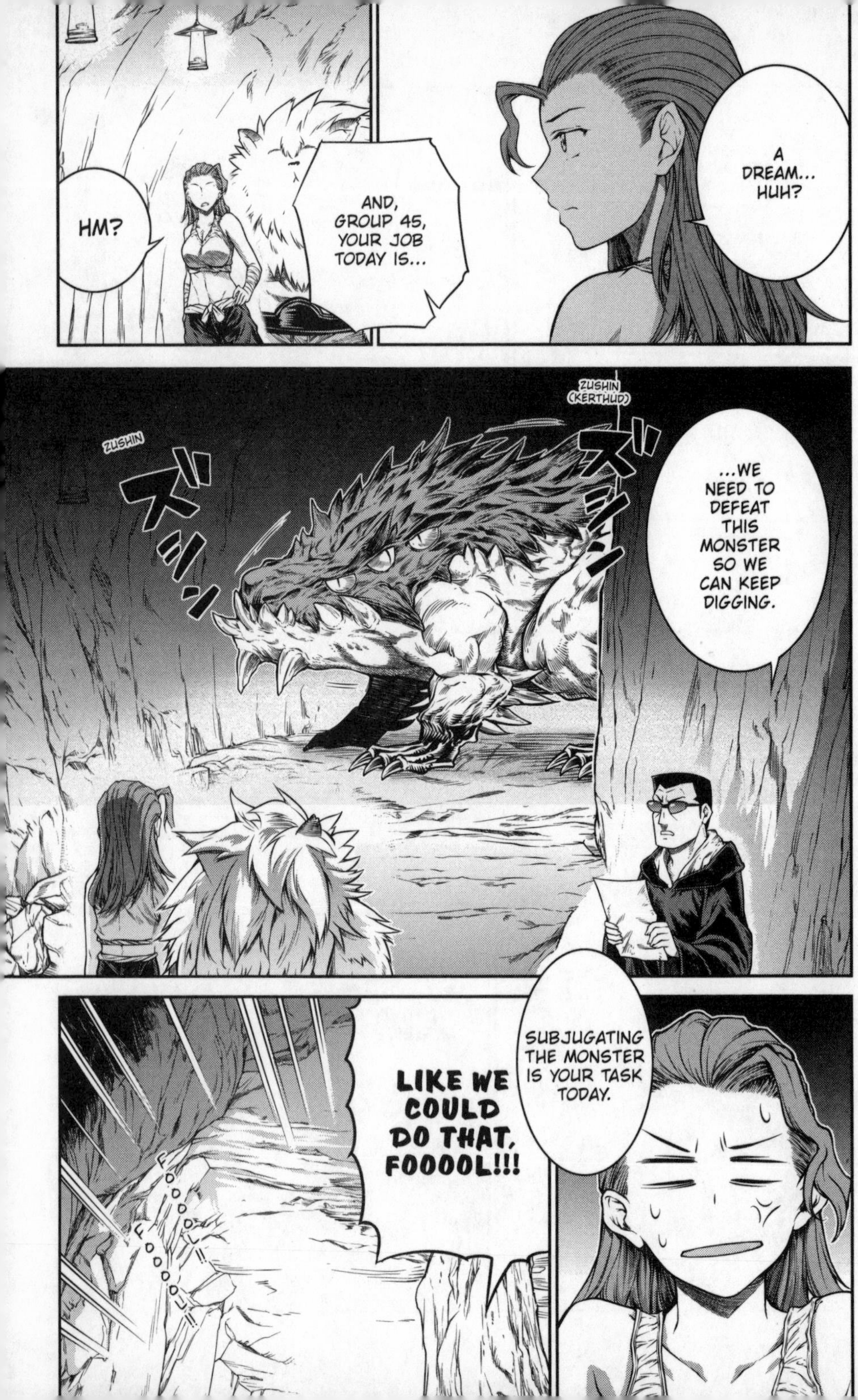
A DREAM... HUH?
AND, GROUP 45, YOUR JOB TODAY IS...
HM?
ZUSHIN (KERTHUD)
...WE NEED TO DEFEAT THIS MONSTER SO WE CAN KEEP DIGGING.
ZUSHIN
SUBJUGATING THE MONSTER IS YOUR TASK TODAY.
LIKE WE COULD DO THAT, FOOOOL!!!

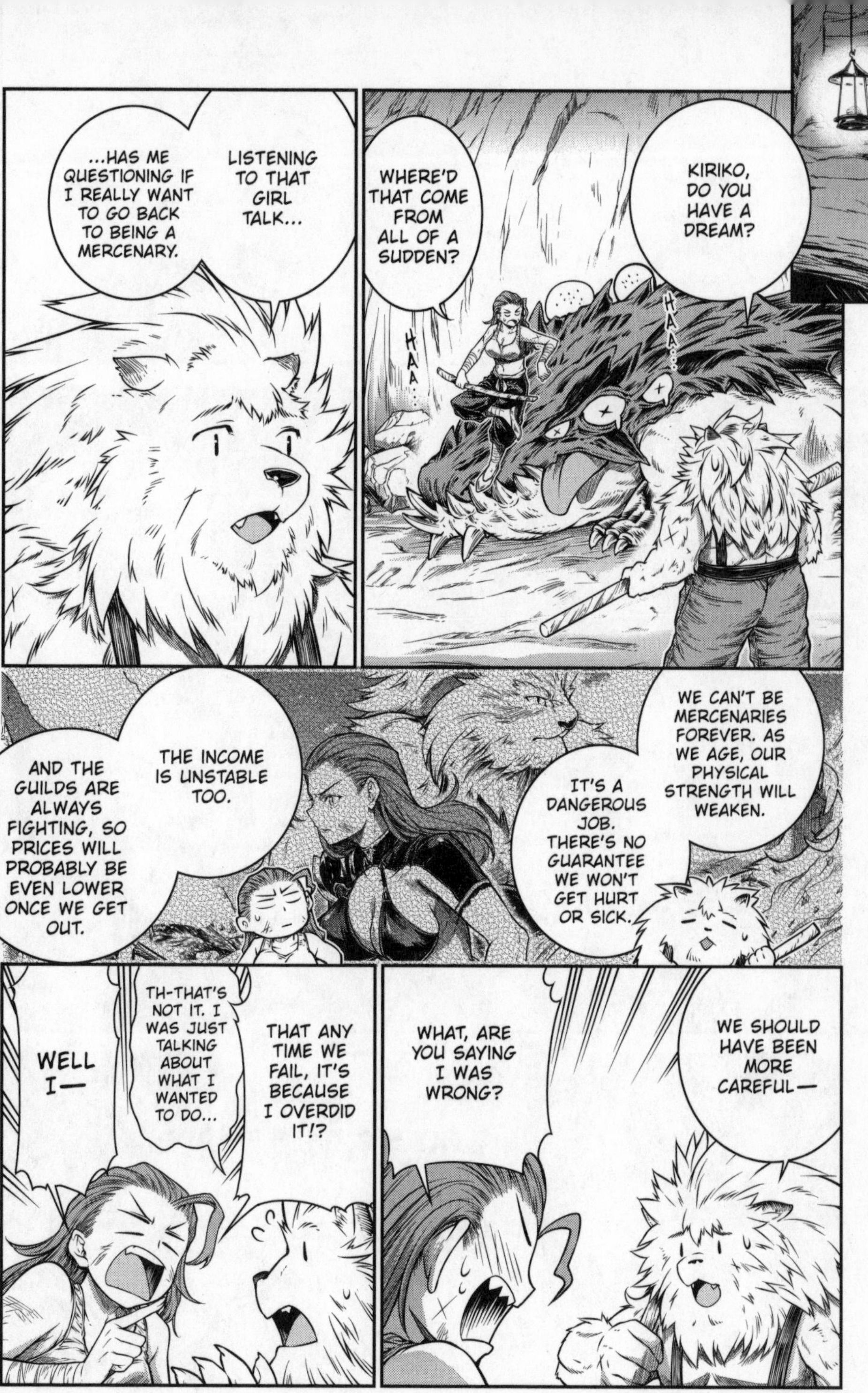
KIRIKO, DO YOU HAVE A DREAM?
HAA...
WHERE'D THAT COME FROM ALL OF A SUDDEN?
HAA...
LISTENING TO THAT GIRL TALK...
...HAS ME QUESTIONING IF I REALLY WANT TO GO BACK TO BEING A MERCENARY.
WE CAN'T BE MERCENARIES FOREVER. AS WE AGE, OUR PHYSICAL STRENGTH WILL WEAKEN.
IT'S A DANGEROUS JOB. THERE'S NO GUARANTEE WE WON'T GET HURT OR SICK.
THE INCOME IS UNSTABLE TOO.
AND THE GUILDS ARE ALWAYS FIGHTING, SO PRICES WILL PROBABLY BE EVEN LOWER ONCE WE GET OUT.
WE SHOULD HAVE BEEN MORE CAREFUL—
WHAT, ARE YOU SAYING I WAS WRONG?
THAT ANY TIME WE FAIL, IT'S BECAUSE I OVERDID IT!?
TH-THAT'S NOT IT. I WAS JUST TALKING ABOUT WHAT I WANTED TO DO...
WELL I—

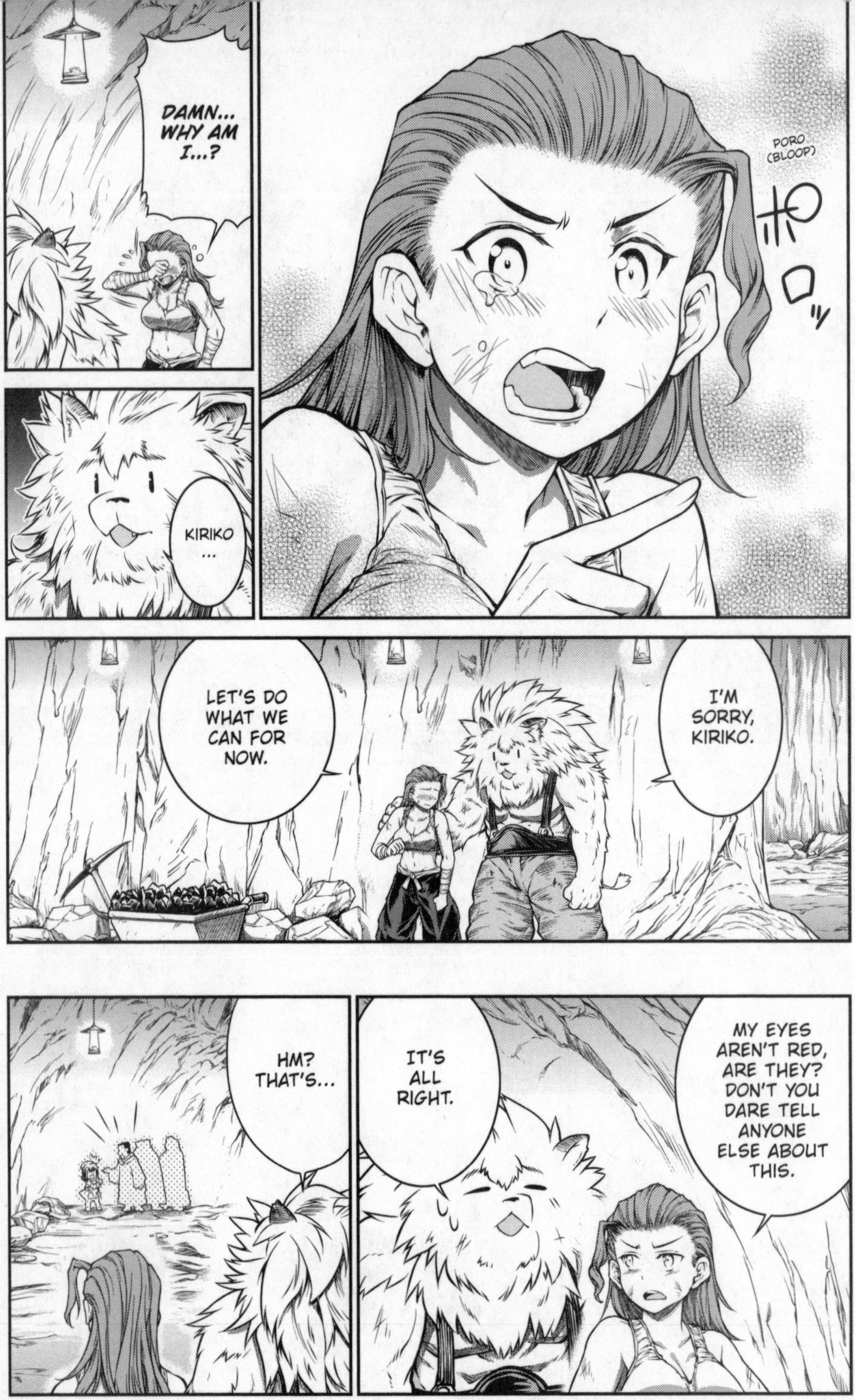
PORO (BLOOP)
ポロッ
DAMN... WHY AM I...?
KIRIKO...
I'M SORRY, KIRIKO.
LET'S DO WHAT WE CAN FOR NOW.
MY EYES AREN'T RED, ARE THEY? DON'T YOU DARE TELL ANYONE ELSE ABOUT THIS.
IT'S ALL RIGHT.
HM? THAT'S...

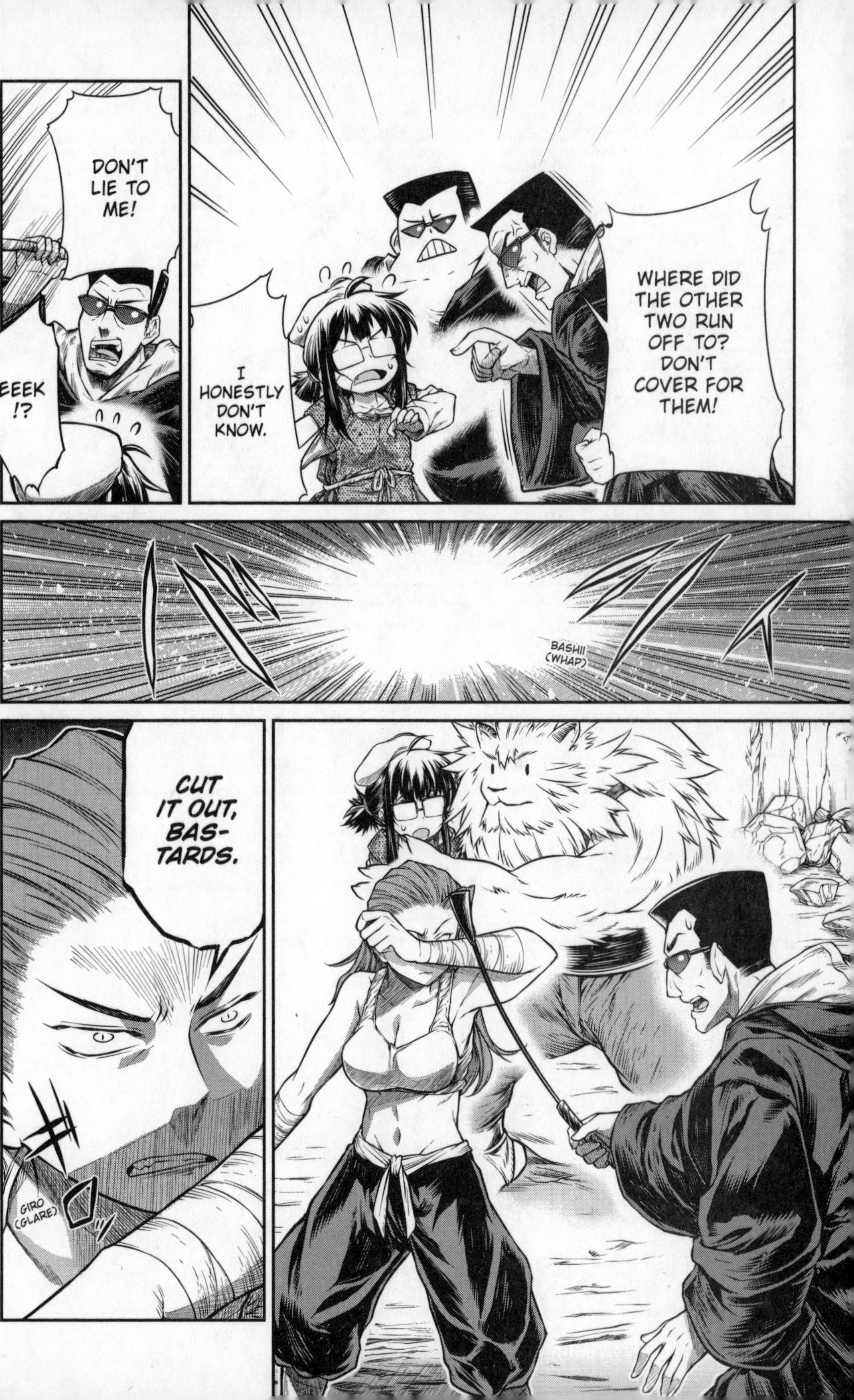
WHERE DID THE OTHER TWO RUN OFF TO? DON'T COVER FOR THEM!
I HONESTLY DON'T KNOW.
DON'T LIE TO ME!
EEEK !?
BASHII (WHAP)
CUT IT OUT, BAS-TARDS.
GIRO (GLARE)

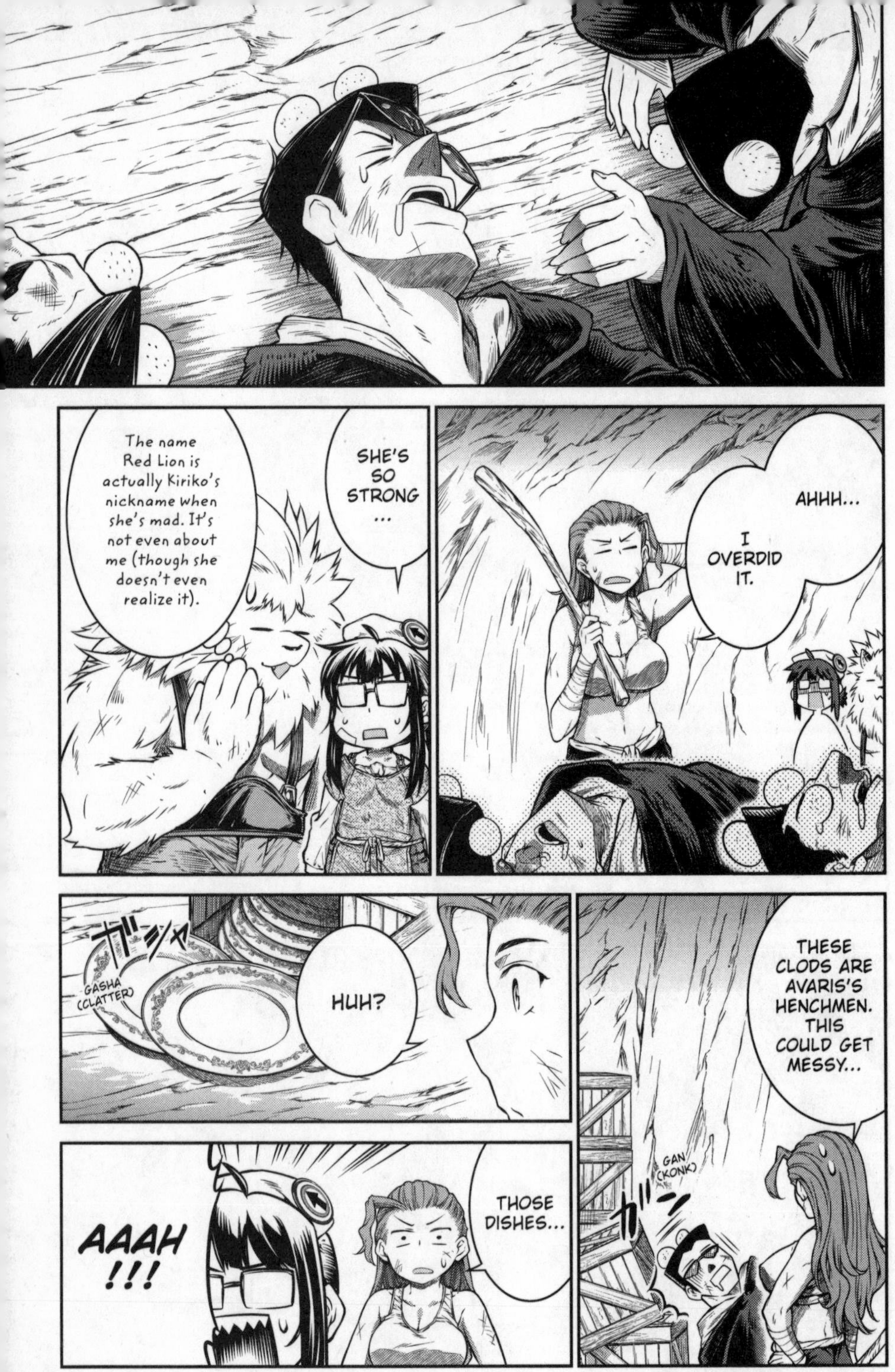
AHHH...
I OVERDID IT.
SHE'S SO STRONG...
The name Red Lion is actually Kiriko's nickname when she's mad. It's not even about me (though she doesn't even realize it).
THESE CLODS ARE AVARIS'S HENCHMEN. THIS COULD GET MESSY...
GAN (KONK)
GASHA (CLATTER)
HUH?
THOSE DISHES...
AAAH!!!

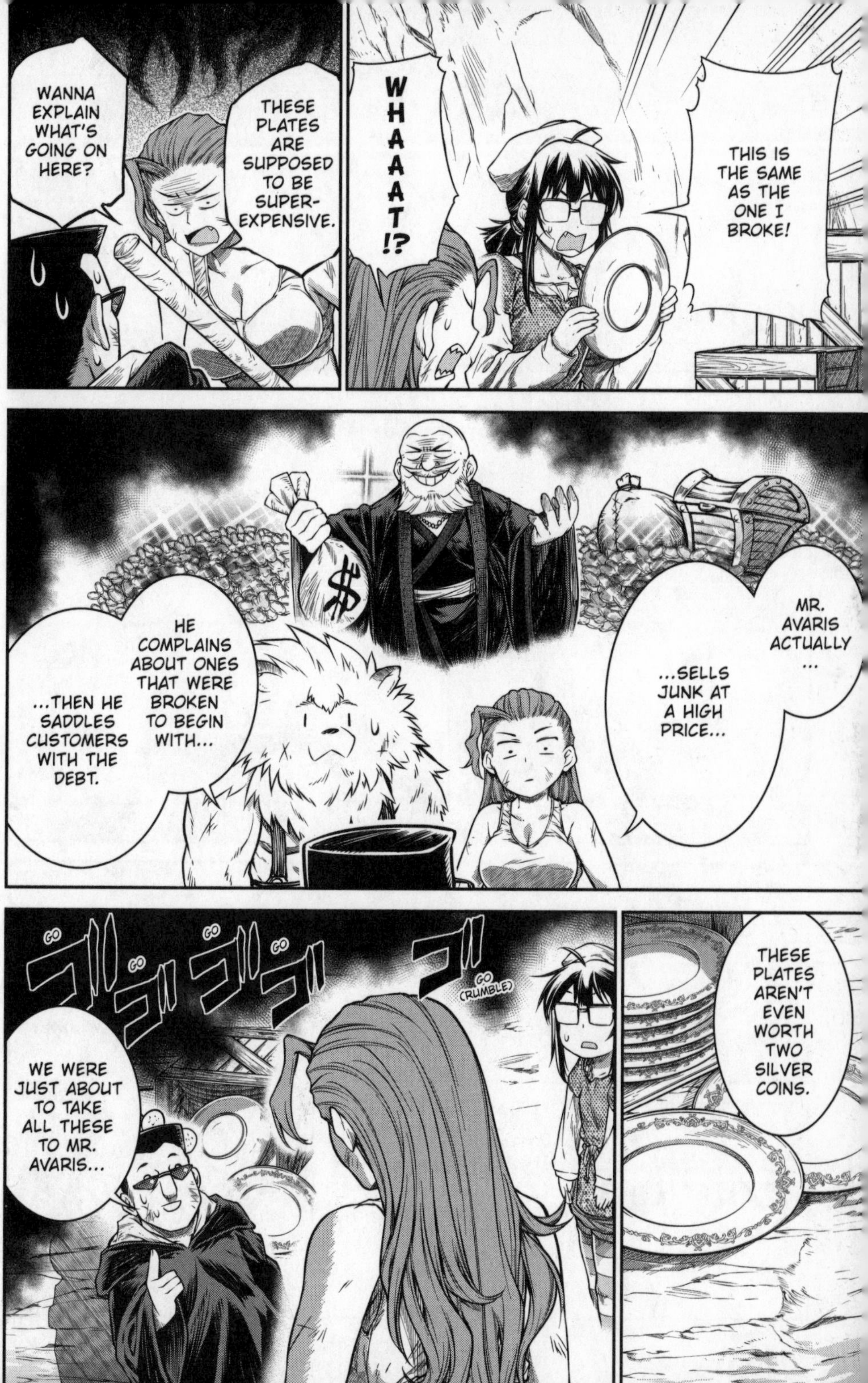
THIS IS THE SAME AS THE ONE I BROKE!
WHAAAT!?
THESE PLATES ARE SUPPOSED TO BE SUPER-EXPENSIVE.
WANNA EXPLAIN WHAT'S GOING ON HERE?
MR. AVARIS ACTUALLY ...
...SELLS JUNK AT A HIGH PRICE...
HE COMPLAINS ABOUT ONES THAT WERE BROKEN TO BEGIN WITH...
...THEN HE SADDLES CUSTOMERS WITH THE DEBT.
THESE PLATES AREN'T EVEN WORTH TWO SILVER COINS.
GO GO GO GO GO (RUMBLE)
WE WERE JUST ABOUT TO TAKE ALL THESE TO MR. AVARIS...

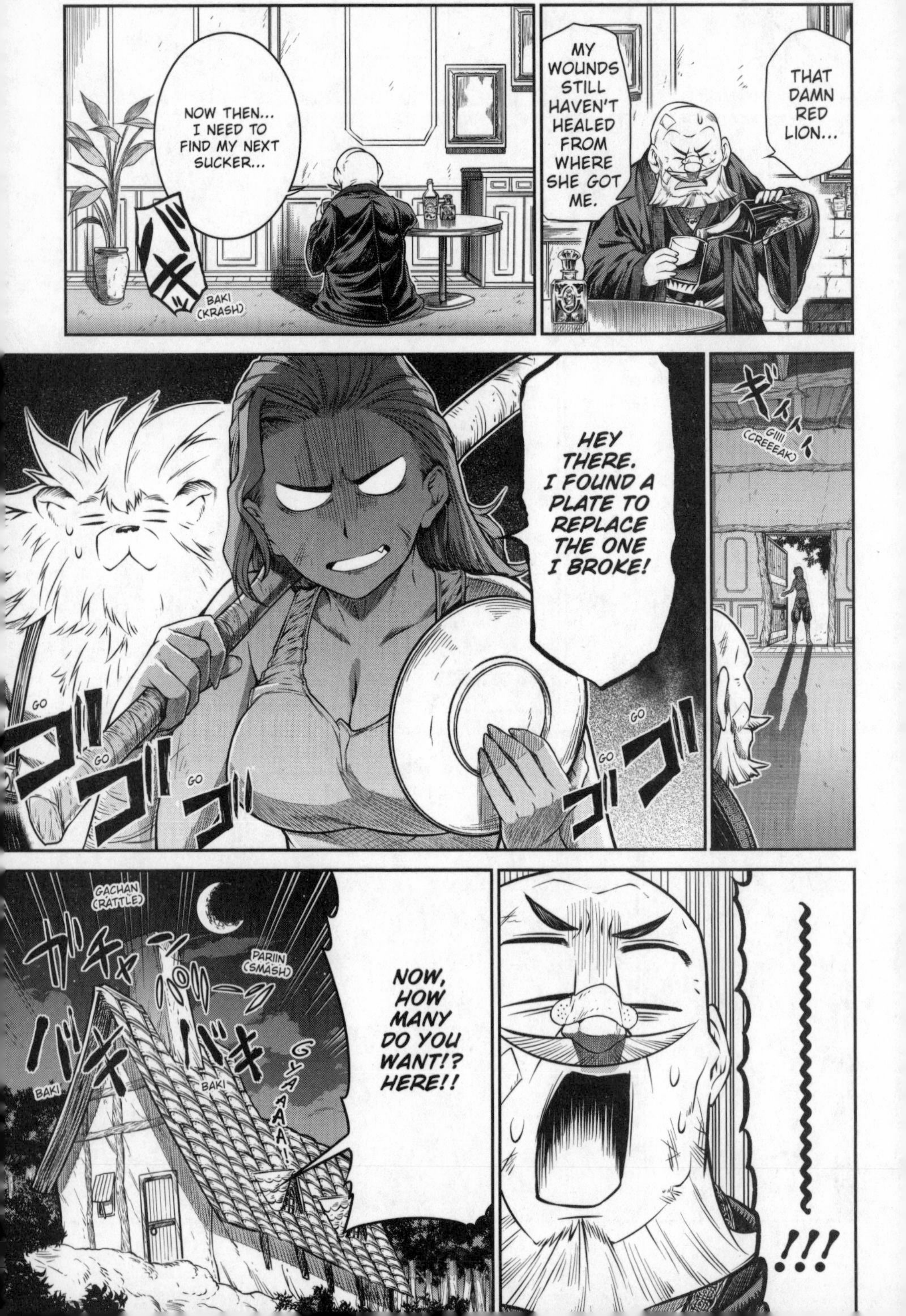
THAT DAMN RED LION...
MY WOUNDS STILL HAVEN'T HEALED FROM WHERE SHE GOT ME.
NOW THEN... I NEED TO FIND MY NEXT SUCKER...
BAKI (KRASH)
GIII (CREEEAK)
HEY THERE. I FOUND A PLATE TO REPLACE THE ONE I BROKE!
GO
GO
GO
GO
GO
!!!
GACHAN (RATTLE)
PARIIN (SMASH)
NOW, HOW MANY DO YOU WANT!? HERE!!
GYAAAAA!
BAKI
BAKI

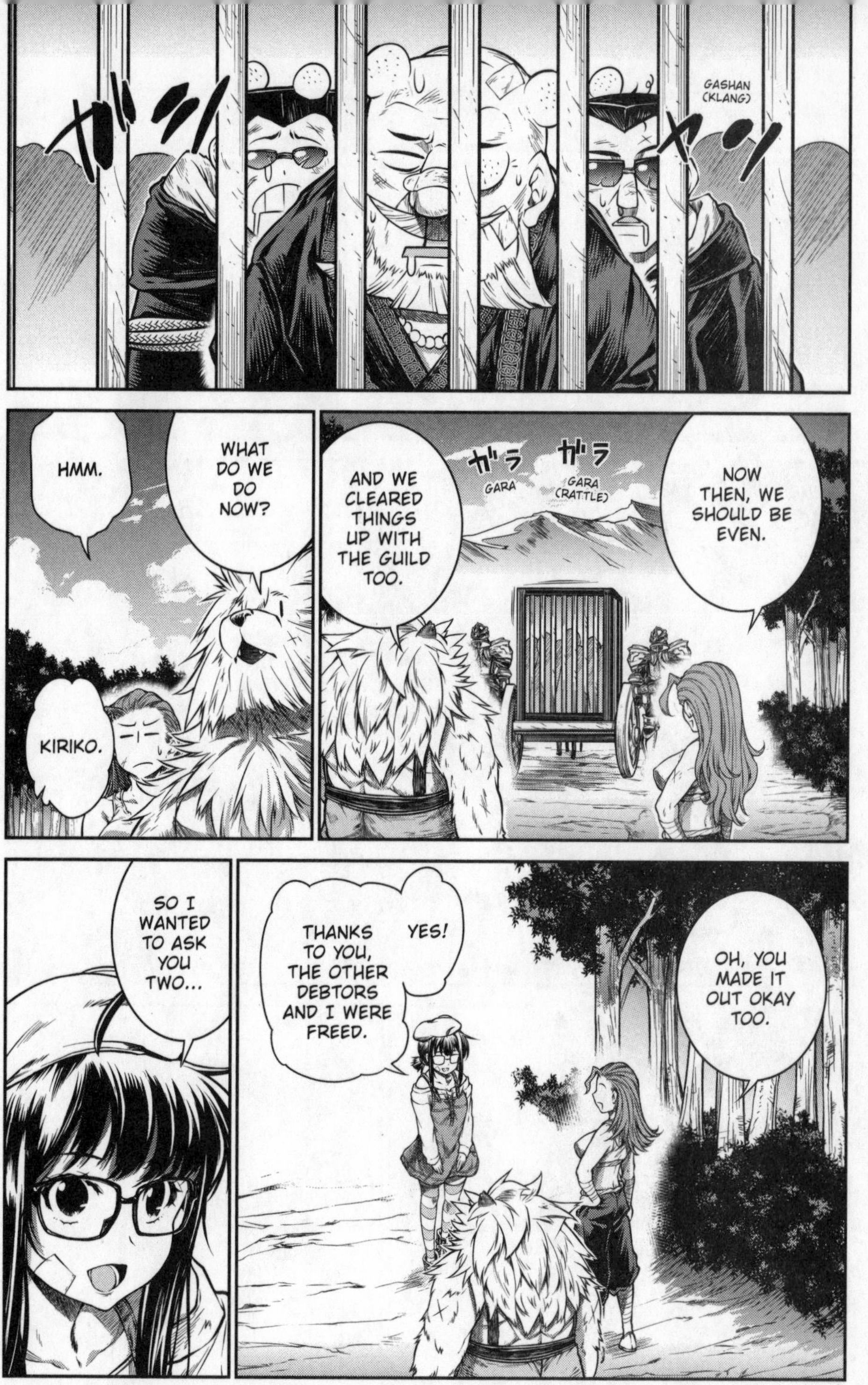
ガシャン
GASHAN (KLANG)
ガラ ガラ
GARA GARA (RATTLE)
NOW THEN, WE SHOULD BE EVEN.
AND WE CLEARED THINGS UP WITH THE GUILD TOO.
WHAT DO WE DO NOW?
HMM.
KIRIKO.
OH, YOU MADE IT OUT OKAY TOO.
YES!
THANKS TO YOU, THE OTHER DEBTORS AND I WERE FREED.
SO I WANTED TO ASK YOU TWO...

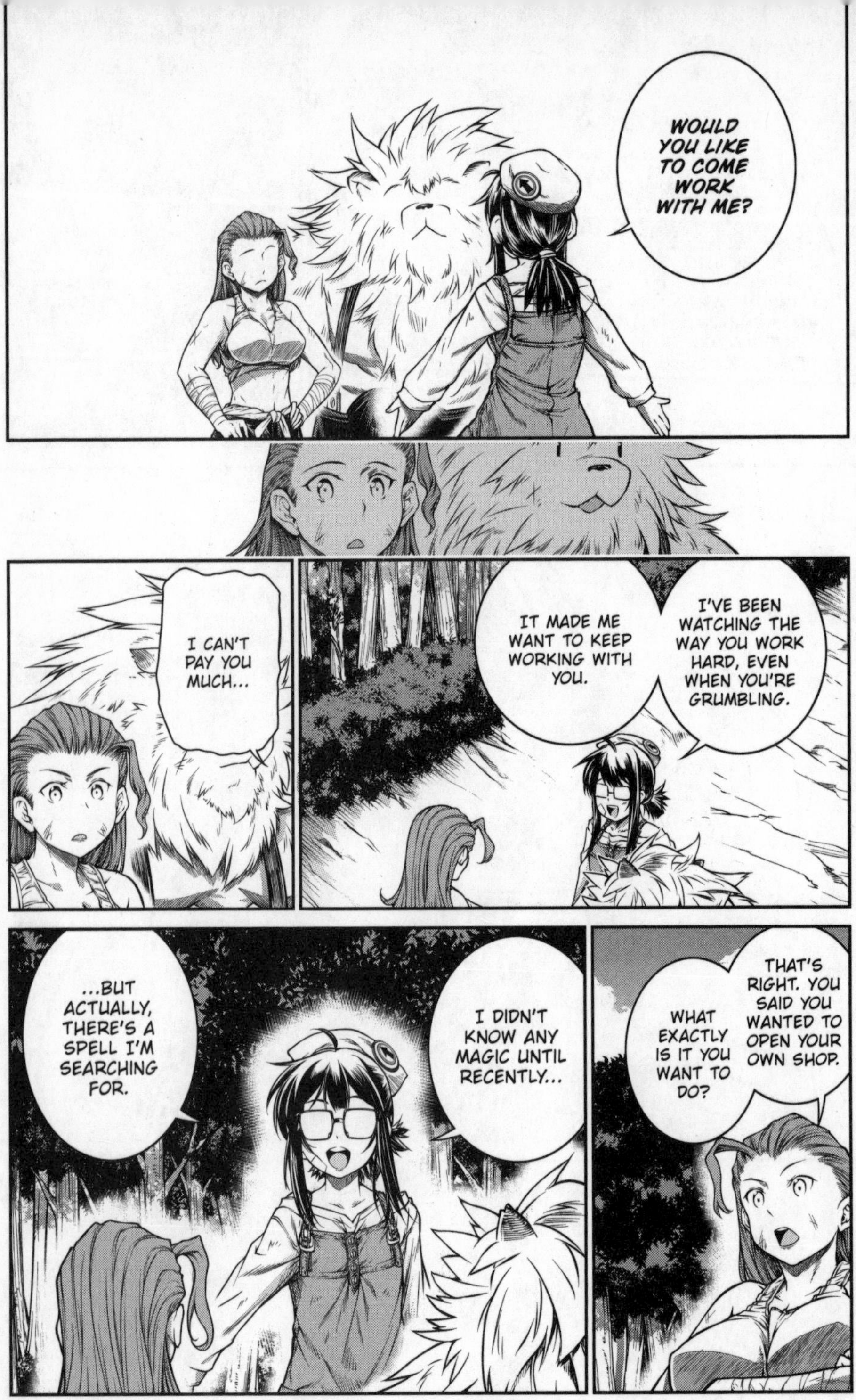
WOULD YOU LIKE TO COME WORK WITH ME?
I'VE BEEN WATCHING THE WAY YOU WORK HARD, EVEN WHEN YOU'RE GRUMBLING.
IT MADE ME WANT TO KEEP WORKING WITH YOU.
I CAN'T PAY YOU MUCH...
THAT'S RIGHT. YOU SAID YOU WANTED TO OPEN YOUR OWN SHOP.
WHAT EXACTLY IS IT YOU WANT TO DO?
I DIDN'T KNOW ANY MAGIC UNTIL RECENTLY...
...BUT ACTUALLY, THERE'S A SPELL I'M SEARCHING FOR.

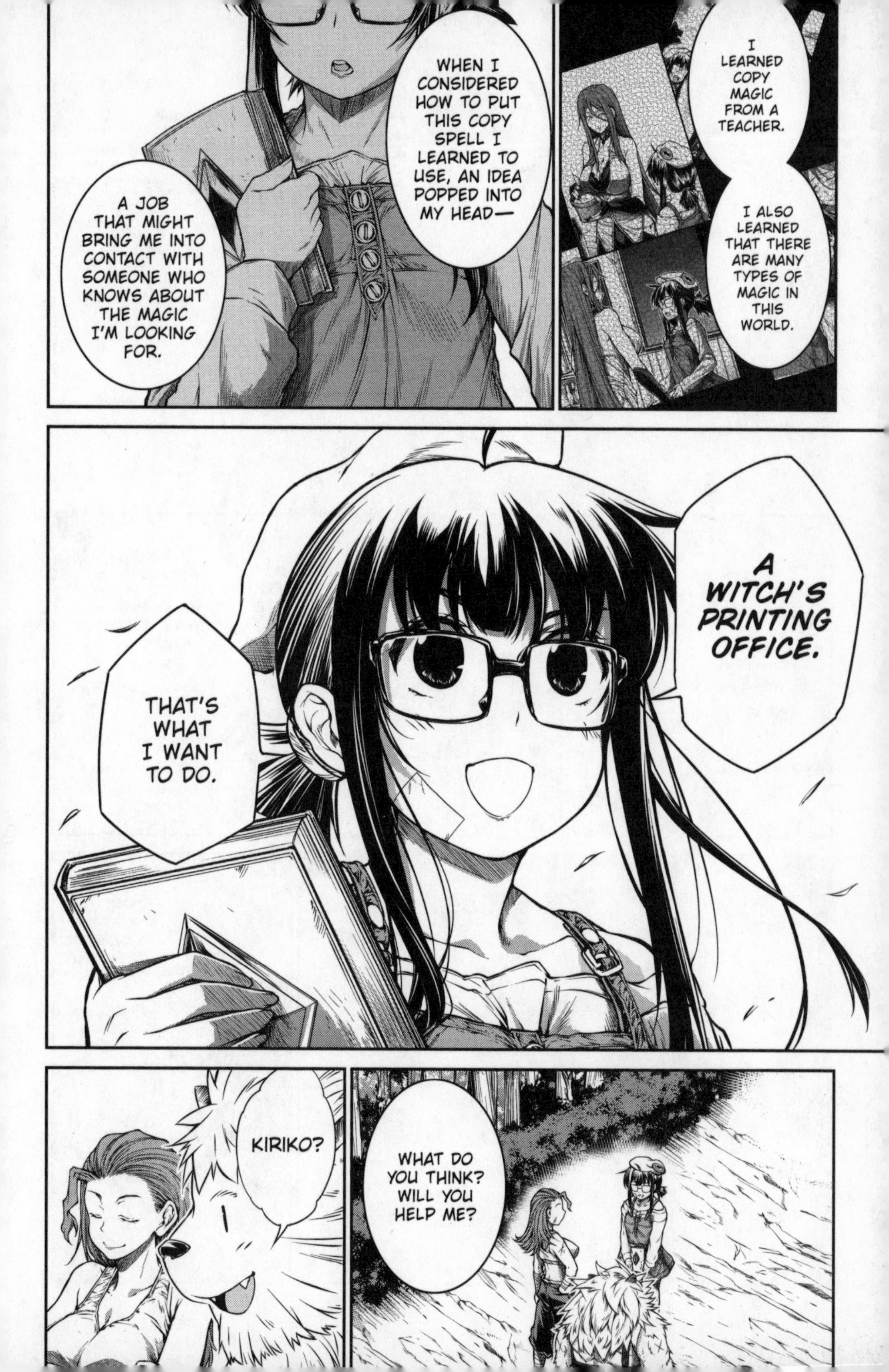
I LEARNED COPY MAGIC FROM A TEACHER.
I ALSO LEARNED THAT THERE ARE MANY TYPES OF MAGIC IN THIS WORLD.
WHEN I CONSIDERED HOW TO PUT THIS COPY SPELL I LEARNED TO USE, AN IDEA POPPED INTO MY HEAD—
A JOB THAT MIGHT BRING ME INTO CONTACT WITH SOMEONE WHO KNOWS ABOUT THE MAGIC I'M LOOKING FOR.
A WITCH'S PRINTING OFFICE.
THAT'S WHAT I WANT TO DO.
WHAT DO YOU THINK? WILL YOU HELP ME?
KIRIKO?

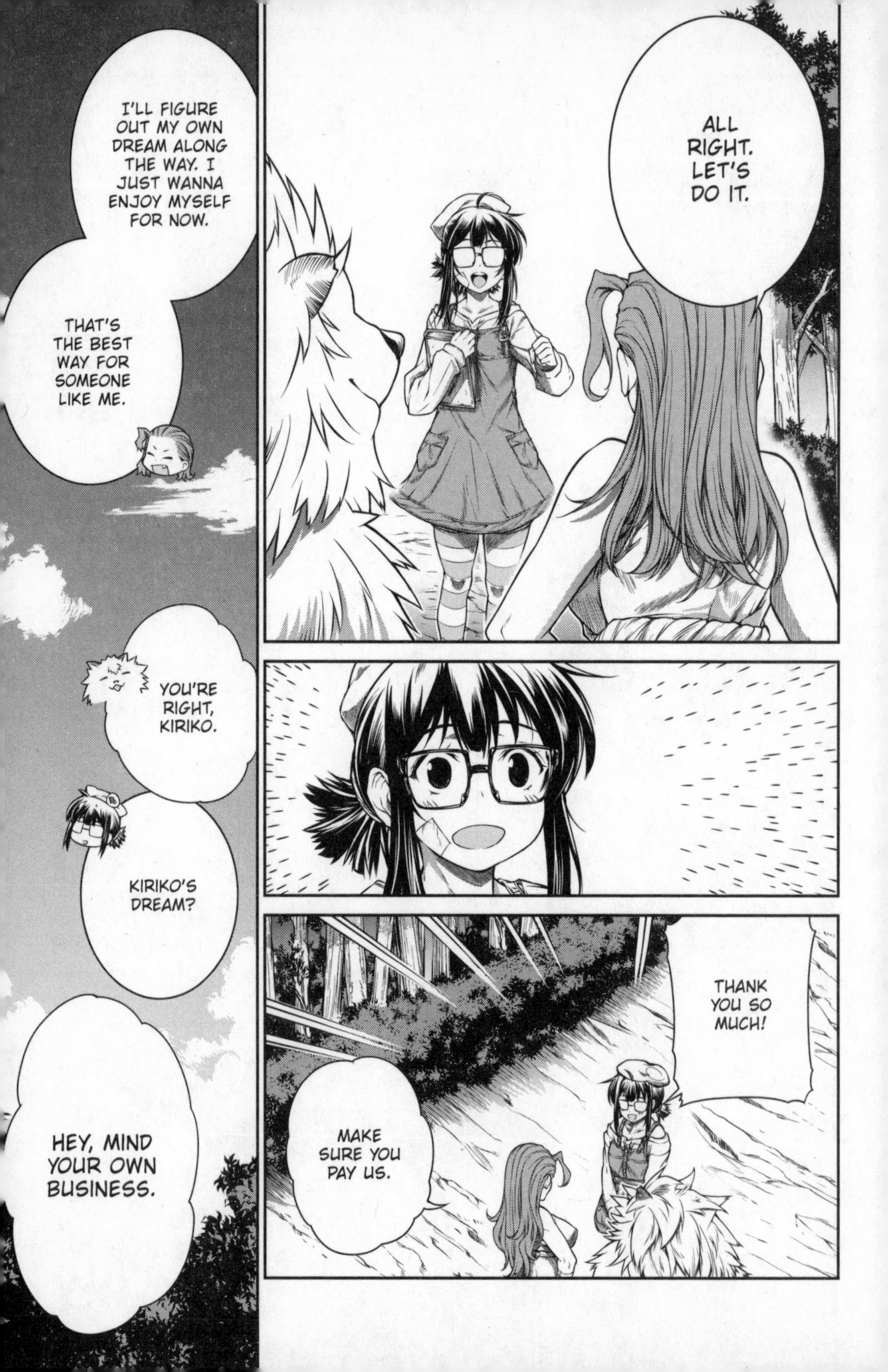
ALL RIGHT. LET'S DO IT.
THANK YOU SO MUCH!
MAKE SURE YOU PAY US.
I'LL FIGURE OUT MY OWN DREAM ALONG THE WAY. I JUST WANNA ENJOY MYSELF FOR NOW.
THAT'S THE BEST WAY FOR SOMEONE LIKE ME.
YOU'RE RIGHT, KIRIKO.
KIRIKO'S DREAM?
HEY, MIND YOUR OWN BUSINESS.

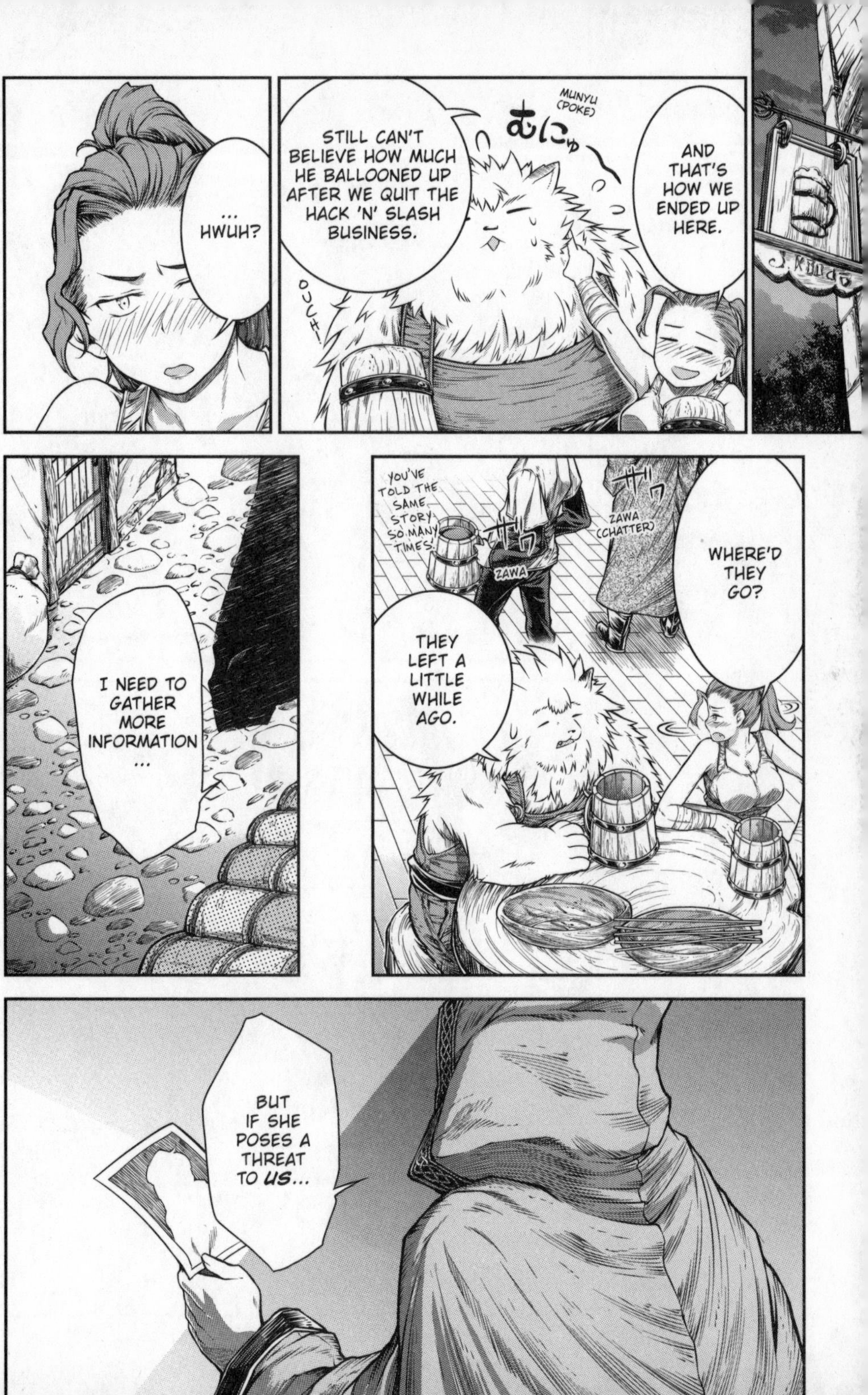
AND THAT'S HOW WE ENDED UP HERE.
MUNYU (POKE)
むにゅ
STILL CAN'T BELIEVE HOW MUCH HE BALLOONED UP AFTER WE QUIT THE HACK 'N' SLASH BUSINESS.
OUCH!
... HWUH?
WHERE'D THEY GO?
ザワ
ZAWA (CHATTER)
YOU'VE TOLD THE SAME STORY SO MANY TIMES!
ザワ
ZAWA
THEY LEFT A LITTLE WHILE AGO.
I NEED TO GATHER MORE INFORMATION ...
BUT IF SHE POSES A THREAT TO US...

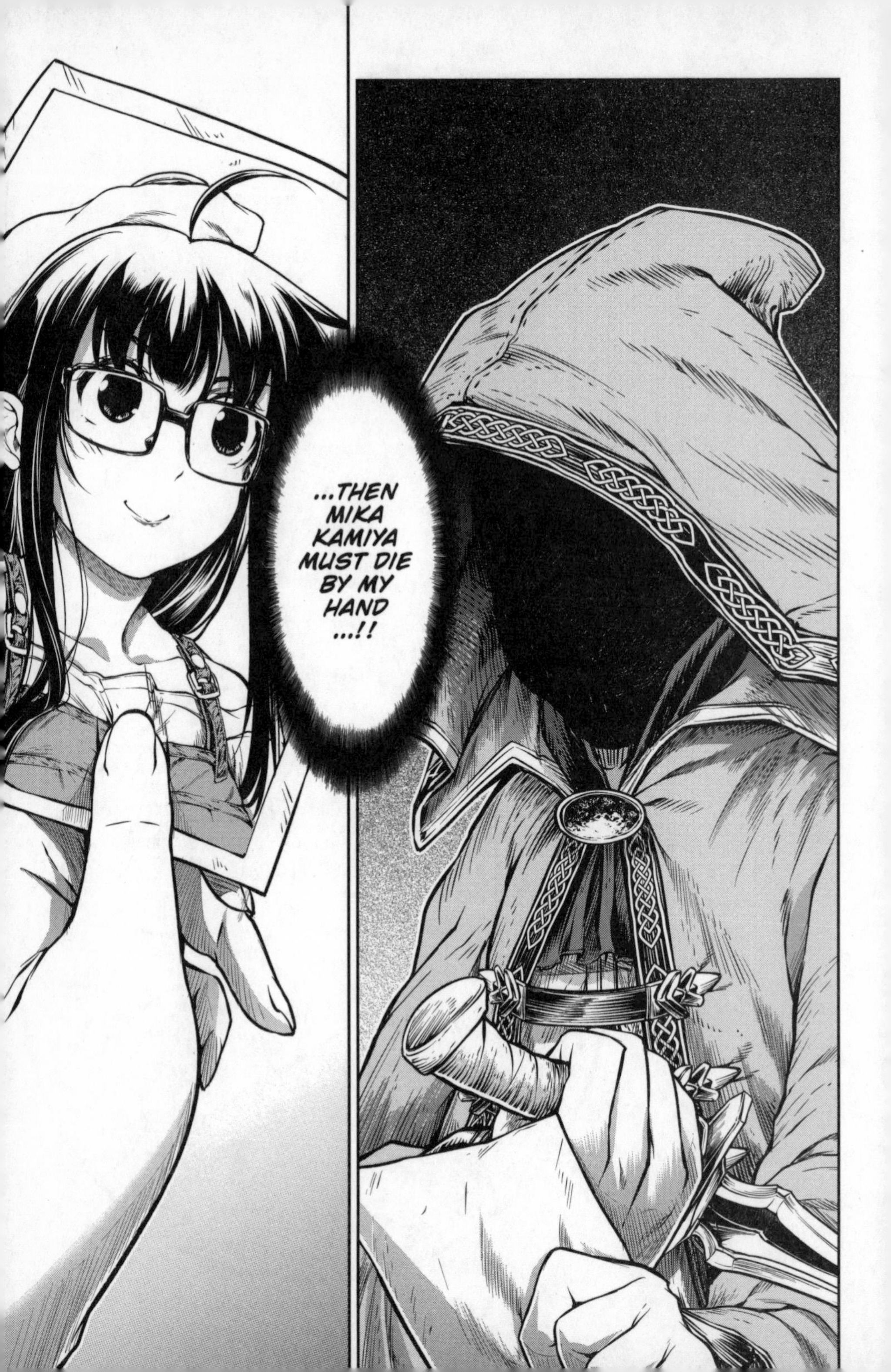
...THEN MIKA KAMIYA MUST DIE BY MY HAND ...!!

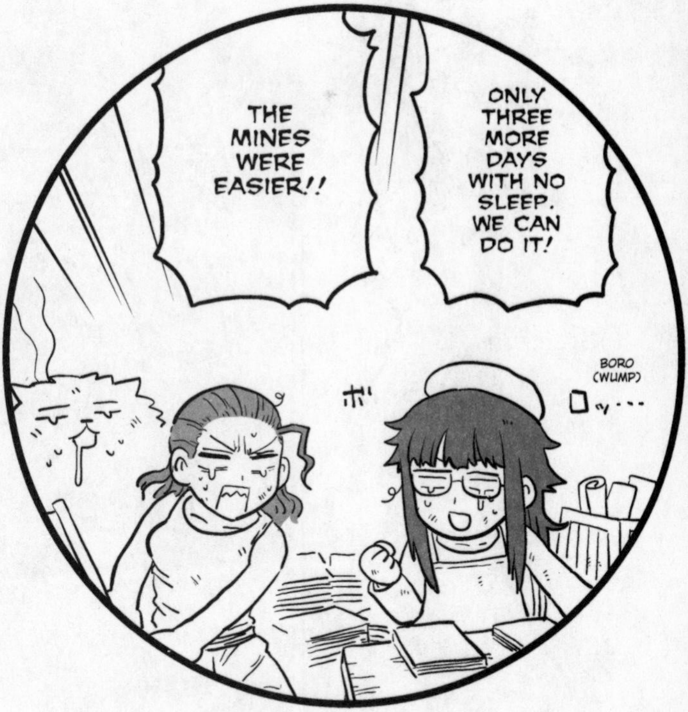
ONLY THREE MORE DAYS WITH NO SLEEP. WE CAN DO IT!
THE MINES WERE EASIER!!
ボロッ…
BORO (WUMP)

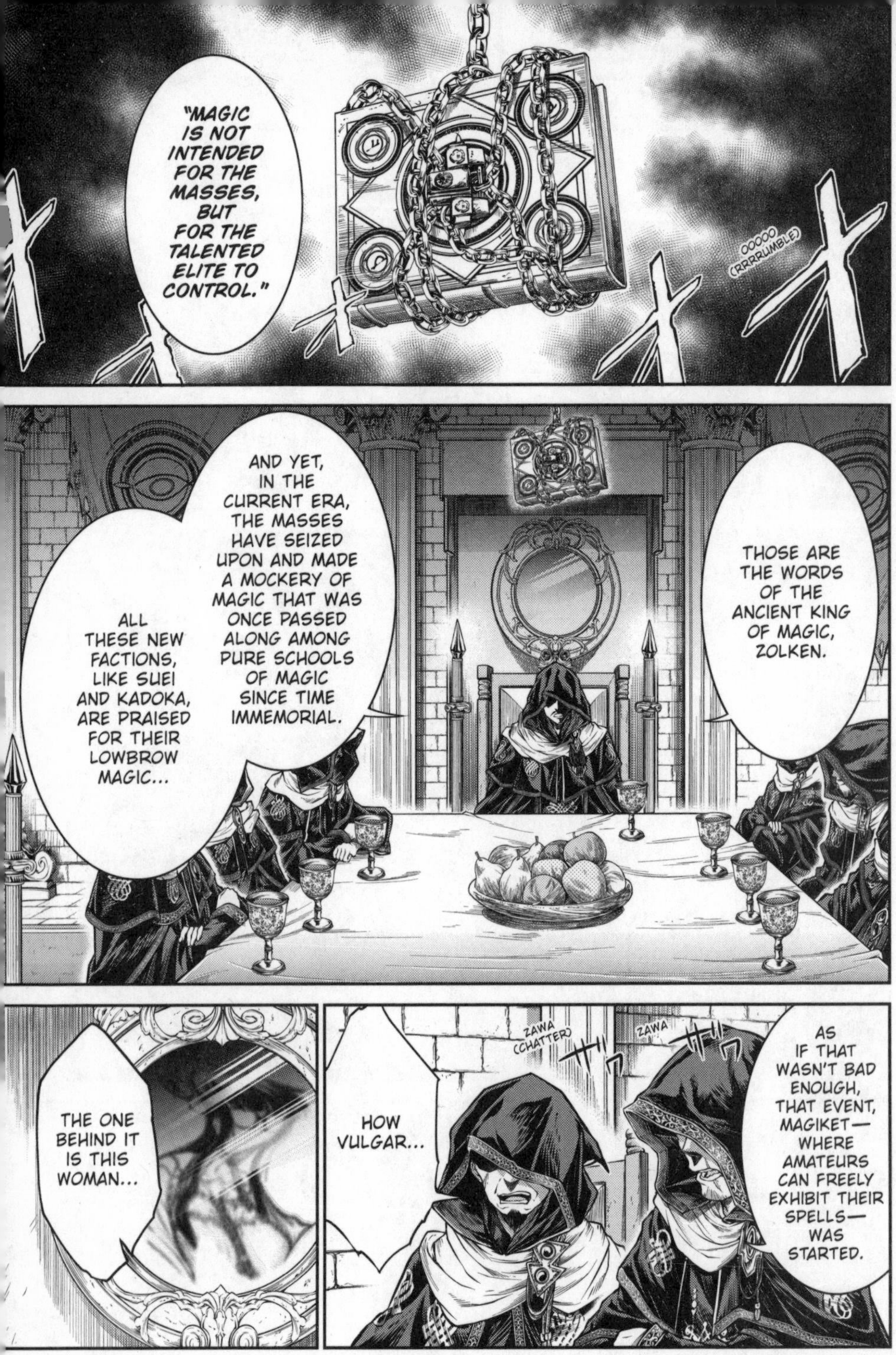
OOOOO (RRRRUMBLE)
"MAGIC IS NOT INTENDED FOR THE MASSES, BUT FOR THE TALENTED ELITE TO CONTROL."
THOSE ARE THE WORDS OF THE ANCIENT KING OF MAGIC, ZOLKEN.
AND YET, IN THE CURRENT ERA, THE MASSES HAVE SEIZED UPON AND MADE A MOCKERY OF MAGIC THAT WAS ONCE PASSED ALONG AMONG PURE SCHOOLS OF MAGIC SINCE TIME IMMEMORIAL.
ALL THESE NEW FACTIONS, LIKE SUEI AND KADOKA, ARE PRAISED FOR THEIR LOWBROW MAGIC...
AS IF THAT WASN'T BAD ENOUGH, THAT EVENT, MAGIKET—WHERE AMATEURS CAN FREELY EXHIBIT THEIR SPELLS—WAS STARTED.
ZAWA
ZAWA (CHATTER)
HOW VULGAR...
THE ONE BEHIND IT IS THIS WOMAN...

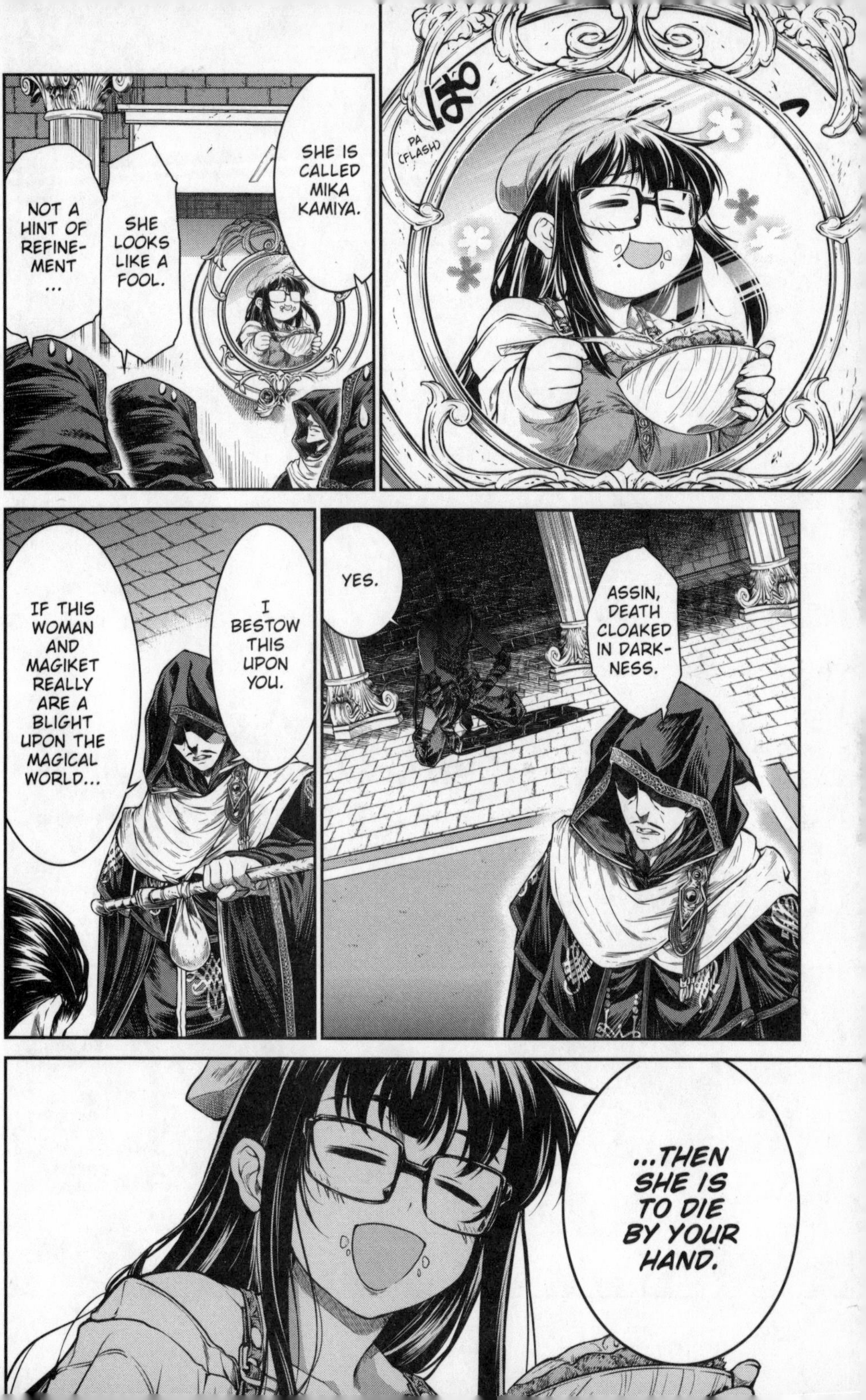
ぽ
PA (FLASH)
SHE IS CALLED MIKA KAMIYA.
SHE LOOKS LIKE A FOOL.
NOT A HINT OF REFINEMENT...
ASSIN, DEATH CLOAKED IN DARKNESS.
YES.
I BESTOW THIS UPON YOU.
IF THIS WOMAN AND MAGIKET REALLY ARE A BLIGHT UPON THE MAGICAL WORLD...
...THEN SHE IS TO DIE BY YOUR HAND.

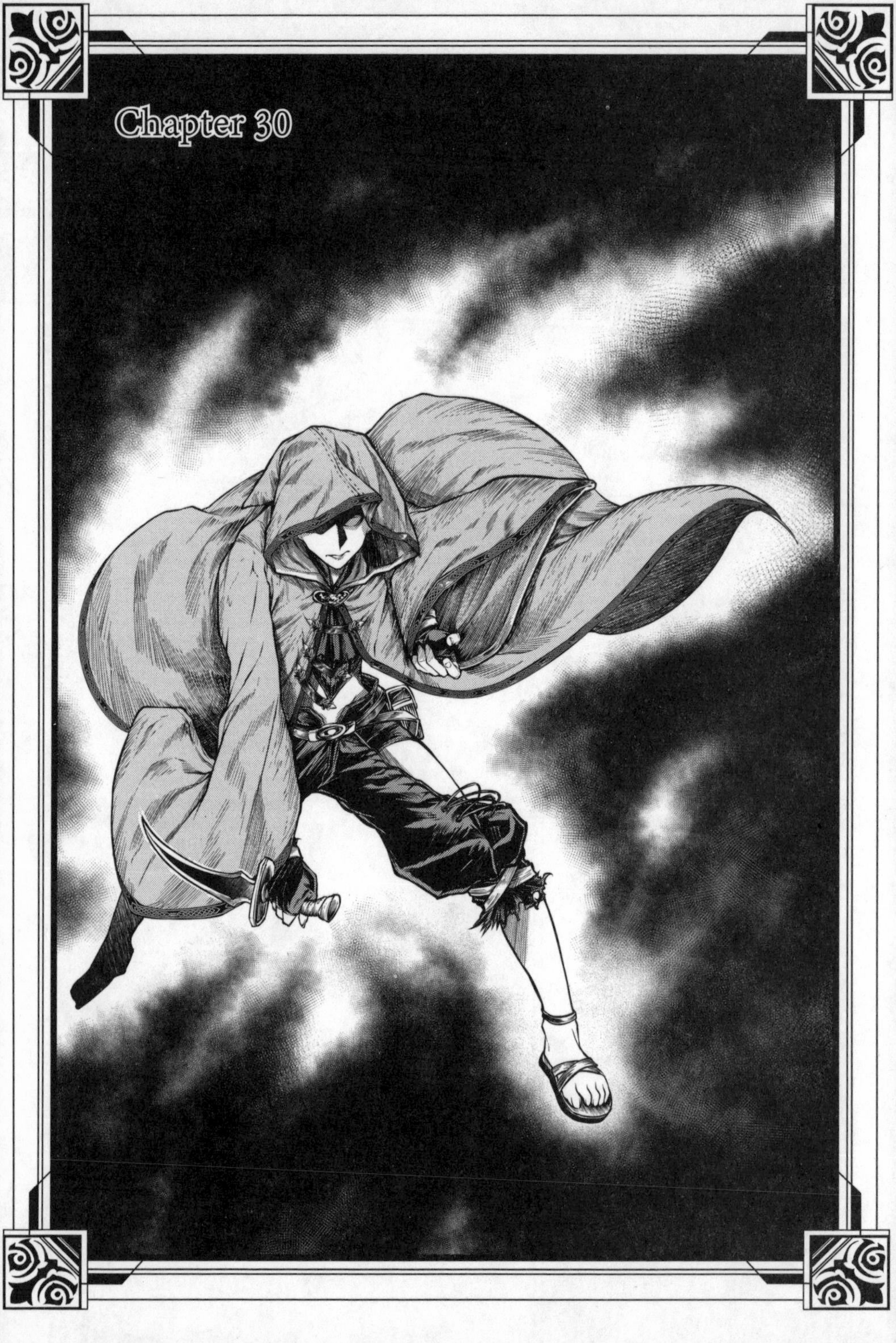
Chapter 30

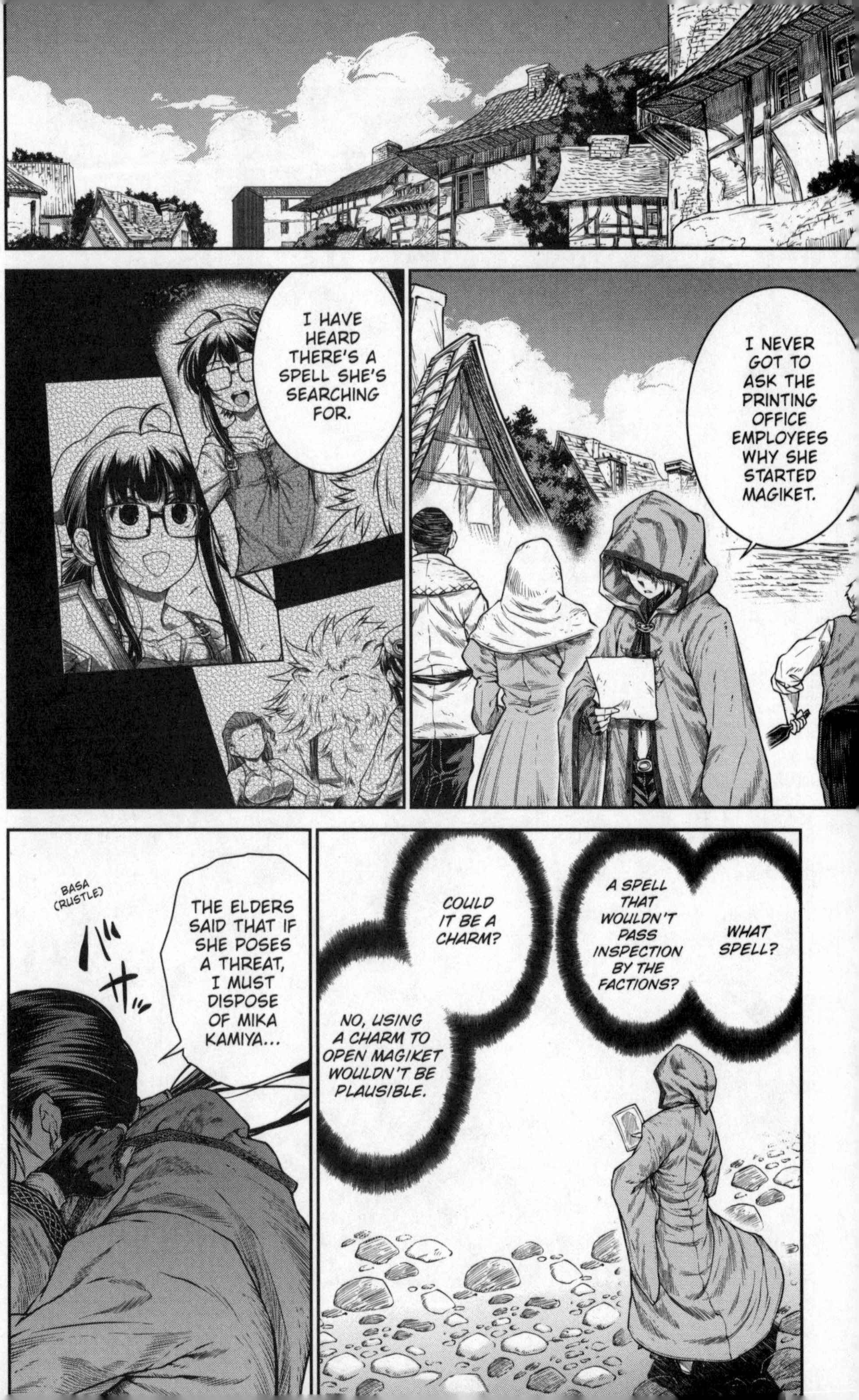
I NEVER GOT TO ASK THE PRINTING OFFICE EMPLOYEES WHY SHE STARTED MAGIKET.
I HAVE HEARD THERE'S A SPELL SHE'S SEARCHING FOR.
WHAT SPELL?
A SPELL THAT WOULDN'T PASS INSPECTION BY THE FACTIONS?
COULD IT BE A CHARM?
NO, USING A CHARM TO OPEN MAGIKET WOULDN'T BE PLAUSIBLE.
THE ELDERS SAID THAT IF SHE POSES A THREAT, I MUST DISPOSE OF MIKA KAMIYA...
BASA (RUSTLE)
バサッ

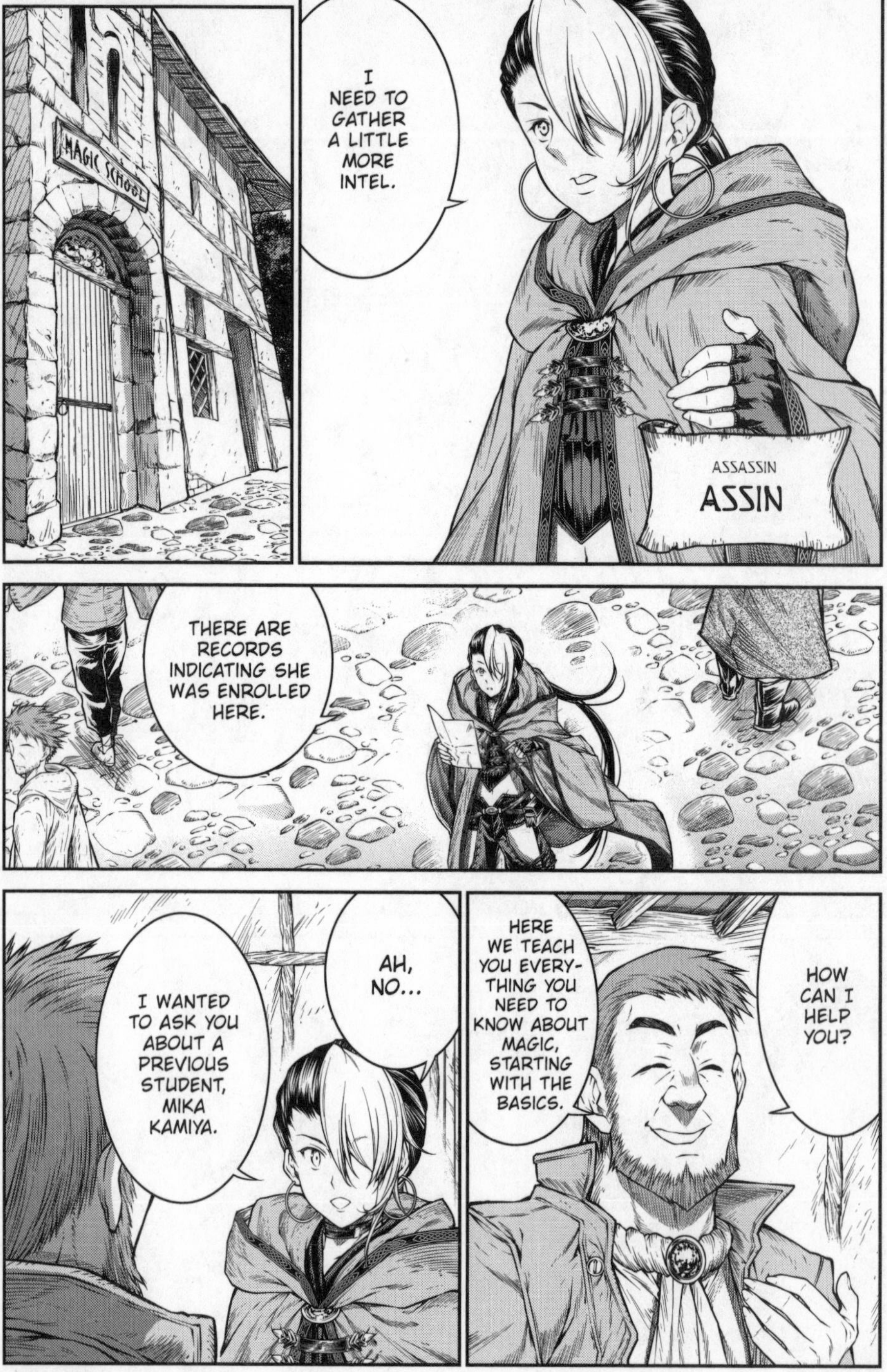
I NEED TO GATHER A LITTLE MORE INTEL.
ASSASSIN
ASSIN
MAGIC SCHOOL
THERE ARE RECORDS INDICATING SHE WAS ENROLLED HERE.
HOW CAN I HELP YOU?
HERE WE TEACH YOU EVERY-THING YOU NEED TO KNOW ABOUT MAGIC, STARTING WITH THE BASICS.
AH, NO...
I WANTED TO ASK YOU ABOUT A PREVIOUS STUDENT, MIKA KAMIYA.

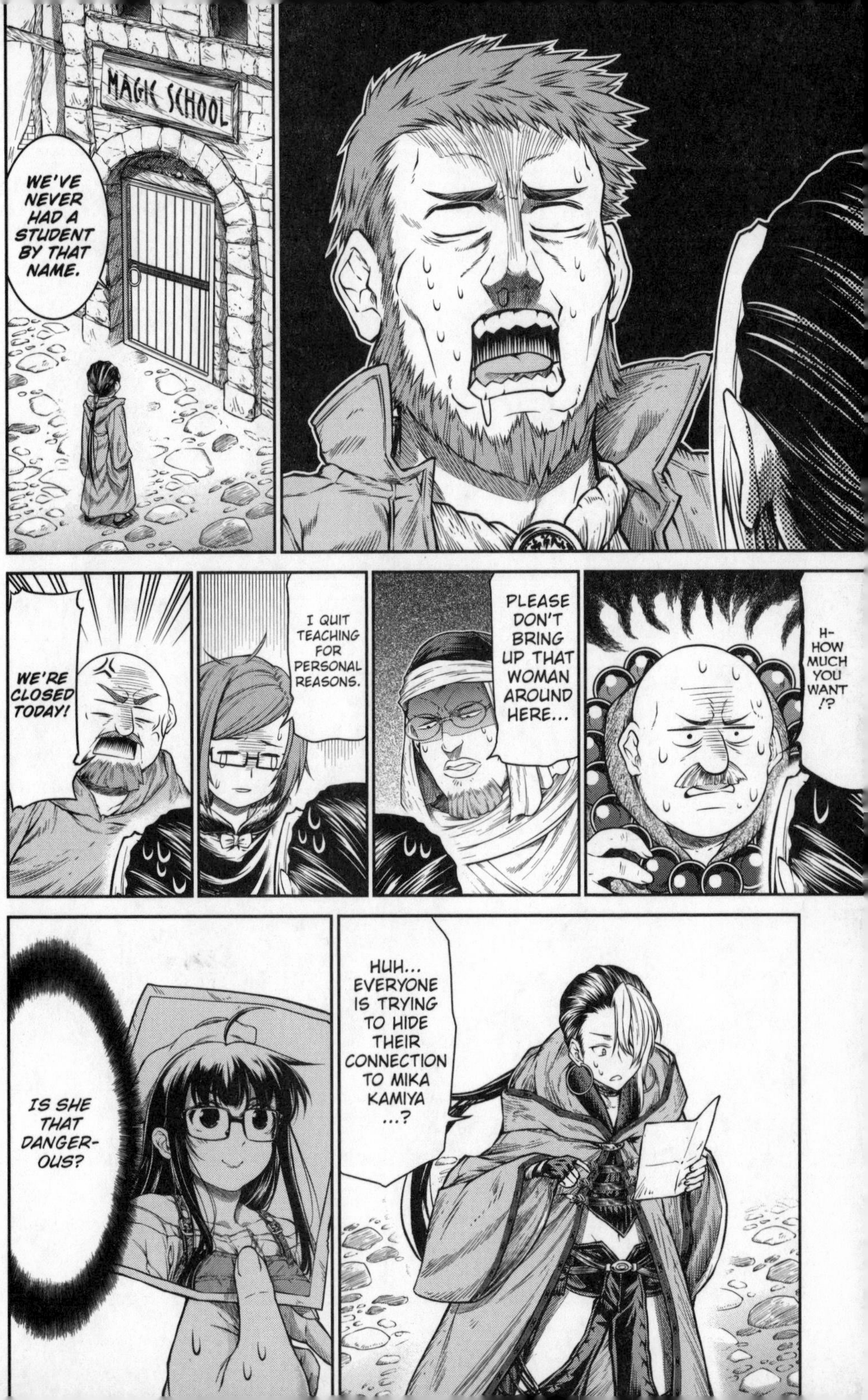
MAGIC SCHOOL
WE'VE NEVER HAD A STUDENT BY THAT NAME.
H-HOW MUCH YOU WANT!?
PLEASE DON'T BRING UP THAT WOMAN AROUND HERE...
I QUIT TEACHING FOR PERSONAL REASONS.
WE'RE CLOSED TODAY!
HUH... EVERYONE IS TRYING TO HIDE THEIR CONNECTION TO MIKA KAMIYA ...?
IS SHE THAT DANGER-OUS?

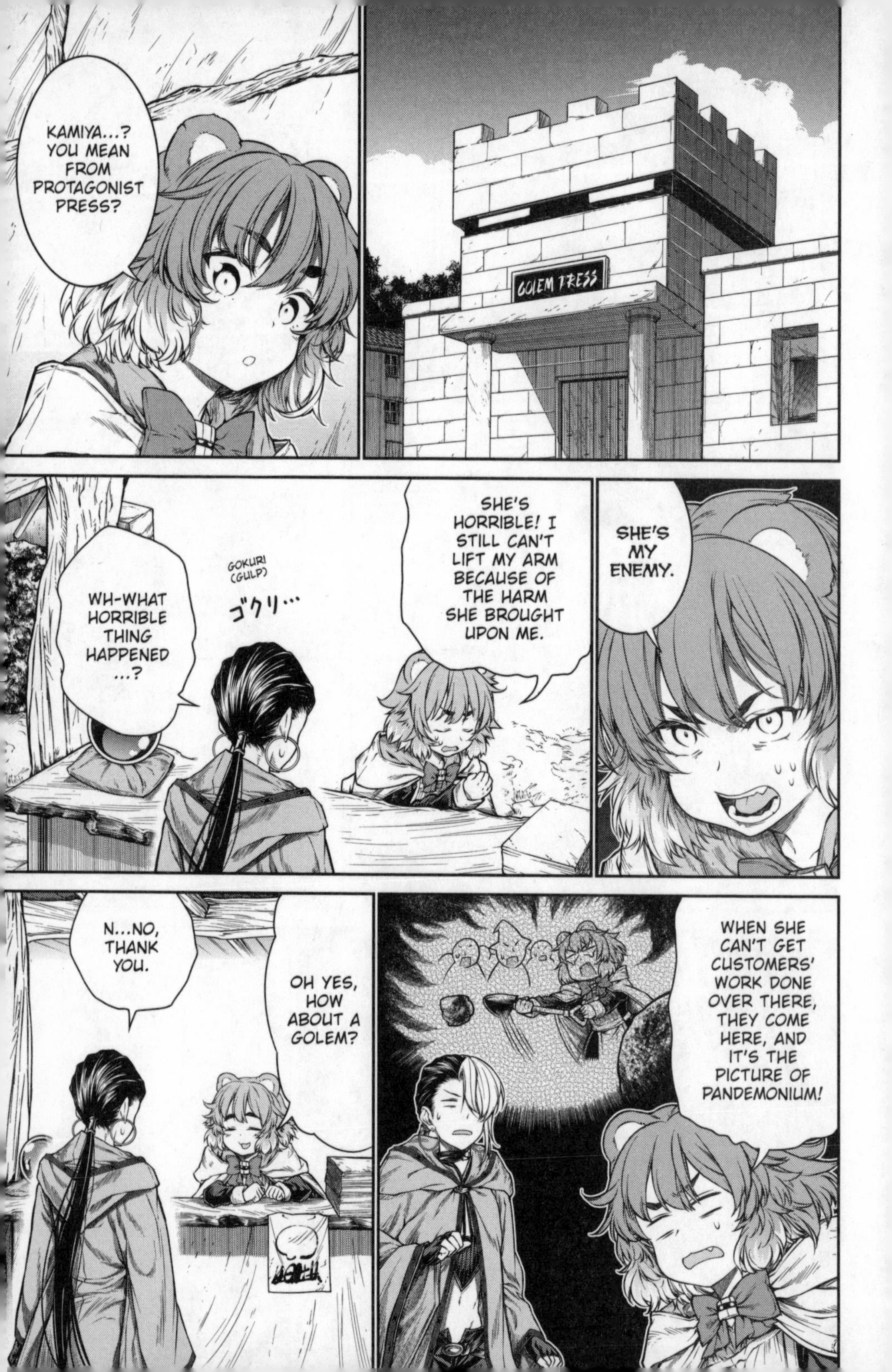
GOLEM PRESS
KAMIYA...? YOU MEAN FROM PROTAGONIST PRESS?
SHE'S MY ENEMY.
SHE'S HORRIBLE! I STILL CAN'T LIFT MY ARM BECAUSE OF THE HARM SHE BROUGHT UPON ME.
GOKURI (GULP)
ゴクリ…
WH-WHAT HORRIBLE THING HAPPENED ...?
WHEN SHE CAN'T GET CUSTOMERS' WORK DONE OVER THERE, THEY COME HERE, AND IT'S THE PICTURE OF PANDEMONIUM!
OH YES, HOW ABOUT A GOLEM?
N...NO, THANK YOU.

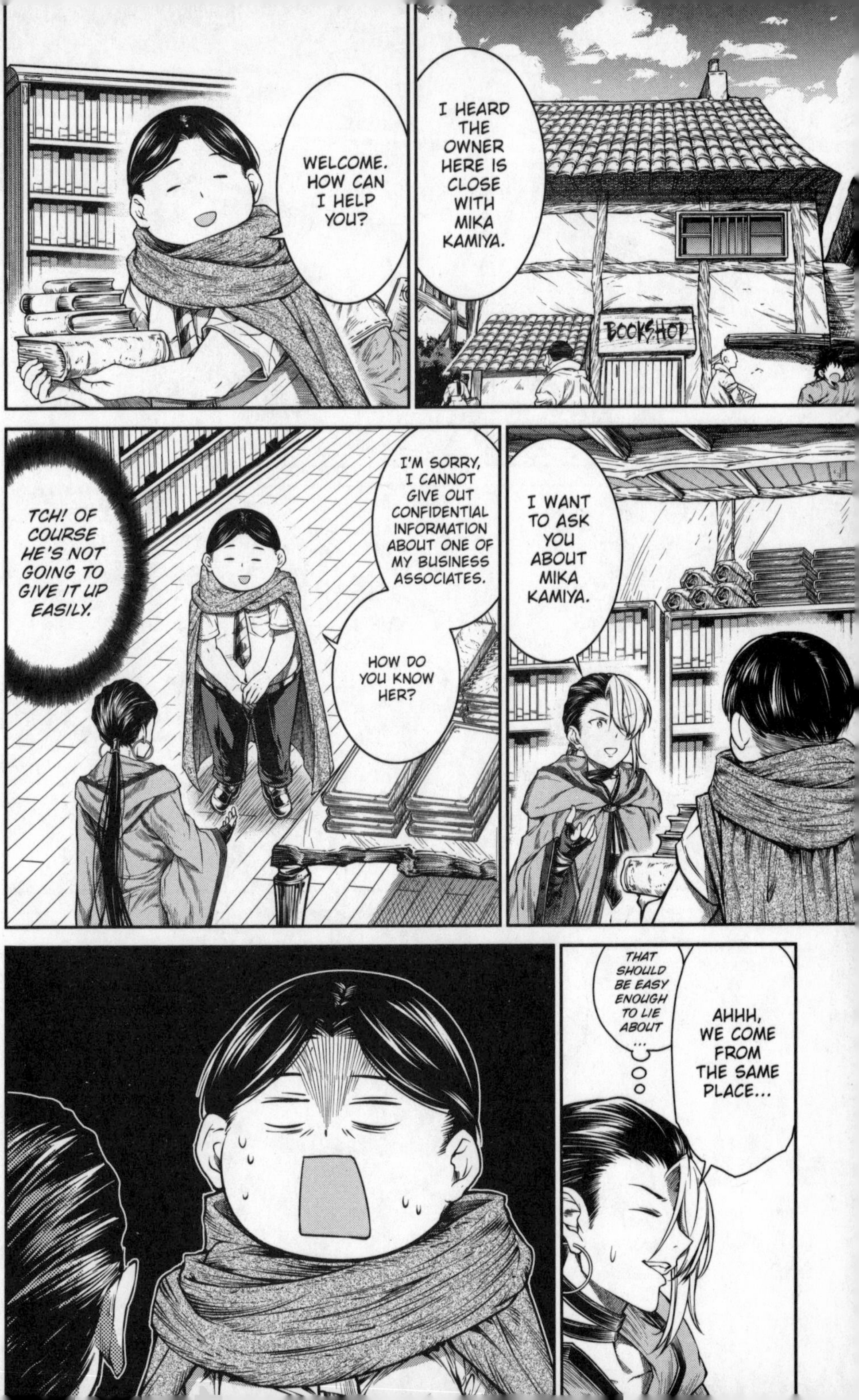
I HEARD THE OWNER HERE IS CLOSE WITH MIKA KAMIYA.
BOOKSHOP
WELCOME. HOW CAN I HELP YOU?
I WANT TO ASK YOU ABOUT MIKA KAMIYA.
I'M SORRY, I CANNOT GIVE OUT CONFIDENTIAL INFORMATION ABOUT ONE OF MY BUSINESS ASSOCIATES.
HOW DO YOU KNOW HER?
TCH! OF COURSE HE'S NOT GOING TO GIVE IT UP EASILY.
AHHH, WE COME FROM THE SAME PLACE...
THAT SHOULD BE EASY ENOUGH TO LIE ABOUT...

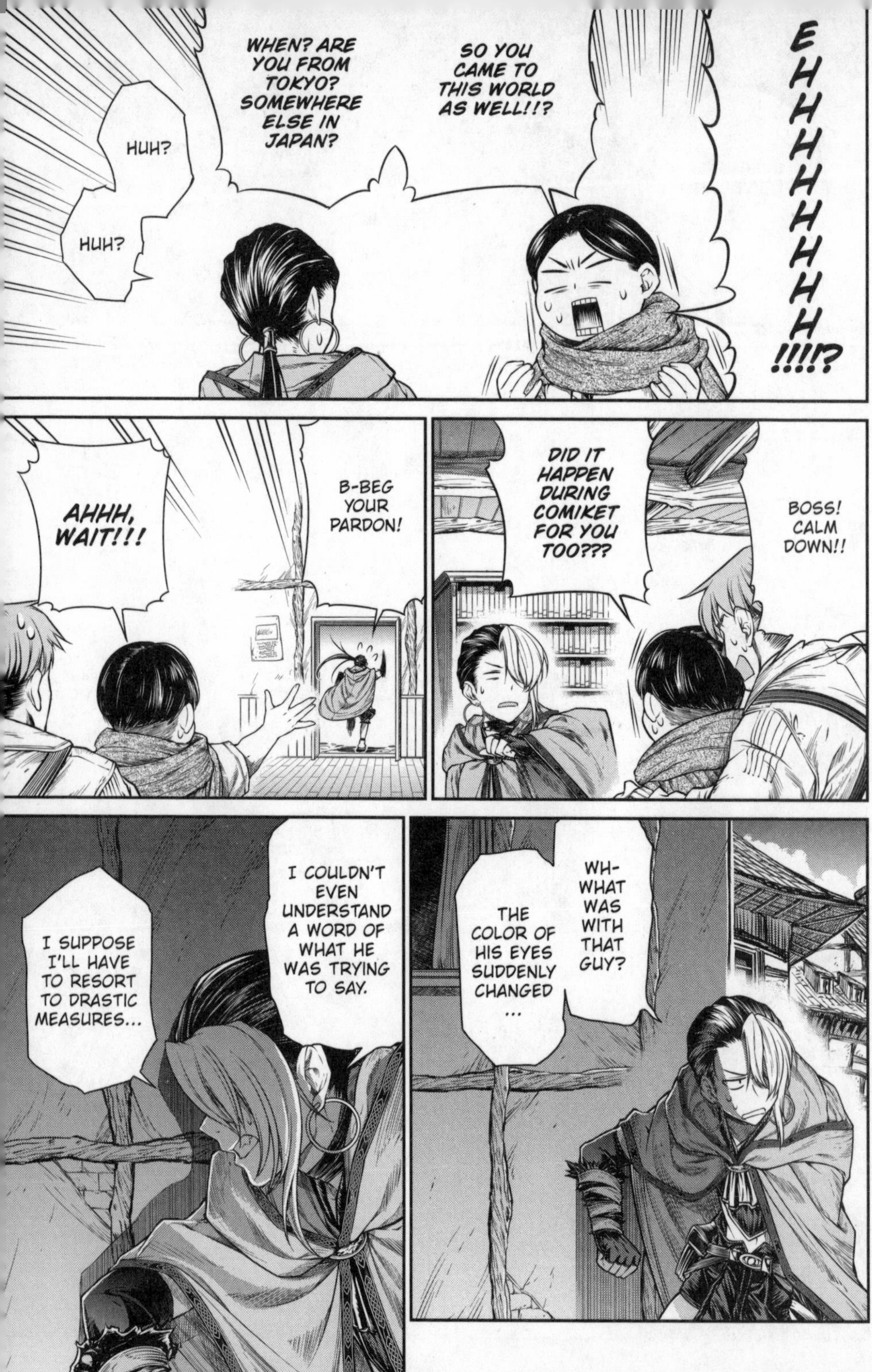
EHHHHHHHH!!!!?
SO YOU CAME TO THIS WORLD AS WELL!!?
WHEN? ARE YOU FROM TOKYO? SOMEWHERE ELSE IN JAPAN?
HUH?
HUH?
BOSS! CALM DOWN!!
DID IT HAPPEN DURING COMIKET FOR YOU TOO???
B-BEG YOUR PARDON!
AHHH, WAIT!!!
WH-WHAT WAS WITH THAT GUY?
THE COLOR OF HIS EYES SUDDENLY CHANGED...
I COULDN'T EVEN UNDERSTAND A WORD OF WHAT HE WAS TRYING TO SAY.
I SUPPOSE I'LL HAVE TO RESORT TO DRASTIC MEASURES...

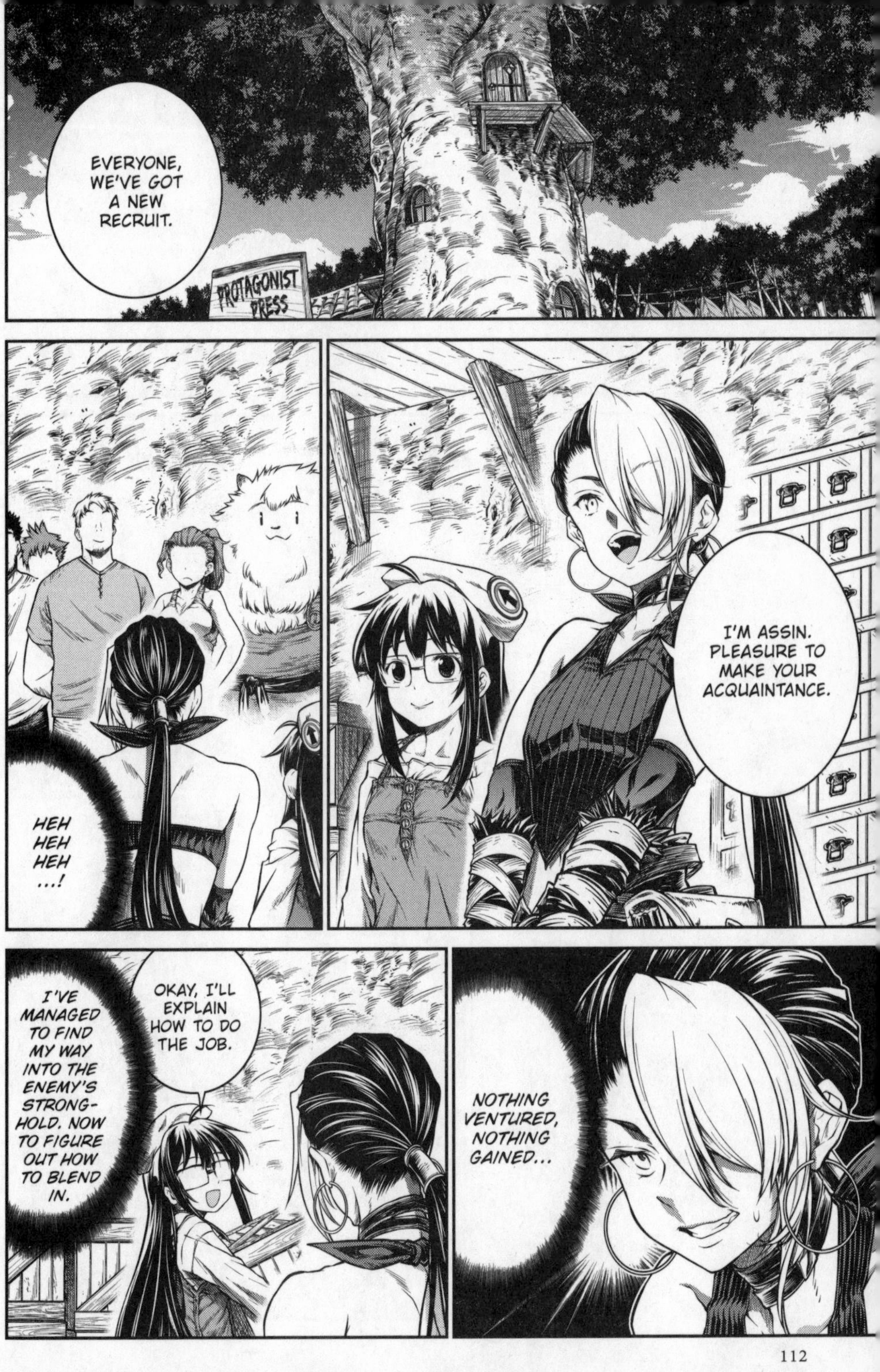
EVERYONE, WE'VE GOT A NEW RECRUIT.
PROTAGONIST PRESS
I'M ASSIN. PLEASURE TO MAKE YOUR ACQUAINTANCE.
HEH HEH HEH ...!
NOTHING VENTURED, NOTHING GAINED...
OKAY, I'LL EXPLAIN HOW TO DO THE JOB.
I'VE MANAGED TO FIND MY WAY INTO THE ENEMY'S STRONG-HOLD. NOW TO FIGURE OUT HOW TO BLEND IN.

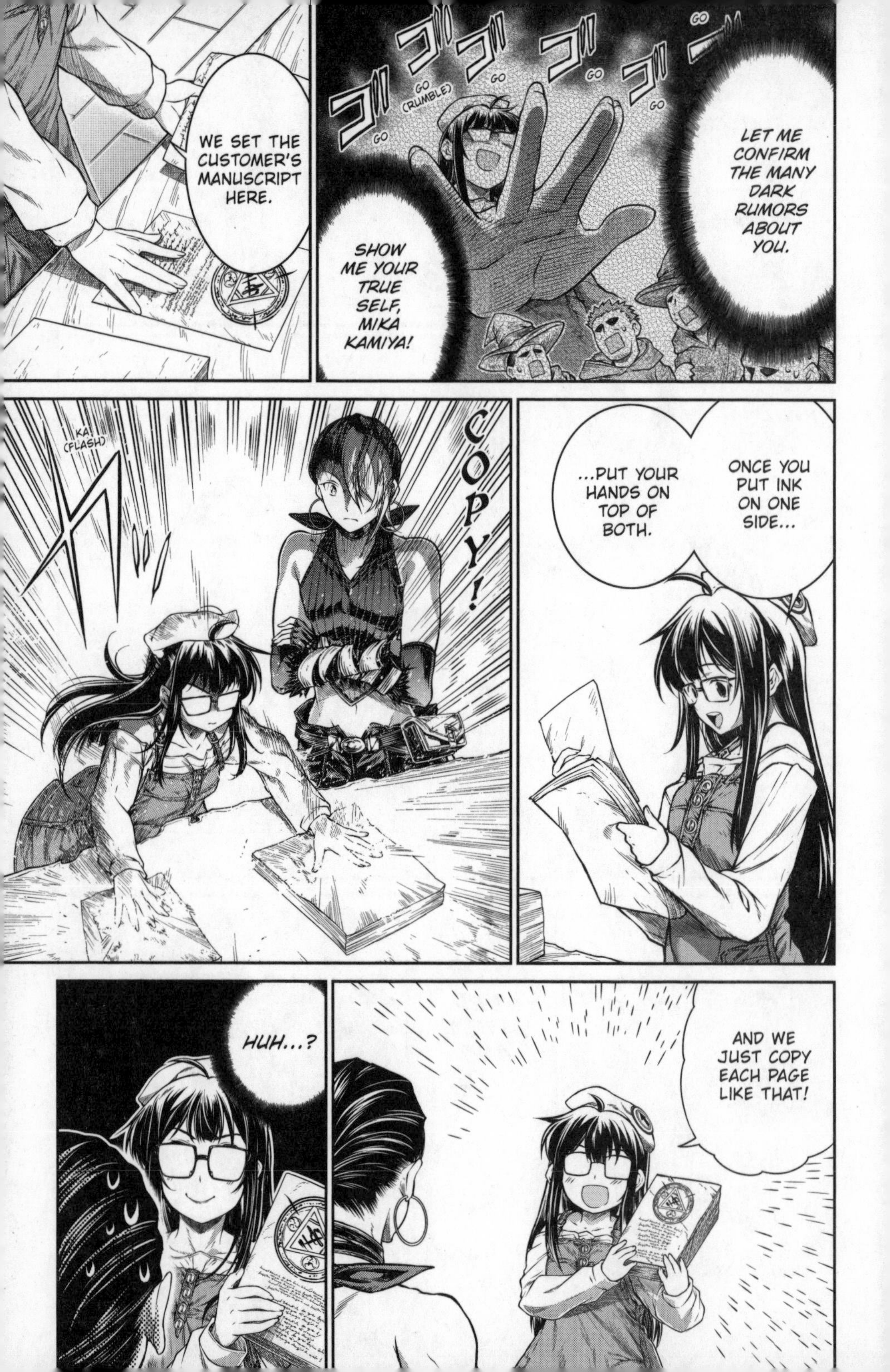
GO GO GO GO
GO (RUMBLE)
GO
LET ME CONFIRM THE MANY DARK RUMORS ABOUT YOU.
SHOW ME YOUR TRUE SELF, MIKA KAMIYA!
WE SET THE CUSTOMER'S MANUSCRIPT HERE.
ONCE YOU PUT INK ON ONE SIDE...
...PUT YOUR HANDS ON TOP OF BOTH.
COPY!
KA (FLASH)
AND WE JUST COPY EACH PAGE LIKE THAT!
HUH...?

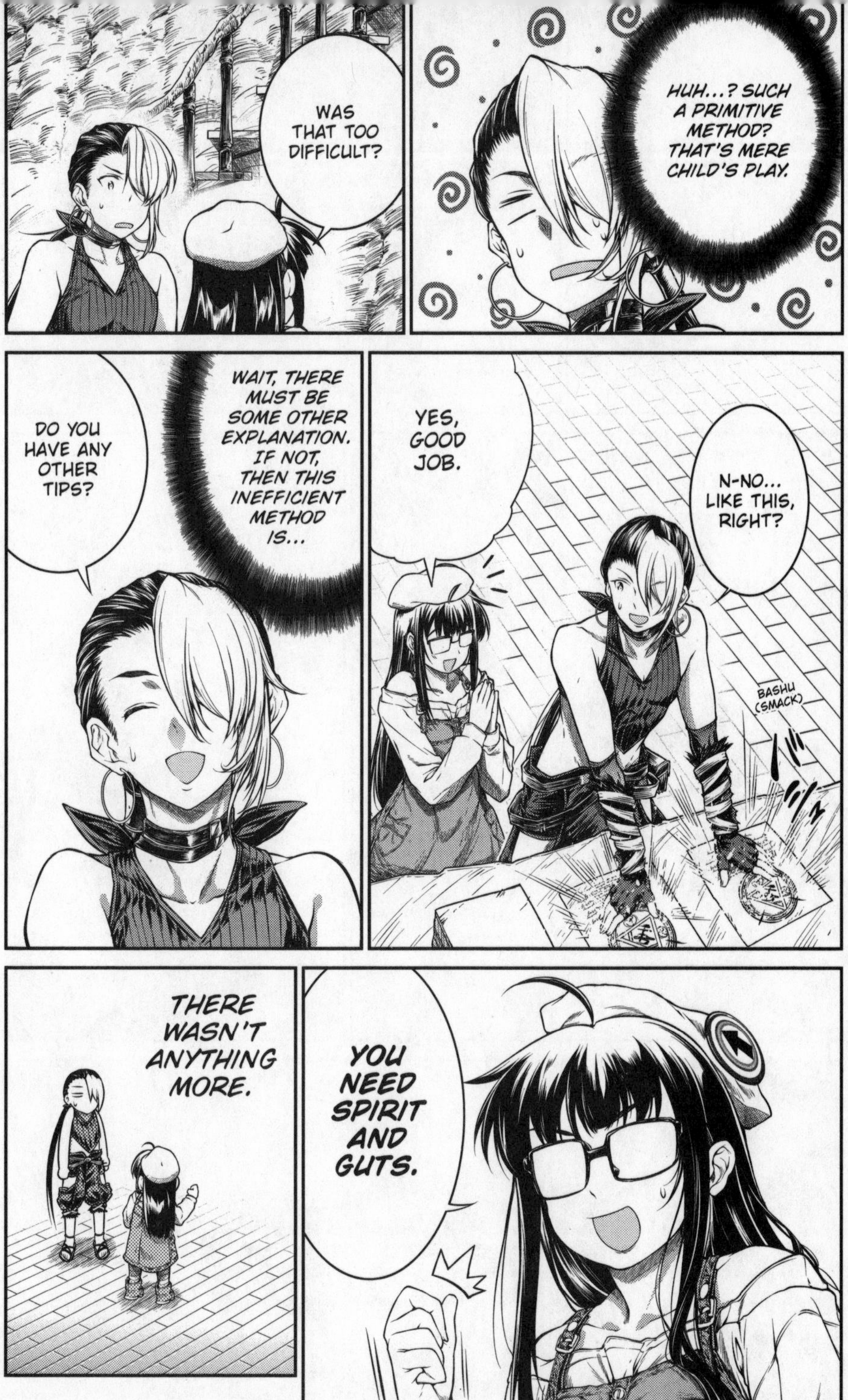
HUH...? SUCH A PRIMITIVE METHOD? THAT'S MERE CHILD'S PLAY.
WAS THAT TOO DIFFICULT?
N-NO... LIKE THIS, RIGHT?
BASHU (SMACK)
YES, GOOD JOB.
WAIT, THERE MUST BE SOME OTHER EXPLANATION. IF NOT, THEN THIS INEFFICIENT METHOD IS...
DO YOU HAVE ANY OTHER TIPS?
YOU NEED SPIRIT AND GUTS.
THERE WASN'T ANYTHING MORE.

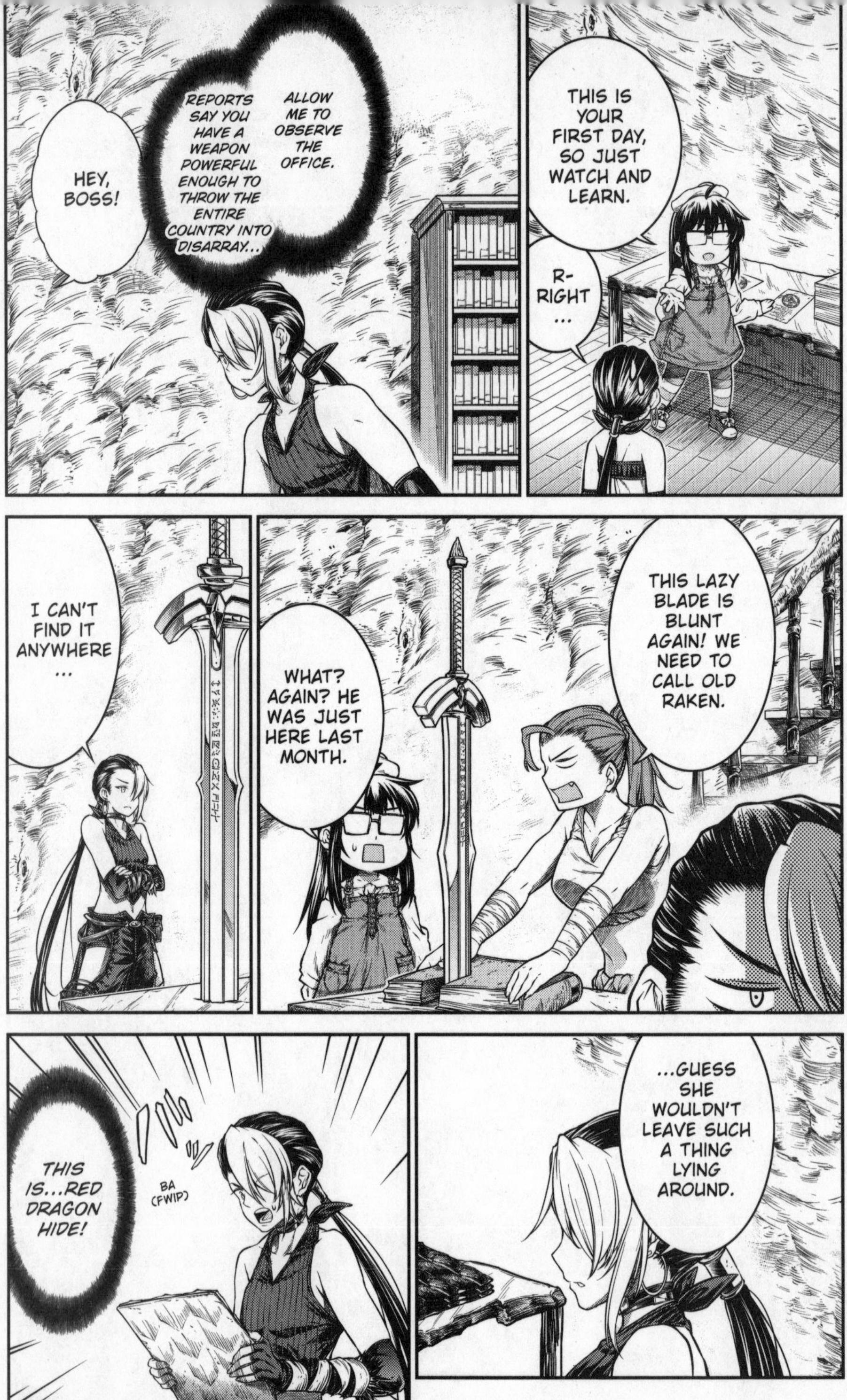
THIS IS YOUR FIRST DAY, SO JUST WATCH AND LEARN.
R-RIGHT...
ALLOW ME TO OBSERVE THE OFFICE.
REPORTS SAY YOU HAVE A WEAPON POWERFUL ENOUGH TO THROW THE ENTIRE COUNTRY INTO DISARRAY...
HEY, BOSS!
THIS LAZY BLADE IS BLUNT AGAIN! WE NEED TO CALL OLD RAKEN.
WHAT? AGAIN? HE WAS JUST HERE LAST MONTH.
I CAN'T FIND IT ANYWHERE...
...GUESS SHE WOULDN'T LEAVE SUCH A THING LYING AROUND.
THIS IS...RED DRAGON HIDE!
BA (FWIP)

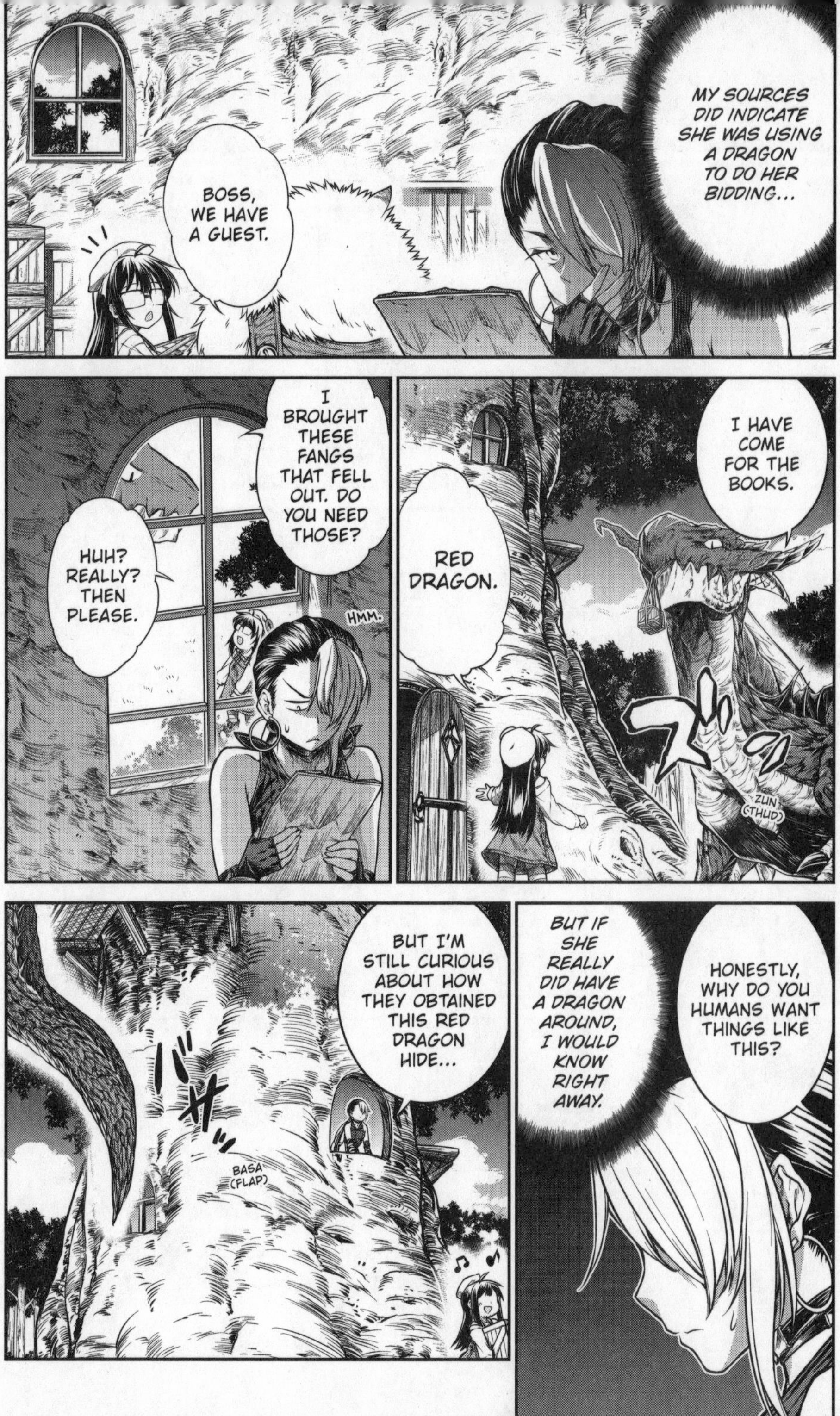
MY SOURCES DID INDICATE SHE WAS USING A DRAGON TO DO HER BIDDING...
BOSS, WE HAVE A GUEST.
I HAVE COME FOR THE BOOKS.
RED DRAGON.
ZUN (THUD)
I BROUGHT THESE FANGS THAT FELL OUT. DO YOU NEED THOSE?
HUH? REALLY? THEN PLEASE.
HMM.
HONESTLY, WHY DO YOU HUMANS WANT THINGS LIKE THIS?
BUT IF SHE REALLY DID HAVE A DRAGON AROUND, I WOULD KNOW RIGHT AWAY.
BUT I'M STILL CURIOUS ABOUT HOW THEY OBTAINED THIS RED DRAGON HIDE...
BASA (FLAP)

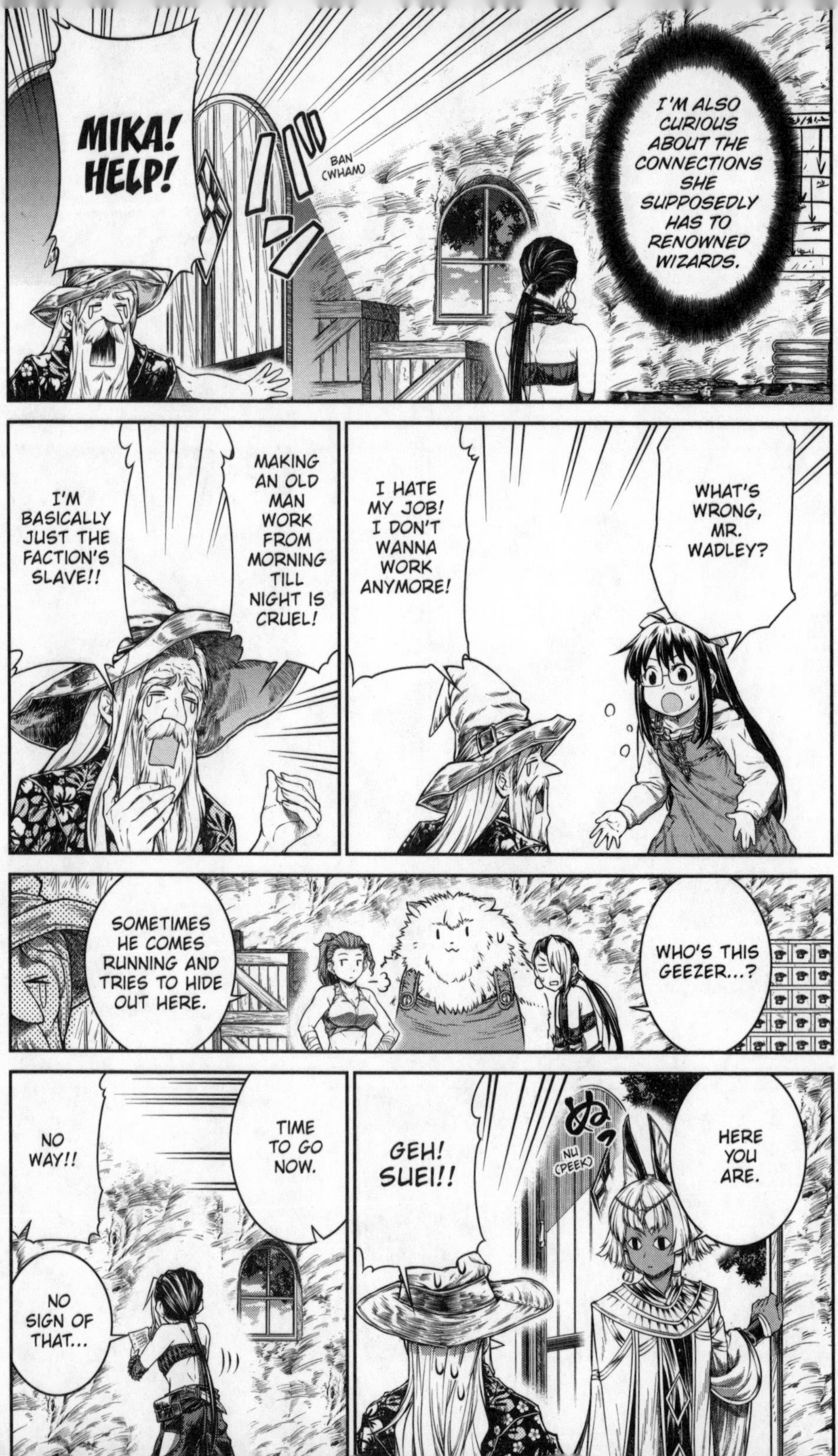
I'M ALSO CURIOUS ABOUT THE CONNECTIONS SHE SUPPOSEDLY HAS TO RENOWNED WIZARDS.
BAN (WHAM)
MIKA! HELP!
WHAT'S WRONG, MR. WADLEY?
I HATE MY JOB! I DON'T WANNA WORK ANYMORE!
MAKING AN OLD MAN WORK FROM MORNING TILL NIGHT IS CRUEL!
I'M BASICALLY JUST THE FACTION'S SLAVE!!
WHO'S THIS GEEZER...?
SOMETIMES HE COMES RUNNING AND TRIES TO HIDE OUT HERE.
HERE YOU ARE.
ぬっ
NU (PEEK)
GEH! SUEI!!
TIME TO GO NOW.
NO WAY!!
NO SIGN OF THAT...

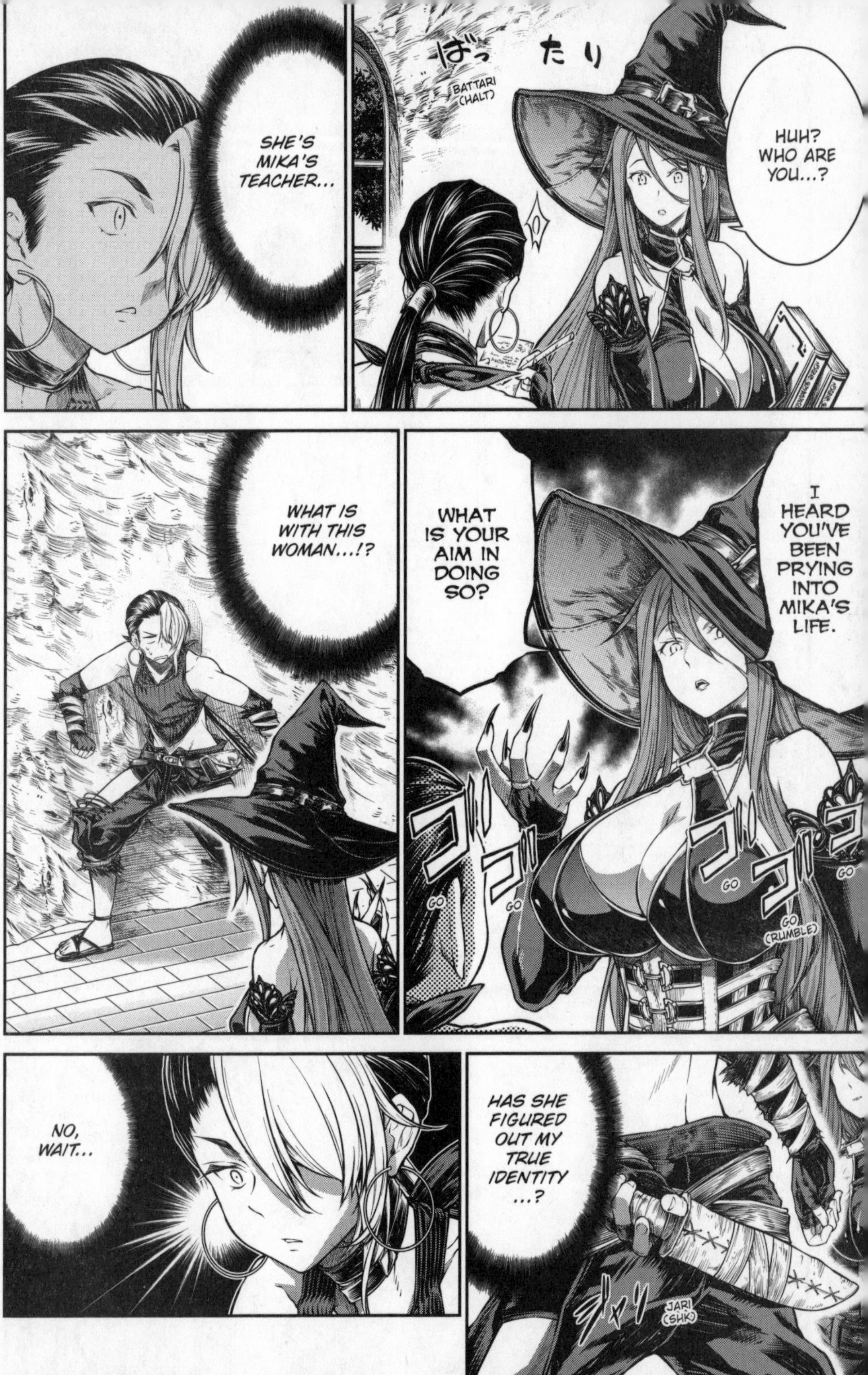

ばったり
BATTARI (HALT)
HUH? WHO ARE YOU...?
SHE'S MIKA'S TEACHER...
I HEARD YOU'VE BEEN PRYING INTO MIKA'S LIFE.
WHAT IS YOUR AIM IN DOING SO?
ゴゴゴ
GO GO GO GO GO (RUMBLE)
WHAT IS WITH THIS WOMAN...!?
HAS SHE FIGURED OUT MY TRUE IDENTITY...?
ジャリ
JARI (SHK)
NO, WAIT...

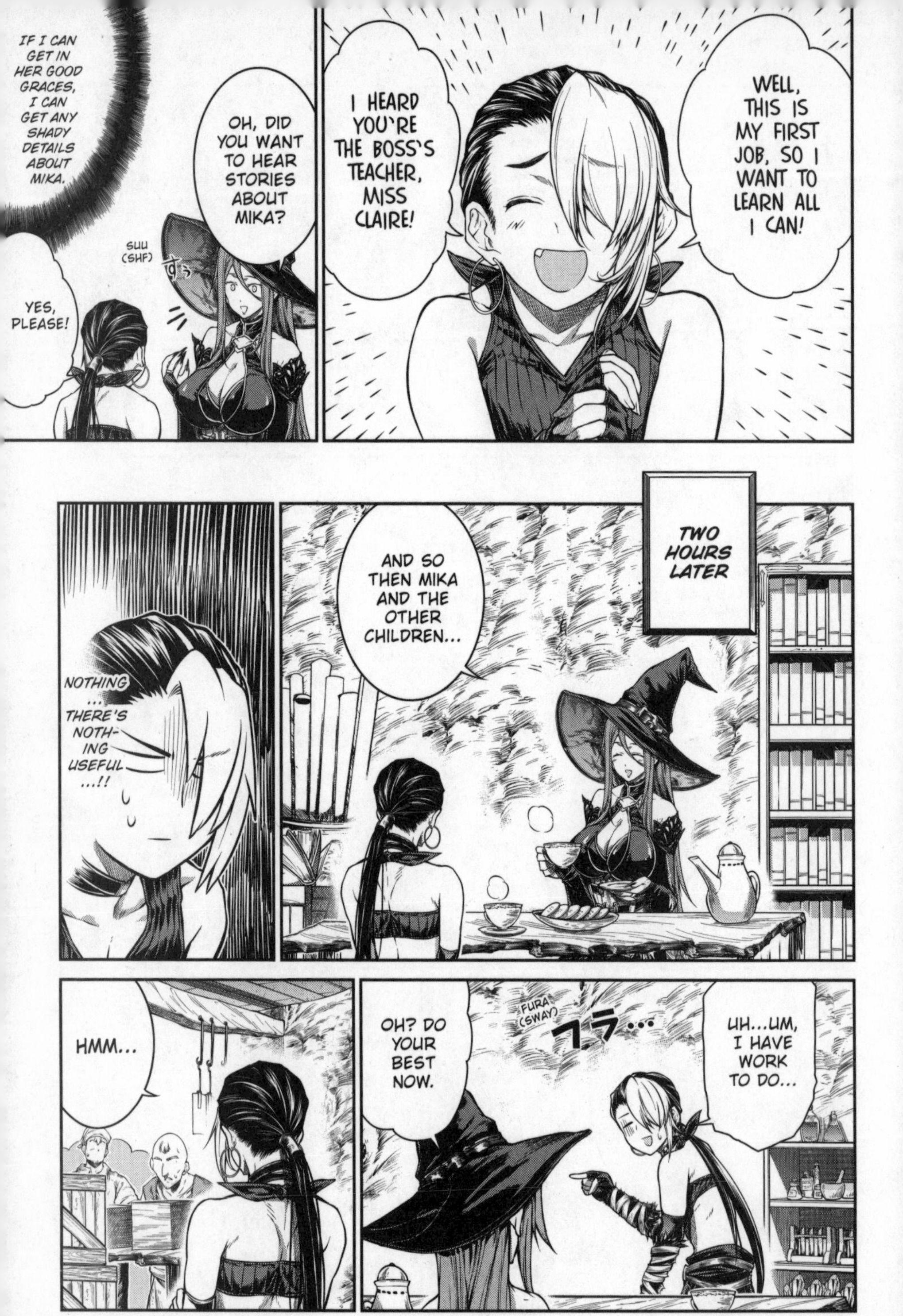

WELL, THIS IS MY FIRST JOB, SO I WANT TO LEARN ALL I CAN!
I HEARD YOU`RE THE BOSS`S TEACHER, MISS CLAIRE!
OH, DID YOU WANT TO HEAR STORIES ABOUT MIKA?
SUU (SHF)
すっ
YES, PLEASE!
IF I CAN GET IN HER GOOD GRACES, I CAN GET ANY SHADY DETAILS ABOUT MIKA.
TWO HOURS LATER
AND SO THEN MIKA AND THE OTHER CHILDREN...
NOTHING ... THERE'S NOTHING USEFUL ...!!
UH...UM, I HAVE WORK TO DO...
FURA (SWAY)
フラ…
OH? DO YOUR BEST NOW.
HMM...

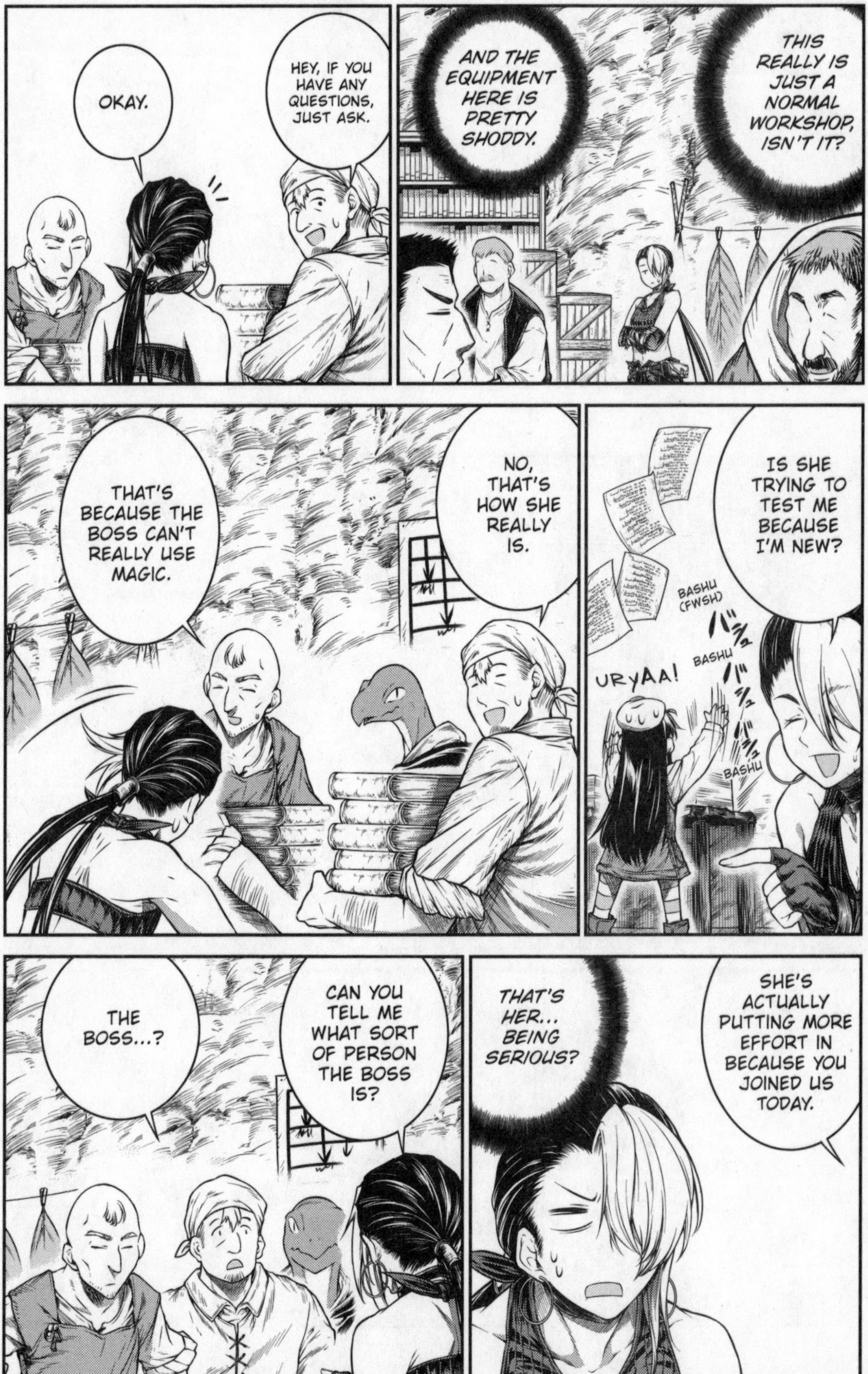
THIS REALLY IS JUST A NORMAL WORKSHOP, ISN'T IT?
AND THE EQUIPMENT HERE IS PRETTY SHODDY.
HEY, IF YOU HAVE ANY QUESTIONS, JUST ASK.
OKAY.
IS SHE TRYING TO TEST ME BECAUSE I'M NEW?
BASHU (FWSH)
バシュ
BASHU
バシュ
バシュ
BASHU
URYAA!
NO, THAT'S HOW SHE REALLY IS.
THAT'S BECAUSE THE BOSS CAN'T REALLY USE MAGIC.
SHE'S ACTUALLY PUTTING MORE EFFORT IN BECAUSE YOU JOINED US TODAY.
THAT'S HER... BEING SERIOUS?
CAN YOU TELL ME WHAT SORT OF PERSON THE BOSS IS?
THE BOSS...?

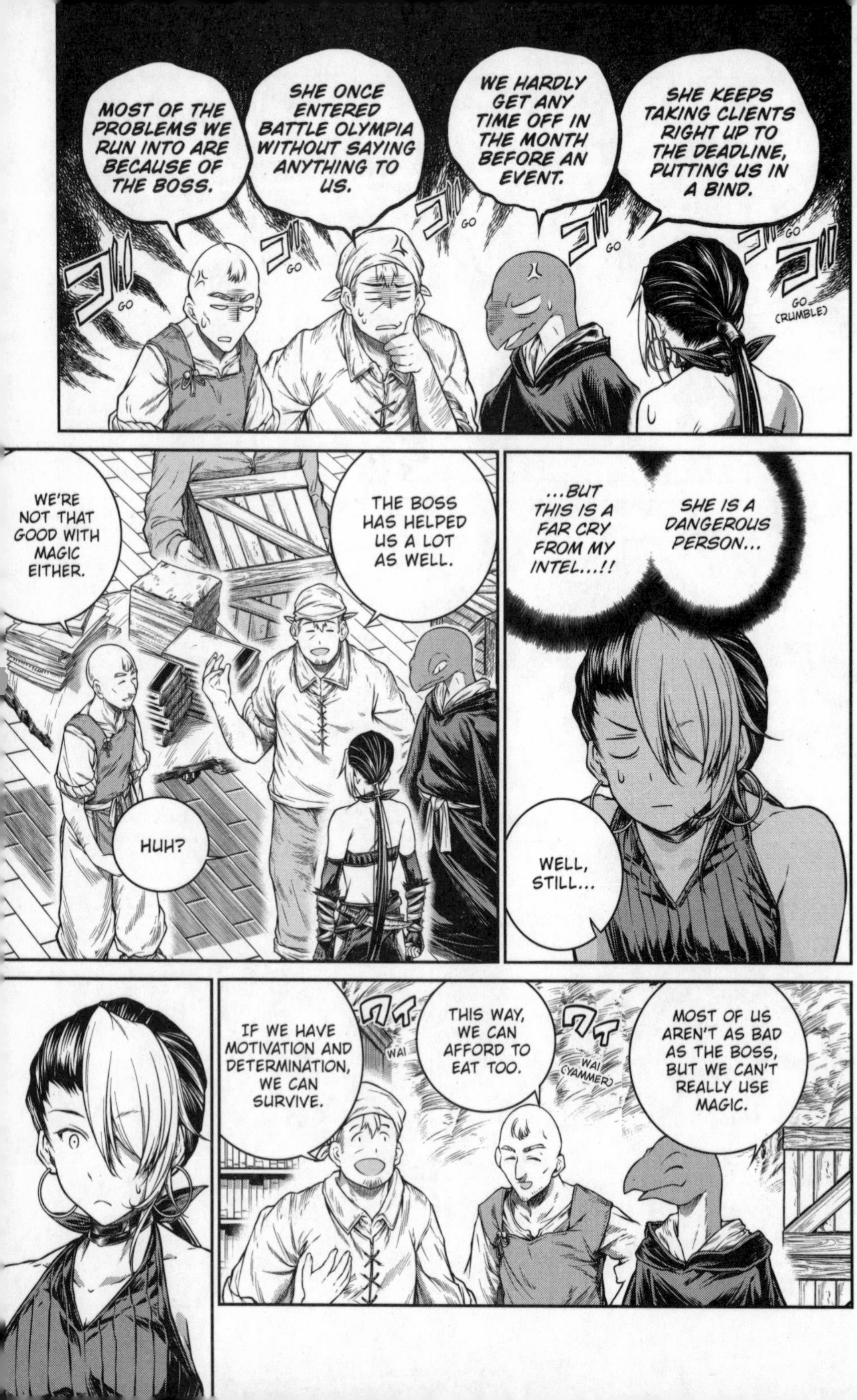
SHE KEEPS TAKING CLIENTS RIGHT UP TO THE DEADLINE, PUTTING US IN A BIND.
WE HARDLY GET ANY TIME OFF IN THE MONTH BEFORE AN EVENT.
SHE ONCE ENTERED BATTLE OLYMPIA WITHOUT SAYING ANYTHING TO US.
MOST OF THE PROBLEMS WE RUN INTO ARE BECAUSE OF THE BOSS.
GO GO GO GO GO (RUMBLE)
SHE IS A DANGEROUS PERSON...
...BUT THIS IS A FAR CRY FROM MY INTEL...!!
WELL, STILL...
THE BOSS HAS HELPED US A LOT AS WELL.
WE'RE NOT THAT GOOD WITH MAGIC EITHER.
HUH?
MOST OF US AREN'T AS BAD AS THE BOSS, BUT WE CAN'T REALLY USE MAGIC.
WAI (YAMMER)
THIS WAY, WE CAN AFFORD TO EAT TOO.
WAI
IF WE HAVE MOTIVATION AND DETERMINATION, WE CAN SURVIVE.

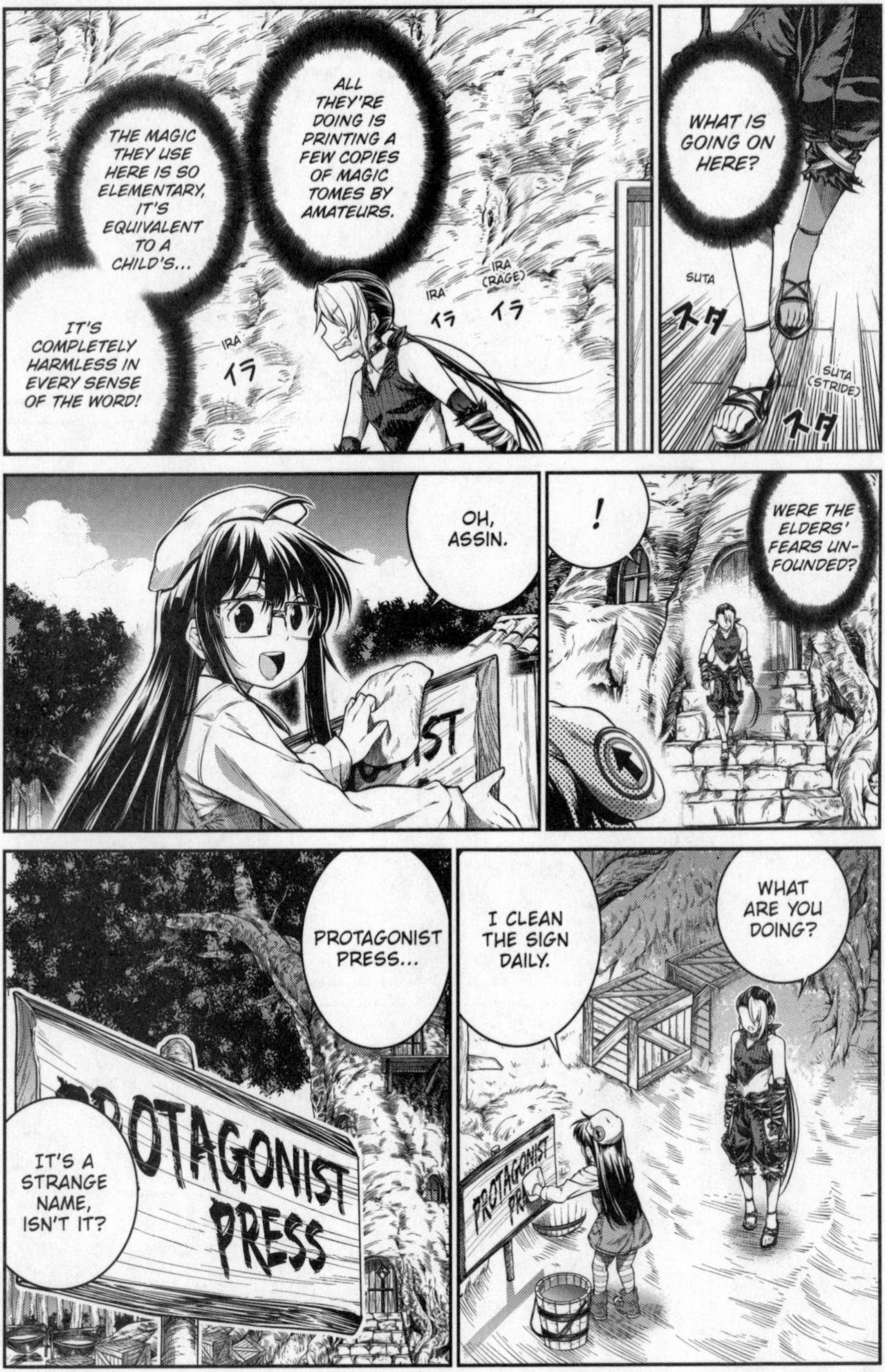
WHAT IS GOING ON HERE?
SUTA
スタ
SUTA (STRIDE)
スタ
ALL THEY'RE DOING IS PRINTING A FEW COPIES OF MAGIC TOMES BY AMATEURS.
THE MAGIC THEY USE HERE IS SO ELEMENTARY, IT'S EQUIVALENT TO A CHILD'S...
IRA (RAGE)
イラ
IRA
イラ
IRA
イラ
IT'S COMPLETELY HARMLESS IN EVERY SENSE OF THE WORD!
WERE THE ELDERS' FEARS UN-FOUNDED?
!
OH, ASSIN.
WHAT ARE YOU DOING?
I CLEAN THE SIGN DAILY.
PROTAGONIST PR
PROTAGONIST PRESS...
PROTAGONIST PRESS
IT'S A STRANGE NAME, ISN'T IT?

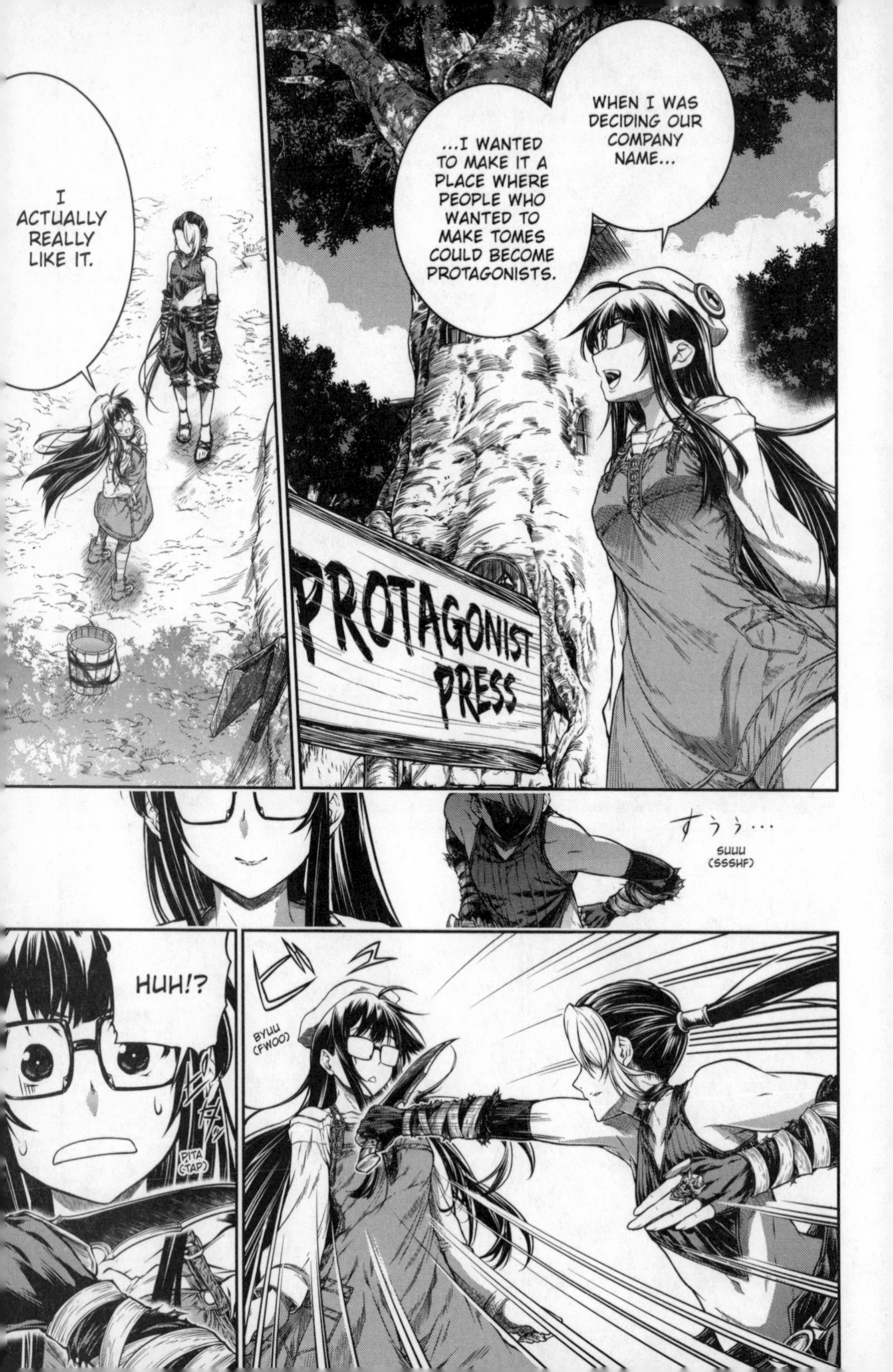
WHEN I WAS DECIDING OUR COMPANY NAME...
...I WANTED TO MAKE IT A PLACE WHERE PEOPLE WHO WANTED TO MAKE TOMES COULD BECOME PROTAGONISTS.
PROTAGONIST PRESS
I ACTUALLY REALLY LIKE IT.
すぅぅ…
SUUU (SSSHF)
BYUU (FWOO)
HUH!?
PITA (TAP)

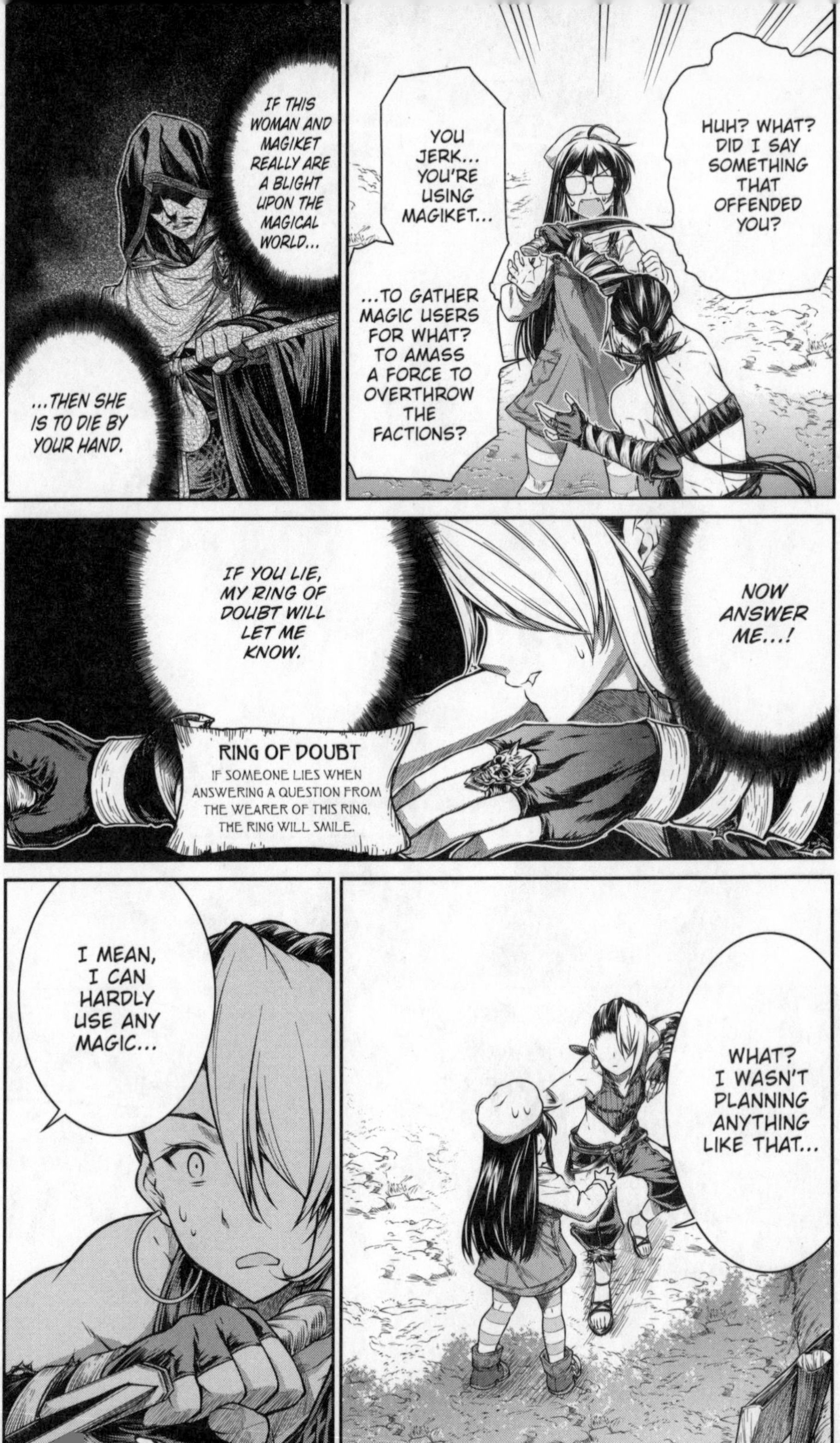
HUH? WHAT? DID I SAY SOMETHING THAT OFFENDED YOU?
YOU JERK... YOU'RE USING MAGIKET...
...TO GATHER MAGIC USERS FOR WHAT? TO AMASS A FORCE TO OVERTHROW THE FACTIONS?
IF THIS WOMAN AND MAGIKET REALLY ARE A BLIGHT UPON THE MAGICAL WORLD...
...THEN SHE IS TO DIE BY YOUR HAND.
NOW ANSWER ME...!
IF YOU LIE, MY RING OF DOUBT WILL LET ME KNOW.
RING OF DOUBT
IF SOMEONE LIES WHEN ANSWERING A QUESTION FROM THE WEARER OF THIS RING, THE RING WILL SMILE.
WHAT? I WASN'T PLANNING ANYTHING LIKE THAT...
I MEAN, I CAN HARDLY USE ANY MAGIC...

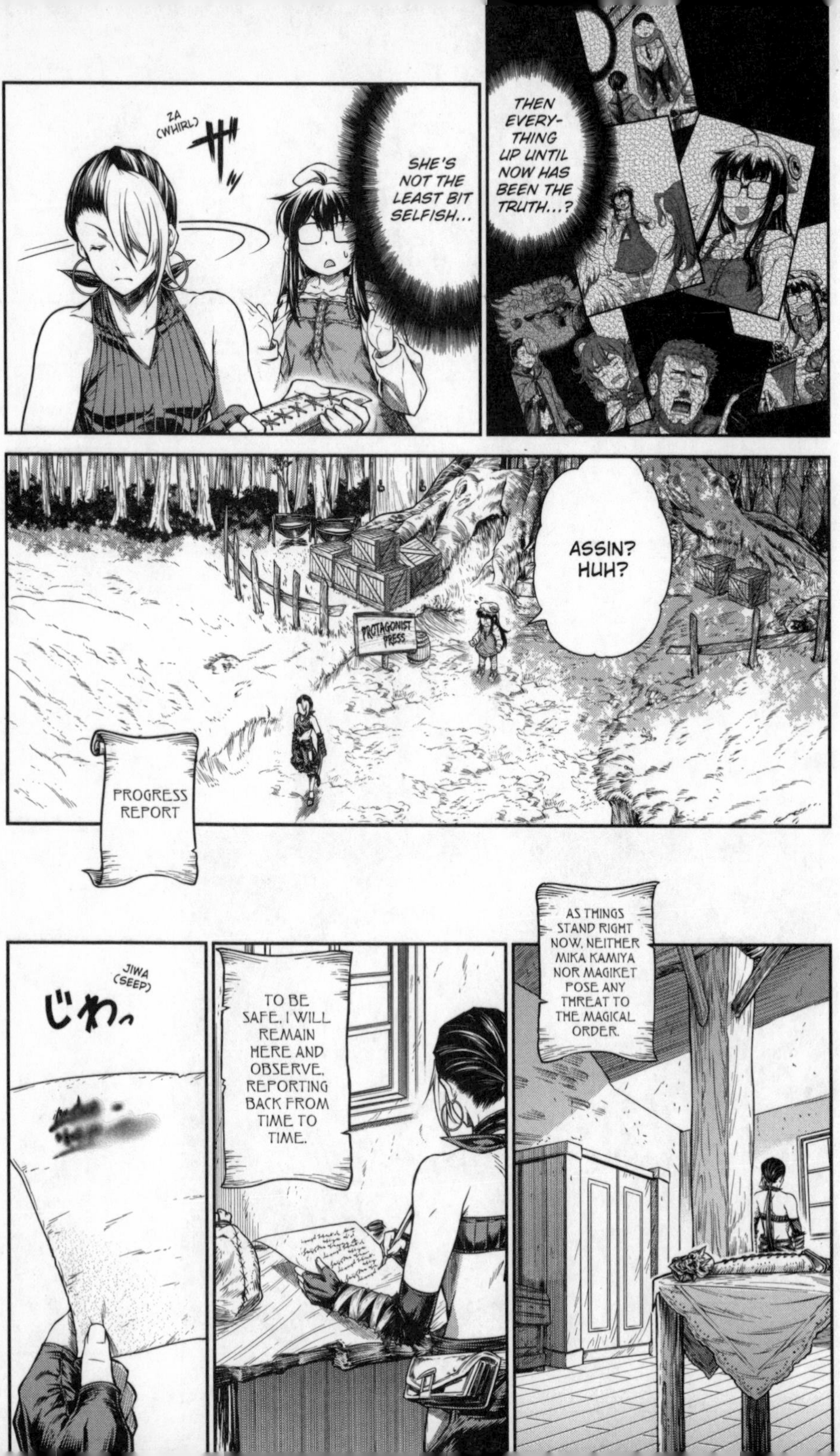

THEN EVERYTHING UP UNTIL NOW HAS BEEN THE TRUTH...?
SHE'S NOT THE LEAST BIT SELFISH...
ZA (WHIRL)
ASSIN? HUH?
PROTAGONIST PRESS
PROGRESS REPORT
AS THINGS STAND RIGHT NOW, NEITHER MIKA KAMIYA NOR MAGIKET POSE ANY THREAT TO THE MAGICAL ORDER.
TO BE SAFE, I WILL REMAIN HERE AND OBSERVE, REPORTING BACK FROM TIME TO TIME.
JIWA (SEEP)
じわっ

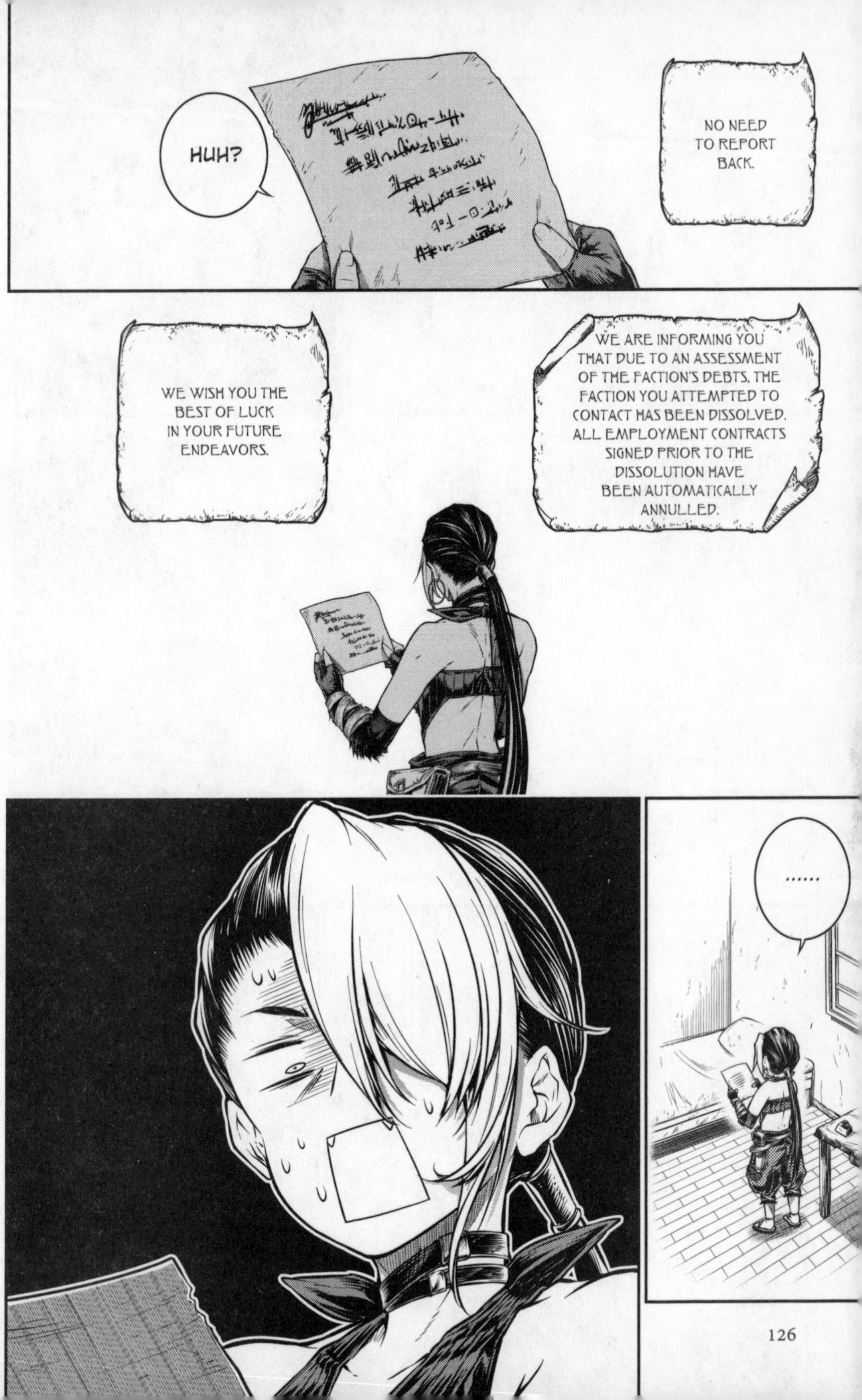
NO NEED TO REPORT BACK.
HUH?
WE ARE INFORMING YOU THAT DUE TO AN ASSESSMENT OF THE FACTION'S DEBTS, THE FACTION YOU ATTEMPTED TO CONTACT HAS BEEN DISSOLVED. ALL EMPLOYMENT CONTRACTS SIGNED PRIOR TO THE DISSOLUTION HAVE BEEN AUTOMATICALLY ANNULLED.
WE WISH YOU THE BEST OF LUCK IN YOUR FUTURE ENDEAVORS.
......

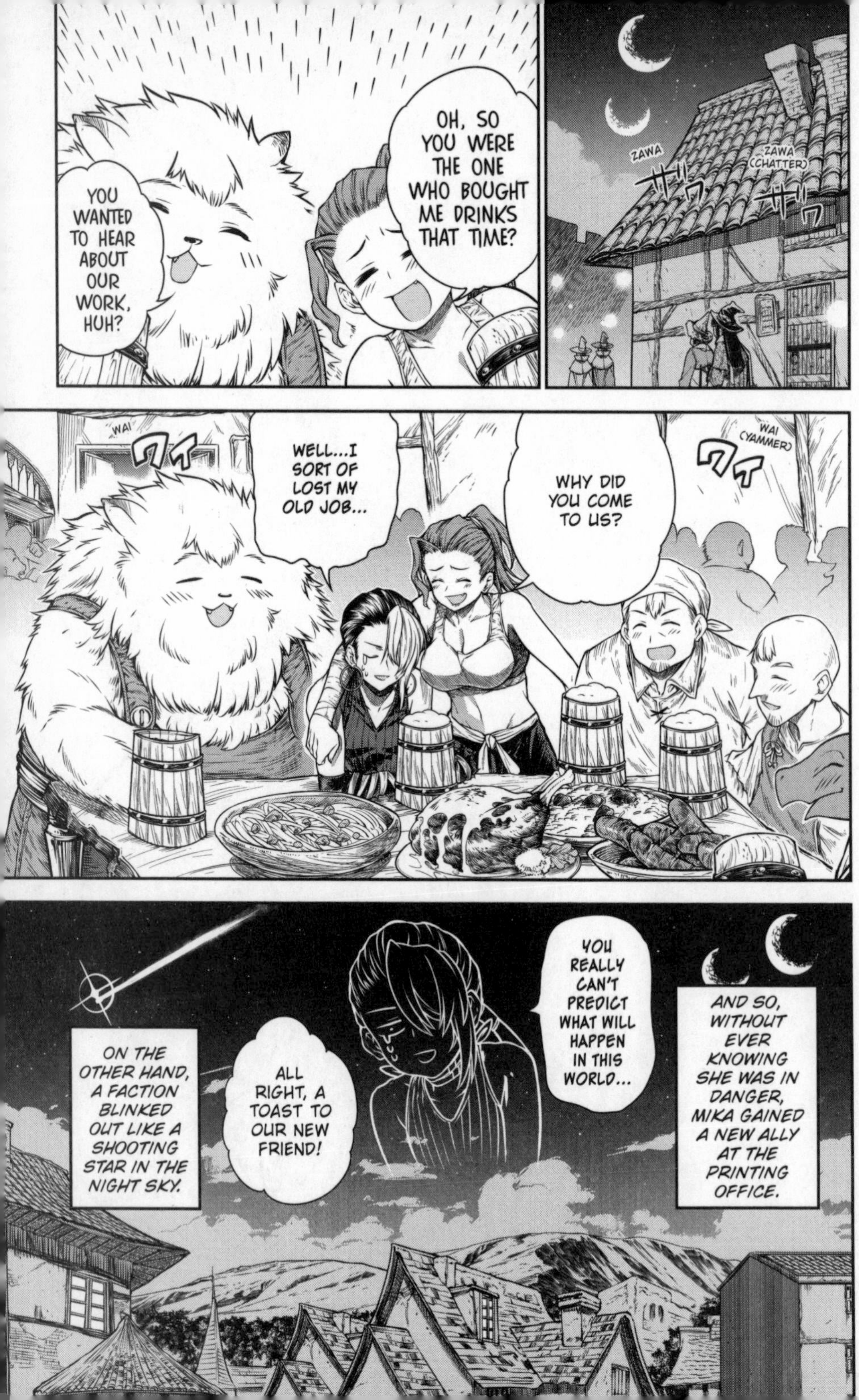
ZAWA (CHATTER)
ZAWA
OH, SO YOU WERE THE ONE WHO BOUGHT ME DRINKS THAT TIME?
YOU WANTED TO HEAR ABOUT OUR WORK, HUH?
WAI (YAMMER)
WHY DID YOU COME TO US?
WELL...I SORT OF LOST MY OLD JOB...
WAI
AND SO, WITHOUT EVER KNOWING SHE WAS IN DANGER, MIKA GAINED A NEW ALLY AT THE PRINTING OFFICE.
YOU REALLY CAN'T PREDICT WHAT WILL HAPPEN IN THIS WORLD...
ALL RIGHT, A TOAST TO OUR NEW FRIEND!
ON THE OTHER HAND, A FACTION BLINKED OUT LIKE A SHOOTING STAR IN THE NIGHT SKY.

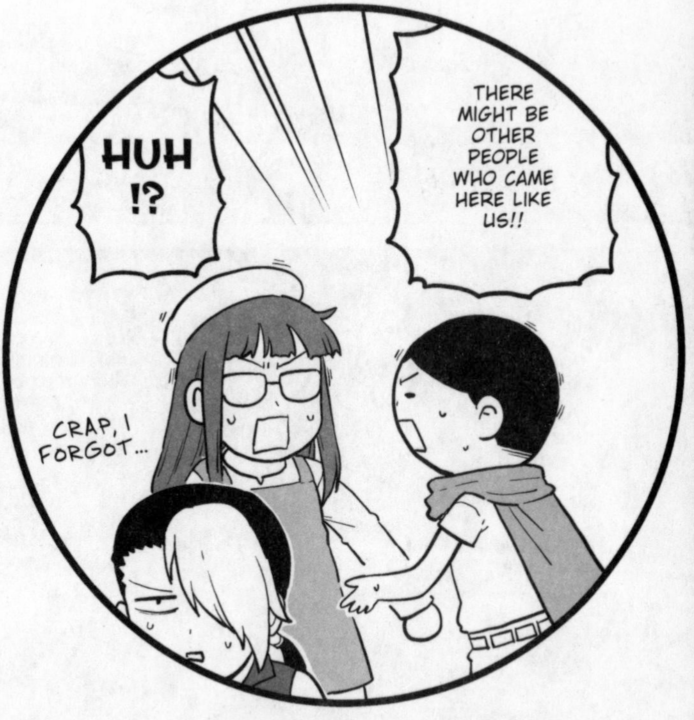
THERE MIGHT BE OTHER PEOPLE WHO CAME HERE LIKE US!!
HUH !?
CRAP, I FORGOT...

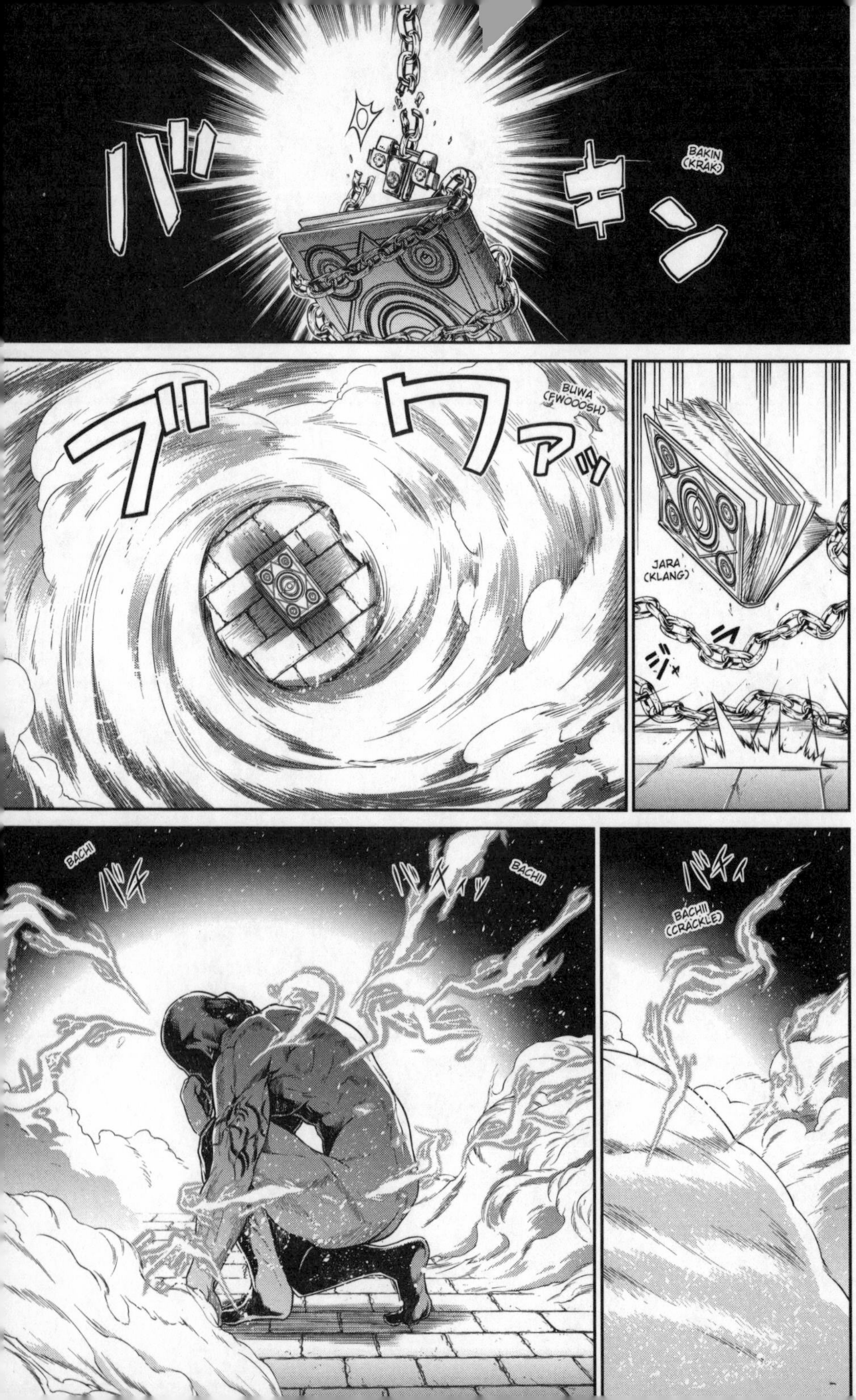
バキン
BAKIN (KRAK)
ジャ
JARA (KLANG)
ブワァッ
BUWA (FWOOOSH)
バチィ
BACHII (CRACKLE)
バチィッ
BACHII
バチ
BACHI

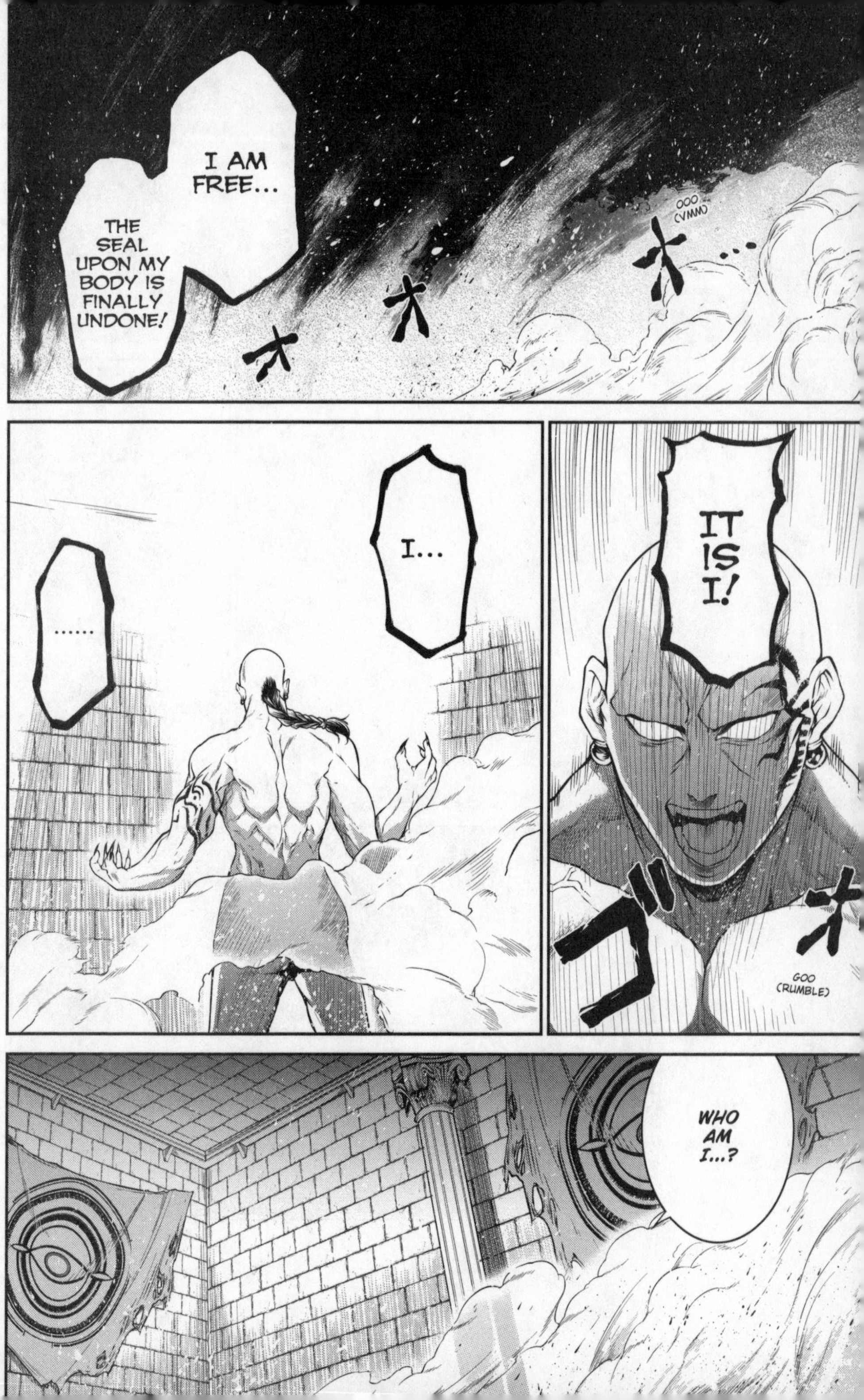
I AM FREE...
THE SEAL UPON MY BODY IS FINALLY UNDONE!
OOO (VMMM)
IT IS I!
GOO (RUMBLE)
I...
......
WHO AM I...?

Chapter 31

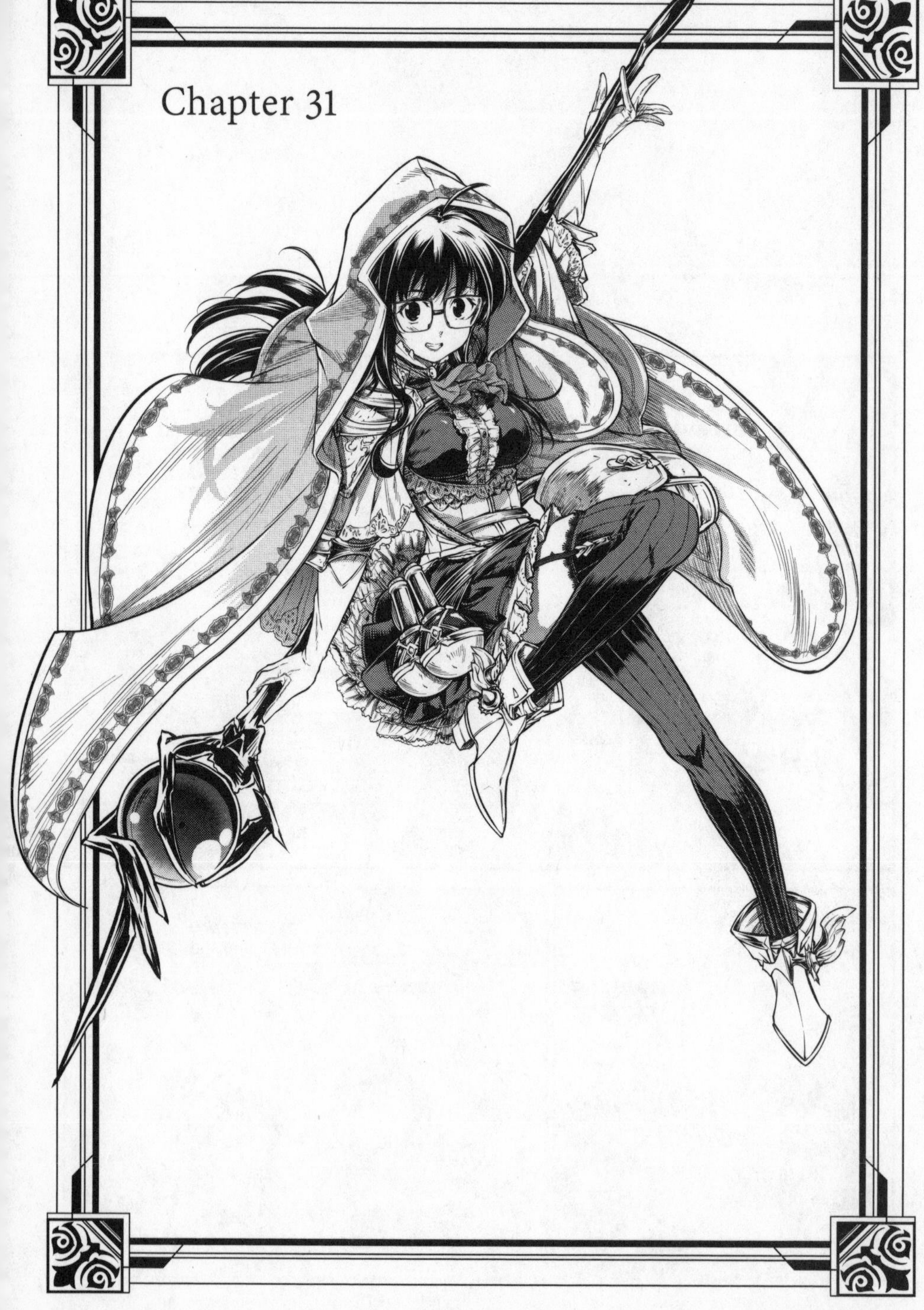

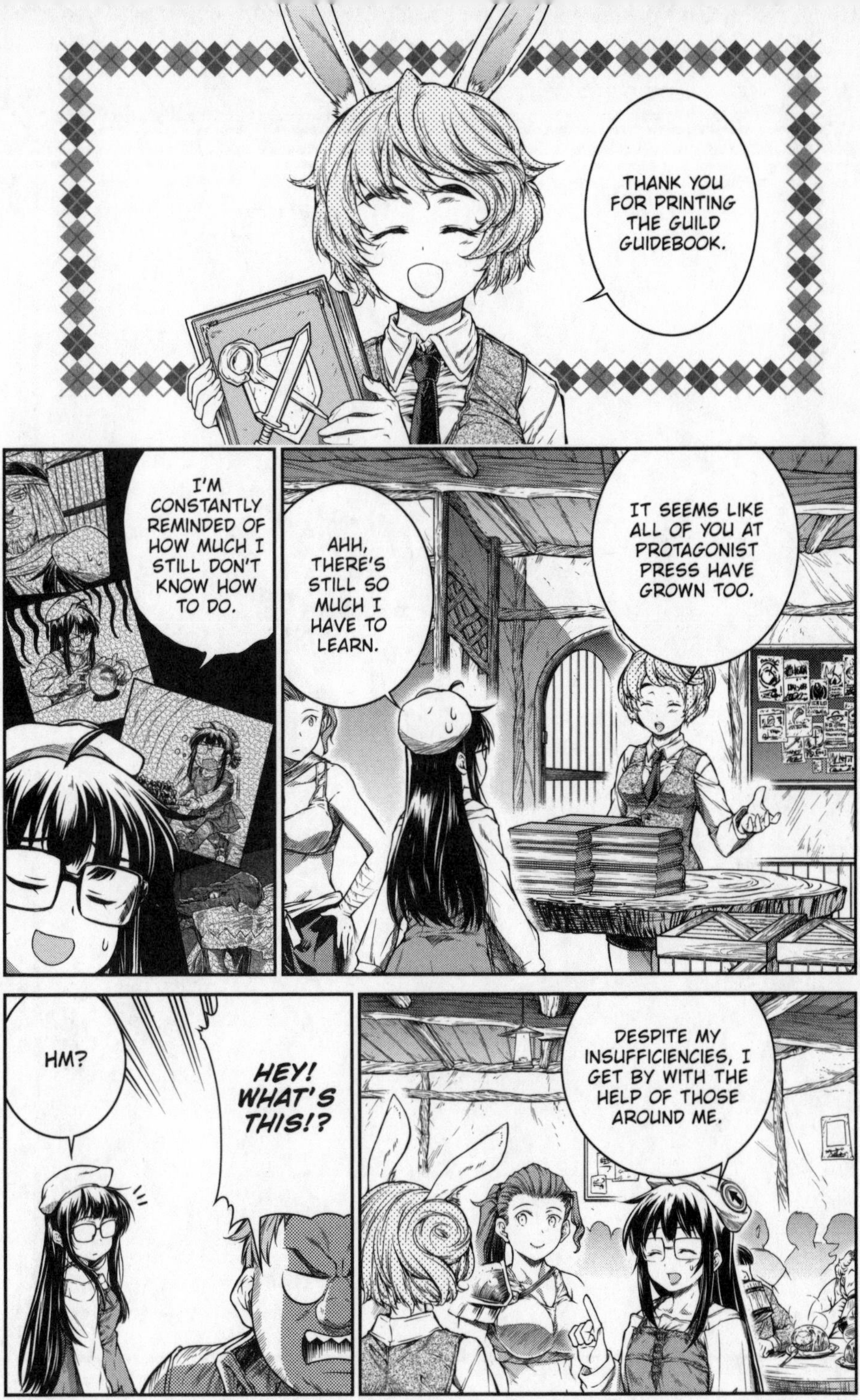
THANK YOU FOR PRINTING THE GUILD GUIDEBOOK.
IT SEEMS LIKE ALL OF YOU AT PROTAGONIST PRESS HAVE GROWN TOO.
AHH, THERE'S STILL SO MUCH I HAVE TO LEARN.
I'M CONSTANTLY REMINDED OF HOW MUCH I STILL DON'T KNOW HOW TO DO.
DESPITE MY INSUFFICIENCIES, I GET BY WITH THE HELP OF THOSE AROUND ME.
HEY! WHAT'S THIS!?
HM?

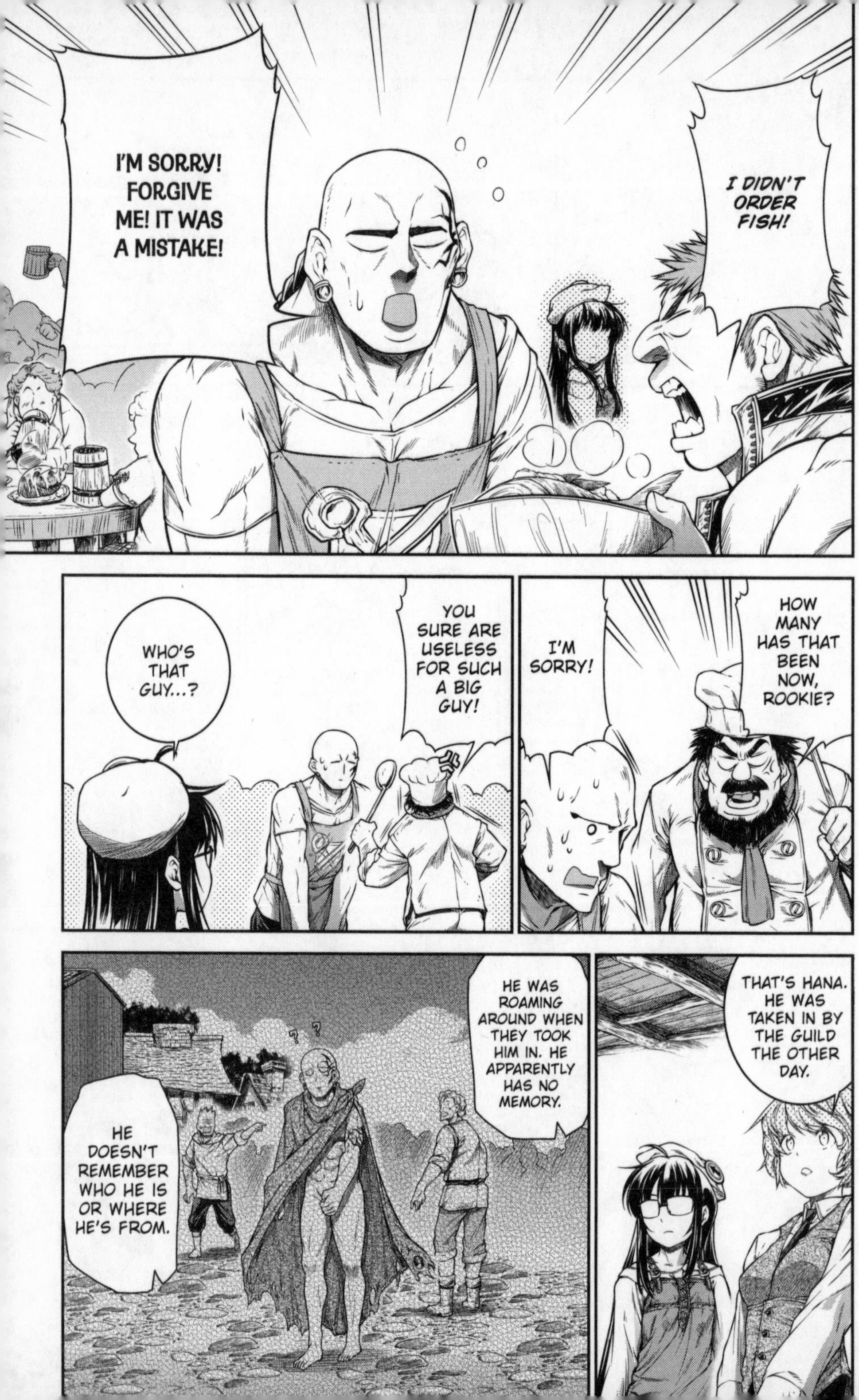
I DIDN'T ORDER FISH!
I'M SORRY! FORGIVE ME! IT WAS A MISTAKE!
HOW MANY HAS THAT BEEN NOW, ROOKIE?
I'M SORRY!
YOU SURE ARE USELESS FOR SUCH A BIG GUY!
WHO'S THAT GUY...?
THAT'S HANA. HE WAS TAKEN IN BY THE GUILD THE OTHER DAY.
HE WAS ROAMING AROUND WHEN THEY TOOK HIM IN. HE APPARENTLY HAS NO MEMORY.
HE DOESN'T REMEMBER WHO HE IS OR WHERE HE'S FROM.

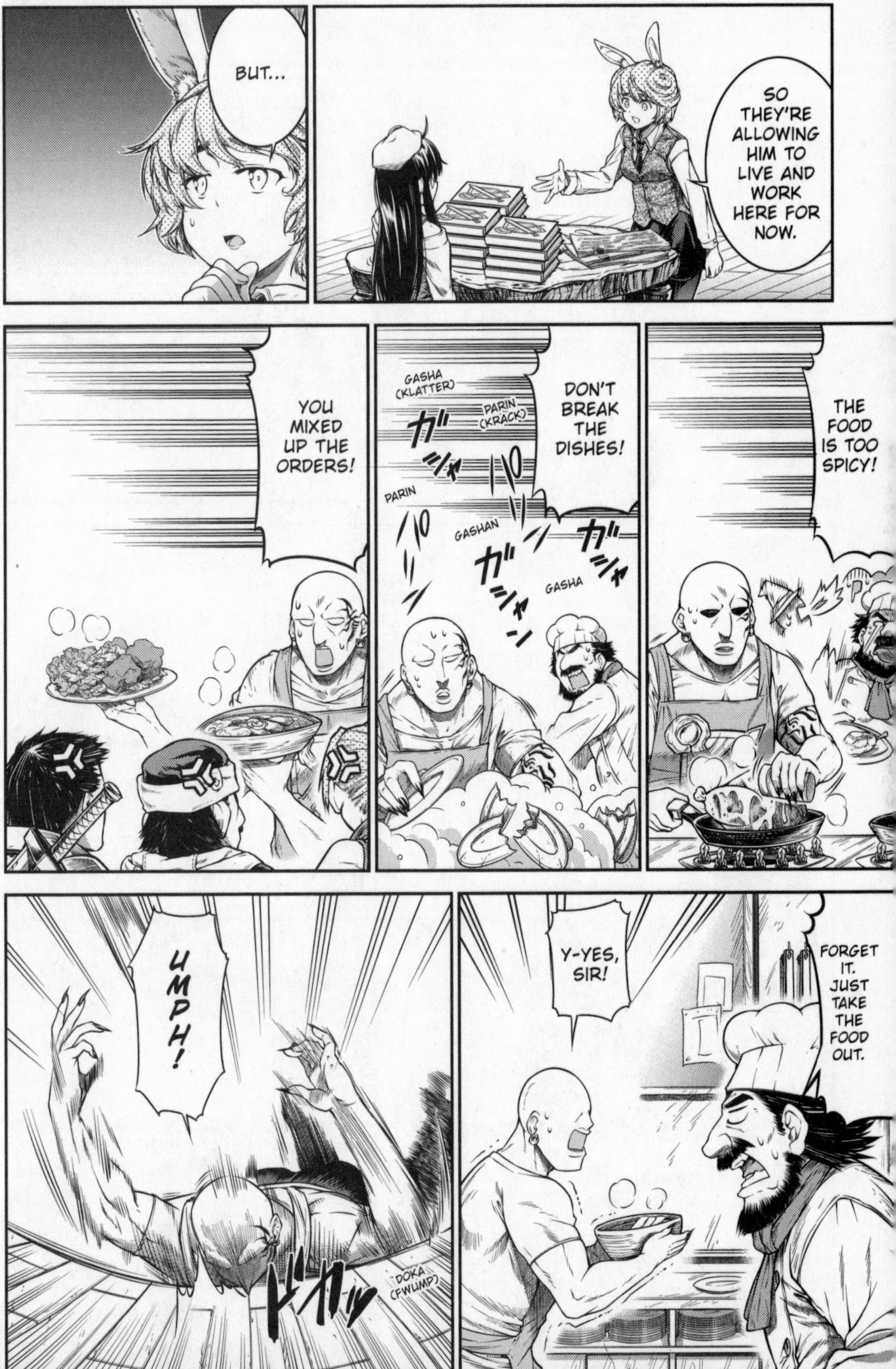
SO THEY'RE ALLOWING HIM TO LIVE AND WORK HERE FOR NOW.
BUT...
THE FOOD IS TOO SPICY!
DON'T BREAK THE DISHES!
GASHA (KLATTER)
PARIN (KRACK)
PARIN
GASHAN
GASHA
YOU MIXED UP THE ORDERS!
FORGET IT. JUST TAKE THE FOOD OUT.
Y-YES, SIR!
UMPH!
DOKA (FWUMP)

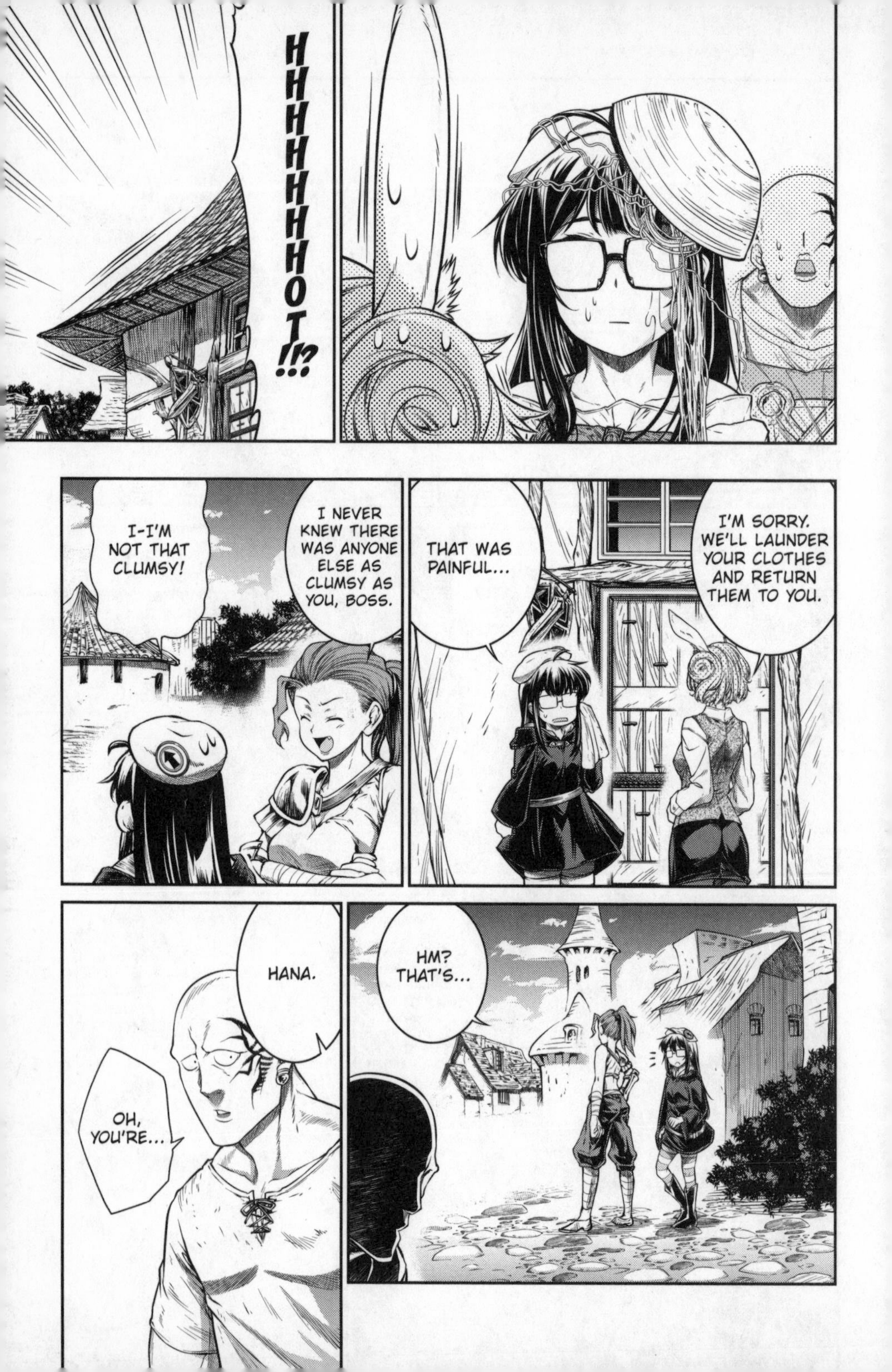
HHHHHHHOT!!?
I'M SORRY. WE'LL LAUNDER YOUR CLOTHES AND RETURN THEM TO YOU.
THAT WAS PAINFUL...
I NEVER KNEW THERE WAS ANYONE ELSE AS CLUMSY AS YOU, BOSS.
I-I'M NOT THAT CLUMSY!
HM? THAT'S...
HANA.
OH, YOU'RE...

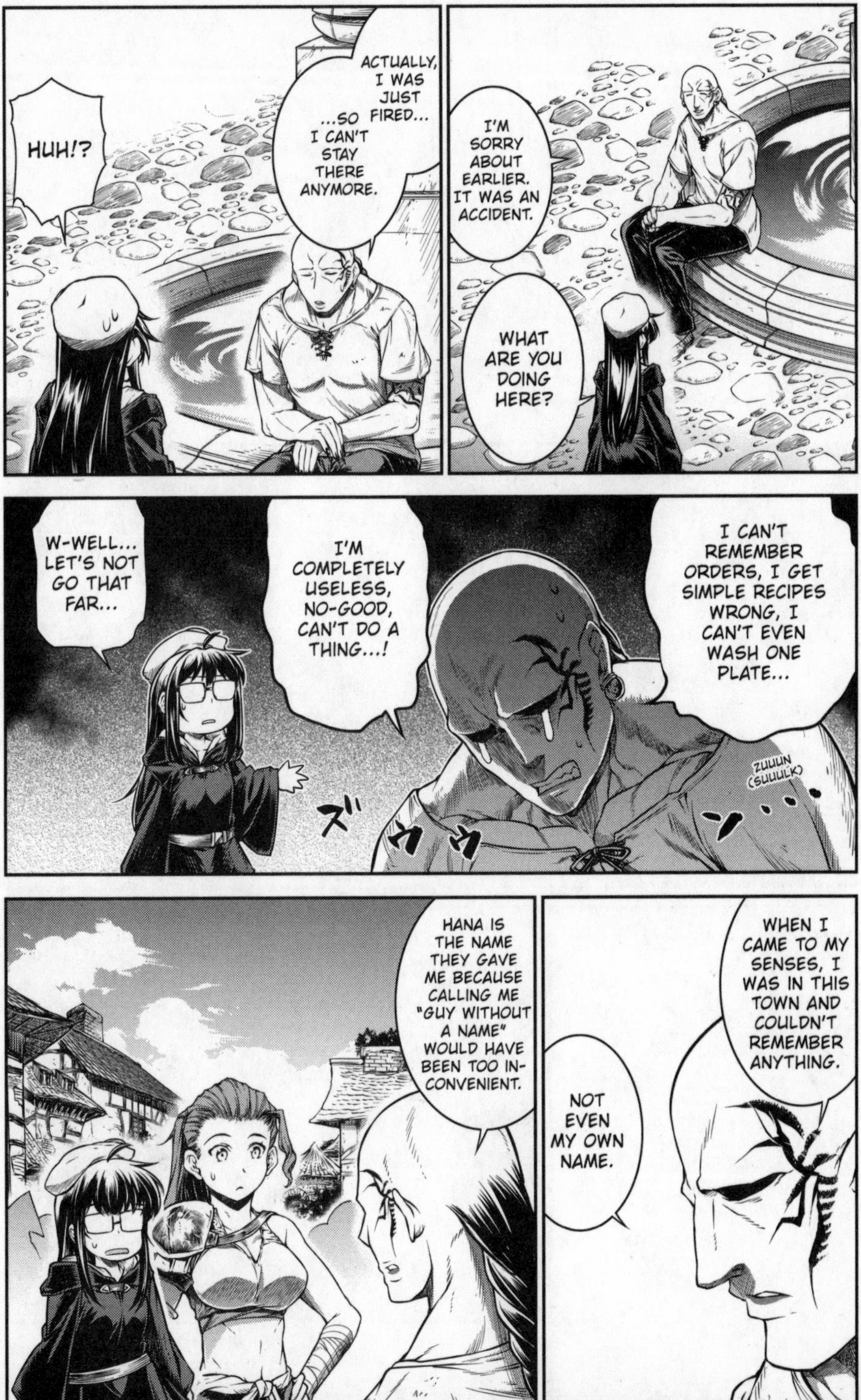
I'M SORRY ABOUT EARLIER. IT WAS AN ACCIDENT.
WHAT ARE YOU DOING HERE?
ACTUALLY, I WAS JUST FIRED... ...SO I CAN'T STAY THERE ANYMORE.
HUH!?
I CAN'T REMEMBER ORDERS, I GET SIMPLE RECIPES WRONG, I CAN'T EVEN WASH ONE PLATE...
ZUUUN (SUUULK)
I'M COMPLETELY USELESS, NO-GOOD, CAN'T DO A THING...!
W-WELL... LET'S NOT GO THAT FAR...
WHEN I CAME TO MY SENSES, I WAS IN THIS TOWN AND COULDN'T REMEMBER ANYTHING.
NOT EVEN MY OWN NAME.
HANA IS THE NAME THEY GAVE ME BECAUSE CALLING ME "GUY WITHOUT A NAME" WOULD HAVE BEEN TOO IN-CONVENIENT.

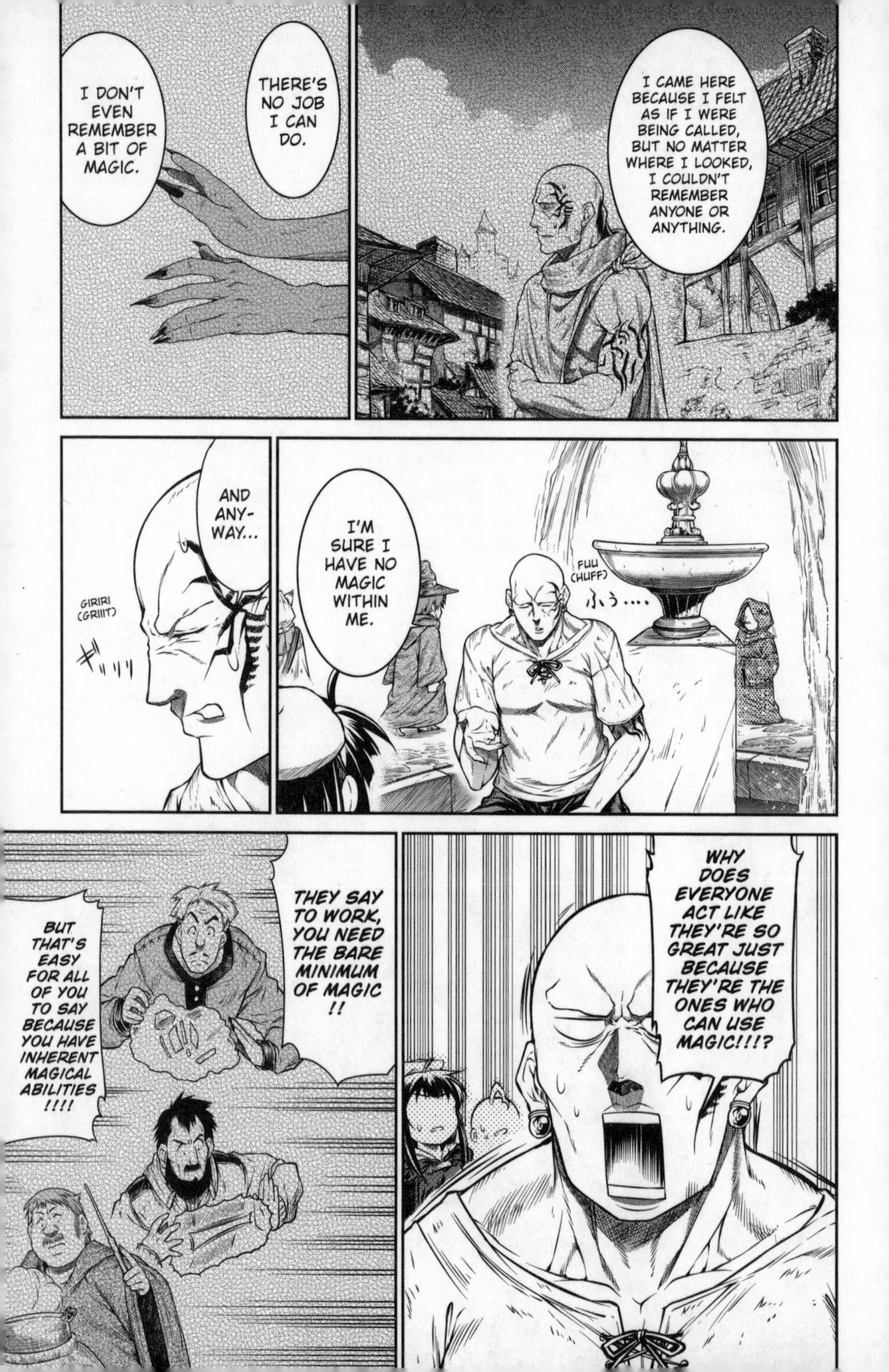
I CAME HERE BECAUSE I FELT AS IF I WERE BEING CALLED, BUT NO MATTER WHERE I LOOKED, I COULDN'T REMEMBER ANYONE OR ANYTHING.
THERE'S NO JOB I CAN DO.
I DON'T EVEN REMEMBER A BIT OF MAGIC.
FUU (CHUFF)
ふう….
I'M SURE I HAVE NO MAGIC WITHIN ME.
AND ANYWAY...
GIRIRI (GRIIIT)
WHY DOES EVERYONE ACT LIKE THEY'RE SO GREAT JUST BECAUSE THEY'RE THE ONES WHO CAN USE MAGIC!!!?
THEY SAY TO WORK, YOU NEED THE BARE MINIMUM OF MAGIC !!
BUT THAT'S EASY FOR ALL OF YOU TO SAY BECAUSE YOU HAVE INHERENT MAGICAL ABILITIES !!!!

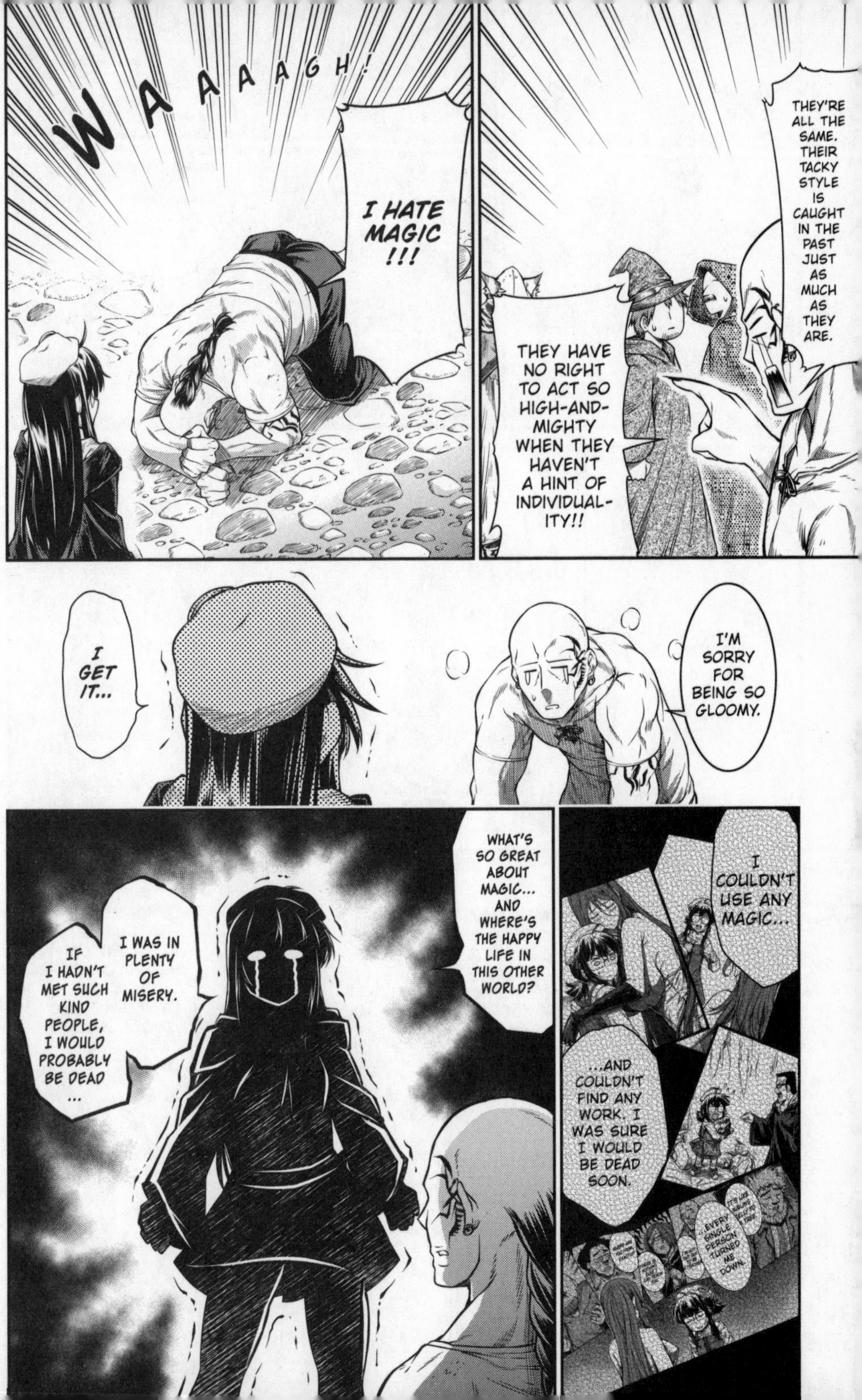

THEY'RE ALL THE SAME. THEIR TACKY STYLE IS CAUGHT IN THE PAST JUST AS MUCH AS THEY ARE.
THEY HAVE NO RIGHT TO ACT SO HIGH-AND-MIGHTY WHEN THEY HAVEN'T A HINT OF INDIVIDUAL-ITY!!
I HATE MAGIC!!!
WAAAAGH!
I'M SORRY FOR BEING SO GLOOMY.
I GET IT...
I COULDN'T USE ANY MAGIC...
...AND COULDN'T FIND ANY WORK. I WAS SURE I WOULD BE DEAD SOON.
...EVERY SINGLE PERSON TURNED ME DOWN.
WHAT'S SO GREAT ABOUT MAGIC... AND WHERE'S THE HAPPY LIFE IN THIS OTHER WORLD?
I WAS IN PLENTY OF MISERY.
IF I HADN'T MET SUCH KIND PEOPLE, I WOULD PROBABLY BE DEAD...

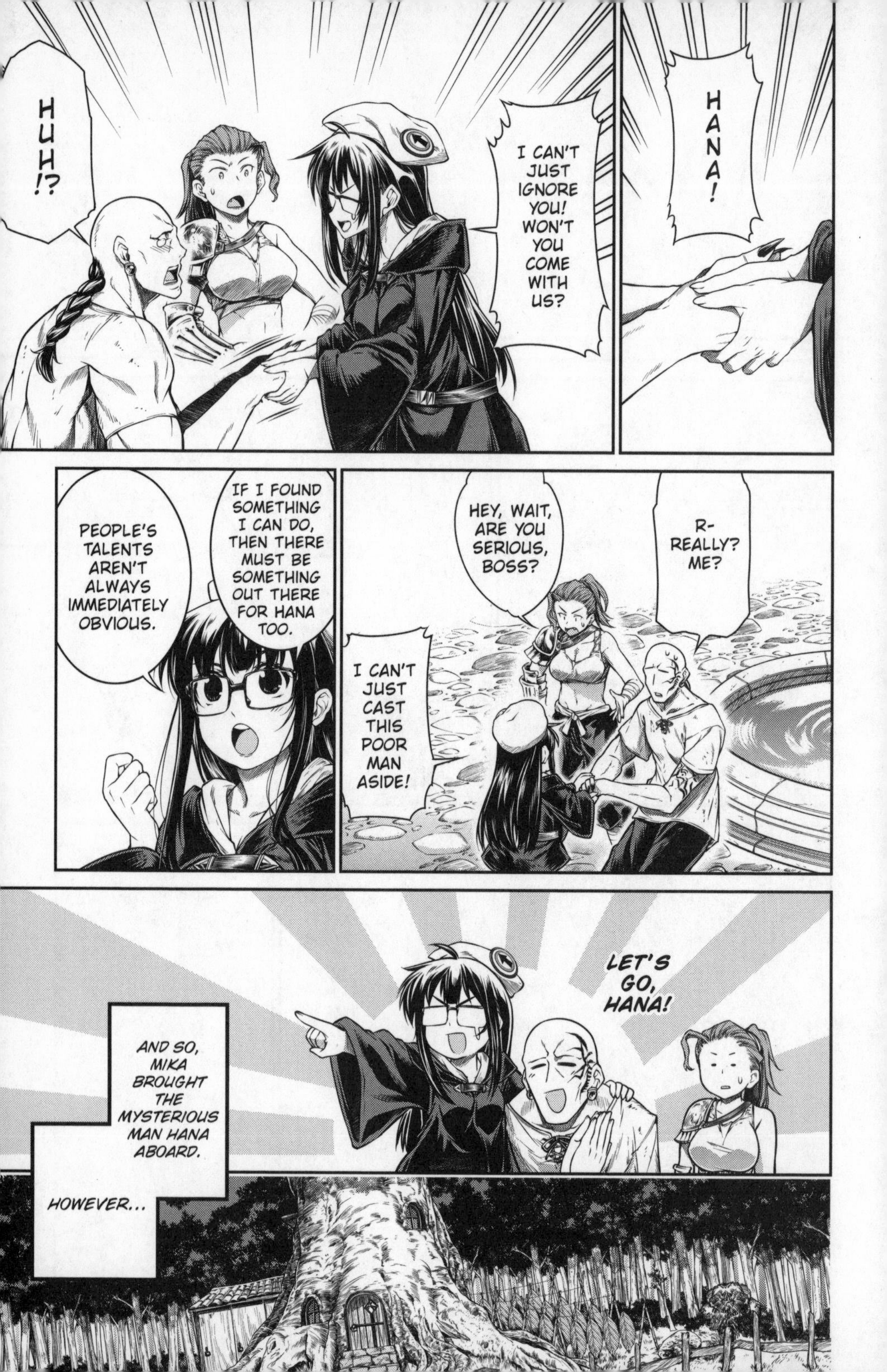
HANA!
I CAN'T JUST IGNORE YOU! WON'T YOU COME WITH US?
HUH!?
R- REALLY? ME?
HEY, WAIT, ARE YOU SERIOUS, BOSS?
I CAN'T JUST CAST THIS POOR MAN ASIDE!
IF I FOUND SOMETHING I CAN DO, THEN THERE MUST BE SOMETHING OUT THERE FOR HANA TOO.
PEOPLE'S TALENTS AREN'T ALWAYS IMMEDIATELY OBVIOUS.
LET'S GO, HANA!
AND SO, MIKA BROUGHT THE MYSTERIOUS MAN HANA ABOARD.
HOWEVER...

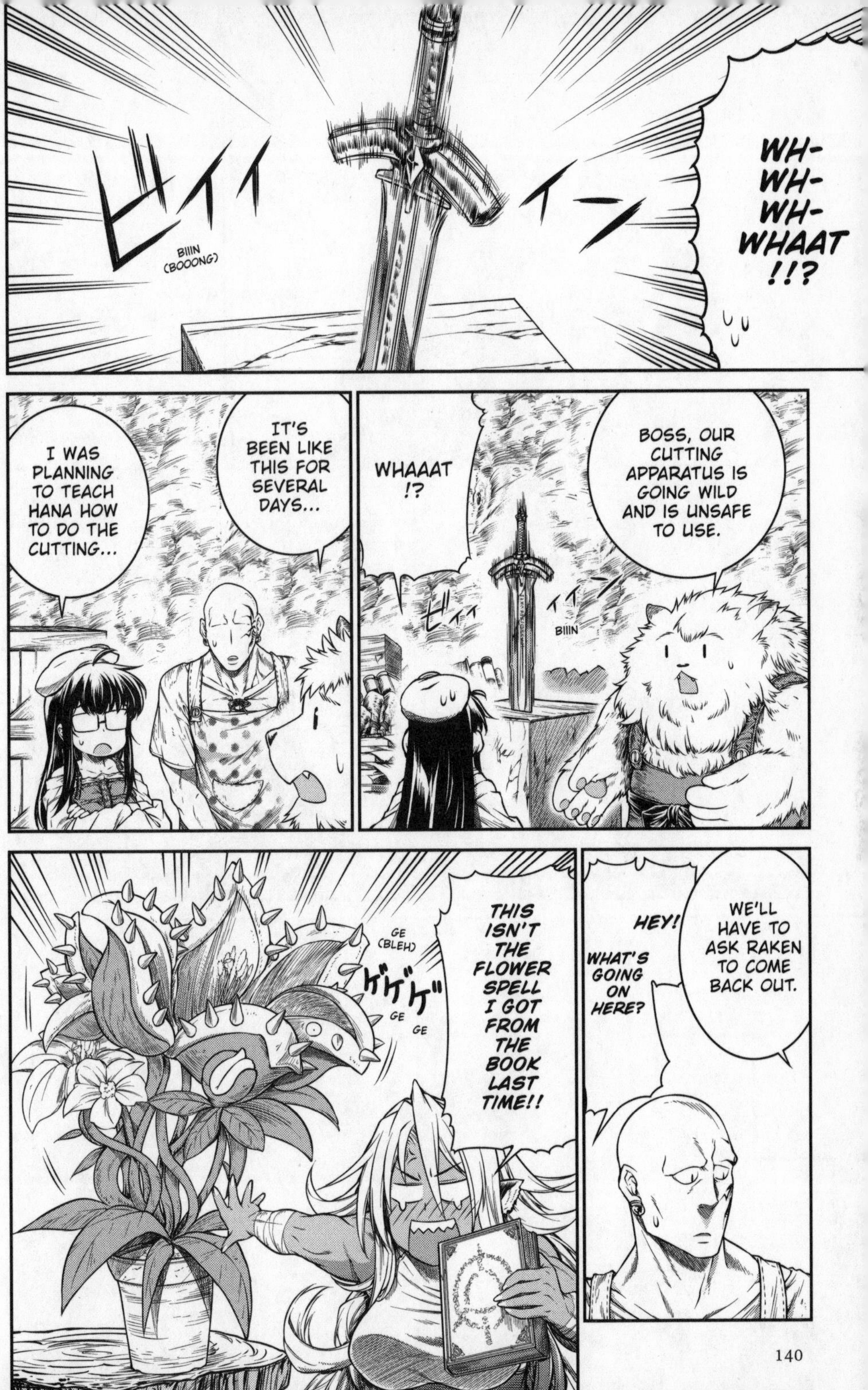
WH-WH-WH-WHAAT!!?
BIIIN (BOOONG)
BOSS, OUR CUTTING APPARATUS IS GOING WILD AND IS UNSAFE TO USE.
BIIIN
WHAAAT!?
IT'S BEEN LIKE THIS FOR SEVERAL DAYS...
I WAS PLANNING TO TEACH HANA HOW TO DO THE CUTTING...
WE'LL HAVE TO ASK RAKEN TO COME BACK OUT.
HEY!
WHAT'S GOING ON HERE?
THIS ISN'T THE FLOWER SPELL I GOT FROM THE BOOK LAST TIME!!
GE (BLEH) GE GE

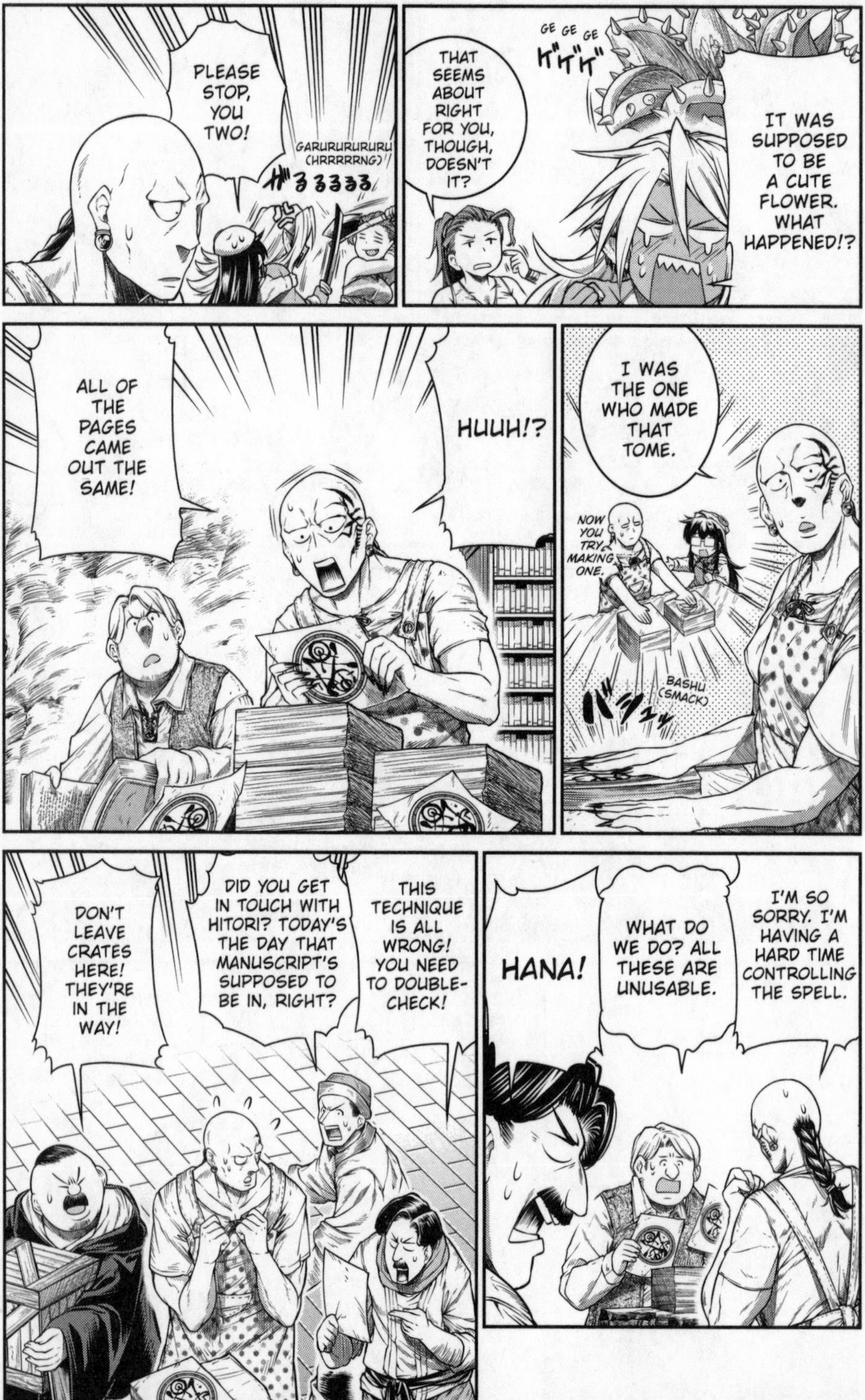
GE GE GE
ゲゲゲ
IT WAS SUPPOSED TO BE A CUTE FLOWER. WHAT HAPPENED!?
THAT SEEMS ABOUT RIGHT FOR YOU, THOUGH, DOESN'T IT?
PLEASE STOP, YOU TWO!
GARURURURURU (HRRRRRNG)
ガるるるるる
I WAS THE ONE WHO MADE THAT TOME.
NOW YOU TRY MAKING ONE.
BASHU (SMACK)
バシュッ
HUUH!?
ALL OF THE PAGES CAME OUT THE SAME!
I'M SO SORRY. I'M HAVING A HARD TIME CONTROLLING THE SPELL.
WHAT DO WE DO? ALL THESE ARE UNUSABLE.
HANA!
THIS TECHNIQUE IS ALL WRONG! YOU NEED TO DOUBLE-CHECK!
DID YOU GET IN TOUCH WITH HITORI? TODAY'S THE DAY THAT MANUSCRIPT'S SUPPOSED TO BE IN, RIGHT?
DON'T LEAVE CRATES HERE! THEY'RE IN THE WAY!

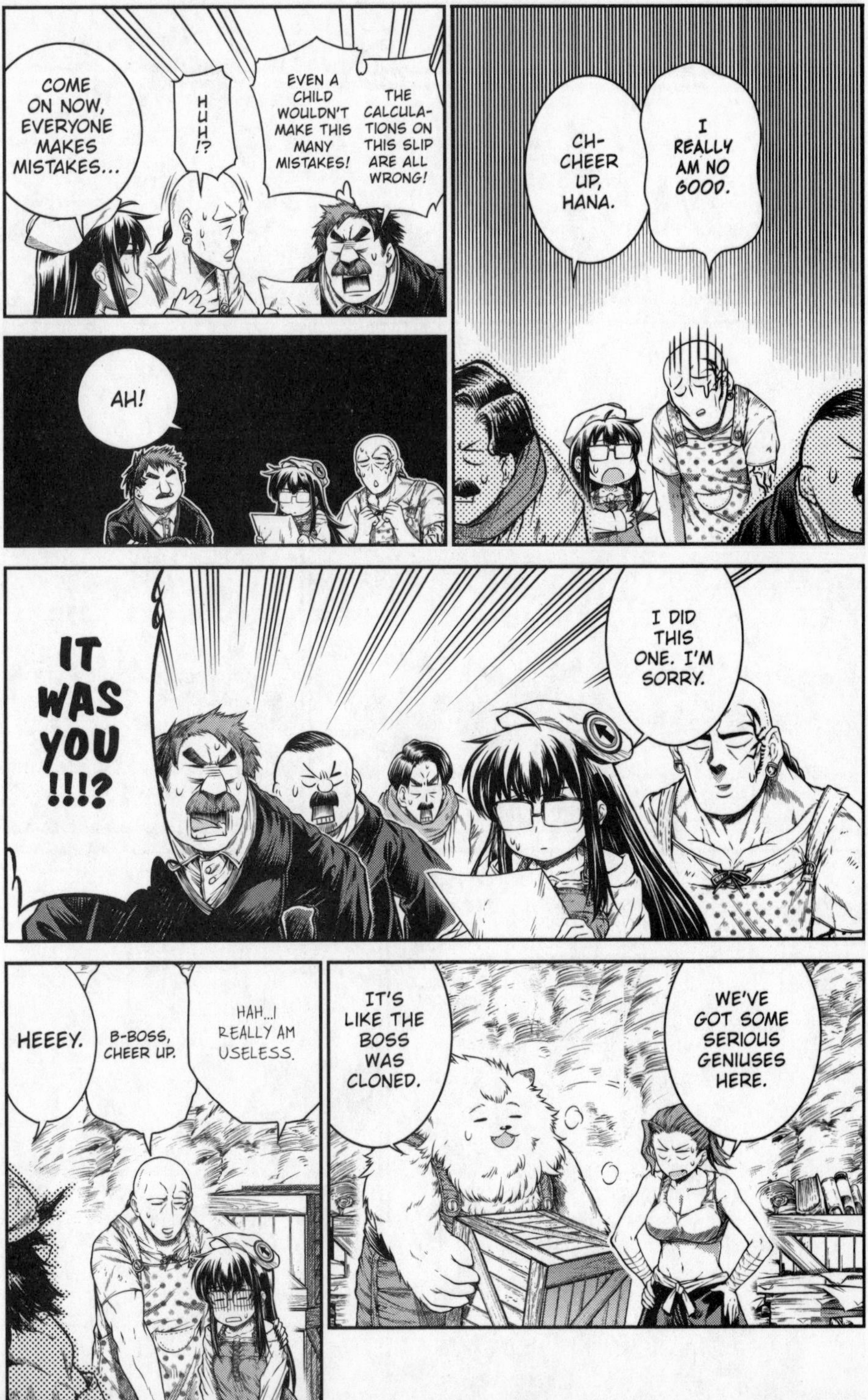
I REALLY AM NO GOOD.
CH-CHEER UP, HANA.
THE CALCULATIONS ON THIS SLIP ARE ALL WRONG!
EVEN A CHILD WOULDN'T MAKE THIS MANY MISTAKES!
HUH!?
COME ON NOW, EVERYONE MAKES MISTAKES...
AH!
I DID THIS ONE. I'M SORRY.
IT WAS YOU!!!?
WE'VE GOT SOME SERIOUS GENIUSES HERE.
IT'S LIKE THE BOSS WAS CLONED.
HAH...I REALLY AM USELESS.
B-BOSS, CHEER UP.
HEEEY.

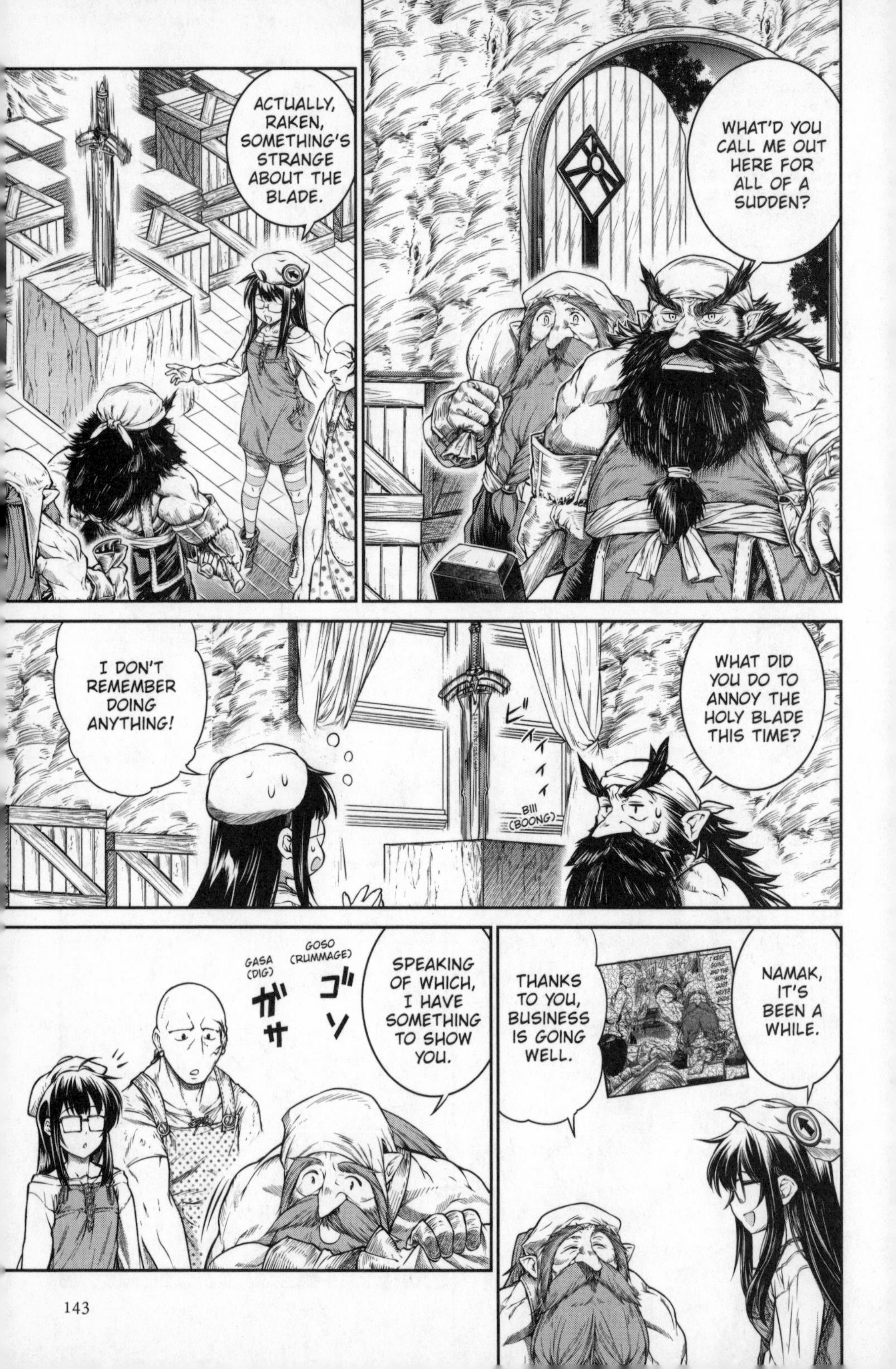
WHAT'D YOU CALL ME OUT HERE FOR ALL OF A SUDDEN?
ACTUALLY, RAKEN, SOMETHING'S STRANGE ABOUT THE BLADE.
WHAT DID YOU DO TO ANNOY THE HOLY BLADE THIS TIME?
ビィィィ
BIII (BOONG)
I DON'T REMEMBER DOING ANYTHING!
NAMAK, IT'S BEEN A WHILE.
I KEEP GOING, AND THE WORK JUST NEVER ENDS
THANKS TO YOU, BUSINESS IS GOING WELL.
SPEAKING OF WHICH, I HAVE SOMETHING TO SHOW YOU.
ゴソ
GOSO (RUMMAGE)
ガサ
GASA (DIG)

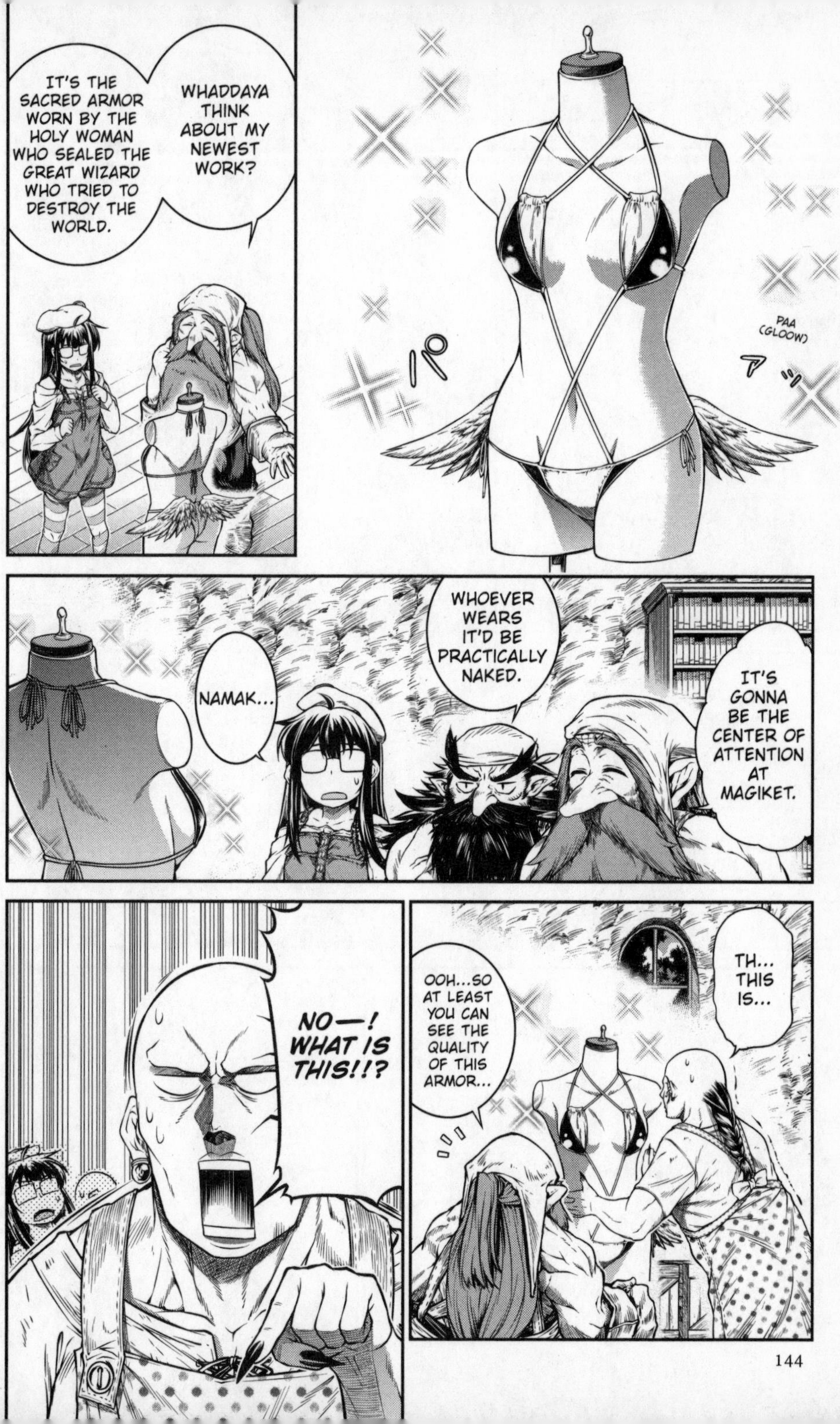
PAA (GLOOW)
WHADDAYA THINK ABOUT MY NEWEST WORK?
IT'S THE SACRED ARMOR WORN BY THE HOLY WOMAN WHO SEALED THE GREAT WIZARD WHO TRIED TO DESTROY THE WORLD.
IT'S GONNA BE THE CENTER OF ATTENTION AT MAGIKET.
WHOEVER WEARS IT'D BE PRACTICALLY NAKED.
NAMAK...
TH... THIS IS...
OOH...SO AT LEAST YOU CAN SEE THE QUALITY OF THIS ARMOR...
NO—! WHAT IS THIS!!?

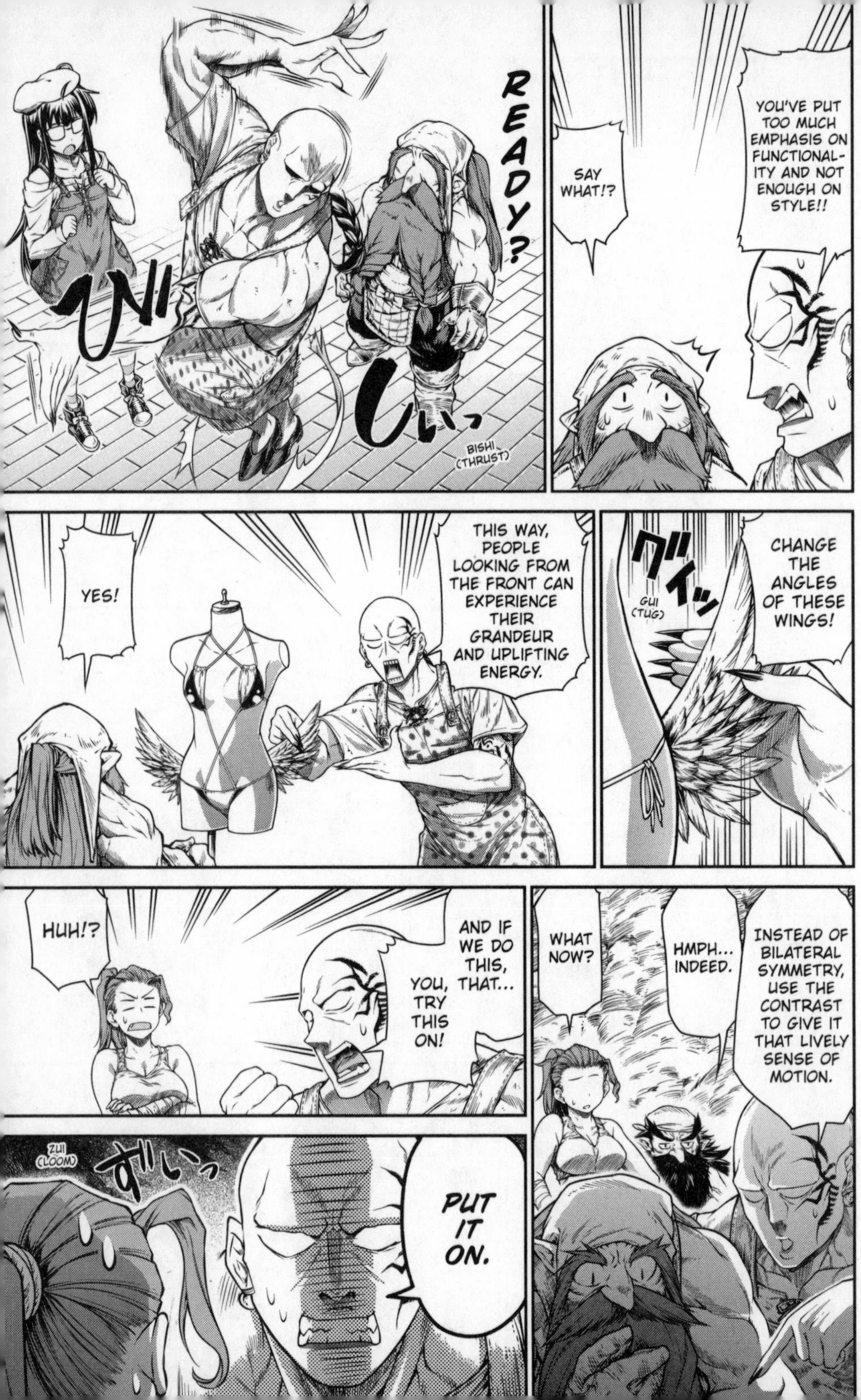

YOU'VE PUT TOO MUCH EMPHASIS ON FUNCTIONALITY AND NOT ENOUGH ON STYLE!!
SAY WHAT!?
READY?
BISHI (THRUST)
GUI (TUG)
CHANGE THE ANGLES OF THESE WINGS!
THIS WAY, PEOPLE LOOKING FROM THE FRONT CAN EXPERIENCE THEIR GRANDEUR AND UPLIFTING ENERGY.
YES!
INSTEAD OF BILATERAL SYMMETRY, USE THE CONTRAST TO GIVE IT THAT LIVELY SENSE OF MOTION.
HMPH... INDEED.
WHAT NOW?
AND IF WE DO THIS, THAT...
YOU, TRY THIS ON!
HUH!?
PUT IT ON.
ZUI (LOOM)

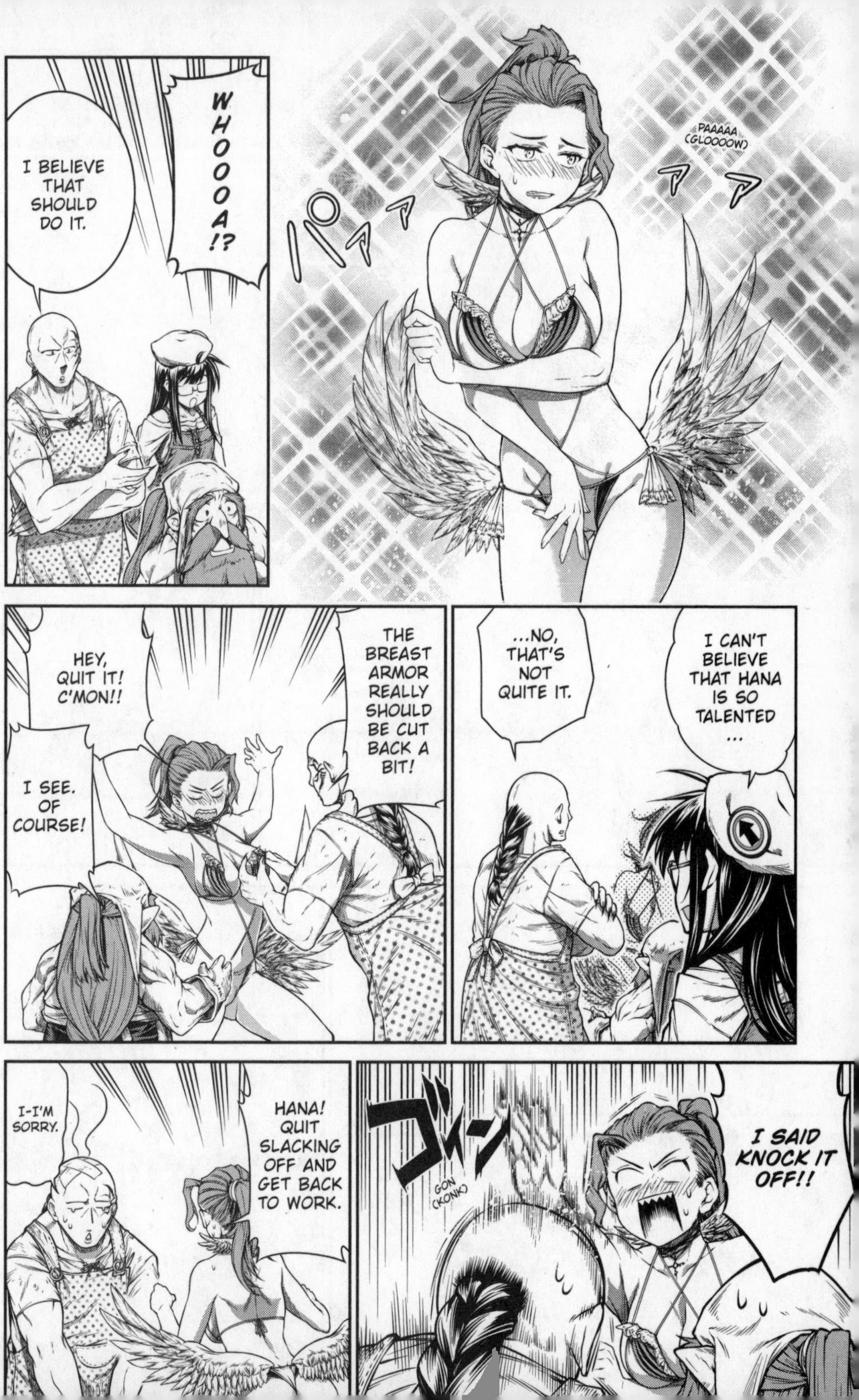
PAAAAA (GLOOOOW)
WHOOOOA!?
I BELIEVE THAT SHOULD DO IT.
I CAN'T BELIEVE THAT HANA IS SO TALENTED ...
...NO, THAT'S NOT QUITE IT.
THE BREAST ARMOR REALLY SHOULD BE CUT BACK A BIT!
HEY, QUIT IT! C'MON!!
I SEE. OF COURSE!
I SAID KNOCK IT OFF!!
GON (KONK)
HANA! QUIT SLACKING OFF AND GET BACK TO WORK.
I-I'M SORRY.

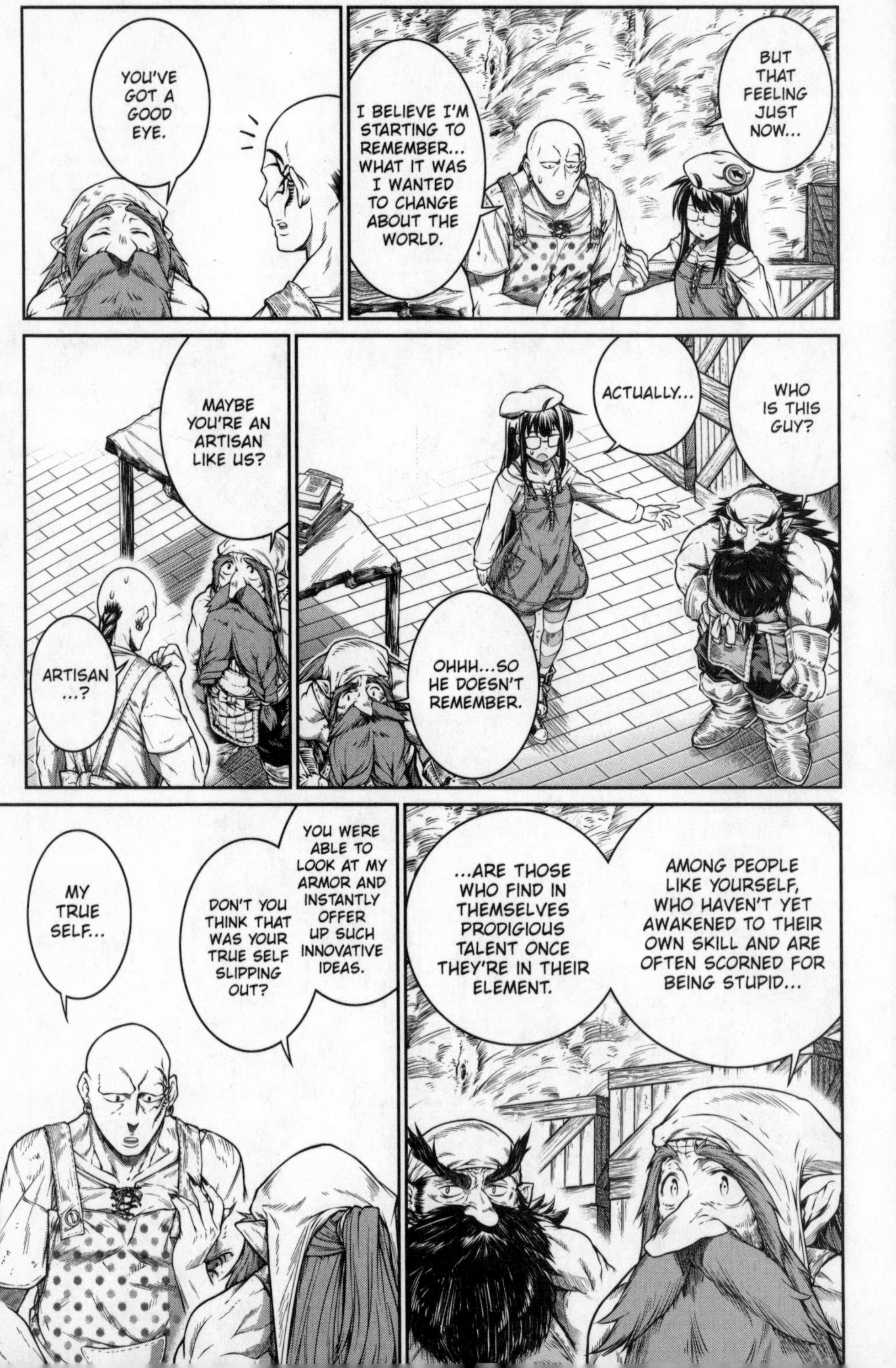
BUT THAT FEELING JUST NOW...
I BELIEVE I'M STARTING TO REMEMBER... WHAT IT WAS I WANTED TO CHANGE ABOUT THE WORLD.
YOU'VE GOT A GOOD EYE.
WHO IS THIS GUY?
ACTUALLY...
OHHH...SO HE DOESN'T REMEMBER.
MAYBE YOU'RE AN ARTISAN LIKE US?
ARTISAN ...?
AMONG PEOPLE LIKE YOURSELF, WHO HAVEN'T YET AWAKENED TO THEIR OWN SKILL AND ARE OFTEN SCORNED FOR BEING STUPID...
...ARE THOSE WHO FIND IN THEMSELVES PRODIGIOUS TALENT ONCE THEY'RE IN THEIR ELEMENT.
YOU WERE ABLE TO LOOK AT MY ARMOR AND INSTANTLY OFFER UP SUCH INNOVATIVE IDEAS.
DON'T YOU THINK THAT WAS YOUR TRUE SELF SLIPPING OUT?
MY TRUE SELF...

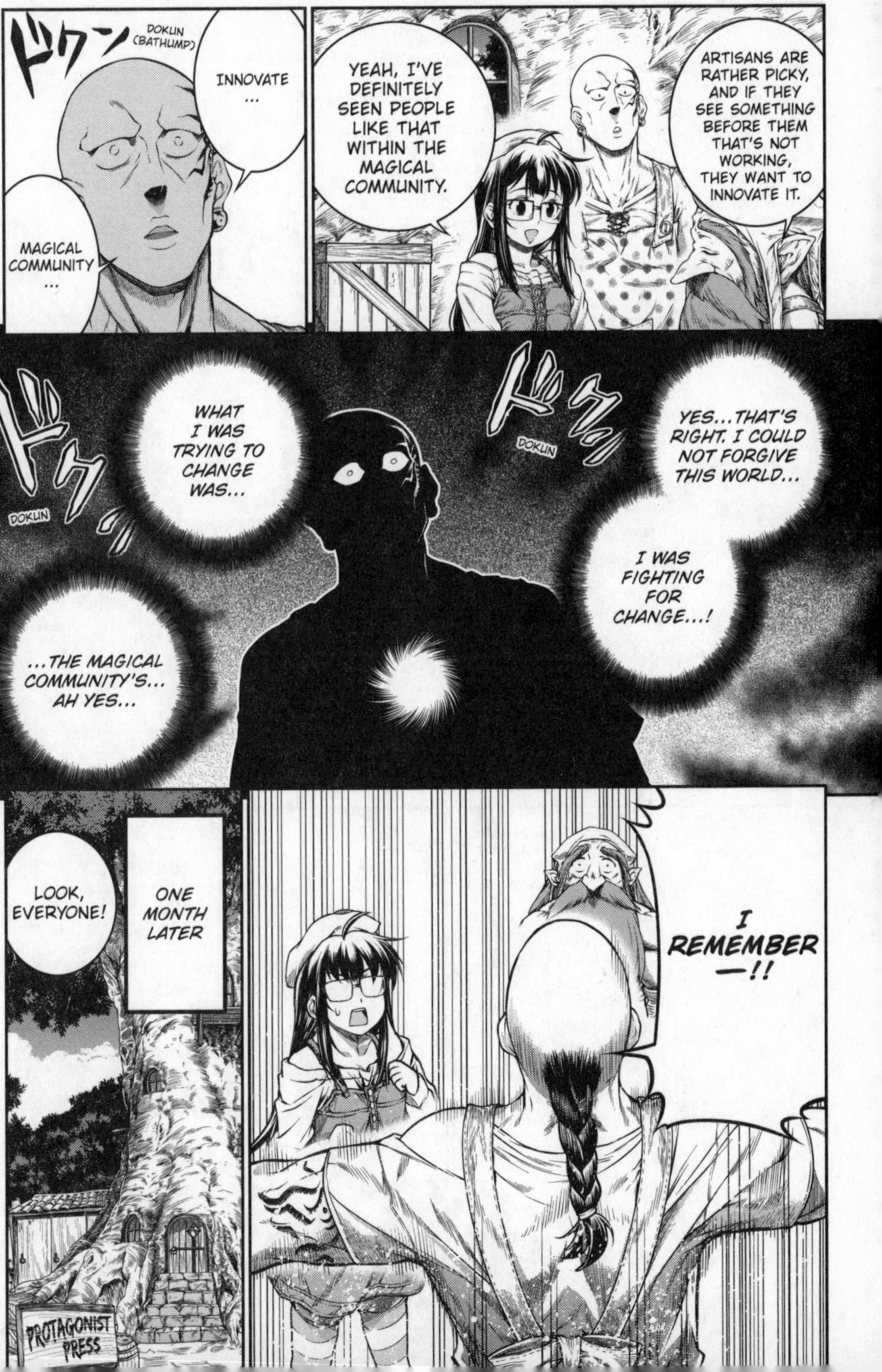
ARTISANS ARE RATHER PICKY, AND IF THEY SEE SOMETHING BEFORE THEM THAT'S NOT WORKING, THEY WANT TO INNOVATE IT.
YEAH, I'VE DEFINITELY SEEN PEOPLE LIKE THAT WITHIN THE MAGICAL COMMUNITY.
ドクン
DOKUN (BATHUMP)
INNOVATE ...
MAGICAL COMMUNITY ...
ドクン
DOKUN
YES...THAT'S RIGHT. I COULD NOT FORGIVE THIS WORLD...
I WAS FIGHTING FOR CHANGE...!
WHAT I WAS TRYING TO CHANGE WAS...
ドクン
DOKUN
...THE MAGICAL COMMUNITY'S... AH YES...
I REMEMBER—!!
ONE MONTH LATER
LOOK, EVERYONE!
PROTAGONIST PRESS

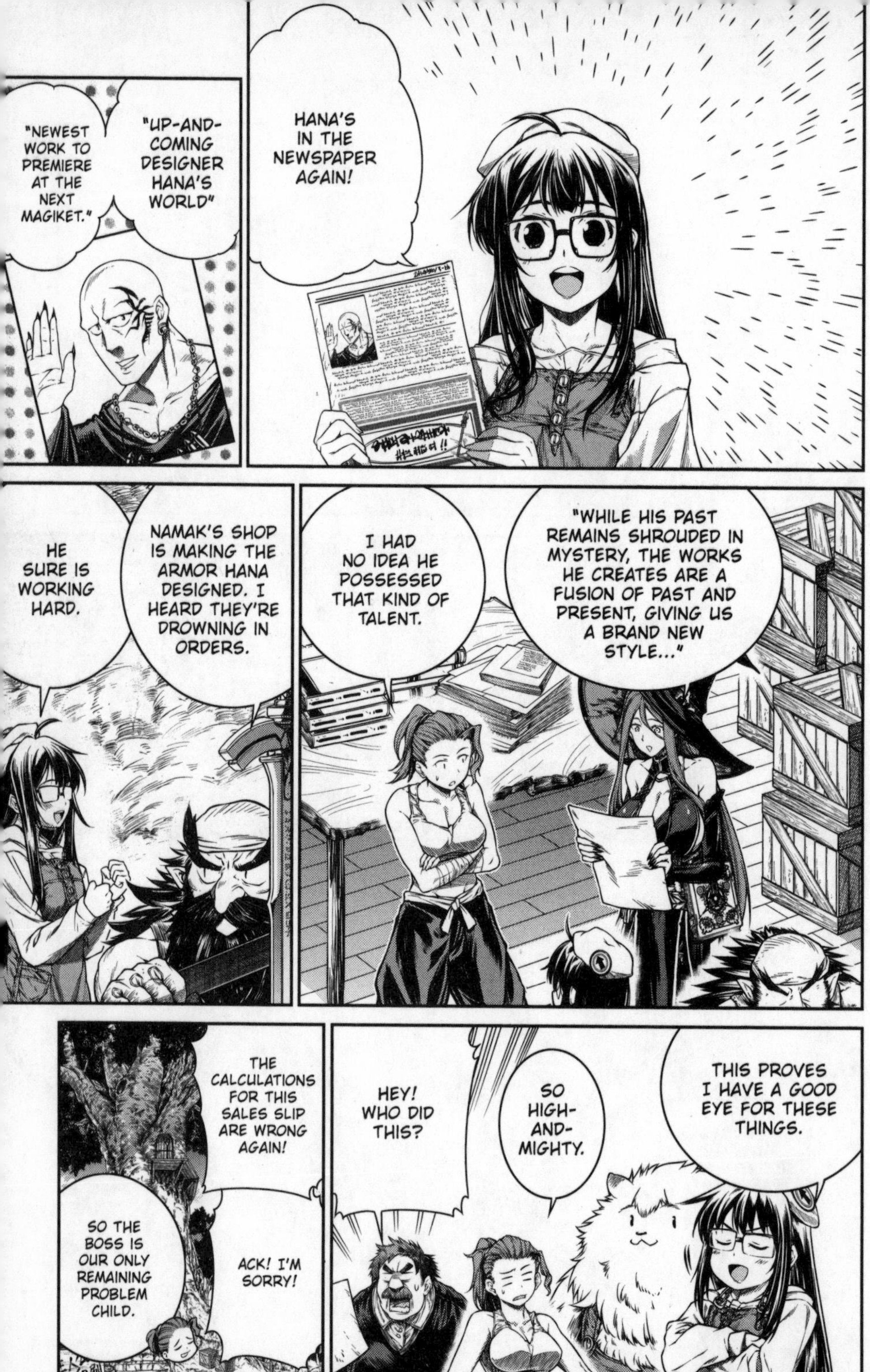
HANA'S IN THE NEWSPAPER AGAIN!
"UP-AND-COMING DESIGNER HANA'S WORLD"
"NEWEST WORK TO PREMIERE AT THE NEXT MAGIKET."
"WHILE HIS PAST REMAINS SHROUDED IN MYSTERY, THE WORKS HE CREATES ARE A FUSION OF PAST AND PRESENT, GIVING US A BRAND NEW STYLE..."
I HAD NO IDEA HE POSSESSED THAT KIND OF TALENT.
NAMAK'S SHOP IS MAKING THE ARMOR HANA DESIGNED. I HEARD THEY'RE DROWNING IN ORDERS.
HE SURE IS WORKING HARD.
THIS PROVES I HAVE A GOOD EYE FOR THESE THINGS.
SO HIGH-AND-MIGHTY.
HEY! WHO DID THIS?
THE CALCULATIONS FOR THIS SALES SLIP ARE WRONG AGAIN!
ACK! I'M SORRY!
SO THE BOSS IS OUR ONLY REMAINING PROBLEM CHILD.

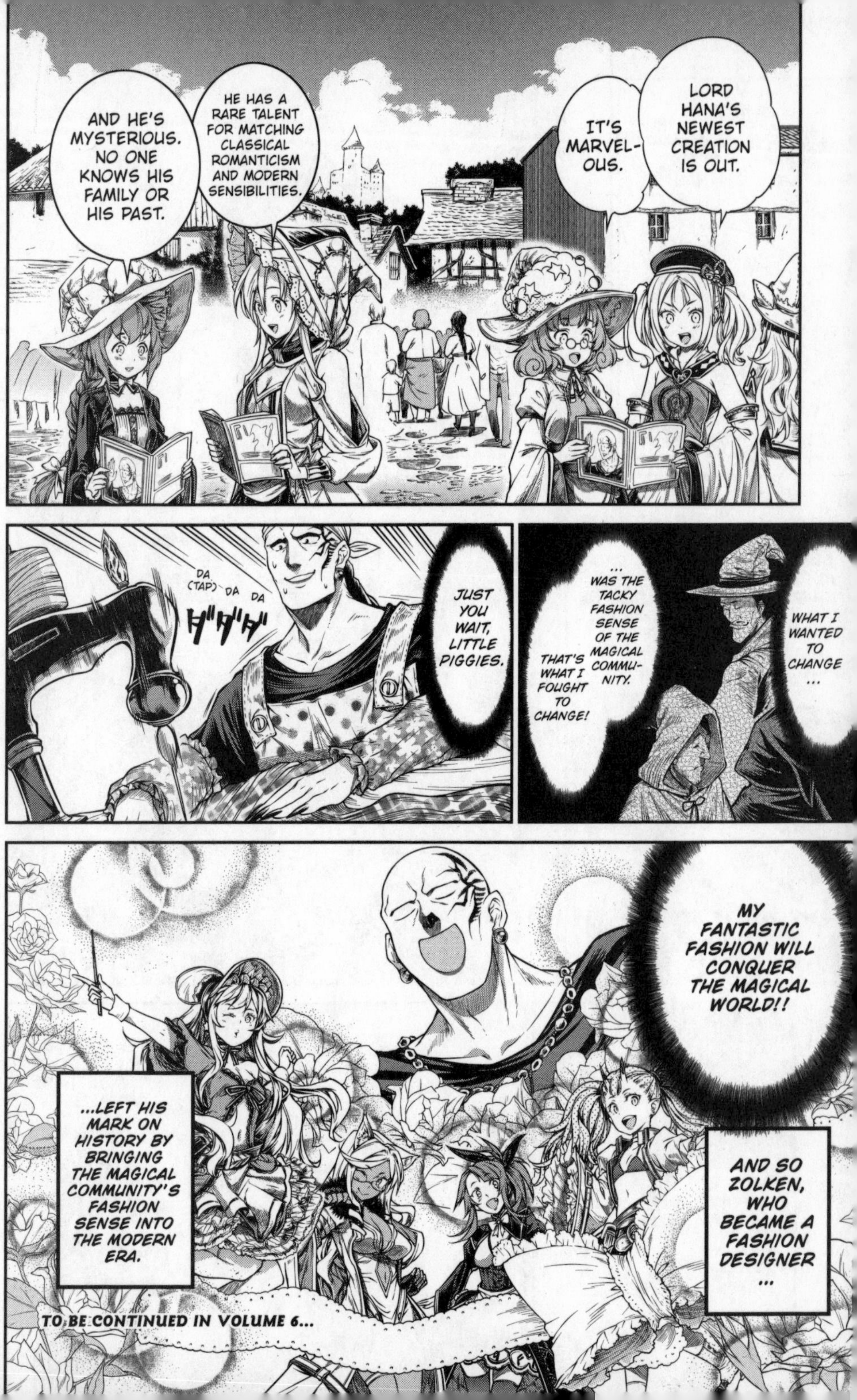
LORD HANA'S NEWEST CREATION IS OUT.
IT'S MARVEL-OUS.
HE HAS A RARE TALENT FOR MATCHING CLASSICAL ROMANTICISM AND MODERN SENSIBILITIES.
AND HE'S MYSTERIOUS. NO ONE KNOWS HIS FAMILY OR HIS PAST.
WHAT I WANTED TO CHANGE ...
...WAS THE TACKY FASHION SENSE OF THE MAGICAL COMMUNITY.
THAT'S WHAT I FOUGHT TO CHANGE!
JUST YOU WAIT, LITTLE PIGGIES.
DA (TAP) DA DA
ダダダ
MY FANTASTIC FASHION WILL CONQUER THE MAGICAL WORLD!!
AND SO ZOLKEN, WHO BECAME A FASHION DESIGNER ...
...LEFT HIS MARK ON HISTORY BY BRINGING THE MAGICAL COMMUNITY'S FASHION SENSE INTO THE MODERN ERA.
TO BE CONTINUED IN VOLUME 6...

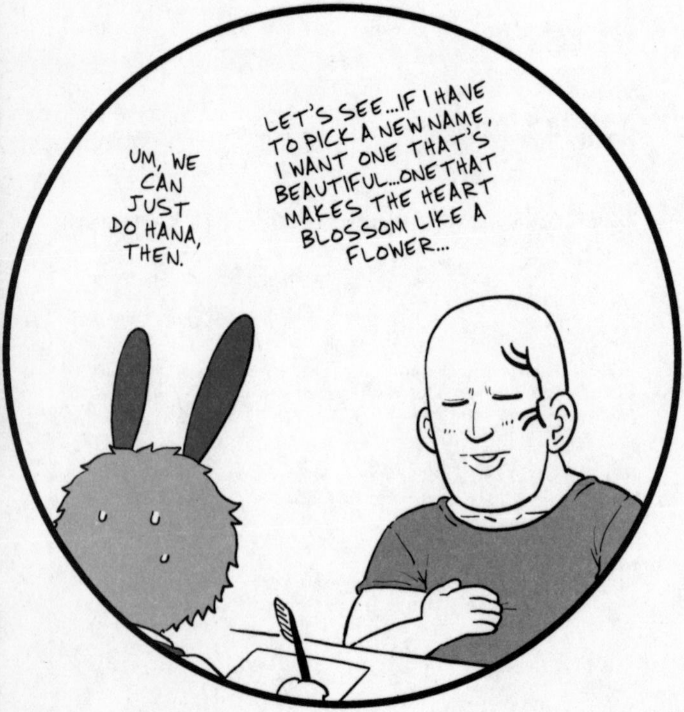
LET'S SEE...IF I HAVE TO PICK A NEW NAME, I WANT ONE THAT'S BEAUTIFUL...ONE THAT MAKES THE HEART BLOSSOM LIKE A FLOWER...
UM, WE CAN JUST DO HANA, THEN.

TRANSLATION NOTES

General
The faction names such as Suei, Kadoka, and Sugak are all references to actual Japanese publishers!

Page 4 – Shinogi Ridge
Shinogi is Japanese for "the ridge on the side of a sword blade" but also has connotations related to Japanese organized crime—namely, the idea of eking out a living day by day through the blade.

Page 14 – Peach Knight
"The Peach Knight accompanied by the three beasts" is a reference to the Japanese fairy tale "Momotarou." In it, a boy is born from a giant peach that was found by a childless old couple, and the boy is named Momotarou. Along his journey to defeat the *oni* (ogres), he meets three animal companions.

Page 25 – Pheasant
One of the three animal companions of Momotarou is a pheasant.

Page 28 – Queen of Ships
"Queen of Ships" in Japanese originally *kifujin*, or "noble lady" in Japanese but written with the fu meaning "rotten" instead of "older (married) woman." Within Boys Love fandom, it refers to a more experienced and mature *fujoshi*. Essentially, if a *fujoshi* is a BL fan*girl*, then a *kifujin* is a BL fan*lady*.

Page 32 – Ntaware
"Ntaware" is a reference to the visual novel *Utawarerumono*. The mask on the cover of the books is similar to that of the main character, Hakuowlo.

Page 40 – Replicatus
Replicatus and Remus's many other golems stylistically resemble the golems of the RPG franchise Dragon Quest, though the latter are not cyclops.

Page 66 – Anywhere Any-Bath Door
This is a double reference to the manga *Doraemon*. The titular Doraemon, a robot cat from the future, can go anywhere he wants using the Anywhere Door. In addition, the character Shizuka is famous for taking lots of baths.

Page 66 – Wall Tile Collection
The name of this spell is referencing the game *Kantai Collection*, which features battleships reimagined as anthropomorphic cute girls.

Page 151 – Hana
Hana means "flower" in Japanese.

Page 155 – *Doujinshi*
Doujinshi are essentially indie published materials typically created by amateur hobbyists in Japan. They are commonly associated with fan comics, but they can also be prose, essays, games, music, or other formats—and can even be 100 percent original work.

Page 157 – Demon Lords
The appearance of the demon lord shown here bears a strong resemblance to Zoma, the final boss of the RPG *Dragon Quest III* and the visual inspiration for the general demon-lord aesthetic found in many Japanese fantasy stories.

Page 158 – Red and green editions
This (along with the mention of monsters that won't fit inside your pocket) is a reference to the first Pokémon games, which were released in Japan as *Pocket Monsters Red* and *Pocket Monsters Green*.

A WITCH'S PRINTING OFFICE

BONUS MANGA COLLECTION

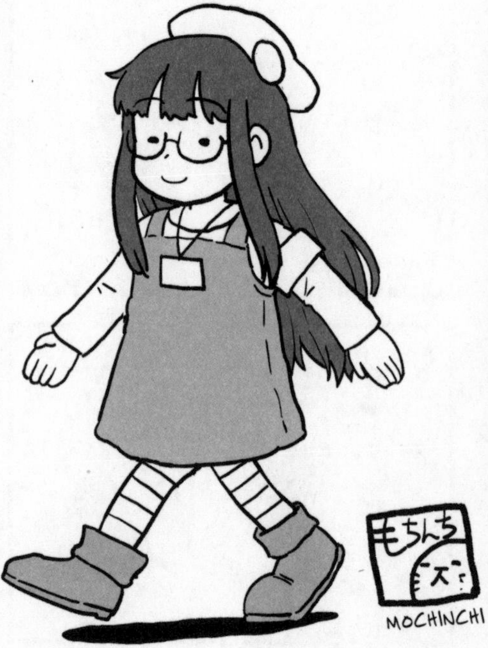
もちんち
MOCHINCHI

OVERNIGHTING IS NOT ALLOWED

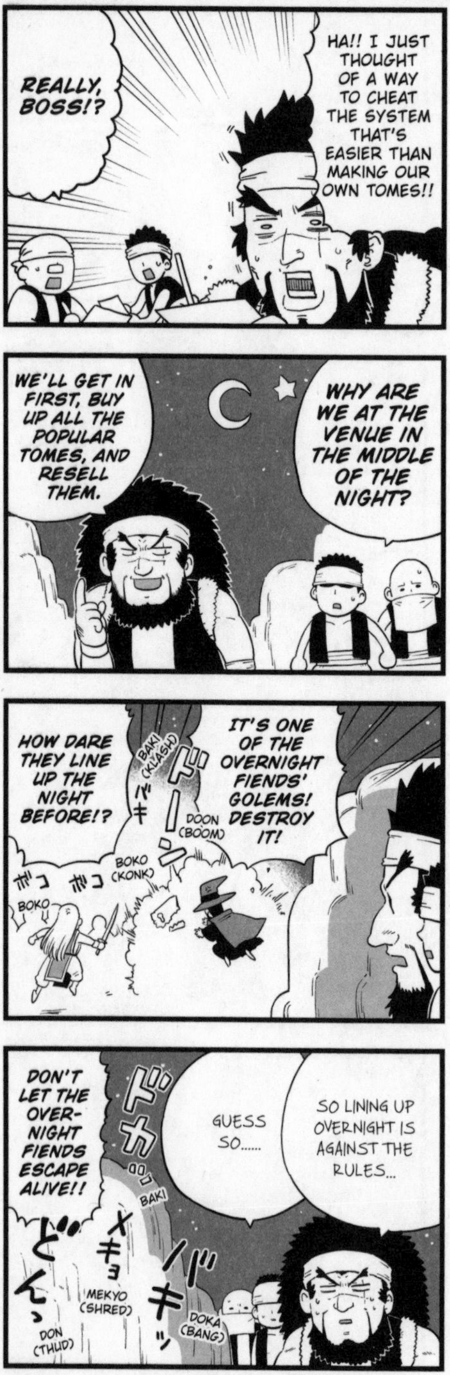
HA!! I JUST THOUGHT OF A WAY TO CHEAT THE SYSTEM THAT'S EASIER THAN MAKING OUR OWN TOMES!!
REALLY, BOSS!?
WHY ARE WE AT THE VENUE IN THE MIDDLE OF THE NIGHT?
WE'LL GET IN FIRST, BUY UP ALL THE POPULAR TOMES, AND RESELL THEM.
IT'S ONE OF THE OVERNIGHT FIENDS' GOLEMS! DESTROY IT!
ドーン
DOON (BOOM)
バキ
BAKI (KLASH)
HOW DARE THEY LINE UP THE NIGHT BEFORE!?
ボコ
BOKO (KONK)
ボコ
BOKO
SO LINING UP OVERNIGHT IS AGAINST THE RULES...
GUESS SO......
DON'T LET THE OVER-NIGHT FIENDS ESCAPE ALIVE!!
ドカッ
DOKA (BANG)
バキッ
BAKI
メキョ
MEKYO (SHRED)
どんっ
DON (THUD)

PERSONAL GROOMING

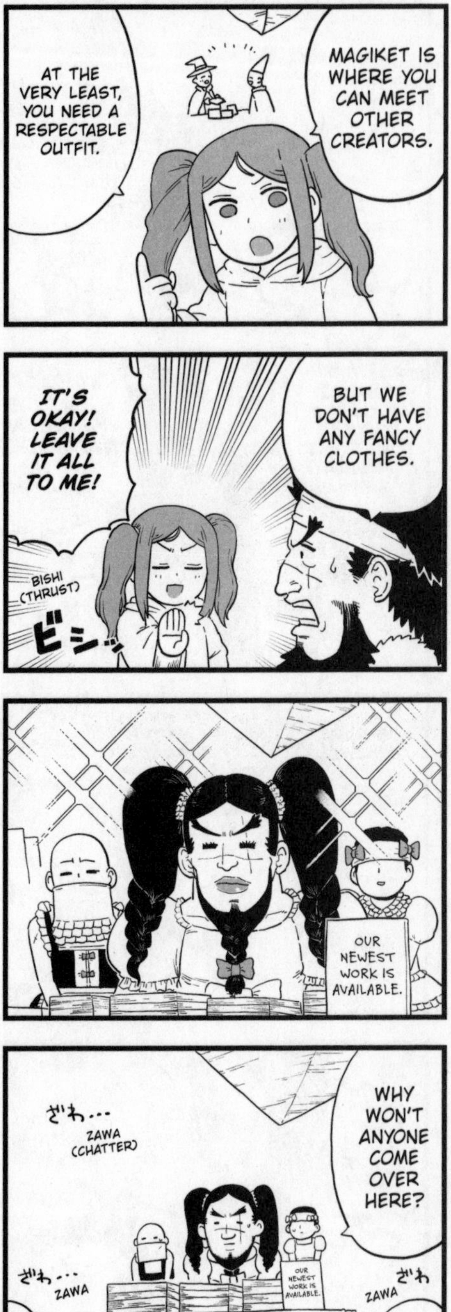
MAGIKET IS WHERE YOU CAN MEET OTHER CREATORS.
AT THE VERY LEAST, YOU NEED A RESPECTABLE OUTFIT.
BUT WE DON'T HAVE ANY FANCY CLOTHES.
IT'S OKAY! LEAVE IT ALL TO ME!
BISHI (THRUST)
ビシッ
OUR NEWEST WORK IS AVAILABLE.
WHY WON'T ANYONE COME OVER HERE?
ざわ
ZAWA
OUR NEWEST WORK IS AVAILABLE.
ざわ…
ZAWA (CHATTER)
ざわ…
ZAWA

GOLEM PRESS

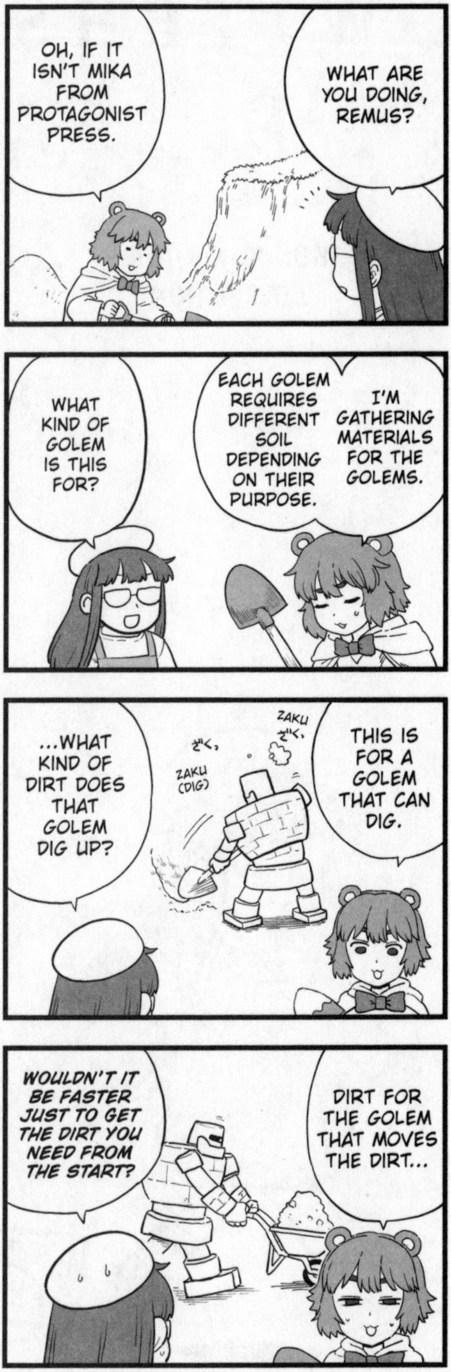
WHAT ARE YOU DOING, REMUS?
OH, IF IT ISN'T MIKA FROM PROTAGONIST PRESS.
I'M GATHERING MATERIALS FOR THE GOLEMS.
EACH GOLEM REQUIRES DIFFERENT SOIL DEPENDING ON THEIR PURPOSE.
WHAT KIND OF GOLEM IS THIS FOR?
THIS IS FOR A GOLEM THAT CAN DIG.
ZAKU ざく
ざく
ZAKU (DIG)
...WHAT KIND OF DIRT DOES THAT GOLEM DIG UP?
DIRT FOR THE GOLEM THAT MOVES THE DIRT...
WOULDN'T IT BE FASTER JUST TO GET THE DIRT YOU NEED FROM THE START?

MIKA AND HER SENPAI ①

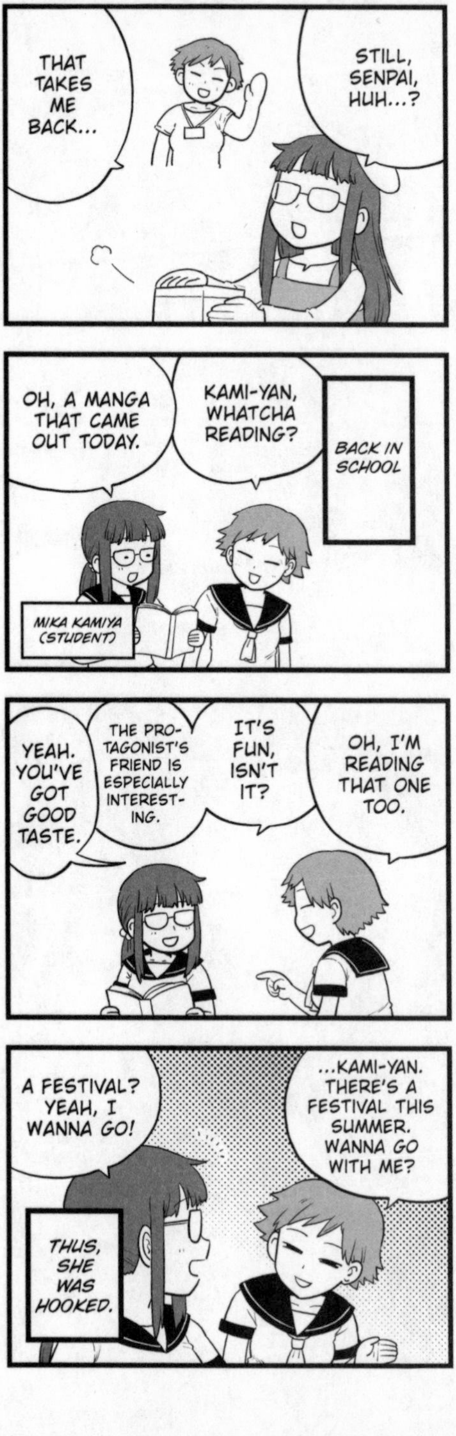
STILL, SENPAI, HUH...?
THAT TAKES ME BACK...
BACK IN SCHOOL
KAMI-YAN, WHATCHA READING?
OH, A MANGA THAT CAME OUT TODAY.
MIKA KAMIYA (STUDENT)
OH, I'M READING THAT ONE TOO.
IT'S FUN, ISN'T IT?
THE PROTAGONIST'S FRIEND IS ESPECIALLY INTERESTING.
YEAH. YOU'VE GOT GOOD TASTE.
...KAMI-YAN. THERE'S A FESTIVAL THIS SUMMER. WANNA GO WITH ME?
A FESTIVAL? YEAH, I WANNA GO!
THUS, SHE WAS HOOKED.

MIKA AND HER SENPAI ②

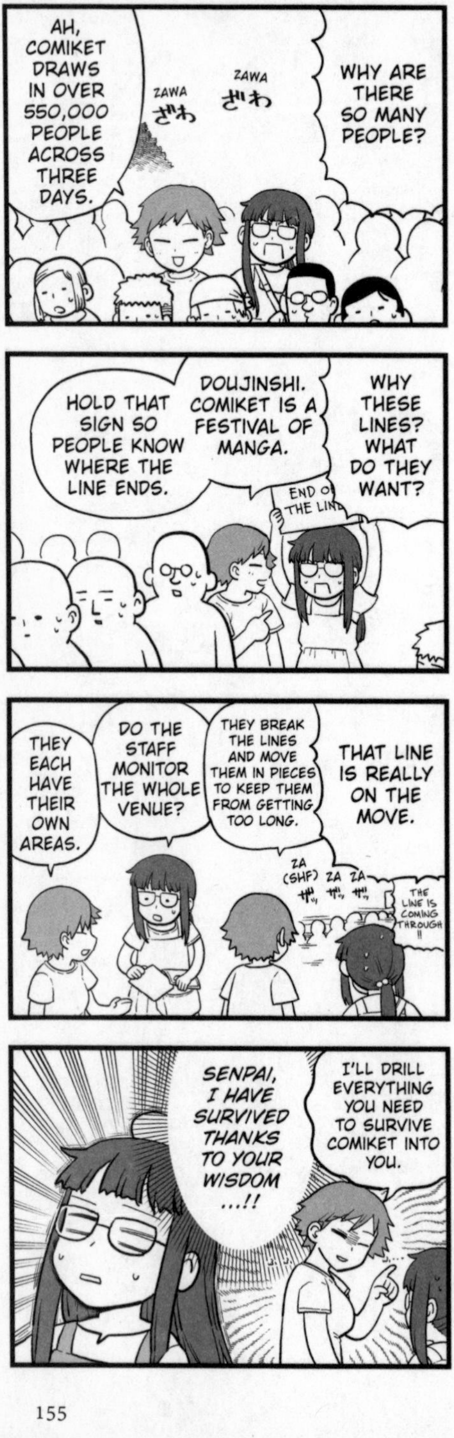
WHY ARE THERE SO MANY PEOPLE?
ZAWA ざわ
ZAWA ざわ
AH, COMIKET DRAWS IN OVER 550,000 PEOPLE ACROSS THREE DAYS.
WHY THESE LINES? WHAT DO THEY WANT?
DOUJINSHI. COMIKET IS A FESTIVAL OF MANGA.
HOLD THAT SIGN SO PEOPLE KNOW WHERE THE LINE ENDS.
END O THE LIN
THAT LINE IS REALLY ON THE MOVE.
THEY BREAK THE LINES AND MOVE THEM IN PIECES TO KEEP THEM FROM GETTING TOO LONG.
DO THE STAFF MONITOR THE WHOLE VENUE?
THEY EACH HAVE THEIR OWN AREAS.
THE LINE IS COMING THROUGH!!
ZA ZA (SHF) ZA ザッ ザッ ザッ
I'LL DRILL EVERYTHING YOU NEED TO SURVIVE COMIKET INTO YOU.
SENPAI, I HAVE SURVIVED THANKS TO YOUR WISDOM ...!!

WHAT MAKES A MEMBER OF THE PRIDE?

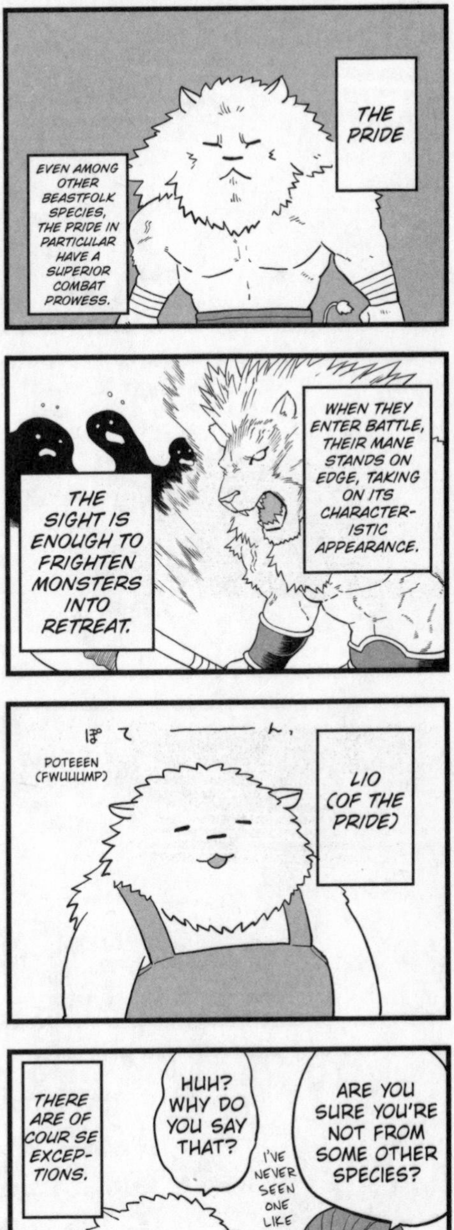
THE PRIDE
EVEN AMONG OTHER BEASTFOLK SPECIES, THE PRIDE IN PARTICULAR HAVE A SUPERIOR COMBAT PROWESS.
WHEN THEY ENTER BATTLE, THEIR MANE STANDS ON EDGE, TAKING ON ITS CHARACTER-ISTIC APPEARANCE.
THE SIGHT IS ENOUGH TO FRIGHTEN MONSTERS INTO RETREAT.
LIO (OF THE PRIDE)
ぽてーーーん
POTEEEN (FWUUUMP)
ARE YOU SURE YOU'RE NOT FROM SOME OTHER SPECIES?
I'VE NEVER SEEN ONE LIKE YOU.
HUH? WHY DO YOU SAY THAT?
THERE ARE OF COUR SE EXCEP-TIONS.
SPECIES GUIDE

ASSIN'S TASK

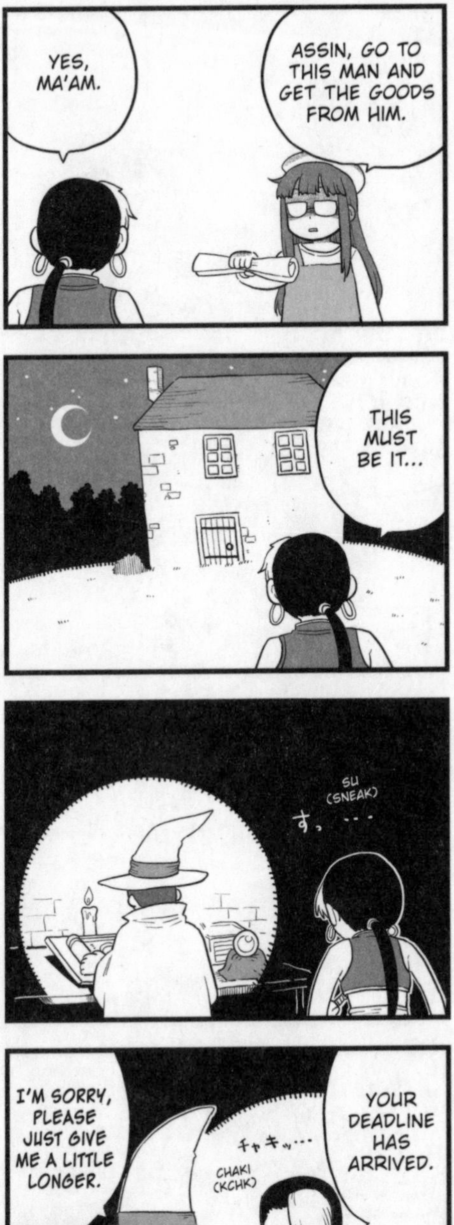
ASSIN, GO TO THIS MAN AND GET THE GOODS FROM HIM.
YES, MA'AM.
THIS MUST BE IT...
すっ...
SU (SNEAK)
YOUR DEADLINE HAS ARRIVED.
チャキッ...
CHAKI (KCHK)
I'M SORRY, PLEASE JUST GIVE ME A LITTLE LONGER.

CHARACTERISTICS OF A MONSTER

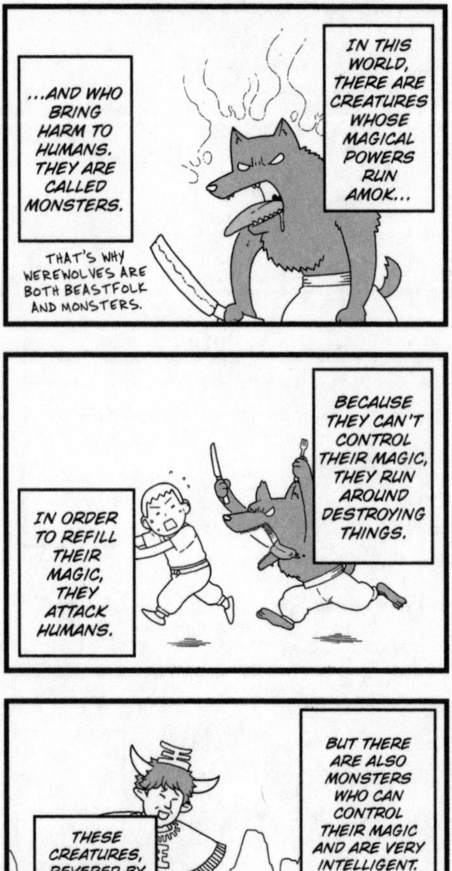
IN THIS WORLD, THERE ARE CREATURES WHOSE MAGICAL POWERS RUN AMOK...
...AND WHO BRING HARM TO HUMANS. THEY ARE CALLED MONSTERS.
THAT'S WHY WEREWOLVES ARE BOTH BEASTFOLK AND MONSTERS.
BECAUSE THEY CAN'T CONTROL THEIR MAGIC, THEY RUN AROUND DESTROYING THINGS.
IN ORDER TO REFILL THEIR MAGIC, THEY ATTACK HUMANS.
BUT THERE ARE ALSO MONSTERS WHO CAN CONTROL THEIR MAGIC AND ARE VERY INTELLIGENT.
THESE CREATURES, REVERED BY THE OTHER MONSTERS, BECOME KNOWN AS DEMON LORDS.
AND SOMETIMES MONSTERS HAVE BETTER MANNERS THAN MAN DOES.
THANK YOU VERY MUCH.
HEY THERE, HUMAN, NO CUTTING IN LINE, PLEASE.

HANA'S TALENT

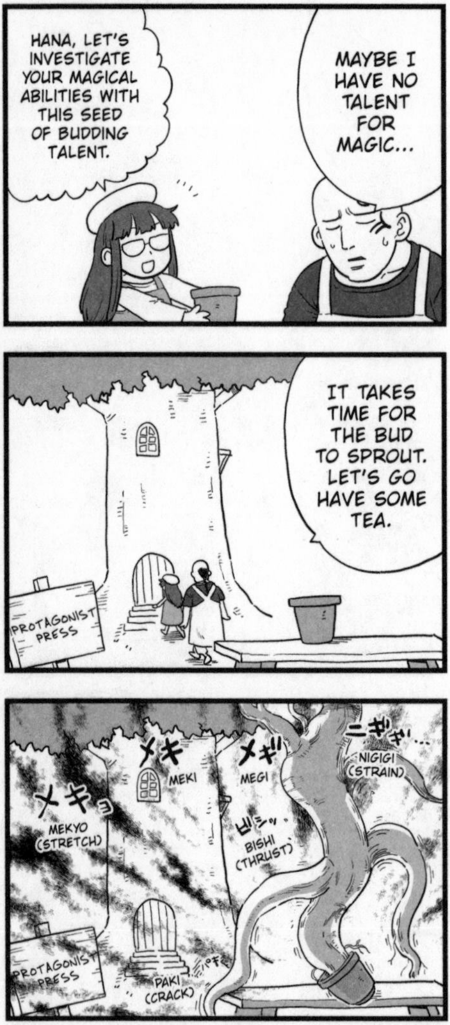
MAYBE I HAVE NO TALENT FOR MAGIC...
HANA, LET'S INVESTIGATE YOUR MAGICAL ABILITIES WITH THIS SEED OF BUDDING TALENT.
IT TAKES TIME FOR THE BUD TO SPROUT. LET'S GO HAVE SOME TEA.
PROTAGONIST PRESS
ニギギ…
NIGIGI (STRAIN)
メギ
MEGI
メキ
MEKI
ビシッ
BISHI (THRUST)
メキョ
MEKYO (STRETCH)
パキ
PAKI (CRACK)
PROTAGONIST PRESS
A GIANT FLOWER MONSTER HAS APPEARED!
RAAWR
WHY SO CLOSE TO THE TOWN?
THAT'S SCARY!!

SEED OF BUDDING TALENT: GETTING IT TO BLOOM WILL REVEAL THAT PERSON'S TALENT (SEE VOLUME 4)

IT WON'T FIT IN YOUR POCKET

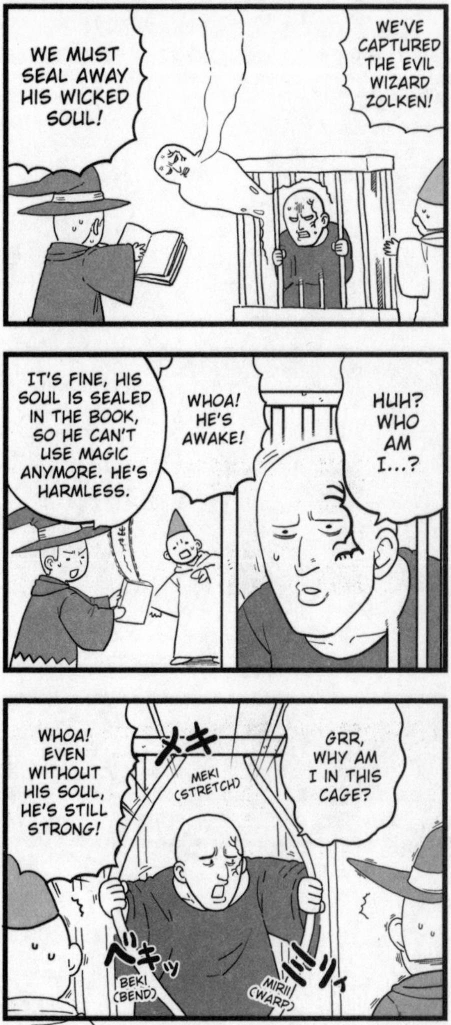
WE'VE CAPTURED THE EVIL WIZARD ZOLKEN!
WE MUST SEAL AWAY HIS WICKED SOUL!
HUH? WHO AM I...?
WHOA! HE'S AWAKE!
IT'S FINE, HIS SOUL IS SEALED IN THE BOOK, SO HE CAN'T USE MAGIC ANYMORE. HE'S HARMLESS.
GRR, WHY AM I IN THIS CAGE?
メキ
MEKI (STRETCH)
WHOA! EVEN WITHOUT HIS SOUL, HE'S STILL STRONG!
ミリィ
MIRII (WARP)
ベキッ
BEKI (BEND)
AND THAT'S HOW ZOLKEN'S BODY ENDED UP SEALED AWAY TOO.
MARK MY WORDS!
I WILL
LATER, THESE BOOKS, WITH MONSTERS SEALED INSIDE, WERE KNOWN AS THE RED AND GREEN EDITIONS.

THE 2020 CORONA CRISIS ①

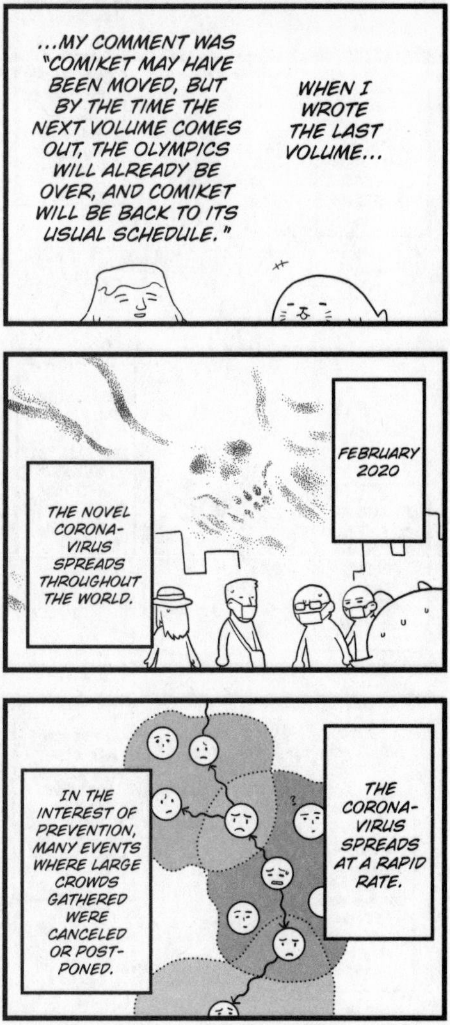
WHEN I WROTE THE LAST VOLUME...
...MY COMMENT WAS "COMIKET MAY HAVE BEEN MOVED, BUT BY THE TIME THE NEXT VOLUME COMES OUT, THE OLYMPICS WILL ALREADY BE OVER, AND COMIKET WILL BE BACK TO ITS USUAL SCHEDULE."
FEBRUARY 2020
THE NOVEL CORONAVIRUS SPREADS THROUGHOUT THE WORLD.
THE CORONAVIRUS SPREADS AT A RAPID RATE.
IN THE INTEREST OF PREVENTION, MANY EVENTS WHERE LARGE CROWDS GATHERED WERE CANCELED OR POSTPONED.
THE OLYMPICS WERE POSTPONED AS WELL...
...AND COMIKET WAS CANCELED...
THAT TIMING WAS AWFUL...
WHYYYYY!?
...ON THE DAY THE PREVIOUS VOLUME WENT ON SALE.
※ COLLECTED VOLUMES ARE FINISHED ABOUT A MONTH BEFORE THEY GO ON SALE.

THE 2020 CORONA CRISIS ②

WHEN THE EVENTS WERE CANCELED, ALL THE PRINTING SHOPS HANDLING THE CATALOGS AND PAMPHLETS SUDDENLY HAD A LOT OF CANCELLATIONS ON THEIR HANDS TOO.
CONCERT
EXHIBITION
EVENT CANCELED
THE EFFECTS RIPPLED OUT TO OTHER INDUSTRIES AND SOME COMPANIES EVEN FOLDED.
THE PRINT SHOP I USED AROUND THE TIME I WAS WORKING ON VOLUME 1 WENT BELLY-UP...
MANY MANGA ARTISTS STARTED TO DRAW DIGITALLY.
ARTISTS WHO USUALLY WORKED WITH THEIR ASSISTANTS IN PERSON ALSO BEGAN TO MOVE ONLINE.
THEY BEGAN SENDING THEIR MANU-SCRIPTS THROUGH THE INTERNET TOO.
I'VE ALWAYS WORKED DIGITALLY, THOUGH.
STAYING AT HOME ALL THE TIME ALSO MADE US CHANGE THE WAY WE READ BOOKS, WITH MANY PEOPLE SWITCHING FROM PAPERBACK TO EBOOKS.
IT'S A TIME OF AN ALMOST DIZZYING AMOUNT OF INNOVA-TIONS.
I WONDER WHAT WILL HAPPEN TO THE MANGA INDUSTRY FROM HERE ON.

GREETINGS

2020

I CAN'T BELIEVE COMIKET WAS CANCELED!

AS SOMEONE WHO CREATED A MANGA INSPIRED BY COMIKET, SEEING THIS HAPPEN IN REAL LIFE IS SHOCKING...

BUT WITHIN THE FICTIONAL WORLD OF MANGA, EVENTS ARE STILL BEING HELD, AND SO THE CHARACTERS' BUSY DAILY LIVES CONTINUE.

NORMALLY, MANGA ARTISTS DON'T VENTURE OUT MUCH, SO EVENTS ARE ONE OF THE FEW PLACES WE CAN INTERACT WITH OTHER CREATORS AND READERS. AS SUCH, IT'S BEEN A BIT OF A LONELY YEAR.

PLEASE TAKE CARE OF YOURSELVES, READERS.

SEE YOU IN THE NEXT VOLUME!

2020.10

もちんち

MOCHINCHI

[BACK PAGE]

■ HELLO. MIYAMA HERE.

THANK YOU VERY MUCH FOR PICKING UP VOLUME 5 OF A WITCH'S PRINTING OFFICE!

IT MAY HAVE ONLY BEEN IN HER MIND, BUT MIKA RETURNED(?) TO HER WORLD IN THIS VOLUME.

I'M CURIOUS TO SEE WHERE MIKA WILL GO FROM HERE. I HOPE YOU WILL ALL ENJOY IT.

WELL THEN, PLEASE ACCEPT MY HEARTFELT THANKS FOR READING.

HANKYUVEYMUH!

A WITCH'S PRINTING OFFICE

5

story **Mochinchi** *art* **Yasuhiro Miyama**

TRANSLATION: AMBER TAMOSAITIS
LETTERING: ERIN HICKMAN

MAHOTSUKAI NO INSATSUJO Vol. 5
©Mochinchi, Yasuhiro Miyama 2020
First published in Japan in 2020 by KADOKAWA CORPORATION, Tokyo.
English translation rights arranged with KADOKAWA CORPORATION, Tokyo
through Tuttle-Mori Agency, Inc., Tokyo.

English translation © 2021 by Yen Press, LLC

Yen Press
150 West 30th Street, 19th Floor
New York, NY 10001

Visit us at yenpress.com
facebook.com/yenpress
twitter.com/yenpress
yenpress.tumblr.com
instagram.com/yenpress

First Yen Press Edition: October 2021

Yen Press is an imprint of Yen Press, LLC.
The Yen Press name and logo are trademarks of Yen Press, LLC.

Library of Congress Control Number: 2019947774

ISBNs: 978-1-9753-3384-3 (paperback)
978-1-9753-3383-6 (ebook)

10 9 8 7 6 5 4 3 2 1

WOR

Printed in the United States of America

A WITCH'S PR

STORY
MOCHINCHI

ART
YASUHIRO MIYAMA

✦

ORIGINAL COVER DESIGN

SAVA DESIGN

COVER PAINTING
SIOKOJI

EDITOR IN CHARGE
KENTARO OGINO

EDITORIAL ASSISTANT
YUSUKE KATO